Walking with the Damned

Walking with the Damned

THE SHOCKING MURDER OF THE MAN WHO FREED 30,000 PRISONERS FROM THE NAZIS

Ted Schwarz

PARAGON HOUSE
New York

First edition, 1992

Published in the United States by
Paragon House
90 Fifth Avenue
New York, N.Y. 10011

Library of Congress Cataloging-in-Publication data

Schwarz, Ted, 1945-
Walking with the damned: the shocking murder of the man who freed 30,000 prisoners from the Nazis / Ted Schwarz.—lst ed.
p. cm.
Includes bibliographical references and index.
ISBN 1-55778-315-2: $19.95
1. Holocaust, Jewish (1939–1945). 2. Bernadotte, Folke, 1895–1948. 3. Diplomats—Sweden—Biography. 4. World War, 1939–1945—Jews—Rescue—Germany. 5. National socialism. 6. Jews—Palestine—Politics and government. 7. Terrorism—Palestine. 8. Israel-Arab War, 1948–1949—Diplomatic history. I. Title.
D804.3.S37 1992
940.53'18—dc20

                                 91-23159
                                     CIP

Manufactured in the United States of America
10 9 8 7 6 5 4 3 2 1

Contents

P_{reface}

IT WOULD BE impossible to write *Walking with the Damned* as a work of fiction. There should have been no connection among the three disparate groups and individuals that make up this story—the revolutionary Jews of Palestine who helped found the nation of Israel, Count Folke Bernadotte, the kin of Swedish royalty, and Heinrich Himmler, a fanatic who was willing to use almost incomprehensibly massive torture and death as a means of social restructuring for all of Europe. Yet in "real life," no one knows how the actions of someone yet to be encountered, living in a different culture, a different nation, might somehow lead him to greatness or cause his destruction in an unforeseen time and place.

It is too simplistic to define the rise of Adolf Hitler's National Socialist party as a time that would pit Germans against Jews. The truth was not formed in black-and-white, except for those whose memories are faulty. In fact, the heroes and the villains were unlike any previously encountered.

The earliest victims of the Nazis were not specifically the Jews. The infamous Dachau concentration camp opened its doors in 1933, a time when the enemies of the state were more likely to be educators, political reformers, Catholic and Protestant religious leaders, and even National Socialists who stood against the megalomania of fanatics within their own party. The idea and practice of genocide came later, and had Hitler triumphed in battle, would have included all the non-

Aryans of the world with the exception of those whose existence as servants for the new Reich would be perceived as valuable to the state.

The villains also did not fit the stereotype. Heinrich Himmler, the most devious and dangerous of all the Nazis to survive deadly political maneuverings, was not a larger-than-life Frankenstein's monster. He was a little man, barely over five feet, six inches tall, with Mongolian, not Aryan, features, lacking in athletic ability, of limited intellect compared with many around him, and a believer in fantasy and myth. Yet he was the creator of the most brutal and efficient killing machine the world had ever seen, and a man who, with his assistant, Reinhard Heydrich, organized the dreaded Schutzstaffel (SS) so that he could take complete control of Germany and whatever territory Hitler conquered in the war.

Other players are not easily classified as hero or villain, including the Jews of Palestine, the "sons of Canaan," who faced overwhelming opposition to a homeland they believed had been promised by God. The Arabs wished to destroy them. The British went from protector to destroyer. And the Palestinian Jews were forced to become both victim of the violence and victimizer, skilled guerrilla terrorists who would ultimately confuse the "good guys" and the "bad guys," murdering a champion of their people in a world where right and wrong could no longer fit a consistent mold.

And there was Folke Bernadotte, a member of the Swedish royal family whose intellectual abilities were limited. He appeared to best fit the role of jovial party host whom everyone liked, even though the guests had long ago learned that he seldom served their drink orders as they had made them. A failure in every business he tried, he would be responsible for saving the lives of more than thirty thousand men, women, and children destined for death in the concentration camps.

Walking with the Damned is the story of disparate but ultimately symbiotic men and women in a world gone mad. And in the end, there would be lives won and lost, treachery, deceit, selflessness, and a man who blundered his way to glory before being murdered by the very people whose needs had assured his moment in history.

SHYLOCK:... *Hath not a Jew eyes? hath not a Jew hands, organs, dimensions, senses, affections, passions? fed with the same food, hurt with the same weapons, subject to the same diseases, healed by the same means, warmed and cooled by the same winter and summer, as a Christian is? If you prick us, do we not bleed? if you tickle us, do we not laugh? if you poison us, do we not die? and if you wrong us, shall we not revenge? If we are like you in the rest, we will resemble you in that. If a Jew wrong a Christian, what is his humility? Revenge. If a Christian wrong a Jew, what should his sufferance be by Christian example? Why, revenge. The villainy you teach me, I will execute, and it shall go hard but I will better the instruction.*

The Merchant of Venice,
ACT III, SCENE I

PART I

Liberator of the Damned

CHAPTER 1

*R*escue from *R*avensbrück

THEY WERE THE ragtag caravan of the damned, their faces gaunt, their bodies emaciated. Most were sick, an unknown number dying, and all of them suffered from parasitic infections.

They should have been joyous, when they saw the white buses with the bright red crosses. Count Folke Bernadotte, the Swedish nobleman who had planned their rescue, envisioned thousands of women and children, faces aglow with happiness, eagerly stepping aboard their caravan to freedom. Instead, there was a mixture of terror, resignation, and defiance as the Ravensbrück concentration-camp inmates wondered what further perverted horror awaited them before their deaths.

One of the Swedish doctors tried to persuade a young French girl that she would be going to a land of safety from which she would ultimately be reunited with her loved ones. His language skills were limited and his explanation halting, but he did not think he had so failed to communicate that she had any reason to stare at him in mounting terror. Later he learned that before she came to Ravensbrück, she had been in an extermination camp where a seemingly kind guard assured her she would soon be joining the mother, from whom she had been separated following the family's arrest by Nazi soldiers.

"And where is my mother?" she had eagerly inquired.

"Up there," he said, laughing and pointing to the smoke rising from the chimney of a crematorium.

3

The rescue workers at Ravensbrück made little effort to separate the healthy from the dying. Everyone knew the ravages of slow starvation had unpredictable results. Someone so emaciated that she looked like a walking skeleton, her breasts shriveled like dried prunes, her brittle hair limp and falling out, her skin cracked, might gradually recover her strength with proper nutrition and live thirty or forty years more. Conversely, a woman who still seemed attractive, her skin aglow with color, her time in the camp relatively short, might be so internally damaged that she would not survive the bus trip.

The only weeding-out process was of the truly insane. The rescue workers tried to avoid the obvious madwomen who wandered the concentration camps, living in a world they could endure only by transforming it in the dark of their minds. Sometimes the madness was manifest in incessant babbling and the inability to carry on a conversation that related to anything concerning the war. At other times the rescuers encountered women who made their worst nightmares seem like a pleasant afternoon romp through an amusement park.

Perhaps the most extreme story was reported by a rescuer from Bergen-Belsen who would later recall: "I saw this one woman in rags, clutching the corpse of a baby. It was stiff, decaying, obviously dead for several days, but the woman did not know that. She went up to every person she saw, asking if they had milk for her infant because she could no longer produce it.

"The woman was in horrible shape. Her eyes seemed hollow, her skin shriveled. And she became more and more manic as the other rescue workers tried to shunt her aside so they could use what little milk they had for the living.

"Finally someone took pity on her, putting a container of milk to the frozen lips of that tiny corpse. A few drops dribbled onto its skin, and the woman's eyes suddenly radiated with joy. It was as though a light had been turned on inside, and for a moment she seemed to glow. She had found someone to help her save her baby. She had achieved the one goal that apparently was keeping her alive. Then she stumbled a few yards from the worker and fell dead, still clutching that infant's corpse.

"We left her there. I don't know what happened to the corpse. It didn't matter. There was no time to worry about her, no time to think. We had too many people to save."

It was a story that horrified most who heard it. However, the former inmates of Ravensbrück only shook their heads sadly when they heard the recounting. They had seen worse among the women whom they left behind.

The inmates of Ravensbrück climbed or were carried onto the buses.

Count Bernadotte, who had organized this rescue through seemingly impossible negotiations with Heinrich Himmler, had an idealized vision of how it would occur. The rescued, he imagined, would sit with dignity, one to a seat, like schoolchildren on a field trip or a family taking a Sunday drive in the country. He had thought of it a little like a Boy Scout outing (he had been a leader in that organization for many years). He may even have envisioned the women lifting their voices in songs of joy and praise. But the count did not travel with the buses. He did not go to the center of the camps where even the SS exterminators "purifying" the Third Reich for the good of the Master Race sometimes felt a tug of conscience over the ultimate pain and terror one human being could inflict upon another. He could still fantasize the rescue as being much like the happy ending of a cinema melodrama.

Folke's sister, the Countess Maria Bernadotte, who traveled with the buses, knew better. She saw the blood, the pain, the faces etched in terror, helplessness, and despair. She knew her brother was immature, a spoiled rich boy with limited intelligence and puppylike enthusiasm. And yet, for once in his life there had been a triumph. It was as though he had calculated the probability of the impossible and come up with the winning number. He did not really understand the camps or what the women were enduring, yet when the Ravensbrück rescue was over, between twenty thousand and thirty thousand members of that tattered army of the damned would be given a second chance at life.

Bernadotte's appeal to Heinrich Himler in March and April 1945 was doomed from any objective view of the Nazi war machine. Himmler was the most powerful man in the Third Reich still accessible during the period when Hitler was focusing all his attention on the military action. The Swedish count had spoken of his desire to save Frenchwomen, then broadened his appeal to include Scandinavian wives of German soldiers, Poles, Jews, and others languishing in the concentration camps. His efforts were preposterous, given the nature of the hostilities and the obvious delight Himmler took in running his efficient death camps. But in his limited way, Bernadotte was as much a "true believer" as the psychopathic leaders of the Reich and in the end he gained concessions.

Countess Maria Bernadotte and the other rescue workers were uncertain they would be able to get their buses into Ravensbrück, so clogged with terrified civilians were the roads along the way.

The caravan consisted of what once would have been the safest vehicles available: twenty-five white Swedish buses, each designed to carry twenty passengers, with the Red Cross insignia clearly painted on the sides and tops. Earlier in the war those markings were like protective shields. The pilots of bombers and the heavily armed infantry hidden near the highways would never shoot at such equipment. The Red Cross was the universal symbol of unconditional love. The organization helped everyone in need, regardless of political affiliation, and all combatants respected them accordingly.

But toward the end of 1944, Adolf Hitler had called for "total war." No one was certain just what that meant, since his able-bodied followers were already giving their lives on the various fronts, the elderly and infirm sacrificing much of their limited food stocks to assure the soldiers were fed. However, to the Allies, with the end of the violence in sight, Hitler's declaration meant that nothing was sacred anymore. Airmen were assigned strategic targets, but if weather, unusually heavy antiaircraft fire, or low fuel prevented them from striking their primary goals, they would dump their explosives where they would do the most damage. Often this meant attacking the civilian population to generate terror that would build anti-Hitler feelings among the people.

Hitler, isolated in his bunker, the concrete-reinforced underground apartment building he shared with Eva Braun, propaganda minister Joseph Goebbels, Goebbels' wife Magda, and their children, imagined greater popular support than he had. The windowless bunker prevented him from witnessing a Berlin in ruins; the offices, apartments, and shops often nothing more than twisted steel, broken glass, and shattered walls. A steady stream of citizens was leaving the city, feet moving to the increasingly loud beat of reverberating cannon fire, rifle shots, and bomb explosions. Once-proud, often wealthy individuals were concerned only with staying alive.

Evacuations were taking place in other cities as well, so the line of empty Swedish buses that had made its way to Ravensbrück in late April 1945 was coveted by the terrified, exhausted refugees. People tried to commandeer the vehicles, to stop them with their bodies, to climb on the roofs and cling for as long as they could.

The drivers dared not stop. The refugees were a pathetic sight, and the rescue workers had great compassion. But the concentration camp refugees were in greater need, and no one was certain if the arrangement Folke Bernadotte had made with Heinrich Himmler would be revoked.

Himmler was already acting in direct contravention of Hitler's orders. At any moment the Germans might change their minds, killing the women who would otherwise soon be on their way to freedom. And so the drivers kept their buses pressing forward, knocking people from their path when necessary, watching the more athletic leap onto the roof or the hood for a few moments, then slide off when they lost their grip. No one was seriously injured by the buses, but even if someone had accidentally been killed, the caravan would not have dared stop.

The Allied pilots knew nothing of the Bernadotte mission. All they saw were bright red "targets" set off against white painted buses in a sea of humanity. They tried to drop their bombs and use their ammunition against the fleeing masses to further demoralize the population. Total war meant that nothing was sacred for either side—not the old, the infirm, women, children, or newborns. Certainly not Red Cross vehicles, no matter what their country of origin. And so, while the caravan was fortunate to evade direct strikes, an occasional plane or two would appear in the sky, move in low, and bring death and destruction all around.

The pilots undoubtedly would have avoided the buses had they known of the mission. But the rescue that was taking place in Ravensbrück (like the rescues from other camps) was a closely guarded secret—if revealed it would cost the lives of as many as thirty thousand inmates whose freedom would have been denied.

As the twenty-five buses carrying doctors and three nurses, including Maria Bernadotte, moved into Ravensbrück, the rescue team discovered another problem. The inmates were in varying degrees of starvation. Some were incontinent, crippled from torture, and/or ravaged by illness. Some, new to the camp, the victims of rape or women who became prostitutes in a desperate effort to stay alive, were pregnant. All were in rags. Many were distinguishable from the dead only by the fact that they could still breathe, open their eyes, and make a few movements with their limbs.

It was originally thought that they could transport the women in several comfortable trips. With each twenty passenger bus filled, five hundred women could be taken out with each caravan. Bernadotte had been so certain that the SS guards would cooperate the rescue workers had envisioned a simple round-robin approach: Select five hundred, load them on the buses, and have the SS gently care for those who remained.

Once the first five hundred were safe, the refueled buses would return for the next five hundred, and the next, and so forth. Before he saw the reports concerning the first rescue, Bernadotte seemed to envision the SS a little like summer sleepaway camp counselors gathering the children together for parents' day. But reality was a nightmare of walking horrors, and the SS guards were part of the Death's Head

Squadron, men selected in large part because of their brutality. The rescue workers soon realized that anyone not moved on that first trip might be dead before a second trip was possible.

Maria Bernadotte and the others quickly packed as many women onto the buses as they could, no matter how cramped they might have to be. They placed women on seats, on the floors, on top of each other. So long as the women could breathe, they were loaded in whatever manner left room for more. By the time the rescue team was done, they managed to pack sixty women per bus—fifteen hundred women traveling to freedom on vehicles meant for one-third that number.

Ravensbrück was fifty-six miles north of Berlin, two-thirds of a mile from the Furstenburg Railroad Station. The buses had to drive northeast to Malmö, Sweden, a trip almost three times that length. It was a drive that, if anything, was worse than the trip to the camps.

No longer did anyone try to climb on board. That was obviously an impossibility for the walking refugees. But the Allied forces were moving closer and the attacks intensified. At least one night of the drive, most of the women had to sleep in the woods for safety. The buses were kept as hidden as they could be, both to protect them and to try to assure the safety of the sickest of the women, who had to be left lying on the floor of the endangered vehicles.

A pregnant Polish woman, near term when the rescuers arrived, went into labor and gave birth during the evacuation. The baby was at once a sign of hope and a greater impetus to get to where proper medical care was possible.

A few of the women talked with their rescuers, desperate to share the horrors of what they had endured so that someone would know, even if they did not survive. They did not speak of themselves, except in the collective. Mostly they talked about individuals who had helped keep them alive.

For example, one British woman had deliberately created the image of being a supporter of the SS while in Ravensbrück. Although an inmate, she made friends with the female guards handling the executions. In that way she managed to learn which women were targeted for death. Then she would alert the other inmates and, together, they would try to find ways to hide the marked victims. Food would be scrounged or stolen, then brought to the prisoners in hiding. They would be nursed back to health if possible—some were so ill that they died despite the efforts to save them. But those who could show that their weight was up and that they were able to work when they came out of hiding were not murdered. Instead they were returned to the labor force, having gained a reprieve that enabled some of them to survive until the rescue.

The brutality of the guards was also mentioned: the Ravensbrück excesses were caused by the women of the SS. These females patrolled with trained attack dogs, which they liked to release against the prisoners for punishment and for pleasure. Often the entire camp would be paraded, then forced to stand for four hours until the weakest began to drop. The first hundred to fall to the ground were taken to the gas chambers, given lethal injections, cremated. Sometimes the victims were dead when they were placed in the ovens—sometimes they were still alive.

One woman who was saved was a French countess who had been part of the Resistance. The guards at Ravensbrück knew from past experience that torture was meaningless. The women of the Resistance had proved immune to physical pain. Not that they could endure torture. They writhed in agony, often begging for a quick death to put them out of their misery. But they would not reveal their plans.

The countess was treated differently. She was given special privileges, better treatment, a ration that would keep her alive a little longer than might otherwise have been the case. When that did not work, she was placed in a small cellar that was wet, windowless, and carefully controlled by the guards. First the holding area would be kept in complete darkness for long periods of time. Then dazzlingly bright arc lights would be turned on, again for prolonged periods. The woman still refused to reveal anything.

Finally, at Christmas 1944, the Countess was given the fine clothing in which she had been arrested and ordered to dress for a special occasion. Then she was taken in to the area where the commandant and his staff were having dinner. There were streamers hanging from the ceiling, a decorated Christmas tree, candles, and a table laden with food and fine wine. Everyone was happy, eating their fill, while the countess sat in a place of honor on the commandant's right—not allowed to eat or drink anything. Then she was returned to her cell, having been given to understand that, when she spoke, the food would be hers to enjoy as well.

The countess said nothing, revered by the other inmates for her strength, about which they bragged during their drive to freedom. (Word of what she had done was given to the medical staff at Malmö, Sweden, who decided to agree to any request she might make. Jokingly she said that she wanted a lipstick and a bottle of champagne. To her surprise, the staff produced them for her.)

When the buses reached Sweden, the women were transferred to hospital trains, many of them taken to a castle in Malmö that had been transformed into a hospital. Their stories had shocked and horrified rescuers, some of whom had narrowly avoided death themselves. But no one spoke to the press of what had taken place. Even when the buses returned again and again, more than fourteen thousand women, two thousand of whom were Jews, didn't discuss the matter. The incidents in Ravensbrück, the conditions of the death camp, the stories of the women who had been rescued, all were kept quiet. The prisoners and their saviors knew that any publicity given to the Bernadotte mission in Ravensbrück would prevent other rescue efforts from other camps.

CHAPTER 2

An Unlikely Hero

THE NEED FOR secrecy have made the Bernadotte rescues, among the most succesful of World War II, little known to the world at large, even now, a half-century after the war. Yet oddly, had they been known, it is not certain how historians would have recorded them.

Folke Bernadotte was not cut from the fabric of the mythical heroes of war. He was a member of the Swedish royal family, but remained the one to whom mostly symbolic duties were given. His intellect was limited, though his enthusiasm for any task to which he was assigned seemed boundless.

He married for love, then found himself in line to inherit his wife's family fortune, an estimated twenty million during the Depression years. He failed at business, including a position as a low-level bank clerk, a job the average high school graduate of the day would have found simple to master, and eventually was accepted for what he was, the ne'er-do-well scion of an otherwise respected family. He was relegated to "good works" and acting as host for events important to the Swedish government. He learned to give good parties, to provide an atmosphere in which people could enjoy each other's company. And behind his back, he was ridiculed and considered a lightweight.

Nevertheless Bernadotte, to some, came to symbolize the hand of God in the affairs of man. They say that biblical history has long revealed that when God wants to prove His presence in our lives, He chooses the most unlikely vessel so that we know He is involved.

Where other compassionate heroes of World War II were often flamboy-ant individualists like Raoul Wallenberg, who stood atop a train hand-ing out passes to Jews so they could escape the Nazi holocaust, Bernadotte was almost unknown. Where others had dedicated their lives to serving God and their fellow man in ways that made risking survival to aid Jews a natural act, Bernadotte had been a self-centered playboy, devoted to his wife and children but to little outside his nar-row world.

Even more amazing than Bernadotte's success was the way he became a catalyst for some of the most dramatic moments in history. It was because of him that Heinrich Himmler would turn against Adolf Hitler in ways that helped signal the winding down of the European theater of World War II. And it was because of him that passions would become so inflamed in the newly formed state of Israel that Yitzak Shamir (much later that nation's prime minister) would arrange for the count's murder, even though he officially represented the newly formed United Nations.

If anyone required proof that Bernadotte qualified for the title "unlikely vessel," it would come in a review of the first forty-some years of his life (he was born in 1895). He was like a handsome, kindly, slightly bumbling uncle who is always welcome, always a perfect guest, from whom little is expected because he has proved he has little to offer.

Even what Bernadotte treasured most, his marriage to Estelle Romaine Manville, an American millionairess, was partially the result of error and confusion. He was a thirty-three-year-old bachelor count of Wisborg, and a member of Sweden's royal family, nephew of King Gustav V. She was ten years his junior when they met at a banquet given by her father, Hiram Edward Manville, while vacationing on the French Riviera. The area was the playground for the rich, where every-one was so important that pretensions vanished. The king traveled as Mr. G, fooling no one but feeling more comfortable about casually relaxing and enjoying the lawn tennis tournaments when not addressed as royalty. Only the unmarried sons of nobility, including Bernadotte, made certain that their titles were discreetly mentioned in the right places to assure the ongoing interest of single American women. It was 1928, the U.S. economy was still strong, and marriage to a count, a duke, an earl, or some similarly titled male was the ultimate souvenir from abroad. The difference between such souvenir marriages and Estelle Manville's interest in Bernadotte was that she and he genuinely came to both like and love each other.

No one was particularly pleased with Bernadotte's sudden interest in what had been a chance dinner partner. The king and the other members of Bernadotte's family did not trust Folke's judgment in matters of the heart. Good or bad, no relationship could be allowed to progress beyond a discreet sexual encounter until it was determined if the woman's ancestry was suitable in its own right. When Folke and Estelle were obviously becoming serious, a study of her background was made.

The individual assigned the task of checking the Manville lineage did not realize that there were two prominent Manville families in the United States. One family represented old money and long time aristocracy. The other was nouveau riche and somewhat crude, even though it could buy its way into some of the same social circles as the other, unrelated Manvilles. The man doing the checking mistakenly decided that Estelle was a "reputable" Manville, and the report he provided the king showed that she was from one of the oldest and wealthiest families in North America, whose ancestors had arrived in the 1600s. Prior to that time, the report noted, the family dated itself from Goeffrey de Magnaville, who had arrived in England with William the Conqueror's invasion force of 1066, an action that eventually resulted in his being named the Earl of Essex.

Just as the king was concerned with Estelle Manville, so Hiram Manville wanted to know more about his future son-in-law's family. He did not want a rich playboy. He wanted a man to whom he could one day leave his business interests, knowing the companies he had founded and that provided his great wealth would continue long after his death.

Hiram quickly learned that all of Folke's uncles and other relatives were sober, serious, brilliant, hard-working, and capable of understanding international business. He assumed that Folke, coming from the same stock, would have the same traits and be able to handle the complex financial decisions necessary when dealing with the large estate Estelle and her husband would inherit.

What neither family realized was that each was deluding itself about the other. The "wrong" Manville woman was about to marry the one member of the Swedish royal family for whom figuring the proper tip for a dinner check was a high point of financial creativity. The only saving grace was that the two of them truly loved each other, and whatever their attraction, it would sustain them through the day of his brutal assassination.

The wedding, which took place in 1928, was an extravaganza that cost the count's father-in-law $250,000 and included a six-foot-high wedding cake. Estelle wore Queen Sophia's wedding veil and a mountain-crystal crown to signify virginity. The ceremony was performed on the Manville estate with 1,450 in attendance.

To the observant, Bernadotte did not seem a great intellect. Certainly he had never shown much ability in his daily life and work. He was as his wife had described him after they were first introduced: "At the first meeting with my future husband I was not really at all gripped by his personality. I wondered to myself whether he wasn't actually quite an ordinary and somewhat self-preoccupied gentleman."

Over time the couple found they shared certain interests. They liked to travel, to entertain, to live lavishly, and to have children. She was attractive, vivacious, and rich. He was good looking, readily led in whatever ways she wanted to go, and even wealthier. The Depression had yet to occur. A couple could consider a mutual dedication to hedonistic pleasures without anyone in their social set being shocked or upset.

The truth of Estelle's background emerged very quickly following the wedding. Estelle was *not* of the noble Manvilles proudly listed in the Social Register. Her father had "new money" made through the manufacture and sale of asbestos products, hardly the type of profession one wished to see mentioned in the newspapers. The only other fame the family would experience came from Estelle's cousin Tommy, who was a firm believer in marriage. He indulged his beliefs eleven times, gaining the reputation as the most frequently married man in America.

Bernadotte's father, his uncles, his grandfathers, and the other family members were, or had been, astute politicians, brilliant leaders, and humanitarians. Folke's first real job was arranged by his father-in-law. Prior to that, Hiram Manville discovered, his daughter's beloved had spent his entire adult life in the Swedish Royal Life Guards Dragoons, riding horses and preparing for battles everyone knew would never occur. Despite a history that implied great honor, the Royal Life Guards Dragoons was by Bernadotte's time essentially a gentleman's club, an anachronism in modern Swedish society. It was a way to claim a career without ever doing meaningful work. Bernadotte was also a hemophiliac, who would bleed to death if he received even a minor wound in battle.

Determined to educate his son-in-law, Hiram Manville arranged for Bernadotte to spend six months in the Lee-Higginson banking house in New York, where Bernadotte was given positions as errand boy and clerk, the type of work offered promising young men just out of their teens who needed to learn the basics of money management. Manville believed that with this training Bernadotte would not inadvertently squander or improperly invest the family fortune when Estelle's inheritance came due.

Even being a gofer seemed to tax Bernadotte's abilities, though he was pleased with the opportunity and applied himself diligently. However, everyone realized there would be no business career in Bernadotte's future. Undaunted by his obvious inability to advance, Bernadotte left the United States when his six months' apprenticeship was over and decided to try studying banking in France. He had not enjoyed the difficulties of his American clerkship, yet he was determined to please both his wife and his father-in-law. Perhaps a cultural problem had limited his efforts. Perhaps a second clerkship, this time in a different country, might somehow transform him into a more competent business person. This time the experience was worse. Even the language became a barrier, much to his surprise; though he was fluent in English, he had long believed his French to be passable at least.

Bernadotte was as doggedly determined to succeed as he was lacking in competence. When he realized that a different language fluency was required for finance than for communicating with French headwaiters, he went to language school and mastered the new tongue. Then he returned to menial clerk-type jobs.

Finally Bernadotte realized that it was time to live life as he had always done, getting by in whatever fit his interests and limited skills. The money would come or it wouldn't. He would succeed or fail with his eventual inheritance. But he was an honest man, caring, loving, and hard-working, if without business ability. Estelle seemed content with that.

The Bernadottes returned to Sweden, where Folke felt most comfortable. Estelle had been raised a citizen of the world, so she was comfortable in the new land. She delighted in preparing their new home, the abandoned building that had once been the headquarters for his military unit, which they leased from the king. She worked with the men remodeling the rooms, turning them into a showplace. Neither she nor her new husband felt any humanitarian obligations concerning the use of their money. Nor were they snobs who thought themselves better than the average citizens. They simply enjoyed life and lived as only the wealthy can.

⚜

A Swedish count had certain responsibilities, among them leadership roles in socially useful organizations. These were not charitable occupations—those so involved were expected to be active leaders. But the skills required were different from those of business leaders. Thus when the opportunity arose for a member of the royal family to become an adult leader of the Swedish Boy Scouts, both Folke and the royal family were pleased.

Bernadotte delighted in working with youth, in the combination of boyish play and quasi-military discipline as well as the frequent camping trips throughout Sweden. He personally escorted Scouts into wilderness areas and taught them the skills he had learned in the military. He was also oddly visionary, seeing the Scouting movement as a way to develop fellowship among nations. Five years later he took great pride in becoming head of the Swedish Scout Union of the Boy Scout Association.

While Folke Bernadotte prepared boys to survive in the woods, others of the royal family were concerned with the events taking place throughout Europe. They were aware of Hitler's rise to power, the violence that seemed increasingly out of control, the potential for war. If war took place, they were in a particularly vulnerable position. Their military was highly skilled and well armed for a small nation, yet its existence was not a deterrent to any larger power determined to dominate the country. Sweden would be forced to become a neutral passageway for troops on all sides or risk domination or total destruction by hostile forces. The next few years would be filled with risks for the Swedish government, dangers that, if mishandled, could lead to the enslavement or annihilation of the Swedish people.

Folke and Estelle had four children, two of whom, Oscar and Gustaf, did not survive early childhood. Gustaf, born in 1930, died from a blood infection of the ear when he was six. (He might have been saved, but the child was frightened of the treatment, which required an injection, and his parents acquiesced to his refusal to have the shot.) Oscar, an infant, had died of an enlarged thymus two years earlier. Such shocks made both of them decide to work with children, Folke becoming involved with the Boy Scouts and Estelle the Girl Scouts.

It was during this period, in 1933, that Bernadotte gained his first experience as a diplomat, a role he treasured for its focus on social niceties. Americans of Swedish descent were mounting a major Swedish exhibition in Chicago, a city with two hundred thousand Swedish inhabitants. Bernadotte was sent to represent the Swedish government and was so well received that he returned to the United States the following year. The effort was more in line with public relations than diplomacy, but he handled it well.

Bernadotte's success in the United States was not matched by similar success in a business venture he attempted in Sweden during this same period. He put up two hundred thousand dollars to become head of an electrical power corporation formed with Baron Baltzer von Platen. The

Swedish company was involved with the long-distance transmission of power, a project that failed, with the company losing everything.

Another Bernadotte project involved the marketing of German machine guns with Major Torsten Lindfors. Bernadotte invested in the company, a business most Swedes found so distasteful that anyone involved, including a member of the royal family, was instantly called a merchant of death. That business also failed.

Folke Bernadotte settled into a life in which he worked with the Scouts, raised his two surviving children, Folke, Jr., and Bertil, and remained relatively ignorant of the shifting politics of the world. He was happy, gregarious, and not very memorable.

In January 1939, as Europe was about to erupt in violence and Germany was living under totalitarian rule, Bernadotte was sent to the United States as Commissioner-General for the Swedish Exhibit at the New York World's Fair, one of the few truly demanding jobs for which he showed some aptitude. He coordinated the site for Sweden's exhibit, then erected and ran one of the most successful pavilions—Swedish Square. He also arranged for a restaurant, Three Crowns (*Tre Kroner*), with a revolving smorgasbord bar. He brought in a highly skilled manager and offered food so popular that the manager, formerly the headwaiter at Stockholm's Strand Hotel, stayed in the United States to open his own Scandinavian restaurant.

Once everything was functioning successfully, Bernadotte and his wife took a trip to the American West. The couple visited Montana, living in a log cabin that was more a wooden mansion than a rustic homestead. They were introduced to the leaders of the Blackfoot tribe whose reservation was nearby, Bernadotte being officially named Ema-do-yena: "He who is idolized by everybody."

The idyllic life in the United States was the last the Bernadottes would know. On November 30, 1939, the Soviet Union sent eight SB bombers over Helsinki in a surprise attack against Finland. The Soviet Union had historically been Sweden's enemy, and Bernadotte was asked to remain in America to raise twenty million dollars and a volunteer corps of Scandinavian-Americans to help Finland in its struggle.

Bernadotte soon discovered that his mission was unrealistic. The American government would not allow an army to be trained in the United States for service on foreign soil. His efforts to raise money to buy airplanes for the Finnish army also met with hostility. He was able to obtain an agreement from the British that if he could get volunteer pilots to go to Canada, they would be given the necessary visas to continue on to Finland. Some of the people recruited proved to be

Communist agents. But before a resistance movement could be orga-nized the Finnish government arranged a peace settlement.

In April 1940, with the Germans sweeping into Denmark and Norway, Bernadotte returned to the Swedish First Cavalry Regiment. He was in his mid-forties, too old to play soldier and too important as a member of the royal family to be placed in any serious danger. Had he been younger and a potential recruit, he would have been dismissed because of his hemophilia. But that was not an issue, and he was asked to become the head of an organization meant to intern foreign person-nel. From his success in this position Bernadotte would unexpectedly be thrown into the world's political arena.

Sweden was a nation in the midst of violent conflict it wanted to avoid, yet whose geography kept it in the midst of action. Pilots who got into trouble over enemy territory might deliberately force-land in Sweden because its neutrality meant they would be safe there. As early as the fall of 1939, two Polish submarines had come aground in Sweden, and several German pilots had landed there. A retreating Norwegian division of more than four thousand men entered the coun-try, along with retreating British and Polish troops. Eventually there would be Americans and Russians; indeed, men and women represent-ing the military forces of all the combatants.

Bernadotte's job was to organize the internment camps, coordinate medical treatment, assist with food and clothing, entertain the men, and generally provide a safe environment until the soldiers could be returned to their own countries. Some of the men tried to escape the camps to return to combat. Others were delighted by the respite that allowed them to stay alive and healthy.

Oddly enough, Bernadotte and the Swedes were the objects of fairly frequent distrust. A neutral nation willing to help people regardless of political ideology or the atrocities committed during the war was diffi-cult for some of the combatants to appreciate.

There were also problems with the Swedish people. In the early stages of the internment program, it was felt that some internees had more freedom than others. Americans and British were frequently allowed leave to go into nearby cities, a fact that delighted local young women and infuriated their parents. Germans and Soviets were gener-ally confined to the camps.

Eventually Bernadotte would handle approximately twelve thousand internees. He was also named chief of the Swedish Army Education Corps, responsible for the ongoing entertainment and education of four hundred thousand Swedish men at arms. This included providing circulating libraries with carefully chosen literature, vocational and correspondence courses, films, and other forms of entertainment.

Bernadotte's actions, no matter how admirable, would have meant little had not the hurricane begun moving more rapidly than anyone expected. Norway and Denmark were controlled by Germany. Finland was harboring German troops in order both to survive and to assure retribution against the Russians. Prince Gustav Adolf, oldest son of Sweden's crown prince, was married to the daughter of an SS general. And Hitler felt that should it be necessary to look to Sweden for assistance, the nation would be pro-German.

In the summer of 1941, Germany requested the right to move troops and armaments across Sweden to Finland. To refuse would mean probable suicide. There were four hundred thousand Swedes under arms, well trained and in excellent condition, but no match for the German military machine. The country would be crushed and the loss of lives greater than anyone dared consider. Yet to allow the passage would mean that all other nations would turn against her. Even worse, the haven of safety would be gone, and Leningrad, among other territories, would probably fall because of the greater ease of attack through Sweden.

The Swedish king had great difficulty deciding what to do. He established a council of state that could rule in the event he was captured, killed, or otherwise unable to govern. To this council he assigned several allies and family members who also had to wrestle with the question of Germany's demand to use Swedish territory for passage. Among the members were Torsten Nothin, Stockholm's governor, a Social Democrat and a close ally of the king; General Thornell, commander-in-chief of the Swedish military and an admirer of the Nazi army; and Folke Bernadotte, who officially represented the crown.

The council was split on the issue, for there were actually pressures not to acquiesce to the Nazi demands. Crown Prince Gustaf Adolf had married two Englishwomen over the years and preferred to speak English in his home. Bernadotte was married to an American and delighted in the West. The king also leaned away from the German demands.

The crown prince used additional pressure as well. He threatened to abdicate if Germany were given unlimited passage, a situation that would place his son (married to an SS man's daughter) on the throne. A compromise was reached. Only one German division was allowed to pass through Sweden, enough that the Allies were irate over the act but not enough to alter the course of the war.

For the first time Folke Bernadotte was forced to involve himself with matters well beyond the life-style he had enjoyed. No longer were parties at the Swedish pavilion his chief distraction. No longer did he worry about the literary merits of the books provided the soldiers or the choice of movies to be shown. Suddenly he had to face the reality that everything he had known all his life might suddenly be destroyed. There was a chance that his country could be crushed, the king imprisoned or killed. His wife, his children, no one was safe.

The final change in Folke Bernadotte came in December 1942, when eighty-three-year-old Prince Carl, head of the Swedish Red Cross, realized that a younger man was needed to replace him. The full butchery of the Nazis was becoming known. If Sweden were ultimately attacked or overrun, the assistance needed would be monumental. If the neutrality remained respected, Sweden would be the only country adequately prepared to step in to assist the people of Poland, Norway, Finland, and the other countries near its borders. Rampant disease, malnutrition, the loss of shelter, victims of torture—the list seemed endless, well beyond the capabilities of an elderly, dying man.

In the spring of 1943, it was decided to move Folke Bernadotte into the post of vice-chairman of the Swedish Red Cross, a position from which he would be trained to take over. His main concern would be prisoners of war, since that was the most immediate need. His background with internees had made him sensitive to this issue and he felt that he could at last make himself useful.

What no one could have anticipated was that Folke Bernadotte, a man who spent his early years becoming a footnote to the history of the Swedish royal family, would become the focal point for violent passion in the two most volatile regions in the world. He would manage to save thousands of lives doomed to death by one of the most vicious and powerful men in the Third Reich. Then he would become the focus for all the hatred engendered by the decades-long abuses in the Middle East, where the people he had saved would elevate his murderers into power positions they still hold.

PART II

Keeper of the Damned

CHAPTER 3

Germany's Other Führer

IF FOLKE BERNADOTTE was God's unlikely vessel, Heinrich Himmler served a parallel mission from Hell. The short, near-sighted, balding, physically weak man with Mongolian features was, during the war years, the true Führer of the Third Reich's civilian population. Adolf Hitler's preoccupation with fighting the war enabled the seemingly innocuous Himmler to gradually take control over the lives of both Germans and the residents of all Nazi-captured territory. His influence ranged from the concentration camps and the dreaded SS units to various government agencies that were likely to risk retribution faster from Himmler than from Hitler.

Though he spent his entire government career skillfully and at times brutally consolidating his power, Himmler probably did not fully recognize what he had achieved. To him Adolf Hitler was a god, a man who transcended this earth, the equivalent of Moses, Elijah, and Jesus Christ in the Judeo-Christian heritage he ultimately disdained. Heinrich Himmler held the self-anointed role of Hitler's pope, apparently infallible when speaking of matters of church and state, life and death. Himmler's job, as he saw it, included creating the Nazi religion, educating Nazi youth, establishing breeding farms for the Nazi future, and protecting the Nazi ideal from all enemies, internal and external.

There was no master plan for Himmler other than avoiding conflict with Hitler, yet over the years Himmler found ways to twist the Führer's goals, convincing him that Himmler's methods were what

Hitler would have decreed had he thought of them first. And when Hitler was adamant about an end with which Himmler disagreed, Himmler was enough of a pragmatist to yield the battle of wits in order to win the ideological war.

Hitler and his propaganda minister, Joseph Goebbels, wanted to exterminate the Jews; Himmler wanted to enslave them—to use their physical skills, their expertise in science, manufacturing, and everything else they might know to better the Reich. Himmler also recognized that the Jews alone were not the enemy. They might be an easily recognizable form of subspecies of human being, but they were not so dangerous as the other subspecies, the Catholics and the Protestants. The Jews happened to live together, centuries of anti-Semitism causing many of them to stay in readily identifiable communities where intermarriage often resulted in similar physical features. But they were just one threat among many.

Himmler saw himself creating two eventual worlds: the slave and the free. The free would be members of the Aryan elite, men qualified to be a part of the SS or who would be capable of serving in other government positions, as well as their wives and children. Many of the slaves would die, of course, some simply because there would be a need for their land—an endless series of "green belts," well-planned idyllic forests, fields, and meadows for recreation and renewal. Inferior races inhabiting the land being annexed would simply be exterminated (on the same logic that herbicides and insecticides were used to eliminate the enemies of food crops). But many other slaves would live to serve their masters, to perform the labor that would assure the good life for the chosen.

The first public statement available in the West concerning Himmler's thoughts about slave laborers came in November 1941, when he spoke with a *New York Times* reporter about the early days of the Reich when he, Goebbels, and others had spoken of their plans for how the Reich would be organized. "Goebbels' attitude was that the Jewish question could only be solved by the total extermination of the Jews. While a Jew remained alive, he would always be an enemy to National Socialist Germany. Therefore any kindness shown them was out of place.

"My view was that it would be enough to expel the Jews. In 1934, I had proposed to the Führer that he should give the Jews a large piece of territory and let them set up an independent state in it. I wanted to help them. We made enquiries in a number of different quarters, but no one wanted to have the Jews."

The territory Himmler had in mind was not Palestine (a likely area given the Zionist movement) but Madagascar, a French possession. Although such a move made sense to Himmler, his attitude that all other "races" should serve the Germans was already clear. Wherever there was land he deemed worthless, the Nazi concepts should be applied. Only when the German government's efforts to find a place to send the Jews was rebuffed did he accept the "logic" of the "inevitable" solution desired by Hitler and Goebbels.

Thus Himmler supported the removal of the Jews to a separate land. Himmler created the idea of Nazi concentration camps long before such facilities were synonymous with wholesale slaughter of humanity and, in a paradox few would comprehend, Himmler was willing to allow mass murder without compassion or reason simply because his Führer wanted it. Concentration camps were not a new concept—they had been used recently by the British during the Boer War. But the idea of using concentration camps as holding facility, research laboratory, center for extermination, and (once the war was over) as a breeding ground for slaves was unique to Heinrich Himmler.

The result of all this was a man who would be important both in the rise of the Jewish state and as the pivotal player in Bernadotte's rescue of thousands from the concentration camps. Yet he never could have anticipated such roles, especially since the realities of both contradicted his earlier stands.

<hr/>

Heinrich Himmler's father Gebhard, until 1897 tutor of Crown Prince Heinrich of Bavaria, married Anna Maria Heyder on July 22, 1897, in Munich, where he had joined the teaching staff of the Wilhelmsgymnasium, a prestigious secondary school. The couple's first child, called Gebhard, was born in July 1898. Heinrich was born on October 7, two years later, and named for the prince, who was his godfather. (This royal association was not sufficient for Himmler; in later years he related himself to the tenth-century Saxon King Heinrich I.)

Heinrich Himmler was born into a country and period in which social class was rigidly defined; status came by the chance of birth and hard work, education, even amassed wealth did not alter it. The Himmler family was middle-class: the father was a professional, and his wife had inherited means from her successful businessman father. An uncle had been a court chaplain and the senior Gebhard was proud of having taught the crown prince—connections that intensified the family's already strong class-consciousness.

Heinrich was raised to have great respect for royalty and the social elite. His father had him provide the names of all of his school classmates, then traced their family histories to see which were important enough for his son to know. Heinrich was instructed which boys he was to befriend and which he was to ignore.

The elder Himmler also raised his son to be single-minded of purpose. If the child made up his mind to do something, he was to let nothing stand in the way of such accomplishment. There was to be no questioning, no soul searching. Once he determined that a path was the right one for him to take, he was to be the best he could possibly be. This trait would later serve him well, both when he decided that he would become a member of Hitler's innercircle despite his apparent lack of qualifications, and when he accepted that death camps rather than slave colonies were to be created.

Heinrich was a sickly child and remained anxious about his health for the rest of his life. Near-sighted and clumsy, he was comfortable withdrawing into the world of books and ideas. Throughout his childhood teachers rejoiced in his high grades and his contemporaries ridiculed his inability to do well at athletics. He attended the Catholic Church regularly, an action his mother felt was of great importance, and played the piano for a while. However, his grades were high because he remembered facts, could work math problems, and otherwise mastered basics, but he never learned the type of abstract reasoning that would later have helped him judge the extremism of others whose ideas he came to think were brilliant.

Life was extremely structured for Heinrich Himmler as a child; his father and mother both comfortable only with highly organized lives. Anna worked out a schedule for housecleaning, shopping, cooking, and all other aspects of the family's daily life, trying to never deviate from it. Gebhard set rules for everything the children, including the youngest, Ernst, born more than five years after Heinrich and never close to his brothers, were to do. He took endless notes on the family, carefully filing all information.

In the summer of 1910 his father decided that Heinrich should keep a diary. As with all aspects of his son's life, Gebhard established not only the structure and form the diary should take, he also made the first entry. The diary was to record every detail of life, no matter how minute or uninteresting. It was to tell where the youngster went, what he did, and the actions of the other family members.

Gebhard monitored his ten-year-old son's entries closely, editing the work, making additional entries as examples of better ways to write, correcting problems he felt should be changed. Because of the accuracy and detail, several facts can be determined from the diary, perhaps the most important being that the diary began during a period when he lived in relative isolation from other children. There are no mentions of other boys and girls in those first few months of entry.

The Himmler diaries gave the earliest clues to Heinrich's ultimate dedication to any man he looked upon as a leader. He felt that he had to establish a routine for school, work, and play, a routine that should not be varied. He felt he must overcome his clumsiness and his tendency to talk too much whenever he overcame enough of his shyness to speak. Yet, though he berated himself, he was also proud that he was working toward such intense self-discipline and held other students in contempt for not making the same effort.

Heinrich would have had trouble with other students at best. His athletic skills were those of a much younger and less coordinated boy, and his poor eyesight forced him to wear glasses at an early age. He was also the teacher's pet, both because of his ability to pass tests and because of his father's reputation as an educator. Thus he endured cruel jokes and the mockery of the other children, something that never outwardly seemed to bother him. He endured whatever occurred, escaping in the one pleasure he and his father truly enjoyed sharing: reading stories about Germany's past military glories. He learned of life in the Middle Ages as well as the exploits of his grandfather, a soldier of fortune, policeman, and minor community official in the 1800s. He became as knowledgeable about Germany's past as many of his teachers.

But always throughout Heinrich's formative years Gebhard encouraged a reverence for royalty. The professor believed that any contact with nobility, no matter how slight, was of great importance. And Heinrich retained this sense of awe and wonder for the cream of society throughout his adult life.

By the time Heinrich was a teenager, he had developed a few close friends who both met his father's standards and respected his own limited abilities. Among these were youths such as Falk Zipperer, who would eventually become a captain in the SS.

In addition to friends, those early teenage years brought a new experience for Himmler—war. Himmler believed in the glory of war, perhaps seeing in the military the discipline, bravery, and skill he feared he lacked. He desperately wanted to become involved in the violence that had begun to sweep Europe in July 1914 when Austria and Serbia went to war. He was intensely patriotic, and his diary carefully noted each German success. For example, for Sunday, August 23, 1914, a portion of the diary entry reads: "The Bavarian troops were very brave in the rough battle. Especially our 16th.... The whole city is bedecked with flags. The French and Belgians scarcely thought they would be chopped up so fast."

Heinrich saw war as a glorious experience that brought out the best in all men. His diaries show tremendous compassion for the enemy, including a trainload of French soldiers who had been wounded and were being transported through Landshut. He reserved his hostility for men who did not go to war and families who failed to support it. Although he believed in Germany, he gloried in battle and hated the civilian population. His fondest dream was to become a soldier, and to that end he decided to increase his strength and improve his health. However, his mother was extremely protective and his diaries record more complaints about colds, stomach trouble, and other minor ailments than a consistency of effort at body-building.

Heinrich Himmler was sixteen when word came that Prince Heinrich, fighting in Romania, had been wounded and died at the age of thirty-two. His family mourned the loss of a friend. But Heinrich Himmler recognized something more: The family no longer had a close attachment to royalty. There would be no security in being able to trade on the old connection as he reached manhood. New leaders would come forward as a result of the changes wrought by the war, and Heinrich would have to learn new allegiances.

By 1917, Heinrich could no longer contain his enthusiasm for the military. His brother Gebhard was in the military, and his friend, Falk Zipperer had quit the gymnasium to enter the officer training program of the Second Bavarian Infantry Regiment. Heinrich wanted to leave school as well, but since he did not turn seventeen until October, he needed his parents' permission.

Gebhard, Sr., realized that Heinrich was not to be denied. He began contacting his royal acquaintances in an effort to place Heinrich in the officer training program of the elite First or Second Infantry Regiment. He made it clear that he was against his son actually entering the service before his seventeenth birthday and that if the war ended, he wanted his son to complete his gymnasium education.

The royal contacts exerted their influence, as they did for boys of similar background in other areas of the country. So even as Heinrich decided to make the military his life's work, he was being rejected: The line of qualified applicants was too long for him to stand out.

Gebhard Himmler then began contacting the leaders of the twenty-three regiments of the Bavarian army in an effort to get his son accepted somewhere, but no one wanted to train new officers; they wanted youths for cannon fodder, fighting the war.

Success came for young Himmler on January 1, 1918, when the

Eleventh Infantry Regiment accepted him for officer training, a program that took one to two years to complete. Every few months of training resulted in increased responsibility for the officer candidate. At least that was how it had worked before the war and during the period when casualties were relatively light.

Heinrich was delighted to be a soldier at last. He was less pleased to discover that a soldier's living conditions were spartan and the work hard. All his life he had lived under the rigid, consistent rules established by his father and experienced the structured home environment created by his mother. He had had privilege in both his school and his personal life. He had wanted for nothing.

Suddenly Heinrich was neither special nor in the type of controlled environment he understood. He was homesick to the point of devastation whenever he failed to get mail from his parents. The letters he wrote were a combination of whining complaints concerning the soldier's life and chastisement of his family for not writing with greater frequency.

Heinrich's endless complaints were totally unrealistic, considering the fact that the country was facing defeat in a protracted, highly destructive war. He wanted a room that was warm and comfortably furnished, including a bed lacking in bedbugs. He wanted more and better food, and extra money from his family so he could go to the beerhall restaurants in town. He needed better clothing and better control over his clothing, which was sometimes mixed up with others'. And he needed food packages, if only to ensure that he would have an adequate supply, enabling him to reduce his dependence upon the restaurants in the town.

Heinrich may have bragged of the glory of war, but he was terrified to see active duty. During his first week of officer's training, the new recruits were teased with a story that they were going to have their training stopped so they could be sent to the front, where they were most needed. He was frightened of this possibility, complaining to his parents, then lying about his fear when he learned the rumor was a joke. He claimed that he was only disappointed that he would not get to be an officer as planned. Yet the truth was that he was coming to understand that military duty was far more exciting when experienced with the imagination than when bullets might be flying all about. Reality could get him wounded or killed.

Heinrich moved through the course with adequate success, complaining most of the time. He reduced his demands for packages from home by the middle of 1918 because he became aware that the civilians were suffering more than the soldiers. Consumer goods were almost nonexistent. Items of clothing too worn to be of use could not be replaced. He was forced to mature enough to begin providing assistance to his family, no longer eating in restaurants—though continually complaining about the poor quality of military food.

The training also seemed to return to Heinrich a desire to see actual combat. He knew that the war was going badly for Germany; perhaps he visualized himself making a difference, the lone soldier leading his nation to glory. Whatever the case, his total military role came the second week of October when he and a fellow officer-in-training, Robert Kistler, were given a chance to drill recruits. It was his first position of true military command—and his last. Although he would later brag about actually seeing combat, the war ended before he was able to leave the training fields. Even more humiliating in his mind was the fact that his brother had received the equivalent of a warrant officer's field commission because of his success in combat.

The war was over but a greatly reduced army was staying together. Approximately a hundred thousand men would be allowed to remain in uniform, and Heinrich wanted to be a part of that force. He stayed in Regensburg, the city to which he had been assigned for his officer training, working as a regular soldier helping with the demobilization records. He hoped that in this manner he would avoid discharge, be selected to finish his officer training, and then become a part of the new military system.

The end of the war brought intense social unrest throughout Germany. Consumer goods were scarce, inflation was rampant, and there were frequent acts of violence by civilians against the remaining soldiers. It seemed most practical for Heinrich to leave the service despite his plans and return to the gymnasium for his last two years. The school program had run eight years when he and so many others had left to go to war. After the armistice, the decision was made to offer a special course for returning soldiers. Those with two years or less to complete would be given accelerated training for six months. The subjects would be the same, but the learning schedule was intensified and the classroom hours were longer.

The program proved uncomfortable for Heinrich. He was reunited with such friends as Falk Zipperer, but his father was his homeroom teacher and carefully maintained records on all the former soldiers' progress. The only freedom he retained was the writing of poetry, some of which was published in the local newspaper, the subjects ranging from the beauty of spring to revenge against France.

Gebhard Himmler wanted his son to concentrate on the classics but did allow his son's intense reading of science fiction writers such as

Jules Verne. What he did not realize was that his son already tended to mingle fantasy and reality, to see the imaginative worlds created by fiction writers as possible in life.

Germany was in the midst of political as well as social turmoil. The end of the war at first brought to power a coalition of moderate Socialists, Democrats, and Catholics. The idea was to give the people a democratic government composed of several different viewpoints. However, many of the citizens preferred what amounted to the totalitarian rule that had existed with the domination of the royal family.

The internal fighting led to active violence, the assassination of Kurt Eisner, the Socialist minister president of Bavaria, and the seizure of the Munich government by radical forces of the left. On April 6, 1919, Munich was declared a Soviet republic; a combination of paramilitary units and volunteer auxiliaries began amassing men and weapons in Landshut. They were being led by such men as Gregor Strasser, a radical pharmacist who would eventually become second in command of the Nazi party. Captain Ernst Roehm, a violent, aggressive homosexual already hated by many but later appointed chief of the Sturmabteilungen (the SA—Hitler's political fighting force, often called the Brown Shirts because of their uniform), was also stationed there.

Once safely away from violence but near to a massing military force, Heinrich's dreams of a military career were again kindled. By the time the army units began their advance on Munich, Heinrich was ready to rejoin the army. Although he continued his studies at the gymnasium, eventually finishing the school program, he had visions of becoming part of the new military elite of Germany. He joined the Landshut auxiliary (Freikorps) and the reserve company of the Oberland auxiliary.

Under terms of the Treaty of Versailles Germany was officially demilitarized and the number of men under arms strictly limited. The Allied powers did not look upon local paramilitary and auxiliary forces as threats, though, seeing them as local police handling civilian matters. They were not aware that the Freikorps members were planning to merge themselves into the military after the overthrow of the Soviet leadership in Munich.

By the time the Freikorps members made their move to become a part of the regular army (Reichswehr), Himmler had made one of his series of bad decisions: He had become deputy to the commander of the Freikorps Oberland, severing his connection with the Landshut group. When the Freikorps units were brought into the regular army on August 26, 1919, the one group excluded was the Oberland unit.

The next stage of Himmler's life was inconsistent with anything that had come before. He decided to work on a farm, learning agriculture firsthand before enrolling in an agricultural school. Degrees in agriculture required both classroom and practical experience, usually gained at the end of the course. Working on the farm before entering the classroom would count toward his graduation.

No one knows why Heinrich made this decision. Such work was manual labor and would continue to be low-status even after he received advanced training. The young man would have to associate with peasants, something he was as loath to consider as was his father. The ideal would have been the ongoing study of the humanities. Failing that, he could have entered the field of engineering, an area that attracted Heinrich's younger brother, Ernst, who became an expert on the elimination of interference in the transmission of radio waves.

The family need not have worried. It quickly became clear that Heinrich was as enthusiastic about the manual labor of farming as he had been about the reality of military training.

Gebhard, Sr., had become the rector (head) of the Ingolstadt Gymnasium, a major promotion both financially and in status, requiring the family to leave Landshut. They were able to locate a farm in Oberhaunstadt, a short distance from Ingolstadt, where Heinrich would do his year's practical work before going back to school. Their son was soon constantly in touch, both bragging about his schedule and in desperate need of better food, money, and someone to clean his dirty laundry.

Doubtless to his great relief, the combination of hard work and exhaustion left him genuinely ill from the bacterial infection known as paratyphus. The symptoms—fainting, fever, intestinal trouble—were similar to those of typhoid fever but much milder and readily treated with the medicine of the day. He had to be hospitalized, needing close attention for ten days but staying for three weeks, reveling in his short-term role as an invalid. He gained special attention from his worried mother as well, thanking her by constantly reporting every detail of his stay, from his bowel movements to his newest ache.

The doctors treating Himmler's infection also diagnosed heart hypertrophy, a condition in which the heart becomes enlarged. The condition required careful attention to diet, rest, and light exercise for a year, after which the patient was considered recovered. Many of the returning servicemen, including Heinrich's friend Falk Zipperer, shared this diagnosis—which was later shown to be nonsense. The men were suffering from exhaustion and the results of a poor diet caused by the food shortages—there was no enlargement of their hearts. Once they took the time to eat properly, rest, and gradually rebuild their bodies, they were fine.

This period led to two circumstances of great importance to the future actions of Heinrich Himmler. The first was a lifelong hypochondria, the tendency to seek every ache and pain he could find, then glorify it into a grave illness. He was forever seeking consolation at the hands of the wives of his associates as well as treatment by a series of doctors, some legitimate, some bogus. He also became susceptible to members of the medical profession in other ways, including letting their political and personal beliefs influence his own each time he had some form of therapy.

The illness also gave Himmler time to continue reading intensely. He studied everything from science fiction and adventure novels, two loves he was by then embarrassed to admit, to books on history, the war, and numerous political theories as to how the Germans could have lost. Many of these were racist and anti-Semitic, often blaming a coalition of the British and the Jews for Germany's troubles.

There is no indication that during the period through 1920 Himmler had come to any firm conclusion about the Jews. His reading included not only anti-Semitic tracts but also those of the Zionist movement. It discussed the Eastern European Jews who had moved into Germany and the actions of groups working to move those Jews to Palestine for resettlement.

Anti-Semitism was widespread in Bavaria. The conservative Catholic lay leaders were constantly seeking the reason why Germans could have been defeated. A secret coalition between Jews and Freemasons, a semisecret charitable organization, was declared the probable cause for Germany's difficulties. It was easier to hate such a minority than to look to possible internal problems with the government leadership that would be more difficult to solve.

The next couple of years moved quickly for Himmler. He returned to school, studying chemistry, fertilizers, and other aspects of agriculture. He became fascinated with raising different types of plants, including the creation of hybrids. Eventually this training would help mold his belief that the ideal Aryan emerged from peasant couples tilling and planting food in a special type of soil. But for the moment his concern was primarily earning his farmer's diploma, an achievement that led to his employment by Stickstoff GmbH (Nitrogen, Ltd.) in Schleissheim, a company testing new types of fertilizers. He also stayed active in politics and paramilitary groups, joining the Reichskriegsflagge, a group of little importance except for the fact that it was one in which Captain Ernst Roehm took an interest. It was a nationalistic group whose sympathies were similar to those of the members of the National Socialist Party—the Nazis—one of whose leaders was a man named Adolf Hitler.

Himmler's first serious postwar involvement with the military was characteristically inglorious. The Reichswehr was firmly established in ways the Allies never intended. They saw it as a small army of men to handle internal concerns but incapable of threatening world peace. The Germans saw it as an elite unit, a hundred thousand soldiers of the highest order, physically fit, mentally superior, men who could respond to any crisis in a manner equal to forces several times their size.

He attempted to join the various units, but each time the recruiting officers declared the intense, slight young man unfit. He also lost his job with the chemical laboratory because of business problems that forced the company to release all new employees.

The one moment of near-glory Himmler experienced was when Adolf Hitler gathered a group of Bavarian nationalists and called on them to help him attack the democratic government (the "November Republic") of Berlin. On November 8, 1923, Heinrich Himmler and his older brother Gebhard went to the Lowenbraukeller, a Munich beer hall, where Captain Roehm prepared them for action. At the same time, Hitler and other followers took the leaders of the government into custody. When word reached the Lowenbraukeller, the men shouted with joy.

Heinrich and Gebhard, in military uniform, proceeded to march to their objective, the Bavarian headquarters of the Reichswehr. Heinrich proudly displayed the flag of the old imperial Germany. Then they occupied the army headquarters building and barricaded the streets. There they spent the night, waiting for violence that never occurred.

The next morning was a comedy of errors. First came the loyalist forces of the new government, bringing in armored cars and riflemen, though no shots were fired. They had been soldiers with the rebels during World War I and had no intention of killing their friends if bloodshed could be avoided.

After the loyalists came three thousand National Socialist followers whose job it was to relieve the rebels inside the building. At the same time, the government leaders were released, a few shots were fired, and Hitler and his fellow leaders went racing for cover.

The end came swiftly. A total of twenty men died in the brief skirmish. Hitler, Roehm, and a few others were arrested. The loyalists asked the defiant Himmler for his gun, then watched as he walked home. He was not taken seriously enough to even bother arresting.

Hitler was jailed in Landsberg Prison, a place sympathetic to the Nazis who had participated in what came to be known as the Beer Hall Putsch. Hitler was given a spacious cell, newspapers, books, a chance to walk in the garden daily, as many visitors as he desired, and an inmate servant to clean his cell. He was given a special table in the dining hall and so much food that he gained weight. When he turned thirty-five while living in his cell, the gifts, flowers, and food that arrived came in such quantities that several additional rooms had to be used for storage.

While in prison Hitler wrote his autobiography, *Four and a Half Years of Struggle Against Lies, Stupidity, and Cowardice.* The material was almost as bombastic as the original title—which was shortened by the publisher to *My Struggle (Mein Kampf).* The rambling text attacked all manner of individuals for the problems that were facing Germany, and related the answer to everyone's problems: He was to become the dictator of a racially pure state that would expand into Russian territory so everyone would have enough land.

Hitler's jail reading was somewhat similar to that of Himmler—history, economics, politics, mass psychology, and racist literature. Hitler came to the conclusion that all the problems of his people were caused by a combination of Marxists and Jews. He also realized that if he could manipulate people into thinking that a single enemy was causing their problems, he could control them. He needed to have a strong message, although it did not have to be truthful. And he needed enough muscle to use physical terror to keep in line everyone who might otherwise not go along with his teachings.

Hitler was released on parole on December 20, 1924, at a time when the Nazi party was banned and the SA could not gather. The country's economy was improving and the National Socialist Party no longer had an appeal for the people. Industry was on the rise because of American postwar aid loans and people were again at work. His efforts were going to be more difficult, but he still had a hard-core group of followers on whom he could rely.

Hitler's followers had tried to maintain their paramilitary style, though with limited success. A large stock of World War I imperial German army tropical shirts was discovered in Austria in 1924. They were an unattractive brown in color, but the quantity was adequate for the immediate needs of the officially outlawed, secretly operating SA members. The price was also right, so low there was no less expensive way to buy a uniform shirt. Although Hitler hated the shirts, by the time the Nazi party could consider spending more money on better uniforms, brown had become a color of pride. All future SA uniforms retained the color, only the design and decorations being altered.

Hitler's release brought a quiet resurgence of the generally outlawed Nazi party. Neither Hitler nor other Nazi leaders were allowed to hold meetings or make speeches in any area where they had previously been strong. They could still speak in Saxonia and Thuringia, though only because they were so minor a political force that they could muster too few followers at public gatherings to be considered a threat to the other parties in the area.

The ban on the SA resulted in Hitler forming a new group of supporters called the Protective Guards or Schutzstaffeln (SS). There was no money for additional uniforms so the men purchased their own clothing, black shirts, slacks, and jackets to distinguish them from the Brown Shirts (SA).

The SS members liked to look upon themselves as an elite group since they were few in number and could travel to places where the SA was banned. They were intensely loyal to Hitler, and he realized that, though they were unimportant to the National Socialist party in 1925, they did have some value for him. He decided to make them all newspaper advertising-space salesmen for the Nazi newspaper *Der Völkischer Beobachter*. He even drafted a constitution for the establishment of the SS that defined the advancement of the fortunes of the newspaper as the duty of every SS man. What Hitler failed to mention to his loyal followers was that not only was he the strongest leader emerging from the National Socialists, he was also part owner of the newspaper.

Heinrich Himmler's quest for military success changed during this period—he now simply wanted to serve a politically active organization. He went to the Landshut office of the Nazi party and talked with the local leader, Gregor Strasser (a former chemist and fanatical adherent of the idea that German nationalism could be mingled with socialism in order to ensure a government that was protector of the common people). Strasser liked Himmler but had no work for him. He promised to keep him in mind and, a few weeks later, offered Himmler the job of secretary of the Nazi party in the area. They also developed a friendship unrelated to politics, both men having an interest and background in chemistry.

Himmler's function was far more important than it seemed. The work was menial, paying 120 marks, much of which he was expected to donate back to the party even though the donation left him with less than a subsistence wage. The Nazis wanted to be sure their actions seemed businesslike, though if Himmler had insisted upon keeping the official salary, the party would not have been able to afford him.

Himmler was asked to make contact with all former members of the Nazi party as well as to recruit new ones. At the same time, Strasser was directed to coordinate publicity in connection with the Nazi newspaper. Between them they would gradually gain intimate knowledge of both the political organization's high command and the rank-and-file.

Strasser was too busy for all of his duties so he frequently asked Himmler to work with the SS men who were selling advertising space, giving them their orders and collecting information from them. During this period the SS men were also asked to work as reporters, since they were visiting businesses and walking the streets on a daily basis. The reporting actually meant spying on the opposition parties, especially those on the left.

Himmler understood the potential for the SS men better than anyone. As Hitler's bodyguards they were respectable to both the leader and his closest followers. They were also acting as community spies, giving all information collected to Himmler, who carefully indexed and filed it. And they were a source of revenue for the party newspaper, making them crucial to all propaganda efforts. That latter situation earned Himmler the title of assistant propaganda chief of the National Socialist Workers party.

Himmler had a dual goal during this period. First, he wanted to be viewed as critically important to the Nazi leadership. Himmler kept a picture of Hitler over his desk and according to witnesses would periodically pretend that the photograph was Hitler himself and that Himmler was having his first meeting with the leader. He would check to see that no one was looking, then practice aloud all the things he might say to the Führer. His actions were a joke to those who overheard him, yet they were also a sign of his intense loyalty to someone he felt worthy of respect.

His second mission was to become a major force within the Nazi party. Those around him dismissed the odd little man as someone of little importance. They saw the menial tasks he was doing as those that no one who mattered should have to do. They did not view them from Himmler's vantage.

Himmler recognized that he had daily access to the most important information available for a fledgling party. His SS men were uncovering not only the actions of Hitler's enemies, they were also providing him information on the new and returning party members. Strengths, weaknesses, personal life-styles, income, family circumstances, and other details were carefully recorded. Himmler was gaining the information he needed for blackmail and other forms of control.

There was another benefit to being seen as an office boy for Strasser. Himmler was at first invisible, then later accepted as a part of Hitler's inner circle.

The first meeting with Hitler was almost as shattering as Himmler's rejection by the military units. Hitler saw Himmler as a faithful but meaningless figure working with Strasser. He did not shake hands. He did not speak. He treated Himmler as furniture, ignoring him as he went about his business.

That Hitler ignored Himmler also suggested trust. What Hitler did out of indifference several of the Nazi leaders read as acceptance. They became accustomed to Himmler's presence, eventually seeing him as one of their own, talking freely in front of him. He knew enough to always be subservient, to never express his own opinions or desires. He became the trusted messenger, the link between the various Nazi leaders and the central party. He provided them with information about other areas and thus were they were quite willing to tell him what was happening in their commands.

The Nazi party was not considered much of a threat to the existing power structure in 1926, so the ban on the SA was lifted. The SS was no longer needed and, though not abolished, was relegated to a position of little importance. However, Hitler wanted to reward Himmler for his loyalty. He knew that the man was impressed by titles, no matter how meaningless, so he named him deputy leader of the SS and doubled his salary, most of which he was allowed to keep. It was a small price for undying subservience.

Himmler's life took an odd twist the next couple of years. Filled with pride, he still longed to be somehow involved with the land. He wanted to try farming of one sort or another without losing his new high status (even if that status existed only in his own mind).

In 1927 a lonely Heinrich Himmler was sent to Berlin, where he met Margarete Concerzowo. She was from Bromberg, Poland, a fact that should have made her fail to meet the Aryan standards he would later demand of the women marrying men in the SS. However, Himmler, like other Germans, saw the entire province of Pomerania, the area in which Bromberg was located, as part of Western Prussia. Thus he could court her without compromising his expressed principles.

Marga, as Concerzowo was called by her friends, was seven years older than Himmler and equally lonely. He was cold, shy around others. She was aloof. Neither seemed to have many friends, yet he found her beautiful and she seemed to enjoy being pursued. They were married by the end of the year, although they rarely spent time together.

Marga came to the marriage with enough money for Heinrich to try his hand at agriculture once more. They bought some land, built a chicken coop, and began experimenting with the breeding of chickens to improve egg quality. He utilized folk wisdom concerning various plants and herbs to try and create gardens whose growth would have medicinal value.

Himmler later discussed his goal for the small farming operation he had developed. He hated doctors and the use of chemicals to treat the sick. He was convinced that in nature was the secret for everything related to health. He wanted to develop plants that would take the place of pharmaceuticals. He hoped that in such a manner he would eliminate doctors, an odd ambition for a man who was such a hypochondriac that he would maintain a private physician throughout the war.

There was little need for the SS during the first few months of his marriage, so Himmler spent much of his time on the farm or talking philosophy with like-minded Nazis. Two of the most important in his development of a personal philosophy were Alfred Rosenberg and R. Walther Darré, both friends of Hitler.

Rosenberg believed that each race had a unique type of blood as well as other characteristics that set it apart. Germans were part of the Nordic race, the world's strongest, which had survived at least from 2633 B.C. in the form of Queen Medinet-Gurob, whose image was found in 1927 during archeological excavations in Egypt. All members of the Nordic race had blond hair and they had gotten stronger with each generation, even as other races were weakening or dying. The Germans were aristocrats, their race the image of the soul. When you had the right blood, no other qualities mattered.

The Rosenberg theories were part racist, part pseudo-scientific, and part incomprehensible, though brilliantly presented. Hitler had a limited education and felt that only a great scholar could speak and write the way Rosenberg did.

Himmler had an excellent grasp of German history, but rather odd philosophies of life. Darré was the man who most guided the "knowledge" he was gaining from Rosenberg.

Darré, the more practical of the two Nazi philosophers, was the proponent of what would become the justification in Himmler's mind for the murder of millions—not just Jews but all non-Aryans. It is hard to know how serious Darré might have been and how much he was amusing himself. Darré was racist and an anti-Semite, but when he used as his historic example the tenth-century Saxon king, Heinrich I, he may have been making a joke at Himmler's expense. If this was the case, by the time it was obvious that Himmler was serious about the concept the young Nazi leader had gained too much power for Darré to dare to contradict what he had said.

Himmler, fascinated, went to Hitler to suggest an even greater future for the SS. He said, "If I had power to rule this exquisite handful of men in his spirit, I could help in perpetuating the Nordic race for ever. They could become a bulwark against the wave of Jewish influences which threatens to drown our beloved people. They could be symbols of the greatness of the German race of which we are the guardians."

The accounts of insiders prior to their deaths describe Hitler's reaction as ambiguous. He found Himmler amusing, especially his pride in military uniforms and empty titles. He also found him a zealot in areas that were foolish. He was said to have commented on the ridiculousness of Himmler's search for a glorious past, feeling that the truth was that the Germans had been barely surviving on the land during a period when the truly great civilizations flourished. Hitler was looking to the present and the future to bring the Reich to glory, not a past he held in disdain.

Even some of the religious beliefs Himmler expressed seemed naive at best. Himmler, raised a Catholic, was struggling with the teachings of the Church as they related to his growing anti-Semitism and sexual awakenings. (He had been extremely naive about sexual matters as a young adult, secretly mixing books on sex with what, to his father, would be the more acceptable tomes on history, race, and politics he read.) He was outraged by the idea that Jesus Christ was Jewish or might have been teaching others from a heritage of Judaism. He was not certain whether to denounce Jesus entirely or embrace a theology that somehow equated Jesus with Aryanism.

Eventually he became fascinated with the occult, Satanism, and pagan religions, spending large sums of money on archeological searches based on what Hitler felt were crackpot ideas.

Himmler's anti-Semitism was most blatant during those early years. He believed in an international conspiracy where somehow all Jews were linked together for their own ends. It was a subtle force more dangerous than any government, any army he later told his physician, Felix Kersten. "The Jew can stand any climate," claimed Himmler. "In places where non-Jews can't live, the Jew manages, conducts a flourishing business and lives happily. This question of climate is also the reason why Jewish blood and Jewish traits always dominate in racial mixtures."

There was also an anti-Catholic bias in Himmler that most people did not recognize. "Pope Gregory VII was a friend of the Jews," he told his personal physician, Felix Kersten, during the war years. "His election was financed by them. His son also became Pope. The grandson of this Pope, Jewish again, was also a Pope. That was the state of affairs in the so-called Holy Church. This Gregory VII announced that nobody could give orders to the Pope, for he was sacred; he was able to depose princes and emperors; God had put all power into his hands; he could even release subjects from their allegiance. For that's what this Jewish fellow did and a German emperor had to stand for three days barefoot in the snow doing penance to him. What blasphemous arrogance and what confusion to the Germanic conception of Loyalty this man brought into the world! That took place in the year 1077 and, in Bismark's own words, it still sears the soul!"

But there was more to the anti-Catholic feelings than the relationship of Jews to one Pope. Himmler wanted to have a religion that was uniquely German, without a god but with loyalty and devotion to Hitler; he would establish it and his research into Germany's past would help form the proper basis for the beliefs.

During the early 1930s he also began to see all Christians, especially Catholics, as a threat to be destroyed. They were counter religions, stressing sensitivity to peoples and attitudes that belied the glory he saw must be limited to the Aryan elite.

One of the plans Himmler began to implement, though it was stopped by the loss of the war, was the takeover, and subsequent internal destruction of the Catholic Church. Himmler admired the hierarchy of the Church as an organization. Many of the ways he created his own state religion seemed based on the idea of the pope (Hitler would be considered a god with only his successors fitting the pope category) and the equivalent of the council of cardinals. The top leaders of the Reich, including Himmler, the "first among equals" in his politico/religious fantasy, would gather after Hitler's death and elect a new Führer. But following an organizational concept did not mean allowing the Church to survive.

Himmler ultimately worked to destroy the Catholic Church from within. SS schools for small children were established over time, and these were directed to prepare a number of boys for entering the priesthood. They would be superb specimens of pure-blooded, Aryan manhood. They would be flawlessly educated for their mission, their bodies and minds shaped by the concepts Himmler was developing as his perverted form of truth. Then, when they could be trusted to never deviate from the new Germanic religion, they would enter seminaries, becoming priests. They would learn and perform the rituals, care for congregations in the manner "real" priests were asked to do, and generally act in the manner of moles—spies who had to be activated. Then, when the time was right, the true values of these mole priests would be revealed as they smashed the Catholic Church from within.

The Christians, like the Jews before them, would be enslaved to work for the Aryans. Extermination would be carried out where necessary.

Those kept alive would be held in controlled circumstances—a country, a village, a concentration camp—except when needed for helping to run aspects of the Reich.

Yet because Himmler was physically innocuous, and because Hitler and the others enjoyed saying yes to the man they considered a toady, they had no understanding of the power base he was implementing. They had a war to run. Himmler had a nation to put under his complete control, and he was succeeding with far greater skill than the generals were showing on the battlefields.

Hitler made the same mistake as the men around him, underestimating the plans Himmler was both developing and quietly implementing. Hitler did not realize that the man who seemed to worshipfully glorify the Führer's presence was marking time, subconsciously seeking a reason to take total control of the nation.

In those early years, all Hitler saw was Himmler's intense loyalty and excellent work. He knew of Himmler's embracing the theories (and his own interpretations) of Rosenberg and Darré. Yet either because of or despite all this, Hitler named Heinrich Himmler Reichsführer of the SS Black Guards on January 6, 1929, setting in motion the most efficient killing machine the world had ever seen. This appointment also confirmed in Himmler's mind that Hitler approved whatever "research" and subsequent action he might wish to take.

What began with a hollow gesture on Hitler's part was developing into an elite force that could endanger every German, Aryan or not. The SA remained the "army" of the Nazi party, fighting in the streets and acting as muscle during rallies. The SS continued functioning much as it had when the men sold advertising space, acting as reporter/spies in the streets. Heinrich Himmler established a large discretionary fund from contributions made by supporters and those who feared him. He had his men wear plain clothing and infiltrate all enemy groups they could—Freemasons, Communists, Socialists, Catholics, Jews, and others. He also had a special locked file on the members of the Nazi party. It contained their strengths, weaknesses, and histories. The information would be used for advancing his own power, either by blackmail or—if necessary—by using the information to arrange for their murders.

Heinrich Himmler, the toady who had been a joke incapable of getting himself arrested during the Beer Hall Putsch, was rapidly making himself one of the most powerful men in Germany. And no one noticed.

CHAPTER 4

Consolidation of Nazi Power

AFTER THE WAR it was easy enough to dismiss Heinrich Himmler as a sadistic, lucky bureaucratic plodder who knew his place within the Nazi structure. The defeat of the Third Reich enabled historians and journalists to focus on the men who fought the war: Hitler, the madman who took on the world and succeeded far beyond what should have been the limitations of his resources; Goebbels, the propaganda minister, who mobilized a nation into believing it could accomplish what should have been seen as impossible; and Hermann Göring, the former military pilot, who became the most powerful minister of the new government. Each of these men contributed to Germany's military accomplishments and ultimate defeat in ways that have caused the public to ignore the truth about Himmler. He has become infamous because of the concentration camps he created and ran, not because of the power he quietly acquired that would have given him full control of the new Reich.

It is not possible to determine when Heinrich Himmler decided to take control of the Third Reich; not until the war was coming to an end did he choose to defy Hitler's orders without concern for the consequences. But at least ten years earlier he had begun deliberately to consolidate his power in ways very few fully understood.

◆◆◆

The political change in Germany began on January 30, 1933, when President Paul von Hindenburg named Adolf Hitler chancellor of the nation. Throughout 1932, Hitler had used the SA to create violence throughout the nation to offset his failed bids for political office. There were four hundred thousand Storm Troopers by then, a force so large that, wherever they were directed to riot, the police could not stop them.

June and July saw almost five hundred separate incidents of violence in Prussia alone, with four hundred people wounded and eighty-two killed. Yet each time an effort was made to bring Hitler into a coalition government (his National Socialist Party never won a majority in any election) Hitler adamantly refused. He wanted absolute power and did not care that the elections were revealing a decline in popular support. Since his followers were so violent, and since Hindenburg wanted peace within the country at any price, the aged president, pressured by Göring, felt that appointing Hitler chancellor was the ideal compromise.

The position of chancellor, limited as it was by law, seemed a safe one for the fiery Nazi. The president acted as overseer, and the National Socialists had to share their power with the conservatives. What was not anticipated was that an emotionally disturbed Dutch youth, twenty-four-year-old Marinus van der Lubbe, would set the Reichstag (Parliament) building in Berlin aflame, and that this individual act of sabotage could be used by Hitler and his supporters to cement their final acquisition of power.

Shortly after 10:00 P.M., on February 27, Hitler and Joseph Goebbels, his propaganda minister, received the news of the Reichstag fire. Hitler was elated. He had been convinced that the Communists were going to revolt against the government. He knew that once they did, he could create a state of national emergency and force a change in the government's power structure. When he reached the scene of the fire, he reportedly said: "Now we will show them! Anyone in our path will be mowed down. The German people have been soft too long! Every Communist official must be shot! All Communist sympathizers must be locked up! and that goes for the Social Democrats, too!"

The Communists knew no more about what had taken place than did most Nazis, but they had their own version of the violence. Van der Lubbe was a pawn, they claimed. Everyone knew that minister of the interior in Prussia Hermann Göring's official residence was linked with the Reichstag by an underground tunnel that contained heating pipes. They reasoned that a team of Storm Troopers used the tunnel to enter the parliament building secretly. There they had placed incendiary devices that would detonate about the time that their pawn, van der Lubbe, entered the building. Because the Dutch youth was known to be a radical Communist, he was the perfect scapegoat.

National elections were to be held on March 5 and Hitler was determined to consolidate his power as well as he could before that. The Nazi daily newspaper released a report on February 28 "proving" the conspiracy by the Communists who were planning to use the fire as the trigger for wide-scale revolution and civil war. Hitler, the appointed chancellor, used his power to temporarily ban all publications by both the Social Democrats and the Communists. This action effectively prevented the opposition from giving their side of what happened, at least until after the elections the following week.

Göring took matters a step further for Hitler. He gathered a list of names of four thousand Communist party leaders. These were politicians and bureaucrats, not rebels. They were functionaries whose only crime was their political affiliation. In fact, the list had been compiled by the Social Democrats, who, though left-wing, had no love for either the Communists or the National Socialists. But long before dawn of February 28, 1933, the list was given to brown-shirted Storm Troopers and police.

The idea was not to make mass arrests, though many of the people named on the list were jailed. It was to spread terror, to eliminate opposition through fear. Göring realized that if the action was taken quickly and before there could be witnesses, everyone would think that the arrests were a legitimate means of putting down a serious crime. More important, the most powerful Communists could be shot or drowned, lesser figures beaten. Such action would send messages to all concerned that they dared not speak against the Nazis if they wanted to remain both alive and in good health.

The night of violence did not have the expected impact. Many opposition leaders were murdered or rendered harmless through fear, but the public's opinion of the parties did not seem to change. When the elections were held, the Nazis did gain 92 seats in the Reichstag, but they only earned 44 percent of the vote. The Nationalists retained the 52 seats they had previously held, enough influence to prevent Hitler from being able to fight the left without a coalition arrangement. And the left wing, which he had tried to destroy using the Reichstag fire as his excuse, stayed extremely stable. The Social Democrats retained 120 of 121 seats, while the Communists lost 19 seats, holding 81 out of their previous 100.

There was a more important payoff for Hitler than the power in the parliament, however. On February 28, using the threat of a Communist civil war as justification, Hitler prepared an emergency decree that eliminated all civil liberties, as well as giving the central government control of the federal states, which previously had a large degree of autonomy. Anyone believed involved with a crime could be sent to jail without a hearing or the right to an attorney. A trial might be held, and it might absolve the individual, but in the meantime it would be possible to spend more time in jail than the sentence normally handed down for the same crime under the former system.

The police could look into all aspects of a citizen's life. Mail could be read, telegrams opened, telephone calls monitored. Crimes such as sabotage and arson were made punishable by death. But the most important freedom denied to the public was freedom of the press—newspapers, magazines, and radio. The takeover of the media had, in fact, been planned long before the Reichstag fire. Hitler knew that the only way to keep people from uniting or from complaining about the excesses necessary for taking control of the government was to keep them from knowing the truth.

At first he engaged in a propaganda campaign to convince the public that enemies of the state owned the media. Eher Verlag and subsidiary companies were controlled by the Nazis. All other media were owned by various religious groups, including Jews, business people, and political interests. A diversity of ideas could be obtained anywhere in Germany. All sides of issues and complete coverage of events taking place in the various cities had been available to the public. But after the elimination of the right to a free press, the Nazis put pressure on all media owners to sell to Eher Verlag. There was no negotiation of price. It was understood that the transactions would be made or the people involved would be destroyed.

Once there was no chance for opposition and no publications that could discuss the ramifications of his acts, Hitler created the Reich Press Law, which was passed on October 3, 1933. Journalism became a "public vocation" under government regulation. Anyone involved with the communications business had to be a German citizen, an Aryan, and not married to a Jew. Nothing could be published except as approved by Joseph Goebbels. Just nine months had elapsed between Hitler's appointment as chancellor and his quashing of all dissent.

Himmler learned two lessons from the 1933 actions. The first was that terror is a key element in controlling people. If you could move swiftly, over-reacting brutally to a perceived threat, the fear that would remain would be such that you would not have to continue the brutality. Anyone else facing the same threat would be unlikely to resist, knowing what happened to those who came before. The other lesson was that when the press is controlled, rumor can be an effective communication device. Power came from manipulating people's perception of events as much as the events themselves.

Himmler was learning, but he was not advancing. He became acting president of the Munich police when Hitler moved into power in 1933. Later he was also made the head of the Bavarian political police, both minor jobs. Yet Himmler understood his situation better than the others.

A few months earlier, Göring had used his position as minister of the interior for Prussia to take control of the ninety-thousand-man police force. This gave him power over Berlin and surrounding areas, power he used to end freedom of the press and assembly. He also banned demonstrations by the Communist party, the primary opposition force.

Göring was a chillingly honest man, comfortable with admitting his dedication to death. On March 3, 1933, for example, he declared "My business is not to dispense justice but to destroy and exterminate." Earlier he had ordered the police to work with the SS and the Storm Troopers, essentially tolerating their violence while suppressing even the most peaceful among his adversaries. He ordered the police to shoot any opposition, regardless of whether the person was simply being vocal or actually endangering lives. He wanted the men accustomed to bloodshed for the slightest provocation, and any man who did not kill was ordered punished. He claimed that he was ultimately responsible, that they were acting in his place even though he might not know of the incident until after the fact.

Again Himmler learned. He could see that by hardening his SS men to death, he could get them to do anything he desired. He wanted them comfortable murdering in cold blood because he knew that with such an earned reputation, fear would control as many people as barbed wire.

Hitler's Consolidation of Power

The election of March 5 introduced what Hitler called Gleichschaltung (coordination), actually a means of establishing central control of the formerly independent state governments. Hitler sent Storm Troopers into each of the seventeen states, ordering them to incite riots among the people. He then used the violence as an excuse to take control of the area in the name of the state government. Ten days after the election, his goal was achieved.

Hitler began making political ties that would give him absolute power and purging the government of opposition. He also worked with Goebbels, who handled propaganda and communication within the country, to link the Nazis with the great leaders of the past. The German people were anxious to regain the self-respect they had lost following the end of World War I. They had been defeated, disarmed, and subject to overwhelming inflation. Hitler wanted a balance of fear and respect, something that could best be accomplished by linking him with the aged Hindenburg and the glories of Prussian history. The people delighted in what he was saying and hoped that, despite the violence that had occurred in his name, Hitler would be able to lead them to new accomplishments.

On March 23, Hitler placed the Law for the Removal of the Distress of People and Reich (also known as the Enabling Act) before the members of the parliament. The leaders were meeting in the Kroll Opera House while the Reichstag was being restored. Entry was limited and Hitler lined the aisles with SS men and Storm Troopers, a show of force meant to intimidate the deputies.

Hitler claimed that he did not want to end civil liberties. He wanted the public to be completely free. Private property, the churches, and other concerns would all be respected. The only reason for the Enabling Act was to give him special powers should there be renewed problems in the country. Since his plans called for ending unemployment and helping the economic well-being of the citizens, it would obviously take an anarchist or revolutionary to challenge the good of the public and force him to use the extraordinary powers he was requesting. The fact that he, alone, would be the one to decide when he could assume absolute dictatorship under the law, and that he was to be given a four-year mandate for this power, was downplayed. At least at first.

The longer Hitler spoke, the more the man revealed about himself. He began quietly, his words implying a hopeful and better future. But by the time he was finished, he made it clear that such absolute dictatorial power would be his whether the Reichstag approved it or not. There would be violence until he achieved his end.

The members of parliament already knew that Hitler was ready to go to any lengths to have his way. A two-thirds majority of the members present was necessary. Hitler had already jailed the eighty-one Communist deputies in order to eliminate their chance to vote. He could use his emergency powers to arrest the less vocal Social Democrats if need be, though he wanted to have some opposition members present to make the vote appear to be legitimate.

Hitler's speech seemed to go too far for some members. The Catholic Center party seldom sided with the Communists because of their religious differences, but they were not supporters of Hitler's National

Socialists, either. For this reason Hitler had been making promises concerning the use of dictatorial powers, explaining that he would invoke no authority without the president's approval. However, since the powers were total, such a promise was an obvious lie, and the members of the Catholic Center party feared his actions.

A debate was held among the members of the Catholic Center party. As with so many in Germany during this period, they decided to go along with Hitler and vote for the Enabling Act. They justified their action by deciding that any opposition would result in Hitler's firing their members from civil-service positions, reducing their power to oppose him within the government. Yet the nature of the act was such that all opposition was impossible from the time of its passage. Between the emergency powers assumed on February 28 and the Enabling Act, the Third Reich had officially taken control of Germany.

The actions came swiftly because there were no longer free media to rouse public opposition. Nazis and Nazi sympathizers took control of the German states, the civil service, and numerous other aspects of public life. Hitler issued more than four hundred decrees that systematically excluded his enemies, including the nation's five hundred thousand Jews, from being a part of what had been normal daily life. The decrees affected where they could work, their ability to be published, their political involvement and even their access to the legal system.

The actions against the Jews did not occur so swiftly as Hitler would have liked. He and Goebbels were extreme anti-Semites, determined to exterminate all Jews from the face of the earth. This obsession colored everything they did and was a weakness spotted by Himmler, who preferred to use the Jews as laborers, taking advantage of whatever special skills they might have. To him, they were no worse than the Catholics, the Protestants, and others. All those not of the master race of Aryans were little higher than animals. Thus he was not so shocked as Hitler when Germans, including his beloved Aryans, continued to accept Jews in their midst.

For example, on April 1, Hitler wanted to show the Jews how little they meant to society. It was a Saturday and there was to be a one-day boycott of all Jewish businesses. Brown Shirts were out in force to picket all such stores to remind people what was happening. Yet the public continued to shop where they had always shopped, for the most part ignoring or openly defying the Storm Troopers. However, instead of easing off his campaign against the Jews, Hitler felt that he had to move more swiftly.

On May 10, Goebbels organized a rally in front of Berlin's Kroll Opera House. Gangs had been sent into libraries and universities to harass anyone who was not perceived to be pure German. Professors, musicians, singers, actors, and others who were considered to either be of the wrong race or to have the wrong politics were fired, beaten, and/or killed. Books that did not fit Goebbels' ideas of what was proper were placed in a heap outside the opera house and set on fire. The book-fueled bonfire was enormous, lighting the sky as a band of Storm Troopers played patriotic music.

And always public awareness was limited. The newspapers, magazines, and radio stations reported only what they were allowed to report. Ignorance and fear were working together to tighten Hitler's controls.

May first and second had seen further duplicity and power moves. Hitler had placed members of the SA within the labor unions, the most powerful force uniting the workers. Then he declared May 1 a national paid holiday for laborers. There was a joyous celebration, with parades, rallies, speeches, and more than a million workers walking to Tempelhof airfield in Berlin to hear Hitler speak. The next morning the labor leaders were jailed, union funds taken by the SA, and efforts set in motion to eliminate collective bargaining. The workers lost all power and every advance that they had celebrated the day before. Factory owners were back in control, and they were, in turn, run by the Nazis.

By July 14, Hitler had destroyed all opposing political parties. Only the Catholic Church was allowed to maintain a presence, through an agreement that stated that the priests would stay out of politics and the government would leave the Catholic schools free from intervention. However, if they or anyone else attempted to establish political opposition, the penalty was three years in jail.

Hitler's final action in consolidating Nazi power was international. Germany was a part of the League of Nations and the Geneva Disarmament Conference, both of which had forced the Germans to remain essentially unarmed. Hitler explained that he wanted the German people to have the same military strength as other nations. Unless this was allowed, he would order a vote by the German people to see if they wanted to withdraw from the organizations.

The move was a gamble, though not in Germany. The Storm Troopers and Himmler's SS men would assure the outcome of the election. Balloting, which included a vote for new members for the Reichstag, was carefully controlled so the outcome would be what the Nazis wanted. Voting was required, so more than 95 percent of all eligible voters turned out for the election. The people were watched so carefully that almost no one tried to go against Hitler's desires.

The remaining risk was the possible worldwide reaction to what

Hitler had done. The act of rearmament should have resulted in an invasion by other nations. However, Hitler gambled that such an invasion would occur only if the world's leaders thought he was acting as a dictator attempting new conquests. If they thought that the people shared the sentiment that he was to be their elected leader, and if he then spoke of rearmament for national self defense, they would allow the nation to rebuild its military. At best, he would succeed. At worst, he would still be in power, though needing to find another way to rearm the country.

Creation of the Concentration Camps

During this period the idea of the Nazi concentration camp emerged. SA leader Edmund Heines was in Breslau when the mass arrests were taking place. Unable to find an adequate location to hold the prisoners, he arranged for the construction of a barbed-wire stockade. The prisoners were not a high security risk or military men, who might try to escape. Thus such a stockade was extremely effective, and other Storm Troopers copied the concept in different parts of the country.

The SS men were not involved with the mass arrests—those were the jobs of the SA. However, the SS was ordered to accompany the others, partially as back-up, partially as observers. They watched as personal enemies of the SA members were beaten and arrested along with those deemed truly a threat to the political order. Homes were ransacked, and what could not be carried out was often destroyed. The SS men who chose to become involved with the beatings and the vandalism were more violent, less controlled, a foretaste of the real threat within the Third Reich, yet the warning was ignored. Himmler had again done his job better than anyone else when it came to training his men, yet his work was still not recognized for what it was.

Kurt Daluege, a high-ranking Himmler underling, was sent to Berlin to coordinate the activities of the SA and the SS. Himmler believed that the greatest threat being faced at the moment was not from the general public but from dissidents within the Nazi movement. Political opponents were open and forthright. Members of the National Socialist party who were vying for power in the back rooms were the ones who were most dangerous. Himmler wanted them destroyed.

Himmler was still loyal to Hitler during this period, though the people he attacked were sometimes more powerful in his mind than in reality. Gregor Strasser, under whom Himmler had once worked, disagreed with Hitler's policies and retired in 1932. Himmler felt that the man was dangerous even in retirement. Yet he also realized that Gregor

Strasser had too many friends who shared Strasser's anti-Hitler sentiments who might form a powerful coalition against Hitler if he arrested the man. Instead he went after Otto Strasser, Gregor's brother and a man without Gregor's connections, as a warning of what could be in store for him.

Otto escaped, as did other formerly respected Nazis. However, the SS was encouraged to leave messages that would be recognized both by the men who might be tempted to return from their self-imposed exiles and by those within the party ranks who might be tempted to disagree with the leadership. Nazi homes were invaded, the wives of the men who had fled were beaten or raped and their possessions looted or destroyed.

The result of all this was that there were three broad classes of prisoners in those first stockade/concentration camps: the Communists, the Jews, and the Nazis.

Dachau

The first true concentration camp was developed at Dachau near Munich. Dachau was intended for longer-term use than the others, though the quality of life was horrible. There was very little water and only enough food to provide either bare subsistence or slow starvation. The barracks for the men and women who had been arrested were designed to hold far fewer people than had been brought to the camp.

Himmler wanted the Dachau guards to be a social unit, the elite among the elite, who could do whatever was asked of them, so he created what he called the Death Head units.

There were plans for settlement of the Aryans in territory taken from German enemies that would require the moving of the existing population, some of whom would undoubtedly be killed. Political enemies were also slated to die in the earliest of the concentration camps. Nevertheless Himmler, at least, did not consider genocide a viable option for any group of people at that time.

In 1941, Himmler reminisced about those early concepts: "Some years ago the Führer gave me orders to get rid of the Jews. They were to be allowed to take their fortunes and property with them. I made a start and even punished excesses committed by my people which were reported to me. But I was inexorable on one point: the Jews had to leave Germany."

Eventually the Jews would serve as a slave force, according to Himmler's thoughts at the time. He was not altruistic when trying to arrange the deportation of the Jews. He was just hoping to isolate them so that they could be handled in any manner necessary at some time in the future. His feelings were pragmatic, though. When the orders to begin extermination of political prisoners, Jews, and others came through, he was quite willing to obey them.

With such attitudes prevalent in 1933, the Death Head unit of the SS was probably not meant exclusively as an extermination squad but as an elite unit capable of following any order, including murder. This would have fit into Himmler's reasoning.

The SS men who formed this special force wore the skull and cross-bones on their caps and lapels, an insignia similar to that of the historic Death Head Hussars of the Imperial German Guards Regiment commanded by the Crown Prince. The connection was one that later made some of the members claim that the symbol meant that they would serve until their own deaths, a claim belied by the leader of the unit, Theodor Eicke. Eicke was a firm advocate of mass murder as a tool for restructuring German society, a major reason he was chosen as the unit leader.

Himmler chose Theodor Eicke because he shared Himmler's belief that anyone, including Aryans, who was not a Nazi was a subhuman and would ultimately become extinct. But Himmler was also considering taking the future of the Aryan race even further than would occur naturally. He wanted to develop a special breeding program, a concept he had discussed with Walther Darré.

&

Himmler's Breeding Program

The idea of racial breeding appealed to both Darré and Himmler since both were fascinated by farming (Darré eventually became minister of agriculture). The only problem was working out the particulars, something Himmler achieved in 1931 with SS Order No. 65:

> The SS is an association of German men of Nordic determination whose selection is based on special considerations.
>
> In accordance with the National Socialist Weltanschauung, and in recognition of the fact that the future of our people depends on the selection and maintenance of racially and hereditarily healthy good blood, I herewith decree that every single member of the SS who wishes to marry must obtain a Marriage Approval.
>
> The aim is to guarantee the hereditarily healthy valuable clan of German stock of Nordic determination.

> Marriage Approval will be granted or refused solely according to principles of race and hereditary health.
>
> Every SS man who intends to marry has to obtain the Marriage Approval of the Reichsführer SS.

The order continued, explaining that anyone who married without approval would be expelled from the SS. The Race Office would maintain clan records much like the Clan Book, a family history that dated back to 1750, which the men had to keep. The investigations into potential brides' backgrounds would be kept confidential, though usually it was obvious to the men which couples would be approved and which not.

The marriage procedure was rather lengthy. First the family history was determined, the bride and her fiancé looking for any trace of Jewish or Slavic blood going back to 1750. Then she would see a doctor so she could be certified as physically and mentally fit. The doctor would then go to see her parents to assure the SS in writing that the family did not seem to be suffering from any hereditary disease.

Once all the documentation had been gathered, the women went to the Race Office, where an SS doctor determined the position and structure of her womb. He had to be certain that she would become the mother of a minimum of four children who would help to populate the Third Reich. (Himmler and his wife, Marga, had three children.)

Next came careful body measurements—How long were her legs? Her arms? What were the dimensions of her hips and waist? The woman was made to feel like a cow being studied for marketing as breeding stock. She usually felt violated, though the procedure was sexless. In fact, after the war many women admitted that they did not marry SS men they loved because they could not bring themselves to face the humiliation of the marriage check.

Only after all the preparatory work was done, after the measurements matched what Himmler and Darré felt were perfect for Aryan motherhood, was the marriage permitted. The one exception was if the woman's background met all the requirements for heredity and she was already pregnant. Then the ordeal at the Race Office was omitted and a marriage license issued. As a result, many SS men checked the history of their beloved's family, documented the family back to 1750 as required by law, then impregnated their girlfriends so the physical check would be waived.

Eventually Himmler added other breeding means. In 1941 he would develop the concept of the Chosen Women. These would be blond-haired, blue-eyed, pure-blooded Aryan women who would be specially trained in foreign languages and the skills needed for diplomatic work. They would study chess to improve their minds and take part in sports with an emphasis on fencing, which Himmler felt provided both physical and mental exercise. They would be skilled with pistols and train in cooking and housekeeping. All their abilities would be perfected to the highest order, and then they would be made available only to the SS elite and other future leaders of the nation. A man who was already married would divorce his obviously inferior wife, who would be provided with a pension. Should the Chosen Women refuse any request for marriage, the Reichsführer of the SS (Himmler at the time the idea was developed) would decide whether or not that particular marriage had to take place.

The children of the Chosen Women would be specially educated to lead the nation. All would be handled by the state government and the Waffen–SS. In addition, there would be Conception Assistants (single women who were pure Aryan, though not necessarily a part of the Chosen Women) who would have sex with married men of the SS or cohabit with them for the purpose of having babies for the state to raise. There would be Lebensborn, homes for unwed mothers, and both the women and the children would be treated with great respect. The SS would handle everything, especially the education, creating an elite group of pure-bred Germans, their only limitation that they would probably never be allowed to achieve the rank given the sons of the Chosen Women.

But while the Chosen Women concept was in the future, Himmler's creation of the Race Office to handle the concerns of sex and marriage was rapidly assuring the image of the SS as the aristocracy of the Third Reich. It was also growing in size and power, something neither Hitler nor the other leaders expected because they did not recognize Himmler's political maneuvering's.

The SS Entrenches

First Himmler gained permission to have SS men continue to act as bodyguards for Hitler. He then convinced other high officials of the Nazi party to allow the SS to act as their bodyguards as well. The dual action effectively weakened the activities of the SA, which originally greatly outnumbered the Black Shirts. Eventually many of the men who had been leaders in the old German army or elitists like the Himmler family chose to join the SS. They held the Brown Shirts in disdain, considering them an unruly mob.

Himmler encouraged the attitude that the men of the SS were without peer, a law unto themselves who would give their lives for Hitler and the Nazi leaders. The weaker among the SS took advantage of their image and their orders, becoming bullies throughout the cities. They would beat up Jewish boys, usually traveling in groups so they would always outnumber their quarry and thus not risk a humiliating defeat. They would make fun of the Jewish girls—including the most beautiful, who were often held in high regard by the Nazis. They reinforced their importance by deliberately causing problems for others.

The violent posturing of the young men caused many Germans, Aryan and Jew alike, to come to hate as well as to fear the SS. But others became excited by the uniforms and the supreme self-confidence of the men who wore them. Women, both married and single, often hung around the SS barracks, trying to pick up some of the Black Shirts. Their actions were no different than occur at army bases throughout the world, but they terrified Himmler. An SS man might impregnate someone who was not an Aryan. They might fall in love with the wrong women, perhaps marry someone whose heritage was such that the purity of the race would be polluted. It was a possibility that terrified him and the Marriage Order seemed to be a way to assure that the men would use greater discipline in their relationships.

Himmler Takes an Assistant

Himmler's primary assistant during this period was Reinhard Heydrich, a man many considered the most potentially dangerous of the younger recruits in the SS. Tall, handsome, and far more intelligent than Himmler or most of the other leaders of the Reich, he devoted himself to the creation of a police force within the SS. It was believed that he was the one man who could orchestrate a power play within the organization, replacing Himmler or any other leader he might choose. His loyalty seemed to be to the organization, not any individual, and this belief was reinforced by his maintaining files on everyone who might one day prove a threat to the SS rise to power as he viewed it—including Hitler and Himmler.

Göring was the man who, in his capacity as Prussian Minister of the Interior, created the Geheime Staatspolizei (Secret State Police) or Gestapo. But it was Heydrich, with his organizational skills, who effectively turned the Gestapo into a police force so effective and ruthless that it became the most dreaded in the world.

It cannot be known how familiar Himmler was with his assistant's personal files, but he was never seriously at risk. He understood how to manipulate men like Heydrich, playing on their weaknesses to which he was sensitive because of his own shortcomings.

Heydrich had a difficult childhood. His parents ran a music school in Halle; his father was a composer and opera singer, his mother a pianist. Heydrich himself trained on the violin. Since he also had a falsetto voice and was a devout Catholic in a predominantly Protestant city, he was taunted by other children in school. When anti-Semitism increased, the teasing turned more savage. Although an Aryan, his grandmother, after being widowed, had married an elderly man with a last name that sounded Jewish. Although he wasn't, and although the man had no blood connection with Heydrich, the unmerciful teasing was often accompanied by beatings. There were beatings at home, as well, his mother believing firmly in severe corporal punishment for children committing the slightest infraction of family rules.

Heydrich became an anti-Communist as a teenager when, at fifteen, he joined a civil defense unit. The year was 1919 and the country was soon ruined by inflation and depression. His family lost its money and social prominence, and Heydrich decided to join the navy. The navy was small due to the postwar agreements, but its members were considered elite. Education was free, and a pension was given after ten years of service. He joined in 1922 when he was eighteen.

Training was difficult. He was well over six feet tall, but lean rather than muscular. His high-pitched voice and the alleged "Jewish connection" in his family aided the other recruits in making his life miserable.

Heydrich had the same determination as Himmler, persevering and ultimately being assigned to the cruiser Berlin. The ship's first officer, Wilhelm Canaris, knew of Heydrich's musical ability and had him attend Canaris' wife's social gatherings, where he would play the violin and mix with the elite of society. He also developed the hobby of seducing single women, enjoying their favors in every port.

In 1930, when Heydrich had made lieutenant and was well on his way to a solid career, the womanizing got him in trouble. He was engaged to two women at once—one he apparently adored, the other he found a desirable sex partner. When he discovered that the fiancée about whom he cared the least was pregnant, he was uncomfortably confronted by an angry father demanding an immediate wedding. The father was also connected with navy officials, so a hearing was held.

Heydrich utilized an ingenious justification for failing to marry his pregnant "fiancée." He explained that a naval officer of his standing could only marry a pure and innocent woman. He could never marry a woman who engaged in premarital relations, even though he was the man involved. Such a marriage would not be proper for a gentleman.

The navy thought differently. Heydrich was ordered to resign in April 1931, and only Lina von Osten, the "good" fiancée who eventually married him, stood by him. He lost the pension that was just a year away and was faced with the prospect of losing forever the military career he desired.

Heydrich's mother was extremely upset by her son's disgrace and by his choice of what she viewed as an inferior woman in von Osten. However, Lina and her brother were ardent Nazis, as was Heydrich's mother. She recognized that the SS had become the elite of Germany and encouraged her son to join the party so he could interview for a job with the SS.

Himmler was in the process of establishing an intelligence service within the ten-thousand-member SS. He was given the impression that the former naval officer had a background in this field, though Heydrich actually had only a single course in intelligence while a student. However, Heydrich decided to lie in order to get the job and was even able to develop a plan for an SS security service during a twenty-minute test by Himmler.

Himmler was impressed and gave Heydrich the job of organizing an agency to gather intelligence and efficiently communicate the information among all individuals who needed it. Heydrich would also determine who might be enemies of the SS as well as of the Nazis, then find ways to deal with them. By August 1931 he claimed to have uncovered numerous spies and saboteurs. He also was able to identify a Munich police officer who had infiltrated the party and turned him into a double agent.

Heydrich quickly showed his brilliance, both for his work and the politics within the SS and the Nazis. He married Lina von Osten in December of that year, days before the Marriage Order went into effect. That same month he was promoted to major in the SS.

In July 1932 Heydrich assembled a network of spies and counterspies into the Security Service, the SD (Sicherheitsdienst). He separated the SD from the uniformed branches of the SS, making certain that all SD members reported directly to him. More than three thousand men answered only to the main office of the Security Service.

Heydrich also organized the rest of the SS. He established individual departments for security, physical training, communications, medicine and social services, among others. He carefully planned their functions so that each was identical to some function normally handled by the German government. In that way the SS could take complete control of Germany at any time it desired. The bureaucracy to run the country was in place, all under Himmler and his assistant. At any time they chose, the SS could eliminate Hitler, Göring, Goebbels, and the others, becoming the leaders they had previously sworn to serve. (Heydrich would be assassinated early enough in the war not to be able to over-throw Hitler and become the leader of the Reich. But even if revolution was planned, it is doubtful that he would have taken control himself. More likely he envisioned himself as second in command in such a new Nazi regime, a fact overlooked by those around him.)

Himmler understood Heydrich better than anyone else did. Heydrich was brighter than Himmler, more efficient, and equally dedicated to the new Germany. He was committed to the Master Race concept, comfort-able with the isolation or murder of all non-Aryans, and shared Himmler's early interest in letting the skilled workers, doctors, scien-tists, and others among the Jews, Catholics, Communists, Freemasons, and all the other "inferior" enemies be slaves for the Aryans. He was the more natural leader, despite his odd voice. But he was also extreme-ly troubled from his childhood. He had been emotionally abused to such a degree that when a man of Himmler's stature believed in him and trusted him, he was willing to be loyal unto death.

Himmler believed in his own vision of Germany and the German people, convinced that Hitler was the means to achieve Germany's glory. He would set aside his own values to follow Hitler's orders. Yet he was aware that one day Hitler would die, and that other leaders would follow. Thus he was comfortable with the idea that he might one day have to switch loyalties, perhaps taking control himself.

Heydrich seemed even more loyal to Himmler than Himmler was to Hitler. His private comments and his writing all indicate that he would willingly have stayed second in command for life. Heydrich had undy-ing loyalty for the man who had believed in him, even though Himmler's level of intelligence often frustrated him. Frequently he used the device of imagining Himmler in his underpants in order to keep him in perspective. But he also knew that, with his political and psy-chological skills, he could convince Himmler to go along with anything he desired. It was even joked among the other leaders of the SS that Himmler spoke for Heydrich.

For his part, Himmler recognized his dual role of mentor for and stu-dent of Heydrich, though the latter was seldom admitted. He also felt intimidated by Heydrich's intellect, and readily agreed with his subor-dinate's suggestions in order to buy time to better consider what they were discussing. Then he would do whatever he felt was best, telling Heydrich that his decision was based on direct orders from Hitler.

Heydrich also improved the SS. Himmler made his original decisions about the SS men through head measurements and similar meaningless concepts. The result was that while men such as Heydrich were brought into the organization, many individuals with limited education also joined. To compensate for that, Heydrich proposed a group of Knight Schools (Junkerschulen). The Knights would be trained in history, military science, geography, and other disciplines. They would also participate in sports and physical activities meant to improve their bodies. These Knights of the Third Reich would be modeled after the medieval Teutonic Knights (Deutsche Ritterorden), a concept that delighted Himmler. The Teutonic Knights were subservient to God's will, pledging themselves to chastity, poverty, obedience to death, and to doing battle under the sign of the Cross.

Himmler founded the first Knight School in Tölz, Bavaria, then worked on more in conjunction with Dr. Robert Ley. Ley wanted to train young boys who did not quite meet the standards of the SS so that they could serve in civilian areas of the party. The schools would provide their education as well as hardening them against the Christian teachings of the past. He wanted them to believe in their racial superiority so no matter what they were asked to do against others, such actions would seem appropriate.

The Spy

Heydrich brought a new recruit into the SS as his aide: Walter Schellenberg, a twenty-two-year-old who would ultimately play a major role in the lives of both Folke Bernadotte and Heinrich Himmler.

Schellenberg was a man of brilliance, brutality, and cunning who would eventually become one of the top spies in the Third Reich. At the time he joined the SS though, he was tested by being made to serve as an interrogator in the Munich police prison. His job was to extract as much information as possible from prisoners, then send them to Dachau or one of the other concentration camps. He would keep them in dark cells, deprive them of food, and bully them physically. Most of the early prisoners were intellectuals unaccustomed to violence. They ultimately provided whatever information Schellenberg desired, a fact that earned him a promotion to positions requiring more sophisticated methods for gathering intelligence.

By the time Heydrich completed his organization of the SS on behalf of Himmler, the power they wielded was enormous. Hitler was Reichschancellor, but directly under him was Himmler, the chief of the SS and by 1936 the chief of all German police. Directly under Himmler were two men, Kurt Daleuge, the head of the Municipal Police (Ordnungspolizei or Orpo) and Reinhard Heydrich, head of the

Security Police (Sicherheitspolizei or Sipo) and of the Security Service (Sicherheitsdienst or SD). Heydrich's Security Police was responsible for the Criminal Police (Kriminalpolizei or Kripo) and the Gestapo, the Secret State Police (Geheime Staatspolizei). Both foreign and domestic intelligence-gathering agencies fell under the SD.

The one threat that remained to the SS leadership's total domination came from the SA, the brown-shirted Storm Troopers led by Ernst Roehm. The Brown Shirts had been tough street fighters and early loyalists. Roehm saw them as being the basis for the German army as it reestablished past glories. He wanted increased power and an increasingly important role for his men.

Himmler and Heydrich recognized that the Storm Troopers, though undisciplined and untrustworthy compared with the SS, sought to dominate the same political territory. They realized it was necessary to get rid of the SA if they were to consolidate their power.

The question remains how much Himmler knew at this time. Hitler was terrified of plots against his life. He was paranoid and seemed relieved to hear about unconfirmed rumors concerning planned coups, sniper fire, or secret grenade attacks. Heydrich, the man who gathered intelligence, began reporting a growing number of such plots. Often the threat came from some unnamed "Communists" who, in Hitler's mind, were always scheming.

The SS, in the guise of protecting its leader, arranged for Josef Dietrich, a Bavarian SS officer, to take 120 men to Berlin to act as internal security for Hitler. They formed a close bodyguard who would screen all contacts with Hitler. This enabled them to prevent any rivals from presenting to the Führer information that they did not want him to have.

Not that the SS men were part of a plot. They had complete loyalty to Hitler, but they were trained by Himmler and Heydrich. They were led to believe that the dangers were great and cooperated in keeping out anyone they might be directed to stop.

Early in 1934, Roehm made his power move. He wanted his Storm Troopers merged with the army. Only the army could bear arms and the Storm Troopers felt that they, too, should have that right. In addition, he felt that the regular army had always been politically independent of the government, a situation that had no place in the Reich. Ultimately Hitler negotiated a compromise that would make the SA a militia, a compromise Roehm later said he would not keep. He then went so far as to call Hitler a traitor to the country, a man who should take a leave of absence from his position while other leaders resolved the government's problems.

Several forces came into play. There were big money interests, who supported the government but who hated the Brown Shirts because they were little more than street thugs. The SS had also grown, quadrupling in the period between the end of 1931 and the middle of 1932, and it was still growing larger. It had become a force that could take on the SA in a battle. More important, the SS was superbly disciplined and trained, their total loyalty reserved for Hitler.

Roehm made his power moves more blatant. He had his men stage long parades as a show of force. He was also a homosexual who began having obvious affairs, an image Hitler wanted to downplay.

The SA leadership was known to be bi-sexual or homosexual in many instances, but the affairs were expected to be kept private. Roehm's blatant homosexual affairs led to rumors that Hitler might also be bi-sexual. Hitler was not close to women and not known for strong heterosexual desires. Even the marriage to Eva Braun at the end of his life was considered more likely to be a reward for her loyalty rather than a love match. Since some of Hitler's closest male friends in the early days of his political ambitions were openly homosexual, there were suspicions of Hitler as well. However, it is also possible that Roehm became blatant as a way to create rumors concerning Hitler and thus embarrass the Führer.

Frightened for his life if a power struggle erupted, viewing the SS men as the true protective force for his government, and seeing Roehm as a man upon whom he could no longer rely, Hitler decided to destroy the Storm Troopers. It was the decision Heydrich had been encouraging through the manipulation of rumors and the reporting of intelligence, though neither he nor Himmler was involved with the early planning.

Destruction of the SA

Hitler, Göring, and the army generals made the initial decision to destroy the SA. Their targets would be Ernst Roehm and the other SA leaders. Most would be killed. A few would be sent to the concentration camps. The exact dates and places were set, then Himmler was informed of the plans. Himmler and Heydrich would be needed for the detailed planning and execution of the arrests and murders.

The plot moved smoothly and aroused no suspicion. Heydrich used a small number of trusted spies to keep watch over key SA leaders while Himmler traveled the country, talking with SS men in critical areas, expressing his faith in their abilities and reminding them of their need for absolute loyalty to Hitler.

Heydrich and Himmler were consolidating their power even while the plot was developing. A directive was issued making the SD the sole intelligence-gathering organization for the government. Everyone in power had to cooperate with any request the SD made of them.

On June 20, 1934, the final plans were made. Hitler and Himmler met at the chancellery, then drove to Göring's estate. They were to be present for the reburial of the remains of Göring's first wife, Carin, in an elaborate lakeside mausoleum he had built for her.

The ceremony was to be a dramatic one, the corpse brought to the area in a pewter sarcophagus carried by a special train. The route the train took had been noted in advance, members of the League of Maidens and the Hitler Youth ordered to be out en masse, saluting, throwing flowers, and holding large German flags that were to be dipped in respect as the train passed by. It was as though a state funeral had been planned for the recently widowed Prime Minister. The truth was that Carin had died almost three years earlier, on October 16, 1931, and the quality of the love Hermann had shared with her seemed to increase in memory that did not reflect reality. But Hitler and Himmler, along with others of the Nazi leadership, agreed to participate in the ceremony, Hitler to accompany Göring to the train station. However, an important incident took place en route.

There are conflicting historical accounts about what did or did not occur. Some records are silent. Others tell of a small girl, carrying flowers, approaching their car as someone, allegedly an SA guard providing security for Göring, fired a bullet that struck Himmler in the arm. There was apparently only that single round, and the man who fired it was never caught. Himmler was said to have exclaimed: "How grateful I am, my Führer, that I was allowed to spill my blood to save your life!"

Exactly what happened remains unclear. It is difficult to believe that a would-be assassin of either man would be satisfied with a single shot. Even if the assassin did not have access to a machine gun, it would seem likely that a rifle with a greater capacity than a single round would have been used (the minimum capacity of a military rifle was five rounds of ammunition). Even if a single shot, bolt action weapon had been used, the time needed to clear the chamber, reload, aim, and fire a second bullet would have been between five and ten seconds maximum. Given the nature of the area and the way the car was being driven, the assassin would have been allowed plenty of time to at least strike the car if not the intended victim. And unless the assassin was on a suicide mission, a highly unlikely scenario since he stopped with one round, the man undoubtedly would have carried a Luger Pistol (standard World War I issue used through the beginning of World War II, at which time it was replaced with the Walther Pistol) with an eight-round magazine to protect himself from capture.

It is most likely that the shooting was a set-up. Only Himmler was hurt, and that wound helped him "prove," if only in his own mind, his loyalty to the Führer. Whether or not one of Göring's men was involved, it is almost certain that Göring did not order the attack. While the reburial of his wife would have been an effective cover, Göring was serious enough about the solemnity of the day that it is highly unlikely he would have participated in a cheap stunt to improve Himmler's image.

On June 30, 1934, Hitler personally went to Roehm's villa in Wiessee, arrested the former SA leader and his friends, and had them shot. Karl Ernst, the Berlin leader of the SA, was murdered as he was about to leave for a holiday cruise. Throughout the country, SS men delighted in attacking those who had been their rivals.

Heydrich and Himmler went to Berlin to the SS headquarters, where SA leaders were being held in the cellars. They ordered them brought to the courtyard, where the best shots among the SS were assembled. One man after another was murdered while Himmler observed how his men handled the executions.

The killings were overwhelming for the SS, though not for Himmler. They were being asked to kill on demand, something for which they had been trained but had never experienced. Few of them proved capable of continuous murder that day, many dropping from the emotional stress of repeated, deliberate shootings of unarmed men who seemed to have done nothing to deserve summary execution.

Himmler, however, was quite comfortable with the killings, considering the victims essentially subhuman, much like any non-Aryan. They may have been part of the Storm Troopers, but when their loyalty to Hitler came into question, killing them was no different from slaughtering chickens for the marketplace. As a result, he concentrated most of his attention on the SS soldiers, seeing which ones did as they were told and which ones appeared to be "weaklings."

Himmler supervised four thousand murders that night, looking upon the blood as the price necessary to establish his power position under Hitler. He also felt that the deaths were like a baptism of blood that showed the world the strength of character and loyalty of the SS. Even Hitler mourned former friends such as Gregor Strasser, who was murdered along with the other enemies of the state. Only Himmler was dispassionate about what had been done.

Heydrich immediately took control of the task of building the SS into the most powerful force in Germany. At the time of the murders there were slightly more than fifty thousand men, including the Action Troops (Verfügungstruppe), an elite fighting force. Heydrich began an intense recruiting drive, seeking specialists in every field, including medicine and law. Training schools would be expanded. The SS would have greater power within the Nazi party. And everywhere in Germany was the symbol of the SS, old Germanic runes that looked like two lightning bolts. They were not a stylized double S meant to stand for Schutz staffeln, but rather the old symbol for Victory: Sieg.

For Himmler there was still one additional plan to be carried out. He needed his own community for the SS elite, a concept derived from history and legend. It would be known as the Burgh of the Holy Order of the SS and was to be located in Westphalia.

The location eventually selected was both practical and the fulfillment of Himmler's fantasy, an area that held the ruins of a foundation for what may once have been a medieval walled castle. This was recreated at a cost of eleven million marks and was designed so that every room was in a different style, none of the furnishings duplicated. A walk through all the rooms was an experience much like visiting a museum that held the history of the German Reich, both real and imagined. Books, artifacts, and priceless antiques were used everywhere. The room dedicated to Heinrich I, the most opulent of all, belonged to Heinrich Himmler.

⚓︎

Death and Dachau

Time was moving swiftly toward the day the world would erupt in violence, the internal policies of the German leadership foretelling the future. First, in 1933, there was Dachau—where the prisoners were mostly political, but their treatment indicated the violence and death to come. For the first few years an effort was made to imply that actions were based on valid law and procedure. Yet even such regulations were terrifyingly brutal.

Originally there was the Order for Protective Custody (Schutzhaftbefehl). The form was simple. It required the prisoner's name, date and place of birth, nationality and religion, and race if the person was a non-Aryan. The form explained: "In accordance with Paragraph 1 of the Order for the Protection of Nation and State, to be taken into protective custody." There were places for the reasons, but most of the forms just used the statement "The investigation of the State Police shows that, by his demeanor and attitude, he endangers the existence and security of State and People."

Dachau was a death camp from the start, though not because of Himmler's orders. The first few weeks there was an attempt to make the camps "legitimate" even if the reasons for imprisoning people were not. The general order of being a danger to the state was often invoked against the extremely elderly who were bedridden as well as against children who had done nothing wrong except to be born to the wrong parents. But once in camp, an attempt was made to maintain a semblance of discipline among the guards. This included a thorough investigation of the death of any inmate not scheduled to die.

The investigation took three days, during which time the prison guard responsible for a death was not allowed to work. Then the investigators would find that the prisoner was killed while trying to escape and the well-rested guard would return to work. Once it became obvious to the guards that none of them would be punished for their actions, it became routine to shoot a prisoner in order to have three days' leave.

In October 1933, Theodor Eicke, working under the direction of Himmler, created specific regulations for the camps. These demanded extreme punishment for any infraction of the rules. Hanging was to be the response for such offenses as loitering, collecting information (true or false), agitating, holding meetings, talking about the camp to others, making inciting speeches, and similar actions. Always there was to be extreme censorship of what was taking place in the camp.

There were minor punishments as well, ranging from solitary confinement to beatings to special-punishment labor units. The idea of total extermination of Jews and other enemies had not yet become government policy, so Himmler was anxious to control any publicity about the camps.

The official statement was that the camps would be for re-education of Germans who would eventually be returned to society as a whole. The re-education would take two to three years, though a flogging might also be prescribed for the behavior that caused the detained individual to need the camps in the first place. Dachau was called a "school for good citizenship," and for a while the camp had signs to this effect.

The task Himmler faced in 1933, before the murders of the SA, was both simple and daunting. He and Heydrich had determined that there were eight million pro-Marxist people in Germany. Some of these could be re-educated in the camps and returned to German society, where they would become constructive members of the Nazi movement. The remainder of those eight million, along with the uncounted number of

Jews who could not be converted because of their race, would remain in the concentration camps.

Dachau was the first camp to be a re-education school. Then came Sachsenhausen in 1936 and Buchenwald in 1937. All of them promised eventual release for prisoners eligible to become Nazis, assuming they were successfully converted. Only later did the camps admit to being places of brutality. For example, the American War Crimes Branch reported 1946 that the average concentration camp was "a factory dealing in death. Hunger and starvation rations, sadism, inadequate clothing, medical neglect, disease, beatings, hangings, freezing, forced-hand hanging, forced suicides, shooting, all played a major role.... Prisoners were murdered at random, spite killings of Jews were common. Injections of poison and shooting in the neck were everyday occurrences.... Epidemics of typhus and spotted fever were permitted to run rampant as a means of eliminating prisoners. Life... meant nothing. Killing became a common thing, so common that a quick death was welcomed."

Dachau became a model camp because it was designed to also house the SS leadership assigned to the area. Small villas were constructed by the prisoners just outside the electrified barbed-wire fence. The prisoners also constructed a barracks for the guards, a riding school, an SS hospital, canteens, and other facilities. The interior facilities for the prisoners were spartan, though, three-tiered bunks being used in barracks surrounding the square.

Some of the camps built before the war also had special barracks units. One small one was used as a movie house for entertainment, as well as the place where all inside executions took place. Buchenwald was famous for its Action Bullet facility. Prisoners were measured for clothing there. However, when a prisoner was marked for death, he would be placed against the measuring area, then shot by a hidden mechanism that sent a bullet through the neck.

Himmler took pride in his compassion for the people in the concentration camps. Many times his mother would discuss friends and acquaintances removed to the camps whom she thought should be spared. All such requests were granted.

In addition, he would sometimes try to spare someone who looked the right type to him. For example, during one visit to Dachau he insisted upon seeing the women's quarters. The women were lined up and he marched past them, studying their facial features, making obscene remarks to those who were "obviously" Jews. Then he noticed one woman who had blond hair and Aryan features. He discovered that she was a German Bible student who had been sent to the camp for being a pacifist who demonstrated against the increasing militarism of the country. She was also married and the mother of two children.

Himmler was deeply moved by her plight. He felt that she had "strayed from the path." He told her that he would order her immediate release if she would sign a document stating that she recognized her Aryan heritage. But such a document would mean denouncing her religious beliefs, something she could not bring herself to do.

The woman was not defiant. Witnesses at the scene said she simply stood, tears streaming down her face, neither refusing nor agreeing, answering him with silence.

Himmler understood what was taking place. Outraged, he announced that she was one of the most dangerous prisoners of all because she also had the advantage of being a part of the Aryan race. He looked upon her as he looked upon any traitor within the Nazi party. Two hours later she was dead.

⚜

The propaganda during the establishment of the camps was positive on the surface. Himmler made a speech in Munich in 1933 in which he said: "Protective custody is an act of care. If I have taken such measures in a rather extensive manner, I have been misunderstood in many places". He added, "You must understand that there was justifiable excitement, annoyance and hostility against those who opposed us. Only by taking them under protective custody was I able to save the personalities who have caused this annoyance. Only in that way was I able to guarantee their security of health and life. But let me say right here, for us the Jews are as much citizens as those of non-Jewish faith. Their lives and property are equally protected. Protective custody where it concerns Jews must be understood in this spirit."

However, even in this early stage, before the purging of the SA and the atrocities to come, Himmler recognized that the Jews might ultimately have to be exterminated. He knew that his idea of enslaving them and others to work for the Aryans went against the desires of Hitler and Goebbels. He could not justify in his own mind the atrocities that would come based strictly on anti-Semitism. He was comfortable with mass murder only if it would help Hitler. Thus, after Heydrich was ordered to spread reports that there had been threats on Hitler's life, threats that preceded the purge, Himmler announced: "Let me say right here if an attempt should be made on the life of the Führer it would result in the greatest pogrom ever. I could not prevent the mass murders which would be the inevitable consequence."

Himmler moved quickly to create an atmosphere where anything was possible. An SS unit entitled Adolf Hitler Bodyguard (Leibstandarte Adolf Hitler) was created, the men issued a black ribbon with Hitler's name to be worn on their arms. They were known as the LAH and were authorized to do anything necessary to protect Hitler.

Soon it was a common sight to see open trucks filled with LAH men race through the streets where Hitler would be traveling. The route would be known in advance, everyone ordered to keep their windows closed as a precaution against snipers. If anyone forgot or deliberately ignored the police order, the LAH would fire into the open window.

The events of 1933 and the purge of 1934 set the stage for the atrocities that would begin in 1935 and ultimately involve all nations of the world. This was also the period when the propaganda developed by Goebbels and other racists such as Julius Streicher, the man who owned Der Stürmer, a weekly Nazi newspaper. Streicher was a crude, uneducated man who had befriended Hitler during the days before his arrest in the Beer Hall Putsch.

The Rapid Spread of Anti-Semitism

Streicher was determined to undermine the popular acceptance of Jews. He wanted to debase them, to create an atmosphere of hatred and intolerance. It was a situation supported by the leaders of the Reich because it desensitized the public to any action the government might take, from confiscation of property to murder. For example, the idea of the Jews as God's chosen people had long been discussed by all Judeo-Christian religions, another reason men like Himmler wanted the Nazis to have their own religion. To counter this, Streicher published statements such as:

"A chosen people does not rape women and girls... does not torture animals... does not live by the sweat of others... or drive your parents from home and farm... all of which is what the Jews are doing." There was no proof, of course. There was never any justification for the charges, any crimes by Jews reported in the papers.

This was also the period when Himmler made a clean break with his personal feelings and his public image. No longer would he talk of the rights of Jewish citizens. Himmler began organizing the World League of Anti-Semites, the meetings discussing such problems as Jews as aliens and Jews as the people who caused the problems that started World War I.

Streicher began preparing people for the purging of non-Aryan blood as defined by Himmler by publishing "scientific" information about such matters as "alien albumen." Der Stürmer reported that "Alien albumen is the semen of a man of different race. One single act of cohabitation results in the woman's blood being poisoned—forever. Never again, even if she marries an Aryan, can she give birth to Aryan children—only to bastards in whose breasts dwell two souls and whose physical characteristics prove the mixture of race. These infants are liable to be ugly children of unstable character with a tendency to sickness…. And, of course, we know why Jews are attempting with every means to seduce Aryan girls, why Jewish doctors rape their female Aryan patients under the anesthetic, why Jewish wives even encouraged their husbands to enter into relations with non-Jewish women—so that the German girl, the German woman, should absorb the Jewish poison and never be able to bear German children."

The newspaper began promoting violence by publishing photos of German girls who had been seen in the company of men known or suspected to be Jews. They also published pictures of Jewish men who were believed to associate with German girls. Any SS men who saw such individuals were expected to punish them. A German who was so recognized was guilty of Rassenschande (race shame).

The violence that followed was a forerunner of the Holocaust. Small children were provided cartoons, textbooks, and other materials necessary to teach them the lies of race hatred and anti-Semitism. The idea was to so convince the young of the evil of the Jews that everyone would tolerate whatever actions were taken against them.

The material published by Der Stürmer was horrendously vile. "Scientific studies" were published to show such "truths" as –

the execution of ritual murders is a law of the Talmud Jew… the rules are as follows: "The blood of the victim is tapped by force. On Passover (in memory of the murder of Christ) it is used in wine and matzos. Thus a small part of the blood is poured into the dough of the matzos and into the wine. The mixing is done by the head of the family… who empties a few drops of the fresh and powdered blood into a glass, wets the fingers of the left hand with it and sprays (blesses) with it everything on the table… then they eat and the head of the family exclaims 'May all Gentiles perish as this child whose blood is contained in the bread and wine….' The blood of the slaughtered… is further used by young married Jewish couples, by pregnant Jewesses, for circumcision and so on. Ritual murder is recognized…. The Jew believes he thus absolves himself of his sins.

Once the public had sufficient anger toward the Jews, the Nuremberg

Laws were enacted (in 1935). Jews were denied their citizenship. Jews married to Germans had to leave their spouses. Relations between Germans and Jews were illegal. They were denied access to public transportation, sidewalks, amusement areas, and other places. They had fewer rights than a dog running loose in the city.

Himmler also established his own newspaper, *Das Schwarze Korps* (The Black Corps), using Heydrich to handle the organization. The paper was used to attack Jews and name dissidents and others who needed to be warned before they were beaten, sent to a concentration camp, or murdered. Heydrich supplied the research to reveal anyone who had ever faltered in loyalty to Hitler and the Nazi cause. The editor, Günther d'Alquen, and his writers said whatever was necessary to attack those who might provide trouble for them.

The Catholic Church and its publication, Messenger of King Christ (*Christkoenigsbote*), had the courage to counter the outrageous teachings by the new Das Schwarze Korps. They showed that the paper not only lied but stressed that individual Catholics were beginning to take stands against the idea of a national church formed by the Nazis. The leaders of the paper were sent to Dachau, but it was not uncommon to hear courageous Franciscans preach such ideas as "We prefer a Jew or a Negro with a pure soul to any Aryan sinner!"

On October 7, 1935, Himmler received the following telegram: My dear Party Comrade Himmler, on the occasion of your birthday I am sending you my heartfelt greetings and add my wish that you may in future as hitherto devote your whole strength to the security of the National Socialist Reich. —Adolf Hitler.

The telegram was all the encouragement Himmler needed to take on any and all responsibility. He began having severe stomach pains, a crippling illness most of which was caused by stress. Whatever concerns arose outside the preparations for war, Hitler would allow Himmler to deal with it. And Himmler was always willing. For the next four years his ever-enlarging SS would deal with the Catholics, the Jews, the dissidents among the Nazis, and all the other enemies, real or imagined. Concentration camps increased. Mass extermination was begun. And efforts were made to utilize slave labor in critical manufacturing plants. By the time the Second World War began, Himmler had become the one of most powerful men in the Third Reich. There was no task too small, no request too large. Whatever he or Heydrich could not handle probably could not have been accomplished by any organization.

And it was with Heinrich Himmler, the presumably ineffective toady who was perhaps the most devious man in the Third Reich that Folke Bernadotte would be called upon to negotiate in a critical life-or-death confrontation.

PART III

Rebellion of the Damned

CHAPTER 5

The Jews

THE MIDDLE EAST had, for centuries, been a land in turmoil, filled with feuding nations and conflicting religions, each convinced of a divine right to either dominate the others or live unmolested by those who would annex their property. The Canaan of God's covenant with Abram (Abraham), an Old Testament story that was a basis for the concept of a Jewish nation in the Holy Land, included all the territory between the Jordan River and the Mediterranean from Egypt into Syria.

Judaism, the first recorded monotheistic religion, was named for the tribe of Judah, the fourth of the twelve sons of Jacob (later called Israel, according to Genesis). His descendants eventually entered Canaan, settling near Bethlehem and acquiring most of South Palestine. Men born into this lineage would be some of the most important in Judeo-Christian history—Boaz, Jesse, and David of the Old Testament and Jesus of the New.

To be a Canaanite, a descendant of the Israelis who conquered Canaan in the 13th century B.C., was, at least in the minds of many of Palestine's Jews, to be part of this rich heritage, to be an inheritor of the land whose domination was promised by God. Other Jews, living hundreds or thousands of miles away, came to view Canaan as the Promised Land, the site of the Jewish state in which they believed. Jerusalem was a part of this territory, and the toast "Next year in Jerusalem" was heard during many a ritual Jewish meal celebrated in other lands. (The reference is, in part, to the site of Solomon's Temple, mentioned in 23 Old Testament and all New Testament books. It was the religious center of world Jewry and was said to contain a boxlike Ark holding two stone tablets that symbolized both the Law and the presence of Yahweh—God.)

Still others were contentedly living in Eastern Europe, in America, and in other parts of the world, with no desire to leave what they considered their homes. Yet they felt themselves a part of both the religion and history of Judaism, supporting the idea for a Jewish state and recognizing that it should be in Canaan even if they had no interest in emigrating there.

Yet because the Middle East had always been a melting pot of religions, with almost every belief imaginable based in the land, there was strong anti-Semitic feeling. The people of ancient Israel were faced with the Canaanites, the Hittites, the Amorites, Perizzites, Hivites, and Jebusites, among others. Each had different histories and beliefs, none of which mattered to those attempting to fulfill God's covenant with Abram.

By more modern times, the polytheistic religions were no longer practiced and monotheistic beliefs prevailed. There were Jews, Christians, Muslims, and others, all believing in one God, all seeing the same territory as a Holy Land, and most feeling that their presence was either ordained by God or at least pleasing to Him. The establishment of a single group that would dominate either sacred territory or the economics of the mostly desert land was likely to bring a hostile response from all other factions. And though no one could have foreseen such a situation, it was this early history that would eventually have a major impact on the life of Folke Bernadotte and the plans of Heinrich Himmler. These individual interests of disparate parties would eventually interact in a way that would bring both great triumph and the murder of a man whose actions helped save Jews from the Holocaust so that they might survive in triumph in the Holy Land.

The Jewish Homeland

The idea of a Jewish homeland had been in the minds of many of the world's Jews at least since the end of the nineteenth century. Serious lobbying of European governments was initiated by Theodor Herzl, who saw in the creation of a Jewish state a chance to diminish the problem of anti-Semitism. In their own land, Jews would no longer be forced into ghettos or forced to take the jobs that a nation's majority population did not desire. They could live in peace, flourishing as both individuals and a nation.

Herzl, who died in 1904, did not believe in simply settling a land and then being recognized by other governments. His work as head of the World Zionist Congress he convened in Basel, Switzerland, in 1897 was meant to gain a charter recognizing the Jewish right to a homeland. He felt that the charter, signed by the nations of the world, must precede any actual settlement.

Twenty years after that first World Zionist Congress, Britain's Lord Arthur Balfour became the first government leader willing to make Herzl's dream a reality. He prepared what came to be known as the Balfour Declaration, a document designed to bring about the Zionist home. The Jewish home would be established in Palestine if the Balfour Declaration was approved, but even its presentation in Parliament brought hope to Jews throughout the world.

The Balfour Declaration took three years to work its way through the English Parliament, during which it was rewritten many times. Originally Balfour wrote "the establishment of Palestine" for the home, but the ultimate document simply said "the establishment in Palestine," a difference that assured eventual territorial disputes. Balfour called the location *the* national home; this was changed to *a* national home. The differences were subtle but quite important. From the start there would be territorial concerns as the Arabs and the Jews had to define the lands they would separately control.

The Zionists were happy about one point, though. Balfour saw the Jews as a race—"the Jewish people"—while most Jews saw themselves as part of a religion. The latter were known as the assimilationists, and though many of them supported the Zionist movement they were anxious to find respite from persecution, not to prove that they were genetically somehow different from others.

The true feelings of the majority of the British people were hard to know. Britain, unlike the United States at that time, was at war with Germany and wanted the political and financial support of American Jews. President Woodrow Wilson also supported the Zionist movement, as did two close advisers, U.S. Supreme Court Associate Justice Louis Brandeis and Rabbi Steven S. Wise. Wise was a rabbi in the reformed movement, a group of Jews who did not believe in Zionism, but he was a strong backer of Herzl's ideas and later established what he called the Free Synagogue, which was a leading proponent of liberal causes.

Sir Herbert Samuel, sent to Palestine to be the British High Commissioner in July 1920, arrived at a time of relative peace in the territory. There had been only one serious outbreak of violence against the idea of the Jewish homeland; that had been led by the mufti Haj Amin el Husseini, the religious leader (mufti) of a group of Palestinian extremists. There were several muftis in the area, the majority of whom had begun working with the Jewish settlers to improve the area. Amin el Husseini, however, was a violent bigot who would develop an alliance with Adolf Hitler. At the time of Samuel's arrival he was in hiding in Lebanon because he had caused his followers to riot against Jews the previous year. That riot had led to the deaths of four Arabs and five Jews, and the wounding of twenty-one Arabs and two-hundred-eleven Jews.

Amin was actually more dangerous than his bigotry indicated. He was a religious zealot who saw himself as keeper of the purest of Muslim traditions. Everywhere he looked, both Arabs and Jews were changing, becoming Westernized. Most of his fellow Muslims were devout, yet they did not follow the ancient traditions. They were becoming Westernized, accepting of other religions.

The mufti Haj Amin el Husseini, born in 1893, was part of the first generation of Arabs who no longer lived exclusively in the desert. Permanent settlements meant an influx of foreign goods. Even Amin (the title *Haj* or *Hajj* indicated that he had made the pilgrimage to Mecca) had succumbed to the new temptations. As a young man he delighted in wearing the gaudiest of Western style clothing, displaying expensive jewels, and dousing himself with perfume. He had also delighted in the appearance of the Jewish girls who, not restricted by Muslim custom, had gone around in shorts.

It was not certain when he became so bitter in his attitude and actions. While Turkey still controlled Palestine, Amin had worked in Jerusalem along with Jews. He confided to his co-workers that he had had no problem with native Jews, respecting them and their customs. However, he hated the outside Zionists and was determined to massacre them as alien invaders. He felt that the Zionists were responsible for bringing progress and prosperity to such a degree that the people could afford the corrupting goods being imported. He wanted to maintain the old ways, living as his people had lived for centuries in the desert, tolerating other faiths providing the people practicing them were natives of the area. It was a warning of what lay ahead that was not taken seriously.

The Jewish settlers were not overly concerned about the violence that had taken place in 1919 because Amin el Husseini was not respected by the vast majority of Arabs. His feelings did not reflect their own. Arabs and Jews were working together for the betterment of Palestine and toward the eventual equitable division of land that would allow for a Jewish state in the midst of the Arab world.

Sir Herbert Samuel was sent to Palestine because it was felt that he would administer with wisdom and fairness. He was of Jewish heritage, yet he was so anxious to bring peace for all people that he pardoned Amin and welcomed him back to Jerusalem. Amin immediately began to work to solidify his power. He hated the Jews, hated the British occupiers of Palestine, hated the other muftis. But violence had only resulted in exile. He needed to build political alliances and mark time until he could position himself to destroy those he saw as his enemies.

Sir Herbert was the perfect pawn. If an extremist stopped using violence, the High Commissioner felt he had changed and should be rewarded for that change. Herbert decided to act upon this belief after the Mufti of Jerusalem died in February 1921. That mufti was the most politically powerful of all the religious leaders and his position was partially elective, partially appointive.

First the Ulema gathered. This was a group of prominent Muslim leaders who held elections to determine the top three candidates, based on number of votes, for Mufti of Jerusalem. Amin took a rather distant fourth place, making him ineligible for any position and making it obvious that he was not under primary consideration.

Amin's followers would not tolerate such an election. They managed to coerce the leading candidate to withdraw, reportedly under threat of death. Amin then moved into the third position, where Sir Herbert—determined to show a complete lack of prejudice—declared him the Mufti of Jerusalem.

The Muslim community was outraged. The man who would soon call himself the Grand Mufti (a self-imposed title of no historic meaning that he used to show he was more important than other muftis) was actually a fraud. He let it be known that he was a direct descendent of the Prophet Muhammad. His followers put great faith in his statements, regardless of how extreme, because of his proclaimed lineage. (The family was actually Yemeni, not Palestinian, and unconnected with the Prophet or anyone else of major importance.)

Life still might have been productive in the Middle East, both Arabs and Jews prospering and living in peace, had not Sir Herbert Samuel continued his misguided effort to make everyone happy. The British government had originally planned to govern Palestine carefully, keeping the peace, encouraging the area's growth, and helping the Zionist movement establish a homeland. Then some of the soldiers and administrators became uncomfortable with their assignment. They were in towns with strange customs and languages. The people were not particularly friendly, more comfortable with the British than they had been with the Turks but still feeling that they were dominated by outsiders.

As a result, some of the soldiers came to fear that they might become targets of violence. The more the new settlements were developed, the greater the chance that the Arabs and Jews would unite against an occupying force, no matter how friendly.

The fears developing among the members of the occupying force played into the hands of Amin as he continued to gain power he should not have had. Samuel, firmly convinced that if he set a positive example of benevolence all the people would be happy, changed the government organization. Instead of the British administering the Muslim affairs, the Muslim leaders would become responsible for their communities. He formed the Supreme Muslim Council and encouraged Amin to be its president.

The year was 1929, and Palestine seemed at peace. Jews and Arabs had been working in harmony for almost nine years. The British troops had no problem with the people, some of the soldiers even married indigenous women. The communities were growing steadily, with the Balfour Agreement holding the hope for an even better future.

Yet there was the underlying fear of the occupation force and the sense among some of the leaders that it might be best to keep tension between Arabs and Jews. When British intelligence officers learned that Haj Amin, now known to his followers as the Grand Mufti, was spreading reports that the Jews were planning to desecrate and destroy Muslim holy places, they did nothing to intervene. The rumors increased, nonextremist Arabs becoming suspicious of Jews who had once been their friends. Then the Grand Mufti let it be known that the Mosque of Omar, on the site of Solomon's Temple, was going to be destroyed. His lies caused fighting to break out near the Western Wall in Jerusalem.

Friday night, August 23, 1929, through early Saturday morning, the violence began. The incident occurred in the city of Hebron, where an Arab mob composed primarily of extremist followers of the Grand Mufti decided to attack Jews least likely to offer resistance. These were elderly men and women as well as religious students of the yeshiva, a training center for orthodox rabbis. The people were peaceful, trusting, neither armed nor accustomed to violence of any kind—perfect victims for a bloodletting by the radicals.

The Grand Mufti's claim that he was going to have violence committed only against the Zionist settlers, "not against the pious and non-political Jews in the land, who had always lived in peace and harmony with the Arabs" should have meant that the Jews of Hebron were safe. The British military leader for the area had left Hebron to confer about violence expected in other areas. The Arabs entered the synagogue, killing as many people as they could find, then moved on to the yeshiva, where only two or three of the students and professors present were able to escape. From there they went to the home of Rabbi Slonim, where thirty-eight men and women had taken refuge. The Arab mob broke through the window, slitting the throats of all who were inside, then removing the breasts of the women and the genitals of the men.

There was only one survivor found in the rabbi's home, an infant whose mother had managed to push him into a cupboard under the kitchen sink. This boy eventually became a decorated officer in the Israeli army during the 1948 war against the Arabs.

When the violence was over and the streets were quiet, Hebron had been radically changed. Most of the Jews who had lived peacefully in the city were dead, their bodies removed as quickly as possible so that the public would not know of the mutilations. Witnesses who had heard the mob shout "The government is with us!," as they attacked the rabbi's home were the victims of attempts to discredit them by the British. And the British governor of Hebron, who had been present when the violence occurred, refused to say why he had not bothered to at least fire a rifle in the air to disperse the mob.

The majority of the Arabs were as upset by the incident as the Jews living outside the city. Overnight their community was ruined. Fear and suspicion were rampant. Some were terrified of Jewish retaliation. Others were frightened of the Grand Mufti and his men. And all were economically shattered, the murdered Jews representing a large enough percentage of their customers that many businesses could not continue to make a profit.

The full story of what took place was eventually known. Sheik Talib Marqa had been the man who represented Haj Amin, gathering a group of fanatical, anti-Jewish Arabs and ordering them to kill the Jews and drink their blood. His skillful oratory had worked them into a frenzy that became completely uncontrollable within minutes. Yet had the British taken action at the start, and there was awareness by at least some of the British authorities concerning what was about to take place the mob could have been dispersed without violence. Instead, their inaction fit into what many of the Jews believed was the deliberate effort to keep an occupied region unstable in order to assure that the presence of the British forces would continue to be needed.

The British seemed to have an unofficial policy in regard to their occupation forces in many parts of the world, including the Middle East. First there was the restoration of order. Turbulent societies were brought under control, warring factions were stopped, and the British brought peace to the region.

Then a paranoia seemed to set in. The British represented an occupation force. They were unfamiliar with the people, the customs, the language of whatever land they were in. Often they did not understand or respect the religious practices of the region and were frequently perceived as considering the natives inferior. The soldiers inadvertently offended the citizens by not understanding or adhering to the local culture, then were irate when they were not respected.

Eventually the British realized that, no matter how turbulent the area had been, they were the outsiders, and outsiders could become a focal point against which all locals might unite. In the case of the Middle East, there may have been hostility among Arab factions, Muslim sects, and between Arabs and Jews, but it was a familiar hostility. Conflicts were based on centuries-old partisan issues involving their shared homeland. Often the issues concerned land sacred to Jews, Christians, and Muslims alike, each having a different reason for revering the territory. Yet these were local concerns that did not change the hostility of all regional factions against an outside occupying force whose ways were foreign to the territory.

The Arabs and Jews, at peace with one another following the start of the British occupation, sharing the same region, economy, and historic life-style, soon looked upon the British as their enemy, and the local people became united in their determination to rid themselves of these outsiders.

There were only three possibilities for the British. The first was to withdraw from the territory. They had brought peace to Palestine. Warring factions had ceased their overt hostility. Everyone, whether Christian, Muslim, or Jew, was earning a similar amount of money, enjoying a life-style equal to his or her neighbor's. No one coveted the wealth of another because almost everyone earned a comparable income. It would be possible to withdraw, safe in the knowledge that the people could continue to live in harmony despite divergent religious beliefs.

But withdrawal meant the abandonment of territory at a time the British were clinging to the empire that had once been theirs. It was only after the war years that demands for independence would be heard throughout the world, countries such as India, Northern Ireland, and others insisting upon change. The idea of abandoning any occupied area was unthinkable during the period immediately following World War I.

The second possibility was to continue business as usual. The troops would operate as they had all along, now becoming a focal point for those who would rally the people against such occupation. This meant that Arabs and Jews would begin working together to rid the land of the British. There could be terrorist attacks, work stoppages, sabotage, and other problems. The soldiers would find themselves living under siege, a terrifying circumstance.

The third approach was the one the British decided to use. If they could create disharmony among the people of the occupied territory, the British would no longer be the enemy. There were Jews, Christians, and several different Muslim groups who could be turned against one another. The people would be so concerned with the various warring factions that no one would take the time to think about the outside forces. More important the British might be seen as peacemakers.

The only problem for the British was that, from the start, they handled this transition poorly. It became obvious that they were deliberately encouraging the most extremist of the Arabs to attack the Jews. There was a perception of bias toward the extremists that not only frightened Jews, causing them to recognize the need to arm for self-defense, but also was of serious concern to moderate Arabs who felt that they could become targeted for violence by both sides.

The result would ultimately thwart British plans for continued dominance. The Middle East would explode in factional violence, but there would be continuing hostility toward the occupying force as well. Instead of a united Arab/Jewish movement against the soldiers, the British would be faced with periodic terrorist attacks from all sides, each working independently of the others. The factions were each seeking to control Palestine in their own ways, creating turmoil yet also making it more difficult for the British to protect themselves from violence.

Although there were attempts to hide all the details, eventually the full horror of that first British-encouraged slaughter was made known. Sixty-three Jews lay dead, another fifty wounded. Most had been disemboweled with daggers. One old man bled to death after being castrated. A Jewish baker was grabbed, his head burned against one of his lighted baking ovens. A rabbi had his eye gouged out before his head was smashed open. Young girls were raped in front of their parents before all were put to death.

The violence of August 1929 did not end that day. For the next week there would be reports of other deaths in both the Old City and the new town of Jerusalem. Details of murders arrived from Deir Yassin, Motza, Lifta, Haifa, Tel Aviv, and elsewhere. A total of 133 Jews died and 339 were wounded, usually in front of government officials and/or

British occupying police. Where Arab police were present, they became involved with the violence. The British merely watched.

As the Jews realized there would be no help from the British and the government officials, a few began to arm themselves and their children. They went to workshops and fashioned sharpened metal ends on wooden poles. Ritual slaughter knives used for killing animals as part of the kosher process became offensive weapons. Knives, hatchets, and other tools were kept not only for work but also for war. This militant attitude was different from the past and it impressed many of the children.

Years later, as they wrote about the struggle against the British and the establishment of the Jewish state, many would speak of how they looked upon the adults who armed themselves as the "new Jews." They spoke of biblical activists such as Ehud ben Gera, slayer of the king of Moab (Judges 3:15), and of Moses slaying the Egyptian (Exodus 2:11). They said that these activists were the role models for their violence, that they were carrying on historic tradition in the face of oppression.

The British eventually responded to the riots by issuing a white paper that restricted Jewish land purchases and immigration—the final act of contempt in the eyes of the Jews. From that moment forward, there would be a war against the British occupation, a war of guerrilla tactics whose "soldiers" would primarily come from the ranks of schoolchildren.

The Child Terrorists

The British did not respect the potential threat of these children as they should have. By 1933, Jewish schoolboys were secretly using print shops to produce posters denouncing the British High Commissioner and the restrictions against immigration. They chose shops owned by the fathers of their schoolmates, using them secretly at night since they knew that the adults would not approve of their tactics. The writing was passionate, undoubtedly naive but the first stand anyone had taken in writing against the actions of the British.

A number of underground organizations existed in Palestine during the period when the schoolchildren were becoming activists in their own right. The groups were more subtle than the children because they understood the ramifications of actions against the British. But one, Haganah Leumit—also known as Haganah-bet, Haganah B, and, more commonly, Irgun (Organization), recognized the need to bring the children into the fold.

A militarist organization, the Irgun wanted to kindle intense nationalism among Hebrew youth, an approach rejected by a second group known as Haganah. Its oath explained much about its spirit and was a factor that appealed to teenage radicals:

> Of my own free will and consent, and without any coercion, I swear to be a loyal soldier of the Irgun Zvai Leumi in the Land of Israel who will defend national property, life and honor, and will help to bring about the full restoration of our people in the land of their forefathers. I accept obedience without any reservations, and promise to keep total secrecy in regard to all I know about the Irgun. I will obey my commanders and carry out all their orders at any place and at any time. So help me the Guardian of Israel.

Irgun members were divided into cells of ten members. While Haganah accepted arms for defensive means when other measures failed, Irgun stressed arms to be used to achieve military victory. Thus all training was meant to create what amounted to miniature terrorist armies. The cells were fighting units that could work alone or in combination with others. The children and adults trained with handguns because their fighting would be close-in, hit-and-run. They also learned to use grenades and other explosives. The cells stockpiled food for when they had to go into hiding and assigned one girl per cell to operate a first-aid station.

As the students proved themselves in the cells, they were sent for more sophisticated training in larger groups. Older youths would teach more advanced fighting, including the use of the Finnish submachine gun, the making of bombs, the use of hand grenades as offensive weapons, and other tactics. The courses ran six months and were taught during times of day when the members were neither at school nor at work. They used locations the British would not spot, including areas of villages where the people were sympathetic and would not report the sounds of weapons being fired during target practice.

In 1936 the role of the Irgun and the Haganah changed. Arab militants began attacking villages with the intent of destroying all the inhabitants. The British police were not willing to have such extremes occur and would come to the aid of the Jews, though not until attacks were underway. The Haganah found itself establishing perimeter defense forces that many of the members of Irgun, primarily under the leadership of Avraham Tehomi, supported. Those individuals decided to merge with the Haganah, protecting the land but not actively pursuing the militant Arabs.

A second group within the Irgun saw no reason to abandon an offensive underground force. Under the ideological leadership of Avraham Stern, they formed the Irgun Zvai Leumi. This organization had as its manifesto a statement made by Stern on April 23, 1937:

> To Those Who Honor The Oath!
> The Irgun Zvai Leumi in the Land of Israel was created because we believe that the Hebrew state will not become a reality without relying on an independent national military body.
> The Jewish Agency now hopes to obtain approval for free action for those under its command in return for subjugation to the foreign rule and surrender to the cantonization plans for this land. The IZL in the Land of Israel is charged with the duty of acting as the only real force that will be called upon and will be able to fight for the re-establishment of the Hebrew nation in the Land of Israel in the face of the plotting of the external enemy and the surrender to those who are willing to betray us from within.
> The IZL in the Land of Israel has been forced by political reality to decide whether to surrender to the power of the government and the Jewish Agency, or to redouble its sacrifice and its risk-taking. Some of our friends were not up to this difficult task. They surrendered to the Agency and left the battlefield. The large loyal majority continues to uphold the original policy of the IZL. All the attempts by the former command of the Irgun to reach a merger with the leftist organization have failed, since the left has not negotiated on the basis of joining forces but of imposing one group's will on the other. Putting the IZL under the authority of the Agency which is ruled by the left is the end of our organization.
> There are two organizations today in this land: one is leftist, run by the left, and to our regret some of our men have joined it. The other is the IZL, which continues to fight for the dignity and the life of the nation being reborn. We believe in the mission of our movement and in its power to re-establish the full independence within the historical borders of the Hebrew state. We believe in Israel's youth's willing to fight and to sacrifice, having set as its life's goal the might and the independence of the nucleus of Hebrew power.
> Anonymous soldiers!
> The nucleus of Hebrew power is prepared for any order or sacrifice. "Only death releases us from duty! "

Avraham Stern's manifesto set in motion the forces that would eventually take the life of Folke Bernadotte. That Stern would be long dead, murdered by British soldiers, would not alter the destiny of his ideas. The group that would come to be known as the Stern gang, a primarily young and often fanatical group, would perpetrate one of the most dramatic and ironic acts in recent history.

CHAPTER 6

The Rise of Jewish Rebels

THE IDEA THAT Jews were fatalists or pacifists when faced with over-whelming violence is not only a long-held misconception but historical-ly naive myth. And the British had particular reason to think of the Jews in Palestine as passive. Not only were they making every effort to work with the Arabs, the only armed battalion of Jewish soldiers fight-ing together anywhere in the world between A.D. 135 and 1918 totaled slightly over five thousand men. These were the 39th Regiment of Royal Fusiliers who marched behind the Star of David through London's Whitechapel on February 2, 1918. They were known as the Jewish Legion and their second lieutenant was the thirty-eight-year-old Vladimir Ze'ev Jabotinsky.

Jabotinsky was an unusual Zionist leader, born in Odessa. His family was wealthy enough to educate him in literature, languages, and the arts. He spoke Yiddish, Hebrew, and six other languages, studied in Switzerland, and moved to Italy. He probably would have lived the life of a scholar had he not returned to Russia for a visit during the period of the pogroms, the systematic violence against Russian Jews. Angered by what he was seeing, he organized self-defense groups to fight offi-cially sanctioned mobs attacking the towns. He also became a dedicat-ed Zionist, determined to establish the structures necessary to have a Jewish state.

World War I seemed the perfect time to establish a Jewish right to Palestine, then part of the Ottoman Empire. He felt that the way to do so was to establish a fighting unit on the side of the Allies, free Palestine from Turkey, and assert the rights of the Jewish people to that territory.

Jabotinsky went to Alexandria, where the British leaders authorized him to establish the Zionist Mule Corps, a Jewish transport outfit. The group came under fire in Gallipoli, proved itself valiant despite not being trained for an active combat role, and asked to see greater action. After the Balfour Declaration passed, the Jewish Legion was allowed to be created.

The results of the Jewish Legion's fighting in Jericho, Shechem, and Jordan were so impressive that even British general Allenby apologized for maligning what he thought would be a weak lot of "small tailors from Whitechapel." By the end of the war, there were three Jewish battalions totaling over five thousand men, all of them combat-experienced. A third had come from Great Britain; the rest were equally split between Palestinians and Americans from the United States and Canada.

Many of these five thousand settled in Palestine after the British mandate went into effect and Jabo, as Jabotinsky was called, hoped to use them to start a strong defense organization. The British refused to allow such a situation, officially disbanding the men. However, when Amin el Husseini instigated the first violence against the Jews in 1920, Jabo organized the Haganah, a self-defense organization that was in violation of British law. As a result, Jabo was arrested, convicted, and sentenced to fifteen years in prison. He only served a few months, though, being released in 1921 under the same amnesty that returned Amin to Jerusalem.

Jabotinsky became frustrated by the slowness of change in the region. The British created immigration quotas for Palestine to assure what they felt would be an orderly building of the Jewish state. They wanted the land and economy to have no more people than could be housed, fed, and employed, while Jabo wanted a free and open nation for Jews where any number would be welcomed at any time.

There was a strong split among the Zionists during this time, Jabotinsky helping found the Union of Revisionist Zionists, many of whose members wanted nothing to do with liberalism and accommodation. They wanted a Jewish state dominating both banks of the Jordan River. Among them was a faction led by Abba Achimeir, a supporter of Mussolini's ideas, who called fascism "the great national movement that will save Europe from its impotent parliaments and from the abominable dictatorship of the Soviets."

Jabotinsky fought such extremist ideas until after the Hebron massacre and the obvious indifference of the British government. By August 1931 Jabo was the head of one faction of Jews meeting at the Seventeenth Zionist Congress in Basel, Switzerland. Numerous political groups were represented, the members coming from several countries of the world, but Jabo had obtained fifty-two supporters among 250 delegates and knew he might dominate in the next year or two. Once he controlled the annual congress, he felt that he could bring Jewish majority rule to Palestine.

The primary opposition against Jabotinsky came from David Ben-Gurion (who would become Israel's first prime minister), who related Jabotinsky to the increasingly powerful Adolf Hitler and looked upon Jabo's followers as no different from the German Brown Shirts, the thugs who bullied Hitler's enemies.

Both Ben-Gurion and Jabotinsky were focusing on the British and the problems within Palestine. A third leader during this period had a more international sense of mission: Chaim Arlosoroff, who had numerous contacts among the most powerful leaders of what was becoming Nazi-dominated Germany. His sister Lisa had been the best friend of Magda Ritschel, who married Dr. Joseph Goebbels, Hitler's propaganda minister. Plans for the extermination of the Jews had not been solidified in the early 1930s, and Arlosoroff knew that Hitler might be supportive of the removal of the Jews to their own country. He subsequently made several trips to Berlin and elsewhere to accomplish such an evacuation.

The problem was that other leaders of the Zionist congress were neither so aware of nor so concerned about German actions before Hitler's assumption of ultimate power. They were more narrowly focused on the actions in Palestine and ultimately considered Arlosoroff a Nazi sympathizer. They did not realize that not only did Arlosoroff feel a mission to save the Jews from what he felt was an increasingly violent Germany, he had also come to hate the British as much as such extremists as Jabotinsky. He realized that despite the Balfour resolution, the British had no intention of allowing a Jewish homeland to become a reality. Immigration quotas were just a screen for a policy that was in direct contradiction to the intention of Balfour.

Later, even the most extreme of the Zionists turned against both the Nazis and the fascists. Jabotinsky even announced "We have to fight to the death against Hitlerism, in every sense of the word." Still, even after that statement, Arlosoroff went to Berlin in April 1933, an action that resulted in intense criticism. It was also during this period that an assassination plot was developed by the Arabs, who seemed to feel that it would be possible to kill Arlosoroff with the fewest repercussions. He was in charge of the Jewish Agency's political department, a position similar to that of foreign minister within an established nation. Killing him during the controversy would help the British and Haj Amin, yet enable the murderers to make a case for the Jews being the assassins. The murder took place on June 16, 1933, and, though Chaim's wife recognized that the killers were Arabs, ultimately there was a cover-up that further inflamed the area.

As Hitler solidified his power German Jews were entering Palestine in record numbers. Britain was attempting to control the influx of the Jews despite the Balfour agreement. The revisionists, led by Jabotinsky, now wanted a Jewish state no matter what it took to obtain it. His followers were ready to use violence if necessary, and they refused to trust the current actions of the British. They did feel that ultimately the British statesmen would honor the promises made under Balfour, but until that occurred, they would use whatever methods were necessary for the building of the Jewish state. They would fight the Arabs, the British, and anyone else.

Ben-Gurion and his followers took the more moderate approach and sought compromise. They were equally dedicated Zionists but were in favor of working with the Arabs. They recognized that the extremists were in the minority and that both Arabs and Jews were suffering under British control.

The leaders of the Haganah, working with the British Criminal Intelligence Division (CID), were sympathetic to the moderates. They convinced Sima Arlosoroff, Chaim's widow, to change her description of her husband's killers. Other witnesses also recanted until the official version of the death was that the killers were revisionist Jewish assassins. Allegedly they based their actions on the ancient Jewish Sicari sect, who carried concealed daggers with which they assassinated the Romans.

Two Jews were arrested for the crime but never convicted. Joseph M. Broadhearst, commander of the British police in Tel Aviv, later wrote of the incident: "We did not have an incriminating evidence, not one real clue, but since the victim was a politically symbolic figure, we had to do something. Thus we decided to arrest a number of militant extremists whose ideas were opposed to those held by the victim. We knew for a fact that none of the accused had been involved in the murder. We were forced to pervert justice for reasons of state."

The killers were later learned to be two Arab youths, Abd el-Majid el-Bukhari, a nineteen-year-old plumber from Jaffa, and his friend Issa Darwish. They were apparently hired as the result of orders by Joseph Goebbels precisely because of the connections that Arlosoroff so proudly hoped to exploit. This connection was with the woman to whom Goebbels was married.

Magda, Goebbels' wife, was the love child of wealthy engineer industrialist Oscar Ritschel and a servant girl, Augustina Bernhardt; they were married for a short while, then divorced. Augustina married Max Friedlander, who adopted the child, though Ritschel remained close, much to the disgust of his second wife.

Friedlander was a Jew, though Ritschel and Bernhardt were Catholic. Since the religion is passed through the mother, Magda would not be considered Jewish under orthodox Jewish teachings unless she converted. Friedlander, a liberal Jew, felt that Magda should be educated in Catholic schools because of her parentage. However, in the Nazi system, Magda would still be a half-Jew and eligible for the death camps.

Magda was educated in convent boarding schools in Germany and Belgium, making friends with students such as Lisa Arlosoroff. She also came to know Dora and Victor (later called Chaim) Arlosoroff, Lisa's brother and sister, and was intrigued by their talk of moving to Palestine, where they planned to live in a kibbutz. She thought seriously about moving with them, becoming a Jew and sharing the communal life in the ancient land. However, love intervened when she was eighteen and she married Günter Quandt, a German industrialist with whom she traveled around the world. She even came to the United States, meeting both President Herbert Hoover and J. Edgar Hoover. (J. Edgar Hoover was so taken by her, according to her half-sister, Ariane Ritschel Sheppard, that he went to Germany to see her after she was divorced.) However, she became involved with Hitler's movement to power, marrying Joseph Goebbels in 1931.

(Magda was Hitler's favorite woman; he considered her the first lady of the Third Reich despite his relationship with Eva Braun. Joseph Goebbels recognized Magda's loyalty, dedication, and importance to Hitler as well as his deep affection for her.) When Magda revealed the fact that the brother of her best friend from school was the minister in charge of foreign affairs for the Jewish Agency in Palestine, Goebbels had to eliminate that connection. First he arranged for the arrest and murder of Max Friedlander in March 1933. Then, in April, when Arlosoroff wrote to Magda to arrange for a meeting with her, a letter intercepted by censors on orders from Goebbels, Arlosoroff's fate was sealed. Goebbels arranged for the assassination to take place in Tel Aviv, where it would not be connected with Germany.

It may now never be known how the two assassins were chosen. Gestapo agents were in Jerusalem and may have hired them directly. More likely the men came recommended by either Amin or someone who shared his sympathies for the Nazis and antagonism against the Jews.

Ironically, Oscar Ritschel, the man Goebbels considered his father-in-law because of the ongoing closeness between Ritschel and Magda, was an ardent anti-Nazi. Ritschel ran an underground railroad for Jews from his home. Each evening he would send his daughter Ariane to her room, lock his wife in their bedroom, then bring the Jews into the basement of his home. There he would provide them with new clothes and a false identity that would move them through Germany to a factory he owned near the border. From there they would slip across to freedom. It was an effort he continued ceaselessly until his death in 1941.

The divisiveness was a strain on all the Jews. The Haganah had worked against those of the same faith but a different ideology. Arabs who had been friends were now suspect. The British could not be trusted to protect anyone. And with the murder of Arlosoroff came the decision by the Arab extremists to wage war on everyone.

The Arab violence was not directed just toward the Jews, as many outsiders believed. Starting in 1933 there was systematic killing of anyone opposed to Amin's ideas. In fact, for the next three years, more Arabs than Jews were killed by the terrorists.

Only the British high command was unconcerned. They allegedly delighted in Arab and Jewish strife and were said to have given orders to the occupying forces meant to assure that the terrorists would not be caught. Disgusted with what was happening, one British soldier gave an anonymous account of his orders in the September 20, 1936, *London New Statesman and Nation*, saying in part: "At night when we are guarding the line against the Arabs who come to blow it up, we often see them at work but are forbidden to fire at them. We may only fire into the air, and they, upon hearing the report, make their escape. But do you think we can give chase? Why, we must go on our hands and knees and find every spent cartridge-case, which must be handed in or woe betide us."

The attacks followed a pattern. Arab terrorist sharpshooters would position themselves in hills overlooking roads. One of the most popular areas was in the Judean Hills, fifteen miles from Jerusalem, near Bab el Wad. Convoys would travel a single road leading to the coast. There would be British soldiers, heavily armed, in a lead car followed by travelers who needed to use the road, whether Arabs or Jews, with a second car of British soldiers bringing up the rear. The protection was meaningless because the hills offered the perfect cover for random shooting of anyone below. The Arabs would let the first car pass, then shoot at all subsequent cars except the last one.

The convoy would stop when rifle and machine-gun fire raked the automobiles. The soldiers would get out, fire in the air, then search the ground for shells as evidence of what had taken place. Meanwhile the terrorists had plenty of time to flee to the nearest village, where they would be drinking coffee and relaxing before news of the latest murders could reach their location.

The British did not want to see the Jews destroyed. They simply wanted to prevent a Jewish majority in Palestine that would allow the Balfour resolution to create an independent state. As a result they began encouraging the Haganah despite the fact that it was illegal for either the Jews or the Arabs to have self-defense units. A small quantity of weapons was issued to the various agricultural settlements, and a few Jews were hired to be what amounted to auxiliary police, called ghafirs, to handle patrols. Such weapons enabled the communities to defend themselves against Arab attack, though they were inadequate for protecting them from ambush on the roads.

Other attacks were successful as well, including the bombing of buildings in the towns, the destruction of communication lines, and the burning of crops. The Haganah reduced its partisan efforts as self-defense became critical for survival.

The British further controlled the violence through a policy (known as havlaga) that allowed Arabs, Jews, and British soldiers to defend themselves against any attack although no one was allowed to pursue the attackers.

Havlaga assured the Arab extremists a success they otherwise would not have had. Their numbers were small and their methods were those of guerrilla fighters. Yet the terrain and the attacks they planned were such that it would have been possible to pursue and kill them. The threat that had been taking lives for years could have been eliminated in a matter of weeks through both retaliatory strikes and arrests. Yet this would have restored stability and revealed the British unwillingness to allow the Jewish state to exist.

Havlaga worked until 1939 because of the nature of the immigrants, the same nature that ultimately, and violently, turned the people against the British and anyone who seemed to represent the British way of thinking.

The British made the mistake of not looking closely at the immigrants who were fleeing Eastern Europe. They saw refugees, often wearing tattered clothes and having few possessions. Certainly there were those who had been wealthy and had escaped with their wealth, but the majority was exhausted, bedraggled, with little strength left to fight.

The truth was that the immigrants were the best, the brightest, and the most militant of the oppressed people. They had been revolutionaries in their own countries, fighting against corruption and violence. They were determined to live, to triumph against all odds. They went along with the British only because they truly believed that the Balfour resolution was official policy and that the Zionist state was desired by the government.

The immigrants were the ones who built the settlements, tilled the land, and created life in the desert. They were fearless against Arab violence because they had learned to not be frightened of attack. They had endured wars and revolutions. The guerrilla attacks were almost meaningless by comparison. Only in 1939, when the British government announced that immigration into Palestine would be stopped in 1944, did the Jews fully understand the truth. British policy was that fifteen thousand Jews per year would be allowed into the country for each of the next five years. Then there would be no more immigration. And this despite the fact that the concentration camps had become known to all, even though the nature of the camps, the systematic extermination of all Jews, had yet to be reported in depth. Such a policy coming at that time meant a nightmare at best, death at worst for hundreds of thousands of Jews who otherwise would have come to Palestine.

Havlaga was not universally accepted by the Jews. There were arguments taking place within the Haganah over the issue of retaliation. In 1931, insiders began referring to the Haganah A and Haganah B, the latter having been formed by a coalition of the Revisionists, the religious party members known as the Mizrachists, the General Zionists, and a few others unconnected with any organization. The Haganah B was also known as the Irgun Zvai Leumi or Irgun, from which the Stern gang ultimately emerged.

The decision by members of the three Haganah factions to resort to violence came in 1936, the start of what may have been the most violent period in Palestine's recent history. Hitler took control of Germany in 1933 and by 1935 it was obvious that the Jews were in serious trouble. Concentration camps were being used for political prisoners, Jews, and others. Jews were being isolated in communities where they were allowed to live. Freedom of the press had been ended, so public awareness of violence was limited. And while the death camps were not yet a major concern, it was obvious that life under the Nazi regime would be a nightmare for the Jews. That year more than sixty thousand Jews entered Palestine, a fraction of the number who wanted admission and would have come if given the chance. With such an influx, it was obvious to Haj Amin that the Jews would soon be the majority in the country, something he felt he could not tolerate.

This time Amin found allies among the leaders of the other Arab parties. They did not share his hatred of Jews, but they did fear the takeover of Palestine by the new refugees. They formed the Arab High Command, naming Amin el Husseini as the leader. What they did not realize was that he did not want a democratic organization to discuss the problem. Once in a position of leadership, he declared himself dictator and silenced all opposition. He arranged for a private army patterned after the Nazi Storm Troopers and financed by the most radical elements in the middle east. At the head of the "army" was Fawzi el Kawukji, a ruthless Arab military commander from Iraq.

The first approach was a terrorist one. There was a general strike by Arab businesses that reduced the supply of food and other necessities to the Jews. Those who were not sympathetic to the cause (and there were many) were physically threatened and coerced into cooperation.

Then came guerrilla action meant to terrorize and destroy. Buses and trucks were ambushed on the roads. Fields and forests were set ablaze, often in a pattern that would isolate a Jewish settlement from all but one side before an attack against it was launched.

At first the Haganah A members reacted as necessary. Then the British, who originally were pleased with the actions, realized that the violence was becoming overwhelming. They recruited what were known as notrim, Jewish supernumerary police, to help defend the country. And the Jews began adjusting the way they did business in order to keep the country moving. When the Arab terrorists shut the port of Jaffa in order to prevent the Jews from obtaining essential supplies, the Jews built a new port in Tel Aviv.

The strength of the defense came not from a superior force but the determination not to be defeated. For the first time the British came to understand the real danger of the Jewish immigrants. They had seen so much hardship, fought against so much life-threatening intolerance, that they would not yield to the pressures brought against them. They carried on in the face of adversity, neither surrendering to death nor fearing it. They could be killed but not intimidated.

The British bias was also evident. There was strong hostility toward the Arabs because they were striking out against the British occupiers as well as the Jews and their own people. Yet only the Jews were regularly searched for weapons—which were illegal when possessed by either Arabs or Jews. Only the Jews would serve time in jail for weapons possession. And only the Grand Mufti was allowed to arrange for government employees to violate the British laws without fear of punishment.

It is not known why the British seemed to fear a Jewish majority more than an Arab one. Perhaps it was fear of a strong Zionist movement that was determined to eliminate the presence of all outsiders while establishing a Jewish nation. Perhaps it was felt that the Arabs were more controllable. Or this fear may have simply resulted from the bigotry of those men in command and decision-making positions. Whatever the case, the bias was obvious to those involved.

Despite the British attitude, there were members of the occupying force who were sympathetic to the Jews and believed, as the increasingly militant members of Haganah B believed, that the war should be taken to the enemy. One of these men was Captain Orde Wingate, who began training the Jews to go on the offensive in the critical year of 1938.

The Grand Mufti had lost all sense of perspective by 1938. He was an ardent Nazi sympathizer who had come to so hate both the British and the Jews that he lost sight of the fact that there were limits to what the occupying forces would tolerate. When he arranged for the murder of the British district commander in Nazareth, the reaction was swift. He was forced to flee to Iraq to avoid arrest and jailing. The Arab High Command was outlawed and the leaders went into exile. However, small groups of Amin followers remained behind to commit terrorist activities, and it was against them that the thirty-five-year-old British captain arranged retaliation.

Wingate created small units of British soldiers sympathetic to the Jewish cause and volunteers from the Haganah. These were trained in counterterrorist activities. They were equipped to operate at night, moving quickly, well-armed and deadly. He called the units the Special Night Squads and moved them about in such a way that they could create pincer actions to trap and destroy the Arab terrorists whenever they encountered them.

The primary field of activity was along the oil pipeline so critical within the country. Battle after battle was fought as saboteurs met the counterterrorists under Wingate's command. As a result of his work, the settlements not only survived; many of the younger members of the Haganah A recognized that it was time for them to go on the offensive against their enemies in a better-organized, more aggressive manner than in the past. And waiting to lead them was Avraham Stern, a man whose intense beliefs resulted in an organization whose members became the most effective terrorists in Palestine and, later, Israel.

CHAPTER 7

Terrorism and the British

TWO STORIES OF death and destruction were unfolding simultaneously. While the world was witnessing much of what was taking place in Germany, isolating that European nation in their minds, seeing the potential for crisis in the change that was occurring, the situation in Palestine, though overlooked by the world press, was almost as explosive. Arabs, Jews, and British were engaged in subtle warfare, with torture and psychological terror playing major roles in the arsenals of all sides.

The growing talk of extremist violence and terrorism among many of the different Jewish factions in Palestine is understandable when seen in the light of what they were facing. First there was the growing danger from the Arab community and the tolerance of mob action against the Jews by the British police. Then came the Munich Conference in September 1938, when the major powers of the world essentially showed that they would do whatever was necessary to appease Adolf Hitler.

On September 28, 1938, Great Britain, France, and Italy were asked to send leaders to Munich at noon the following day to decide the fate of Czechoslovakia. Neither the Czechs nor the Russians were asked to be present, though the Russians had a pact with Czechoslovakia guaranteeing armed support in case of German attack.

The Munich meeting was meant to arrange for Germany to occupy Czechoslovakia peacefully. If that could not be done, Hitler planned to invade by force on October 1. Such an invasion would have been premature and deadly for Hitler. It would have brought an immediate armed response from Moscow, followed by attacks by Britain and France. The German army was incapable of waging such a war and the end would have come quickly, perhaps within a few weeks. The threat of National Socialism would have been over with a minimum of violence outside Germany.

The governments that met at Munich were presumably aware of the limited strength of the German military. Yet they did not want to be responsible for going to war. They apparently felt that by appeasing Hitler, by letting him take control of Czechoslovakia in a bloodless occupation, they could prevent any further violence. In fact, only Winston Churchill, at the time not part of the British government, understood what was taking place. On October 5, he addressed the British House of Commons: "We have sustained a total and unmitigated defeat.... We are in the midst of a disaster of the first magnitude. The road down the Danube... the road to the Black Sea has been opened.... All the countries of Mittel Europa and the Danube Valley, one after another, will be drawn in the vast system of Nazi politics... radiating from Berlin.... And do not suppose that this is the end. It is only the beginning."

But not until November 20, 1938, was the full scope of the loss obvious. Czechoslovakia was forced to give Germany 11,000 square miles of territory where 800,000 Czechs and 2,800,000 Sudeten Germans were living. The territory included the bulk of all raw materials needed to remain an industrialized nation, as well as the major fortifications the country needed for defense. All forms of transportation and communication were also disrupted. The nation had become helpless faster and more effectively than if it had been taken by force of arms.

In Palestine it became obvious to the Jews that the British could not be trusted, though there was disagreement over what Germany's annexation of the Czechoslovakian territory ("repatriation" of Sudetenland Germans, according to Hitler) meant in terms of the Reich's ultimate plans. Jabotinsky, the leader of the Revisionist Zionist movement, felt that no war was imminent. Menachem Begin, increasingly a leader of a younger faction within that movemen' strongly disagreed. Warsaw, Poland, was the site of the Third World Congress Betar (an international gathering for leaders of the Zionist movement) shortly after the Munich Conference, and there he tried to place what was happening in perspective for the members:

> Until now, the Zionist movement's answer (to Arab and British opposition) had consisted of political activity, settlement, mass

immigration, moral pressure, making common cause with the British and maintaining faith in the League of Nations and the conscience of the world. Now, all is changed: the conscience of the world has ceased to react, and the League of Nations has lost its value. Our British partner leads us to the gallows and imprisons the finest of our nation.

Our good friends the British offer us five percent of Eretz Yisrael [The Peel Commission of 1937 suggested that Palestine be divided into Arab and Jewish states west of the Jordan; this was called Eretz Yisrael] and give primary consideration to the Arabs in appeasement of their nationalist ambitions. If we continue on this course, the realization of Zionism will be deferred. We want to fight—to conquer or perish. After political Zionism, after practical Zionism, we must now enter the age of military Zionism. We must amass strength that will not be dependent upon the mercies of others. If such a force is created, the world too will come to our assistance.

The gallows remark actually referred to the execution of nineteen-year-old Shlomo Ben Josef in June 1938. He was a part of Betar, a Revisionist youth movement, and had become enraged when he learned of Arab terrorism along the Safad–Rosh Pinna road. A Jewish-owned taxi was carrying five men and an eighteen-year-old girl when they were ambushed by Arabs. The men were shot and their bodies were systematically chopped to pieces. The girl was forced to watch the mutilations, then raped by each of the terrorists in turn.

Outraged, Ben Josef and two other Betar members, Abraham Shein and Shalom Zurabin, obtained guns and grenades in order to avenge the deaths. However, they were not so skilled as the terrorists.

The boys targeted an Arab bus for their reprisal. They had heard that the terrorists came from the village of Djouni so they waited for a bus to emerge, then hurled a grenade at it. The grenade was either faulty or improperly armed by the boys because it failed to explode. The bus continued on, none of the passengers hurt. However, before the three boys could return home, they were caught by the British police.

The decision was to punish them as harshly as possible as an example to others. Zurabin, eighteen, was found to be mentally ill and was ordered to a mental institution. Shein was initially sentenced to death, then had the sentence commuted to life in prison because he was only seventeen. There was no such leniency for Ben Josef, though, and he became the first Jew to be executed in Palestine since the destruction of the Temple in A.D. 70.

The hanging would have been shocking in any circumstances, given the boy's youth and the fact that his act of reprisal had failed to injure

anyone. But the drama was intensified by international appeals to com-
mute the sentence and intense demonstrations against the British officials. In addition, several men wrote about the death, each for different
reasons, and their writing added impact to the execution. For example,
Reuven Hazan, a Jewish officer, was assigned to guard Ben Josef the
night before his execution in Acre Prison. He later wrote:

> I went to Haifa for a rabbi but couldn't find one to perform the
> last rites. I returned to Acre at 7 in the morning, an hour before the
> execution. At 6 A.M. they had dressed him in his civilian clothes—
> shorts and shirt, socks and work shoes. He was already awake and
> greeted me with a smile. There was no sign of excitement on his
> face. He had written his mother in Poland, "Beloved Mother, don't
> feel sorry for me. Try to forget me. Other sons of the Jewish nation
> finished their lives in far more despicable and tragic fashion."
> When I told him the rabbi had refused to come, he said he would
> resist being taken to execution unless he could make his confession
> to a rabbi. I said the British and the Arabs would not understand
> his resistance, but interpret it as fear. I suggested that he read with
> me some of the Psalms and this might take the place of confession.
> He agreed. So during the hour that remained I read chapters of the
> Bible and he repeated each sentence after me.
>
> Then he insisted upon being hanged in his Betar uniform. "I
> won't die as a civilian—I acted as a soldier and I will die as a sol-
> dier." I told him this was impossible—he would be dragged to the
> gallows by force.
>
> "Very well," he said. "Then I will go." But I had to promise to tell
> his friends that he wanted to wear his uniform.

The death became a rallying cry for many of the young who related
the murder to the poem written by Avraham Stern of the Irgun. The
poem, "The Unknown Soldier," read:

> We are the men without name, without kin,
> Who forever face terror and death,
> Who serve our cause for the length of our lives—
> A service that ends with our breath.
> In the days that are red with the flow of our blood,
> In the nights of blackest despair,
> Through the length and breadth of our land
> We shall raise our banner of strength without fear—
> Not driven like slaves at the master's command,
> Forced to die at the stranger's behest,
> We dream of the time when our people and land
> By freedom and peace will be blessed.

It was not surprising that Begin would refer to the boy's death during his speech. For the older delegates, it was another example of the problems with the British. For the younger, the death was a rallying cry for independence. In both instances, it showed that the Jews could not relate to their occupiers.

Later, during the debate over what to do next, Begin asked angrily: "After Munich, who can have faith in the conscience of the world?"

His words proved prophetic. In April 1939, Hitler had gained control of all of Czechoslovakia. And one month later, Neville Chamberlain, the man who had helped give the Czechs to the Nazis, signed the British white paper that renounced the Balfour Declaration. Jewish immigration to Palestine was to be limited to fifteen thousand a year for five years, then would stop completely. Ultimately the Jewish population of Palestine was to be frozen at one-third the total population. Within ten years, by 1949, Palestine would become an independent state in which the Jews would be a permanent minority. In addition, the Jews would only be allowed to freely buy land in 5 percent of Palestine. Land purchases in the remaining territory could be accomplished only with Arab approval.

The white paper could not have come at a more destructive time. There was a period when Himmler and other Nazi leaders were seeking a way to remove the Jews from Germany. The SS spoke of entjudung (de-Jewification) during the years 1935 through 1938, a time when an exodus from Germany was still possible. Countries willing to accept the Jews—which almost none were—could have saved hundreds of thousands of lives. Countries not willing to allow immigration, such as British territories, reinforced the Nazi idea that the Jews were either so worthless or so dangerous that no one wanted them.

In July 1937, Hitler remained a supporter of sending all the Jews to Palestine. This was not because he shared Himmler's idea of using the Jews as slaves—he still wanted to exterminate them. What intrigued Hitler was the idea of concentrating them in one small area so that eventually they could be destroyed with a single attack. Letting them emigrate to countries such as the United States presented problems when it came time to attack them.

Himmler was also beginning to parrot Hitler's hatred, the first step toward his self-justification for killing those he felt would better be enslaved. In one of the speeches reported throughout the world, he had said: "We shall unremittingly fulfill our task, to be the guarantors of the internal security of Germany, just as the Wehrmacht guarantees the safety of the honor, the greatness, and the peace of the Reich from the outside. We shall take care that never more in Germany, the heart of

Europe, can the Jewish-Bolshevistic revolution of subhumans be kindled internally or by emissaries from abroad. Pitilessly we shall be a merciless executioner's sword for all these forces whose existence and doings we know... whether it be today, or in decades, or in centuries."

On January 21, 1939, Czech foreign minister Chvalkovsky was informed by Hitler's emissaries: "We are going to destroy the Jews. They are not going to get away with what they did on November 9, 1918. The day of reckoning has come." It was a message conveyed nowhere else because the European countries had so thoroughly abandoned and isolated Czechoslovakia. But Britain's Neville Chamberlain was undoubtedly aware of Hitler's address to the Reichstag on January 30. It was the anniversary of his ascension to power and the speech was reported internationally. He stated clearly:

And one more thing I would like now to state on this day memorable perhaps not only for us Germans. I have often been a prophet in my life and was generally laughed at. During my struggle for power, the Jews primarily received with laughter my prophecies that I would someday assume the leadership of the state and thereby of the entire Volk and then, among many other things, achieve a solution of the Jewish problem. I suppose that meanwhile the then-resounding laughter of Jewry in Germany is now choking in their throats.

Today I will be a prophet again: If international finance Jewry within Europe and abroad should succeed once more in plunging the peoples into a world war, then the consequence will be not the Bolshevization of the world and therewith a victory of Jewry, but on the contrary, the destruction of the Jewish race in Europe.

While Hitler was announcing his plans for genocide, the British were taking sides more formally in Palestine. The Arab leaders had refused to sit down with Jewish leaders to reconcile their differences. The Arabs also vastly outnumbered the Jews. It seemed that the best chance for some sort of peace in the Middle East came from working with the Arabs, ignoring the Jews, and concentrating resources for use against the growing dangers in Europe. That decision was formalized with the May 1939 white paper.

The reaction to the white paper, officially announced in England on May 17, was violent. The Palestine Broadcasting Studios were bombed to prevent the announcement from being heard in Palestine. The following day immigration offices were attacked by mobs in Haifa and Tel Aviv. The protesters checked the files to find documents relating to illegal refugees who faced deportation. Then the records were destroyed.

The Arab menace was forgotten. Britain had become the enemy and anyone representing the British cause faced violence or death.

Retaliation by the British had to be swift. They could not go against the mobs, but they could go after the extremists. The members of the Irgun were well known to the police and all but two, David Raziel and Avraham Stern, were arrested immediately. Raziel was finally caught on the twenty-second, but Stern was in Poland on a mission for the Revisionists.

The Stern mission was one that would have both angered and frightened the British authorities had they been aware of it. Anti-Semitism ran rampant in Poland, yet the Polish government was comfortable with having its Jewish population emigrate to Palestine. The Polish officials had also agreed to help Stern by supplying arms and training both the commanders and instructors of the Irgun so that they, in turn, could train forty thousand Jewish youths from throughout Europe. This fighting force would travel to Italy in October 1939 and, from there, stage a one-day attack against Palestine. The force would seize the British government buildings, take control of the British police and military presence, and declare an independent state. The Italians, who also hated the British, were happy to allow their ports to be used for such a mission.

The Polish attitude was difficult to determine. All that was certain was that they willingly provided both instructors and a training camp in Zakofna, a mountain region in the southwest portion of the country. It was a rural farming area where the army officers could teach the Irgun instructors the tactics they would need to handle both a mass operation and guerrilla tactics. The first group completed its training in early May, with other groups scheduled to follow.

Quite separate from Stern's actions in Poland that saved him from arrest, the older Revisionist members were laying their own plans. Jabotinsky and a group of illegals planned to use a boat to stage a night landing in Tel Aviv. Once landed, they, along with the Irgun, would take over the residence of the British High Commissioner, proclaiming a new Jewish state. Jabotinsky would head a provisional government that would not last for very long. The British forces would eventually retake the residence, Government House, arresting Jabotinsky and others with him. However, he believed that so bold an action would result in Jewish leaders throughout the United States and Europe forming governments in exile and providing intense support against the British.

The Jabotinsky plan had little hope of success from the start. The action of the British in arresting the Irgun leaders that May assured its never being attempted. Only Stern had been successful with gaining some training for a few of his men. But even he felt the need to return to

Palestine following the arrests to see what he could do to take command of his organization.

The British action was worse than Stern expected. Ralph Cairns, the assistant superintendent of police, was head of the Jewish section of the Criminal Intelligence Division. He was a brilliant man, fluent in Hebrew, and notorious for his sadism. He delighted in abusing prisoners in the best of circumstances. With the Irgun leaders in jail, he amused himself by using torture on, among others, a Yemenite Jewish girl who had been caught carrying a bomb.

The emotionalism of all sides created problems during this period. Occupying forces used by any nation are invariably youthful. The soldiers are almost always little more than boys, older teens, and youth in their early twenties, often with no more education than high school, if that, and usually away from their home country for the first time in their lives. All they want to do is serve the time required by their government, then return to girlfriends, parents, and friends. They are homesick, often friendly and looking for a good time in a strange area.

In the country where the soldiers are stationed, the force is hated. They are occupiers, forcing their will upon the populace through threat of violence with the weapons they carry. There is suspicion, hatred, and a desire to get them out at any cost. They will ignore, verbally harass, and/or physically attack the boys who, under other circumstances, might be warmly welcomed as visitors.

The occupying soldiers become frightened of the unknown, angered by the impersonal hatred they are encountering and bitter about being misunderstood and mistreated. They may try to avoid mingling with the local people or even be ordered to stay near their barracks. Or they may develop a "tough guy" swagger, verbally and physically attacking the natives to try and instill more fear in the public than they themselves are experiencing.

In a country like Palestine the situation was more extreme. The Arabs and Jews spoke languages and had cultures radically different from those with which the British youths were familiar. They ate different food, had different customs, and seemed quite foreign. When the soldiers became subjected to everything from rocks to knives to gunshots and bombs, they wanted to strike back. Sometimes they could do so by standing aside and letting the Arabs and Jews fight each other. At other times they vented their fear and anger by abusing and torturing those who had tried to hurt them. To their way of thinking, torturing a teenage girl was justified because she was carrying a bomb that threatened their lives.

The Jews saw only an occupying force that was trying to prevent them from living in the manner God had promised from the time of Abraham. They had experienced torture, mutilation, and death at the hands of the Arabs, even during the periods the British seemed to be most friendly toward them. With the ending of the Balfour Declaration, the German actions in Europe, and the ongoing deaths of Jews who could only be saved by the British allowing them to open their borders for immigration, attacking the occupiers seemed necessary. They would fight and kill any of the British occupiers, regardless of their innocence, until Britain felt that the occupation was too costly and allowed the homeland to be established. They were in the right, in their minds, and any violence on the part of the British had to be wrong.

Tragically, when each side can justify its position so strongly, violence increases. Both sides are comfortable with the most extreme inhumanity because each feels that such action ultimately saves more lives than it takes. With the arrests and tortures of the Irgun leaders, Stern rallied the men and women on the outside to wage intense guerrilla warfare against both the British and the Arabs.

In the minds of the Jews, the warfare began May 28, when eighteen Arabs were wounded and five killed in Jerusalem's Rex Cinema. Two days later the guerrilla stronghold of Bir Adas was attacked, and five more Arabs were killed. But the British failed to understand the significance of the actions, so similar to other Arab/Jewish violence.

The two attacks convinced the British that they were safe, that the Jews were simply waging the war they had been fighting for years. However, on June 3, lulled into a false sense of security, the British were unprepared for violence from Jaffa to Jerusalem. Communication and mail centers were bombed, telephone lines slashed, railway lines were destroyed, and other critical services were disrupted.

On August 7, 1939, the battles and the enemies began a radical change. First came the arrest of Avraham Stern in Tel Aviv, where he and three other leaders had been working, an arrest that placed all leaders of the Irgun in jail. Then, approximately two weeks later, the Irgun members succeeded in murdering police inspector Cairns. And finally, on September 1, Hitler marched into Poland, starting World War II and effectively ending the program to train Jewish youths for the attack on the Palestine occupying force. It also marked the beginning of the end for thousands of Polish Jews who suddenly faced confinement and death in the concentration camps.

The war forced changes in the way the Jews viewed the British. Suddenly there was a common enemy more important than the British. Hitler had made clear his plans to eradicate the Jews from Europe and, with his troops storming into Poland, his statements had to be taken seriously. No one knew how many lives were at stake, but the possibility of true genocide was unquestioned everywhere Hitler invaded. It was better to assist Britain against Germany than to risk Hitler's winning the war.

At the same time, the true horror of the British white paper had been revealed by the start of the war. Restrictions on Palestinian immigration had been the same as signing a death warrant for the European Jews. No Western country wanted to accept the people. With all the rhetoric of governments throughout the world, the truth was that immigration was intensely restricted everywhere. The only land that could have been open was Palestine, yet the actions of the British prevented that from happening. The white paper had been a death sentence for an untold number of innocents.

David Ben-Gurion, the chairman of the Jewish Agency, best stated how the Jews of Palestine felt they had to react: "We shall fight the war as if there were no White Paper, and fight the White Paper as if there were no war."

It is difficult to know how anti-Semitic the British governmental leaders might have been. Did they deliberately ignore the fate of the Jews in Eastern Europe or were they so compartmentalized in their thinking that they separated the issue of illegal immigrants from the reason the fleeing Jews were attempting to enter Palestine?

The Haganah established a unit called Mossad, whose members had the job of finding a way to bring Eastern European Jews to safety. This usually meant getting them to Mediterranean, Adriatic, or Black Sea ports or taking them to displaced persons camps. There they would be safe from harm and could be shipped to Palestine.

Prior to the outbreak of war in Europe, Britain had a naval blockade of Palestine with ships ready to shoot incoming vessels laden with illegal refugees. The Mossad leaders risked their own deaths with each shipment they accompanied, yet the men and women who accepted this task felt that it was worth the risk.

Mossad used both large and small boats, though the members gradually began relying on smaller vessels whenever possible. They would use code words to indicate the cargo being shipped (a ship carrying fourteen hundred refugees might result in a radioed message that a shipment of fourteen hundred books was on the way). While many of the vessels were turned away, by using large numbers of smaller vessels the British were increasingly thwarted and had to increase their own vigilance.

Many felt that the threat to the Jews might cause a relaxation of the immigration laws or reduced compliance with the law. The humanitarian act would have been for the captains of the British vessels to not watch so closely for the immigrants. But this was not to prove the case.

For example, with Hitler about to enter Poland, a group of Polish Jewish emigrés set sail on the SS *Tigerhill* from a Romanian port. Before they could leave, the British pressured the government to keep the ship from sailing. Only when Mossad agent Ruth Aliav was able to contact Romania's King Carol directly was the ship allowed to leave, reaching the coast off Tel Aviv just a few hours after all of the Middle East learned that Hitler had invaded Poland. Yet despite everyone's greatest fear having become reality, the British navy was ordered to open fire on the ship to force it back. Three women and one man died in their efforts to flee death.

By 1940 the British attitude toward the Jews and the situation in Palestine became obvious. The German concentration camps were in full operation, increasing both the difficulty and the urgency of trying to flee the Nazis. Yet the British were determined to make examples of those they caught sneaking into Palestine.

In November 1940, the ships *Pacific* and *Milos* carried a total of eighteen hundred refugees into Haifa. Most of the men and women were part of a potential military force trained in European camps along the line established so briefly within Poland. However, regardless of their mission, a return to Europe would probably mean death.

The eighteen hundred were arrested by the British and, for a while, it was believed that they would be returned to the Nazis. Fortunately, the decision was made to take them to the Indian Ocean island of Mauritius, which was being used as a detention facility. The announcement of their arrest was accompanied by the statement: "Their ultimate disposal will be a matter of consideration at the end of the war; but it is not proposed that they shall remain in the colony to which they are sent, or that they should go to Palestine. Similar action will be taken in the case of any further parties who may succeed in reaching Palestine with a view to illegal entry."

For the first time the Haganah made a serious mistake in trying to protect the people and fight the British. They decided to set off an explosive on the ship the British would use for transportation. The idea was to cripple the vessel, forcing it to stay in port, then attempt to sneak the people off the boat during the subsequent confusion.

Ships of any value were being used for the war effort. All that were available for a mission such as transporting illegals to an island holding facility were of extremely poor quality. Such was the case with the *Patria*, a French ship obtained as the Nazis were occupying that country. No one had wanted the German government to commandeer the vessel, though that might have been a better idea than the sabotage.

The *Patria* was a much older ship than anyone realized, poorly maintained, and the hull was not as well made as they thought. A barrel of dynamite was attached to the side by men who had trained for such sabotage missions. But when it exploded, the ship seemed almost to disintegrate. Of the illegals on board, 240 met their death, along with fifty crew members. Numerous others were injured, many of them having to be rescued from sections of the sinking ship or from the waters of the Mediterranean.

The British had no compassion for anyone involved—including the illegals, who had no idea that such a rescue attempt was going to be tried. They made an example of the emigrés, placing all who lived in the Palestinian detention camp known as Athlit.

The detention camp became crowded quickly. The *Atlantic* arrived in Haifa with 1,875 refugees. They had succeeded in passing through the blockade but were arrested upon arrival, then sent to Athlit.

The use of both the military and civilian vessels to handle a refugee problem during wartime was an idea that most of the world's leaders found outrageous. The British High Commissioner justified his actions by saying that it was likely that Communists had joined the emigrés in order to smuggle themselves and their ideas into Palestine. From there they would create serious political problems for the country.

At first the British government felt that deportation to a British colony was best for all involved. In November 1940, the statement was made that "His Majesty's Government are not lacking in sympathy for refugees from territories under German control." It then went on to state the deportation policy:

> But... they can only regard a revival of illegal Jewish immigration at the present juncture as likely to affect the local situation most adversely, and to prove a serious menace to British interests in the Middle East. They have accordingly decided that the passengers [of the two vessels]... shall be deported to a British colony... and shall be detained there for the duration of the war. Their ultimate disposal will be a matter for consideration at the end of the war, but it is not proposed that they shall remain in the colony to which they are sent or that they shall go to Palestine.

Then came the 1941 sinking of the *Patria* and a backlash of public opinion against the refugees. The most tragic result came after 769 refugees managed to reach Istanbul on a cattle ship, the *Struma*. Based on Britain's statement, the Turkish government felt it could not allow anyone to stay in Turkish territorial waters. In early 1942 the ship was sent back into the Black Sea, where it was sunk by a German mine on February 23. All passengers but one were lost. Even more tragic, the incident occurred after the British had relented and agreed to allow entry permits for all children under sixteen, a message that did not arrive before the vessel had sailed.

The *Struma's* sinking created a great outcry against British policy. The British tried to explain that they were worried about the infiltration of Nazi spies among the men, women, and children trying to immigrate. Yet by this time there was information available concerning the concentration camps. The mass murders were known, as was some of the intense hatred of the Nazi high command against all non-Aryans. The idea that the refugees might have Nazi spies or sympathizers among them was ridiculous.

The Jews of Palestine faced a dual crisis. Approximately two-thirds of them had families in areas overrun by the Nazis or being threatened by Nazi domination. They felt that they needed to support the British action against Germany and many of them wished to fight the Nazis. At the same time, they were hostile to the British action in Palestine and determined to eliminate the domination at any cost.

Several viewpoints were coming into play. There were those among the Jews who wished to suspend hostilities toward the British and unite for the fight against Germany. There were those who wanted to wage a two-front action, fighting with the British in Europe and against the British in Palestine. And there were those who were hostile to the European Jewish problem. They considered themselves the sons of Canaan, though none of the most militant could trace their unbroken ancestry in the land to more than three generations. They looked upon the Jews of Poland, Germany, Austria, and elsewhere in Europe as the Diaspora—the dispersed who had left Canaan and deserved whatever God wrought. They saw no reason to worry about Hitler, their only concern being for the Jews of Palestine and the fight against the British. The Nazi menace was not personal to them.

The British were also facing problems. They felt that they needed Arab support in the Middle East. There were large territories without a British presence, land where the Nazis could gain a foothold and use the people to attack. Typical was a government memorandum of November 21, 1940:

The situation in Iraq, where there are no British troops, is particularly unsatisfactory, and the Chiefs of Staff fear that serious military consequences may result unless a better atmosphere is created. In Egypt also, there is sympathy with Arab discontent, which might at any time express itself in a manner highly inconvenient to us in the Nile Valley. The Arab leaders in Syria and Palestine are in close contact with those in Iraq... but in spite of this tendency to turn towards the Axis there is still widespread dislike of Nazism and a bitter hatred of Italy and distrust of Italian ambitions... all our Arab friends, Ibn Saud in particular, are constantly urging us, in our own interests, to make a definite effort to rally Arab opinion to our side.

Despite all the conflicts, a large number of Palestinian Jews wanted to fight against Hitler. As of September 1939, eighty-six thousand Jewish men and fifty thousand Jewish women registered with the government for the military. The only stipulation made by the Jewish Agency was that the volunteers be placed in all-Jewish units. However, the government still felt that there had to be mixed Arab-Jewish units in order to maintain the balance believed necessary for the defense of Palestine.

By October, efforts were being made to find alternative ways to utilize the Jewish volunteers. One concept was to take a thousand Jews to England to train them as officers, then have them return to organize twenty thousand men and women into an army that would handle internal security in Palestine. It would take four months of intensive training to have the officers ready, a seemingly realistic time frame. Other men and women from among the 136,000 registered volunteers would be trained to fight in the Western Desert. Then a thousand more would be given officer training, following which they would train fifteen thousand men for a special force that would be a mobile unit. The special force would be sent anywhere in the world that the British felt was necessary.

The problem was that the logical planning taking place within the British government was in contrast to the wishes of the leaders of the Colonial Office responsible for the maintenance of peace in Palestine.

Winston Churchill felt that no matter where else the Jews were used, it was important to have them take over the keeping of the peace in Palestine. The British regular battalions were all well-trained and well-armed. They belonged in Europe, fighting Hitler, not acting as police officers in Palestine. He wanted to train and arm both Arabs and Jews, giving each authority over their respective communities. They would not only keep the peace among their own people but could maintain a check and balance against each other. They would all have the same weapons, the same skills, and the same mandates. Thus a balance would be maintained and there would be nothing to gain by continuing the hostilities against each other.

By February 1940, opposition against Churchill's views was too strong for him to counter. There had been civil war in Palestine, followed by years of tension. It was believed that there was a good chance that violence would break out between Arabs and Jews the moment the British troops left.

But the violence between Arabs and Jews had escalated in large measure because of the presence of the British. In addition, the covert actions of the Jewish rebels were such that the reduction in British manpower would ease some of the tensions. But former Prime Minister Neville Chamberlain's government could not see the value of the change, a fact that disgusted Churchill. Colonial Secretary Malcolm MacDonald later noted Churchill's reaction:

> It might have been thought a matter for satisfaction that the Jews in Palestine should possess arms, and be capable of providing for their own defence. They were the only friends we had in that country, and they were much more under our control than the scattered Arab population... the sound policy for Great Britain at the beginning of the war would have been to build up, as soon as possible, a strong Jewish armed force in Palestine. In this way we should have been able to use elsewhere the large and costly British cavalry force, which was now to replace the eleven infantry battalions hitherto locked up in Palestine. It was an extraordinary position that at a time when the war was probably entering its most dangerous phase, we should station in Palestine a garrison one quarter of the size of the garrison of India—and this for forcing through a policy which, in his opinion, was unpopular in Palestine and Great Britain alike.

The problem with Churchill's logic was that it did not address the perceived fears of others. Arming Palestinian Jews was likely to be interpreted as supporting the eventual Jewish domination of Palestine, an action that would cause problems with the Arabs and Muslims and in India, where rebellion against British rule was also taking place.

Churchill countered by showing that the Palestinian policy his predecessor had instigated was a failure by the fact that twenty thousand British soldiers had to be retained in Palestine in order to keep the peace: "Should the war go heavily into Egypt, all these troops will have to be withdrawn, and the position of the Jewish colonists will be one of the greatest danger." He further pointed out that the troops handling Palestine were among the elite of the British armed forces. He also said that he felt that, given the nature of the war, there would not be a back-lash by the Arabs.

The reaction in the Colonial Office was changing in 1940. Churchill stressed that the British soldiers in Palestine might have to be with-drawn on a moment's notice to fight in the European theater. There was growing pressure from Zionists in the United States and Britain to allow the Jews to fight in the military. One idea was to recruit Jews and Arabs in equal numbers, then turn them into mixed fighting units of a thousand men per side. However, the Colonial Office officials felt more comfortable staying with five hundred-man battalions trained to fight internationally. They still feared an adverse reaction from the Arabs against armed troops in Palestine.

In September 1940 a new proposal came to raise a Jewish force con-sisting of ten thousand men, two-thirds of whom would come from the United States, one-third from Palestine. They would be trained in England, fight where assigned, then have to return to their country of origin. This would prevent American Zionists interested in settling in Palestine from being able to do so.

The Jews were enthusiastic for several reasons. The first was that enough was known about the Nazi actions for them to feel that the war was, in large measure, one that had their people as a primary target. They would be able to protect other Jews from the devastation taking place.

A second motivation was the belief that if they proved themselves in combat against the Nazis, they would ultimately be rewarded when it came time for peace. There would be a greater chance for a Jewish homeland and the elimination of British control. They would be respected for what help they gave to the Allied powers and, hopefully, then be rewarded with support for their cause in Palestine.

For every scheme there were new objections. Britain knew it would be running out of oil in a few years. The British empire would eventual-ly have to utilize the resources of the Middle East. The wrong policy toward Arabs and Jews today could translate into economic disaster perhaps thirty years later.

There was also the fear that the Americans would assume that the reward for the Jewish armed forces would be control of Palestine. This would lead to postwar problems that could be avoided at the start.

And most important of all was the concern that if the Germans moved through the Balkans to the Mediterranean, the Middle East would become a critical theater of war. The Axis powers would want the Arabs to join with them and the Arabs would be most inclined to do so if they felt threatened by changes in the Jewish position in Palestine.

Arab politics forced the British to change. A coup d'etat in April 1941 brought Rashid Ali to power in Iraq. He was strongly pro-German and the Nazis were anxious to utilize him to fight against the British while they, in turn, attacked Russia and had Rommel move against Egypt. Syrian air bases were used for refueling and maintenance of German planes, and it would only be a matter of time before Rashid Ali was given the military equipment needed to go after Britain.

Rashid Ali had also shown his position against Britain by taking all British citizens living in Iraq and moving them into a concentrated, guarded area. He said that if Britain bombed Iraq from the air, the hostages would all be killed. In the meantime, Amin el Husseini had come back from exile and was working with Rashid Ali and the Nazis, adding to the political change in the Middle East.

The answer to the problem was an uncomfortable one. General Sir Archibald Wavell, commander-in-chief of the Middle East, negotiated with the Irgun to have its members attack an oil refinery near Baghdad. The action would distract the military and give the British time for other maneuvers. It would also be ground sabotage, so the British citizens being held hostage would be less likely to be harmed.

The Irgun leaders agreed, though they wanted permission to go beyond the single attack. They wanted the opportunity to either capture or kill Amin. Wavell dared not give approval of any attack against the Arab leader. Instead, he authorized the destruction of the refinery and made it clear that he did not want to know anything else that might be done.

The attack proved a nightmare. Four Irgun members—David Raziel (code name Ben Moshe), Yaacov Meridor, Yaacov "Sika" Amrami, and Yaacov Tarazi—flew to the only British holding in Iraq, Habbaniya. There they found that their mission was changed. They were to gather intelligence concerning the strength of the Iraqi defense forces.

The initial action took place on May 17. Two of the men, Amrami and Meridor, used a small boat to travel flooded lowland to see what they could find. The other two, along with a British major and his aide, would return to the camp to wait. But before they could complete that action, a German plane spotted the car they were using. A bomb killed the major and Raziel, the aide surviving though badly wounded. Tarazi was unhurt, as were the two men who had taken the boat. It was a serious and totally unexpected blow to the Irgun. The German plane had seen them by accident, its weapons so limited that had the bomb missed its target, all would have survived.

The men felt compelled to do some work in the area, Meridor helping with the sabotage of a bridge southwest of Baghdad before returning to

Palestine to take over the Irgun. Relationships between the British and the Jews seemed to improve, though the Irgun became suspicious of what was happening. The British intelligence division seemed to be working with the Haganah in ways that were theoretically supportive. Yet though both sides were exchanging information, the Irgun leaders felt that the British were deliberately providing misinformation. It was also believed that both the Haganah and the Jewish Agency were working to eliminate Avraham Stern and the Stern gang. The Irgun leadership did not feel that Stern's efforts to achieve an armed uprising against the British was realistic, yet they generally respected Stern's anti-British actions and sentiments. They were not willing to act in a manner that might destroy the group.

The main difference between Jabotinsky, Raziel, and (after the Iraq fiasco) Meridor of Irgun and Stern, leader of LEHI (the so-called Stern gang), was that Stern saw only one course of action, one goal. The leaders of the Irgun felt that Stern was blinded to any alternatives as well as to the probable reactions to the plans he might put into effect. Stern and his followers had a fanatic's devotion that did not allow for detours from their ultimate goal of ridding Palestine of the British and establishing their own nation.

By the early 1940s, LEHI's tactics had been called into question by the other Jewish groups. Relatively well-funded and well-armed, the Haganah was an underground militia and the Irgun the equivalent of an underground army. LEHI was a terrorist organization, the one form of warfare available to those who are too weak to mass a confrontational force. The past claims of high-minded purpose were suppressed. The group needed money, weapons, and to make an impact. Terror seemed the only way.

The British policies reinforced LEHI's fanaticism. The 1939 white paper restricting immigration to Palestine proved to the members that the British would not listen to reason. Negotiations with the Jewish leadership had obviously failed. The British government was not about to act in a manner that would do justice to the Jewish concerns.

By the time war in Europe was taking place, LEHI was making overtures to the Arabs. Stern came to believe that Arabs and Jews shared a common enemy and that they should fight together against the British. He understood that there had been vicious riots and murders by the Arabs, though he saw them as correctable misunderstandings. He knew that once the two groups communicated, the Arabs would see that their enemy was Britain. They had been against each other only because the British maneuvered such a confrontation, not because they had fundamental differences with each other.

Stern also saw the fascists of Italy as possible allies against Britain. He felt that in many instances the anti-Semitism of some of the Axis powers did not mean that they would be against a Jewish state. Great help had come from Poland preceding its collapse before the Germans. Yet Poland was also perceived as being anti-Semitic and the government helped the Jews form a military unit up until the Nazi invasion ended such assistance.

The problem with LEHI was that after the split with the Irgun it had great need of money and limited resources. A few hundred dedicated loyalists and probably an equal number of supporters believed in Stern but would not get involved in his more violent activities. The only answer seemed to be to steal money from a bank.

The first bank robbery occurred in Tel Aviv in September 1940. Five thousand pounds was taken from the Anglo-Palestine bank, enough to buy the makings of bombs and to help obtain handguns and other weapons. A second bank robbery attempt, this time in Jerusalem, failed. However, a bombing against a British government immigration office in Haifa that December was effective.

By 1941, both Stern and LEHI were seen by the British and by many Jews as unrealistically out of control. The Irgun had made contacts with the French Underground concerning a possible link-up if Palestine fell to the Germans, a clear and present threat. Despite RAF bombing of Syrian airfields, 120 German planes had landed in Syria by June 4. It became necessary four days later for the British and other Allied troops to invade both Syria and Lebanon. Rashid Ali's forces had been stopped. Iraq was occupied, and the Middle East was filled with Allied troops. However, the invasion and occupation forces were badly needed elsewhere. They had been sent into the countries as a reaction to the growing Nazi presence. They were stretched thin, outnumbered, and lacking in order. There is a chance that, had the Middle Eastern countries' leaders known just how weak the Allies were at the time of the invasion, they would have continued fighting and ultimately triumphed. Instead, many of them surrendered on the assumption that they would otherwise be devastatingly outgunned.

The German troops were moving swiftly into Russia. Opposition was being overwhelmed and the Nazi military strategy appeared flawless. When that operation was completed, it was believed that Rommel would be reinforced, taking control of Cairo and Palestine. The idea of continuing the violent struggle against the British seemed foolish to most Palestinian Jews during the period when everyone was needed to fight the greater threat of Hitler. The British had become the defenders of the Jewish homeland. LEHI's fanaticism seemed unrealistic and

116 · WALKING WITH THE DAMNED

potentially foolish. Even LEHI's reading of the minds of the Italian leadership and other members of the Axis powers who were not obviously obsessively anti-Semitic seemed naive at best, deadly at worst.

Stern's image changed radically for most of the Jews. There had once been a romantic quality to the Stern gang. Posters would appear in the middle of the night, attacking the British occupation and rallying the Jews. Bank robberies and the robberies of wealthy British businesses all had a Robin Hood quality about them. Even the assassinations, when they occurred, were justified by the tortures Jews had endured in the British prisons and holding facilities. Yet that had all been before the war, before the death camps, before the annihilation of the Jews was a primary goal of a major aggressive European power.

There was nothing romantic about the systematic slaughter of millions of Jews. There was nothing courageous about running gun battles against an occupying force that stood between survival and the ultimate victory of the Nazis. The inability of the LEHI members to change from their single-minded purpose cost them the support of the people they felt they were serving.

Stern and his followers were barely tolerable as they pulled two bank robberies in Jerusalem on December 26, 1941. They crossed an unspoken line that assured their destruction on January 9, 1942.

The city was Tel Aviv and they had targeted a Histadrut bank that employed a number of Jews. The employees were honest, hard-working, respectful of their employer. When the armed terrorists burst into the bank demanding money, the employees refused. Shocked by such passive resistance, the Stern gang fired their weapons, killing two male Jewish employees.

The deaths ended almost all support for LEHI. The fanatics recognized the shootings as tragic, a needless waste of life that should not have happened but apparently was unavoidable. The Jewish community saw things differently.

The British had been enemies whose policies were indirectly responsible for the deaths of hundreds, perhaps thousands of potential immigrants. The Arabs were fighting for the same land, the same economic opportunities as the Jews, their occasional fanatics needing to be fought for survival. Such enemies could be understood. Such enemies might die in pursuit of a homeland. That was all acceptable, understandable.

But two Jewish men being murdered in a bank robbery by supposed Zionists thinking of the Promised Land? The killers were not heroic. They were not freedom fighters. They were crazies who would take the lives of the very people they were supposedly trying to protect from tyranny. LEHI had gone too far, and almost every Jew was willing either to cooperate with British intelligence to stop them or would no longer seek ways to obscure the facts. It was only a matter of time before Stern would be captured.

The ultimate fate of the Stern gang was sealed on January 20. Yael Street in Tel Aviv was the location for a LEHI bomb factory, or so the British intelligence unit (which included four Jews) was led to believe. At 9:00 A.M. a bomb exploded in the building, damaging much of the structure but not so much that the British intelligence officers were unable to search the room. Within minutes of the explosion, local constables, special investigators, and—most important—the leaders of the intelligence unit swarmed through the upper floor of the building, looking for evidence and bodies. Then, at 9:20 A.M., a much more powerful explosion destroyed the building completely, killing the four Jewish officers and most of the intelligence-agency leadership. The supposed headquarters for a bomb factory had been a trap. The first explosion was meant to bring law enforcement to the structure. The second explosion, carefully timed, was meant to kill all the investigators.

By February the British, in cooperation with many anti-LEHI Jewish groups, were rounding up members of the Stern gang before more violence could take place. Two-way radios were confiscated, making coordination of delicately timed actions more difficult. Members were arrested in endless sweeps of the community. A genuine bomb factory was discovered, its contents seized before more people could be killed. And safe houses once operated by sympathetic members of the Irgun and the Haganah were closed to Stern and his followers. No one wanted to have anything to do with Jews who killed Jews, regardless of their motivation.

Only Stern himself had a chance for survival. There were enough people who respected the man and his dedication to a cause to be willing to shelter him if he would not continue with his violence while in hiding. A kibbutz would allow him to stay for so long as he stopped leading terrorist activities. A few members of the Haganah made the same offer. Since his photograph was everywhere, on shop walls and in every newspaper, no one could fail eventually to spot him, and his survival seemed dependent upon compromise. Yet this he would not do.

Stern, using disguises and traveling with one or two of the young women in LEHI, would move his location daily. Always he had a small suitcase with him in order to carry a collapsible cot and some clothing. And always those who let him spend a night had second thoughts, refusing to allow him to return.

Finally there was only one person who would hide him. Tova Svorai, whose husband, Moshe, also a member of the Stern gang, had been shot and arrested two weeks before, agreed to let him stay in the attic apartment she rented in south Tel Aviv. He had a sofa on which to sleep and Tova smuggled letters to the other followers who were still free.

What neither Stern nor Tova Svorai knew was that she had been under surveillance. British intelligence had no idea that she was shielding anyone of importance, but they were certain she was hiding one of the LEHI members they were seeking. They gathered around the building on February 12, then made their move at 10:30 A.M.

The police were frightened of the reaction to their raid and determined not to get in trouble. LEHI was hated more than the British at that time, so the officers persuaded two of Tova Svorai's neighbors—Jewish women who were at home in their apartments down below—to accompany the officers as witnesses. They did not wish to be accused of brutality, perhaps changing the attitudes of the people who had just begun to support them.

The apartment was entered, Stern found hiding in a wardrobe. He was handcuffed and pushed onto the sofa while Tova was arrested, then taken to a patrol car.

The surviving leaders of British intelligence were summoned to the apartment. The witnesses were thanked for their cooperation and allowed to return downstairs. Then all the officers except for the leaders of the intelligence unit were dismissed.

Geoffrey Morton, head of British intelligence, grabbed the handcuffed Stern and pushed him toward the open window. Then he pulled his revolver and shot Stern in the head. Blood splattered the walls, the window, the floor. Still alive, Stern was carried to the street and dumped in the gutter, where he died within moments. The official report, backed up by the "evidence" that Stern had been placed on the sofa but had been shot near the window, indicated that he was killed while "trying to escape." Everyone knew the truth. No one outside LEHI chose to challenge the report.

PART IV

Living with the Damned

CHAPTER 8

Moving to War

HEINRICH HIMMLER, THE least respected man among Hitler's inner circle, revealed himself as the most cunning as the Reich became stronger. His eccentric ideas of religion and history were the substance of many jokes among the Nazi leadership, yet no one openly spoke against them. And when, on June 17, 1936, Himmler was named chief of all German police, he achieved a power domestically greater than anyone in the Reich. He was in charge of all intelligence-gathering, state police agencies, the uniformed and criminal police. He answered only to Hitler, which meant, in essence, he had a free rein, for Hitler was preoccupied with the consolidation of his international power and the forthcoming war.

On July 2, 1936, Himmler participated in a ceremony that further showed his plan for self-glory and power within the Reich. It was the thousandth anniversary of the death of Henry the Fowler, the Saxon duke who became King Heinrich I in A.D. 919 and founded Germany. Heinrich I had also conquered vast land areas in what later became Poland, Russia, and the Slavic area of Czechoslovakia.

Himmler came to believe that it was his destiny to duplicate such conquests, uniting all Aryan people in the process. Prior to the ceremony honoring this early king, Himmler became involved with the creation of the Ancestral Heritage Society, an organization sponsored by wealthy industrialists who either shared Himmler's beliefs or were attempting to gain his favor. Expeditions were launched to study the history of Asian people who had migrated to Europe centuries before Heinrich I began his conquests. Archeological digs were also instituted, all for the purpose of properly defining the true Aryan.

During this period, the Volksdeutsche Mittelstelle (VOMI) was formed as the Liaison Office for Ethnic Germans. This group tracked ethnic Germans whose ancestors had moved into other parts of Eastern Europe following the Middle Ages. The ethnic Germans were to be identified, then encouraged to have children for the Reich. Ultimately they would be used for the eastward expansion of the Reich. In the meantime, it was hoped that the contacts established by VOMI would help Himmler establish SS power and influence in countries outside Germany.

Himmler named Lt. Gen. Werner Lorenz head of VOMI. Lorenz, who had been a pilot in World War I, was a staunch nationalist and a skilled diplomat with people at all social levels. He did not respect Himmler's theories but knew enough to neither openly challenge him nor try to work for his downfall behind the scenes.

By the time of the anniversary of Heinrich I, those who wanted Himmler's favor played to his fantasies. The ceremony took place at Quedlinburg, at the ruins of Burg Dankwarderode, where the king once made his home, and was recorded by Gunther d'Alquen, editor of Das Schwarze Korps, the SS. "A thousand years ago, one of the greatest Germans ever died, but today he is so much alive, so close, that we believe to be seeing him physically in our midst.... Heinrich I, founder of the First German Reich, whose live spirit is an expression of our new, yet so old, mysticism of eternal life." He clearly believed that Himmler was essentially the reincarnation of Heinrich I—or at least he wanted Himmler to feel that he held such a belief.

"Today we stand at the grave of Heinrich I, who died exactly a thousand years ago—a creator of the German Reich and yet a figure who has almost been forgotten," Himmler said in his speech. Befitting the reincarnation of the great warrior, Himmler wore a special dress uniform and a black steel helmet, but at five-six, surrounded by men who were well over six feet and wearing a uniform inappropriate for a small man, he looked absurd. This coincided with the time Himmler was first declaring his ambitions and his hostility toward the Christian Church. Soon there would be new standards for a German religion, followed by Himmler's creation of his own religion—which went against all moral standards except his own. "Open wounds testify to the radical and bloody introduction of Christianity. The Reich was weakened by the perpetual aspirations to power of the spiritual princes and the Church's interference in temporal affairs."

Himmler also introduced the idea of the future betrayal of Russia, another important element of the speech that went unnoticed at the time. Heinrich I had been threatened by hordes of Magyars on horseback who could overwhelm his forces, a situation not unlike the threat facing Nazi Germany from the Soviet. Heinrich I had made a treaty that gave him time to prepare for battle, building the German strength so there could be a surprise attack and victory. Such actions were obviously the way to handle Russia as well, a fact so strongly implied that only the lack of understanding of Himmler's real power as head of the SS kept the words from being seriously heeded.

"We Germans of the twentieth century should know the source of the strength which filled Heinrich I. He was a leader surpassing his people in strength, greatness and sagacity, inspired by the principle of loyalty, ruthless against his enemies, loyal and grateful to his comrades and friends, faithful to his given word, conscientious in keeping treaties, respectful for things which are holy to others. He was a man who never forgot that the strength of the German people lies in the purity of their blood, and he realized that he could not successfully defend his country if petty influences denied him absolute power."

Unspoken during that ceremony was Himmler's fantasy about who he was. Heinrich I's remains had been removed from their original burial site and no one knew where they were. Himmler believed that some divinity had built his own body around those thousand-year-old bones.

The events of the day are best understood in hindsight. They help explain Himmler's future actions as well as the ways in which he would be both manipulated and supported by those aides who understood his fantasies and were willing to play along with them.

It took only a year for Himmler and his brilliant underling Heydrich to reshape German police powers. Despite the abuses that were occurring throughout the nation, despite the establishment of the first concentration camp at Dachau, followed by Sachsenhausen (1936) and Buchenwald (1937), the police had paid lip service to the maintenance of human rights. The officers had followed the law, strictly enforcing codes against wrongdoing, reacting to crime in the same manner that other law enforcement officers went about their business throughout the world. Punishments might be excessive and some of the police might have been increasingly brutal during arrests and detentions. However, the public could always see a cause-and-effect relationship between the laws and the arrests.

In 1937 everything changed. Three concentration camps were in operation. Detention, torture, and murder were secretly established as national policy for control of the people. All opposition, Aryan and non-Aryan, was to be either stifled through fear or destroyed. The enemies of the Reich were defined by Heydrich in an internal memo: Those who had to be stopped were involved with "communism, Marxism, Jewry, the politically active churches, Freemasonry, political malcontents, the nationalist opposition, reactionaries, economic saboteurs, habitual criminals, also abortionists and homosexuals, traitors to the country and the state."

Several different meanings lurked within the list. Russia and other Eastern nations were perceived as critical for Himmler's expansion plans. He felt that the inferior people (non-Aryans) of that region should be destroyed, though such information was secret at the time since Hitler needed a pact with the Soviet Union to buy time for his expansionist plans. Only later would Himmler's speech to the SS generals reveal both his and Hitler's true feelings. The speech, given after the invasion of Russia in 1941, stated in part:

"What happens to a Russian or a Czech does not interest me in the slightest.... Whether these nations live in prosperity or starve to death interests me only insofar as we need them as slaves for our Kultur. Whether ten thousand Russian females fall down dead from exhaustion while digging an antitank ditch interests me only insofar as the antitank ditch for Germany is finished. We Germans, who are the only people in the world who have a decent attitude towards animals, will also assume a decent attitude towards these human animals but it is a crime against our own blood to worry about them and give them ideals."

Thus anyone involved with communism or Marxism was connected with Soviet Russia and had to be destroyed. Malcontents were more broadly defined: Anyone who made a complaint about anything related to the Nazi government was considered a malcontent. Generally punishment was limited to chronic grumblers, men and women who routinely complained about the harshness of the laws, the working conditions, the attitude toward human rights, or anything similar. Jokes could be made about the leadership provided no jokes were made about Hitler (an action for which the humorist faced execution).

Abortionists were hated because the Reich needed as many children as possible to be able to repopulate forested zones to the east which were going to be taken from the Russians and Slavs who currently owned, worked, and/or lived on the land. Homosexuals not only weakened the future by their failure to reproduce, they also were considered likely to commit espionage.

Heydrich arranged for the police to be empowered to move against anyone who offended against morality or was an "antisocial malefactor." Local officials and courts no longer controlled the police. They had become representatives of the nation, subject to the whim of Himmler and Heydrich, no longer responsible to the law. Civilian protection had come to an end. The state was all that mattered, and if it had to be protected from the citizens who objected to its policies, so be it.

No longer did the police react to crime. Arrests were to be made of anyone who might become a danger in the future. This could mean political opponents or someone who listened to the wrong radio programs.

Typical of the extremes to which the government began to go was the arrest of anyone who listened to American jazz, which was increasingly popular in Europe. The music was new, generally having started with black entertainers, and was being broadcast in many countries. It was not part of a propaganda effort; it was simply played because it was enjoyed. However, the Nazis felt that it was "nigger music," inferior melodies reflecting an inferior race, and that anyone listening to it should be placed in a concentration camp.

No proof of the offense of listening was needed. If someone had a radio capable of picking up stations that occasionally played such music, and if a neighbor or family member claimed they overheard such sounds, the person was locked away. In the minds of the new police units it was better to mistakenly send a thousand innocent people to the camps than to allow one guilty person to be free.

The open warfare against the public resulted in internal dissent as well. The extremist leaders, such as Dr. Paul Joseph Goebbels, the Reich propaganda minister, wanted to blame all problems on the Jews. When Hitler was first coming to power in the late 1920s, Goebbels had written a pamphlet, the tenets of which would guide him through the war. He had stated:

> Why are we enemies of the Jews?
> We are enemies of the Jews because we are warriors for the freedom of the German people. The Jew is the cause and the beneficiary of our slavery. He has used the social troubles of our broad masses in order to widen the split between right and left among our people, he has made two halves of Germany. Here is the real reason for the loss of the World War on one side and for the betrayal of the revolution on the other side....
> The Jew has no interest in the solution of the question of German fate. He can't have it, since he lives because it remains unsolved.... He has a better trump in his hand, when a nation lives in slavery than when it is free, busy, self-conscious and self-contained. The Jew has caused our misery, and to-day he lives on our troubles.
> That is the reason why as Nationalists and as Socialists we are enemies of the Jew. He has ruined our race, rotted our morals, cor-

rupted our traditions and broken our power. We can thank him for
being the goats of the world today. As long as we were Germans, he
was a leper among us. Since we have forgotten our Germanic character, he has triumphed over us and our future.

... Anti-Semitism is un-Christian. That is to say then that the
Christian means to look on as the Jew cuts our skin into strips.... In
order to be Christian: you must love your neighbor as yourself! My
neighbor is my comrade in blood and nationality. If I love him, then
I must hate his enemies. He who thinks as a German, must despise
the Jew. One statement depends on the other.

Even Christ saw once that one doesn't find love sufficient in all
situations. When he came across the thieves in the temple, he didn't
say: "Children, love each other!"; instead He took a whip and drove
the pack away.

We are Jew-haters because we admit that we are Germans. The
Jew is our greatest calamity.

It isn't true that we eat a Jew with every breakfast.

But it is true that he is eating us up slowly but surely, together
with all our possessions.

That is going to change, as sure as we are Germans.

The problem was that there had been opposition from the Christians
who were also deemed enemies of the new Reich by Himmler. An effort
was made in 1934 to establish a new religion that would pay lip service
to Christianity but begin to make Naziism the state faith. The supporters called it the German Faith movement (Deutsche Glaubens-
bewegung), and one of its leaders, Professor Ernst Bergmann, developed a twenty-five-point catechism. It was hoped that this would
appease those who were shocked by Goebbels' rantings. The catechism
fit the Nazis' "Positive Christianity" that had been developed by the
party leadership at a time when they still openly adhered to Article 24,
which provided religious freedom for all groups "so far as they are not
a danger to it and do not militate against the moral feelings of the
German race." A few of the twenty-five points stated:

1. The German has his own religion, which flows like the living
water of his own understanding, sentiment, and thought, and is
ingrained in his blood. We deem it to be the German religion, or the
religion of the German people. We understand by it a German
belief expressing the special character and the integrity of our race.

5. The German religion is not to be regarded as a religion of revelation in the Christian form. It is based rather on a natural "revelation" of the divine will on earth and in the human mentality.

6. The German religion is a religion of the people. It has nothing

in common with free thought, atheist propaganda, and the break-down of current religions. We real followers of the German religion hold on to a positive religion.

7. The German religion is not opposed to any Church. What it wants is a German Church representing a religious people.

8. The idea of God is a moral concept, which we believe is based on the eternal creative force of Nature, which works in the world and on man. Belief in a God of another world is of Semitic, not Indo-European, origin. This kind of belief in God is not consonant with true religion and piety.

11. Man is not God. But he is the birthplace of God. God exists and appears in man. He never comes to earth. Therefore, the German religion is the religion of great faith in man.

15. The ethic of the German religion condemns the concept of inherited sin, and also the Judeo-Christian idea of a fallen world and man. This kind of teaching is not only non-Germanic, but also immoral and non-religious. Anyone who practices this concept of sin is a menace to the morality of the people.

17. At the heart of the German religious ethic stands a real under-standing for the welfare of the people and the Fatherland, and not for the blessedness of the individual. Unlike the Christian ethic, the German ethic does not call for the salvation of the individual, but rather for the welfare of the people as a whole.

18. He who belongs to the German religion is not a slave of God, but actually lord of the divine power inside him. German ethics hence reject as non-German the concept of making man passive for receiving grace.

22. We of the German religion think of the Divine in images true to life, male-hero and woman-mother.

23. One of the two religious forms of the German religion is the Nordic Light-Hero, who embodies heroic manliness. This Nordic Light-Hero reflects the high human Mind and the heroic, helpful Leader. This image struggles triumphantly ahead as the Moral Ideal of the people.

24. The mother-child concept is the truest, most loving, sacred, and happiness-inducing of all the symbols of world and life. The mother figure is the original religious figure, from which the God-Father derives its splendor. In the German Church, alongside the manly-heroic figure is the faithful picture of the most blessed moth-er. This is necessary if the church is to be based on the laws of life.

The writing was convoluted and confusing, but it was an important transition for the SS actions. Inhibitions against violence, not just against Jews but against other races, nationalities, even against Nazis who had come to disfavor, were drastically reduced by those who would embrace the new religion that was forming. The concept that man becomes like a god (No.ll) was meant to defuse moral inhibitions. Any action done for "the good of the state" could be justified.

❦

Czechoslovakia was the first test of Himmler's concepts outside Germany. VOMI worked to unite the various ethnic German communities through careful spreading of propaganda. Clubhouses, hospitals, and other facilities for ethnic Germans were financed, a way of helping the people, gathering them for sessions concerning Hitler and his goals, and discovering where the opposition might be. Many of the ethnic Germans were hostile to the activities of the Reich and felt comfortable to say so during the meetings. They did not realize that they were being targeted for the concentration camps through the files VOMI was carefully maintaining.

Hitler was pleased with Himmler and the VOMI because he was nervous about opposition from within the military. No matter how much power Hitler had within the government, he knew that the military historically had been known to act independently of any leader. They were well-armed, well-trained, and recognized how badly they were needed for anyone seeking to obtain or retain power.

In 1934 when Hitler and his followers had their first bloody purge, the army had provided transportation for the SS assassins. They had allowed the radical, violent change to occur, showing their support for Hitler in that manner. But in November 1937, Hitler made a more threatening announcement within his inner circle of military advisers. He said that he planned to have the matter of proper living space for the German people resolved within six years.

Everyone understood what they were hearing. Hitler planned to move east, controlling land even at the risk of war. He would start with Austria and Czechoslovakia. Although he did not mention the country, Himmler's previous statements, coupled with their own awareness of the way the Reich leaders were thinking, meant that Russia was likely to be targeted soon thereafter. It was a feat they knew was impossible, given their manpower, weapons, skill, and the nature of the opposition.

Colonel General Werner Freiherr von Fritsch was the first to object to the plan, explaining why it would not be realistic. His reaction should have sealed his death warrant, but Hitler knew he dared not be too harsh at first. Military leadership was well established, as was the loyalty of the troops to that leadership.

The move against the military was handled in a more subtle way. First came an attack on Fritsch. It was found from the records that a man named Otto Schmidt had reported witnessing a homosexual act between two men, one of them an army officer named Fritsch. Schmidt was a blackmailer and a thief, so his statements tended to be disregarded as self-serving at the time. But with what was happening in the military, they suddenly appeared to be exactly what everyone was seeking.

Hitler's high command was desperate to destroy Fritsch. Himmler, ever the loyal assistant, arranged for the general to be interrogated by the Gestapo while twelve high-ranking SS men, picked for their superior intelligence and almost irrational loyalty to Himmler, sat in an adjoining room. The SS men placed their chairs in a circle, leaned forward, and concentrated all their mental energy on Fritsch, who was unaware of what was taking place. They were helping Himmler mentally overwhelm the general, "forcing" him to confess. Instead, he simply maintained his innocence.

By the time a trial was held, early in 1938, the truth had become known and was repressed at first. The officer involved in the homosexual liaison was a captain, not a general, and his name was Frisch, not Fritsch. The truth might easily have been found, but everyone was too anxious to eliminate the general to properly investigate the charges.

The general was released and returned to the troops as the leaders of the SS gathered in small groups, fearful of what would happen next. Heydrich closeted himself with Schellenberg, the latter an expert shot who came armed to the private meeting. Others also armed themselves, waiting to see if Gestapo headquarters would be attacked by men seeking revenge for the near-destruction of the general. Although there was some indication that rebel troops had planned retaliation, nothing took place. Fritsch returned to his former duties and accepted a formal, public apology. Ironically, a year later, in 1939, he would die in combat.

Himmler, no longer fearing an assault by the military, handled Schmidt in his routine fashion. The man was taken outside and shot.

Hitler, meanwhile, managed to make several changes in the military to give himself slightly more power. In January 1938, War Minister Werner von Blomberg married his secretary, a woman who proved to be a former prostitute. She had posed for obscene photos during her career and some were located by the Criminal Police of Berlin. Himmler and Hitler used these to force his removal from power. Then, during the period when Fritsch was still in trouble, Hitler removed sixteen generals from their command positions, disbanded the war ministry, reassigned forty-four other generals so they would be leading different troops, and established the High Command of the Armed Forces

(OKW). With the restructuring, Hitler became the equivalent of commander-in-chief of the armed forces, assuring himself absolute control once the troops decided against any sort of revolt.

By March, Hitler sent his army into Austria, declaring it a new German state. And by October, he controlled ten thousand square miles of Czechoslovakia. To his delight, these illegal, violent acts were committed without any repercussions from the other nations of the world.

Before the invasion of Czechoslovakia, in July 1938, Hitler increased the power of the VOMI so that it was in control of other agencies that had previously been involved with the ethnic Germans. It did not become a formal part of the SS until three years later, but Himmler made certain that loyal SS men were infiltrated into all positions of leadership right from the start. His actions were reinforced by the naming as foreign minister of Joachim von Ribbentrop, a man with whom Himmler had been friendly for the previous six years.

Ribbentrop had married into great wealth and had the air of a man of intelligence and breeding, something that impressed Himmler, who promoted him to general during the years before he was named foreign minister (an action based on respect, not Ribbentrop's ability). However, the extremely vain Ribbentrop was so pleased that, on becoming foreign minister, he did whatever he could to bring more SS men into high staff positions. Later, when the two men became enemies, Himmler's power base was so strong that Ribbentrop was helpless against him, all because of the favors he did for the SS leader.

It was with Czechoslovakia that Himmler made his first major power move outside German territory. The ethnic Germans of Czechoslovakia lived mostly in the area of the Sudety Mountains in the western part of the country.

VOMI was ordered to infiltrate the Sudetenland, as the area was known, and create unrest. There was economic depression in the country and the ethnic Germans, more than three million strong, felt that they were being unusually punished by the central government. In truth, they were suffering no more than other Czech citizens, but they were isolated enough that propaganda turned them into a highly dissident force.

There was a Sudeten German political party, headed by Konrad Henlein, a moderate loyal to the Czech nation and anxious to see the frustrations of the ethnic Germans resolved in a way that did not endanger the Czech government's stability. As a result, Heydrich's intelligence unit began monitoring all of Henlein's actions, seeking ways to discredit him. They tried to spread stories that he was secretly meeting with the British, a charge no one outside the Nazi government felt was very serious. The best they could do was to gain the support of his chief deputy, Karl Hermann Frank, then isolate the political leader from much of his support.

Since political action and rumor did not work, covert violence was the next step. Initiated in the summer of 1938, the Freikorps Henlein along with members of VOMI began preparing to bring down the government. Instead, on October 1, the Czech leadership, frightened of a war with Germany, gave up the ten thousand square miles that formed the Sudetenland. Henlein, though actually left without serious power, was named an SS general to appease his supporters.

The covert action units moved on to Bratislava, the Slovakian provincial capital. Led by SS general Wilhelm Keppler, they met with the ultranationalist Slovak People's party, a group with limited support who wanted to have Slovakian independence. The party members did not realize Hitler's plans and were anxious to work with the Germans. They also did not realize that, since they were Catholics (several were priests), Himmler already had plans to purge them when the mission was accomplished.

This time violent sabotage was used. Bombs were set off in various locations, including a chocolate factory. The Slovak People's party was not suspected, nor was there any indication of who was committing the violence, a fact that forced the Czech government to declare a state of emergency in Slovakia.

Street demonstrations were organized. More terrorist units infiltrated the area, and finally Slovakia was declared a sovereign state under German protection. German occupation forces arrived by the middle of March, resulting in the Czech leadership capitulating entirely. Rather than risk war, Moravia and Bohemia were also placed under German control. On March 15, Hitler entered Prague, triumphant and with limited violence, none involving outright military action.

Czechoslovakia was desired by Hitler, but Himmler and his followers considered the maneuvers there mere preparations for their first major military effort. The small group of loyalist bodyguards had grown into the most important military force in the Reich. They had also learned how to create political unrest and terrorist violence and to utilize the propaganda value of fear within a nation, not just the concentration camps. They were ready for the true test of what they had learned, what they had become. They were going after Poland.

SS units united with regular German forces on the Polish border. However, Hitler wanted an excuse to attack and Heydrich was put in charge of staging such an incident.

The orders came on August 10, 1939. Alfred Helmut Naujocks, who had been part of the SS for the previous eight years, was told to arrange for an attack against the German radio station near Gleiwitz, a German community on the Polish border. There would be a six-man team, one of whom spoke fluent Polish, and they were to broadcast an announcement that Poland was invading Germany.

Later, during the Nuremberg war trials, Naujocks discussed what he had done. He said that Heydrich explained "Actual proof of these attacks of the Poles is needed for the foreign Press, as well as for German propaganda purposes." He then said of his own involvement:

I was directed to go to Gleiwitz with five or six SD men and wait there until I received a code word from Heydrich indicating that the attack should take place. My instructions were to seize the radio station and hold it long enough to permit a Polish-speaking German, who would be put at my disposal, to broadcast a speech in Polish. Heydrich told me that this speech should state that the time had come for the conflict between the Germans and the Poles and that the Poles should get together and strike down any Germans from whom they met resistance. Heydrich also told me at this time that he expected an attack on Poland by Germany in a few days.

I went to Gleiwitz and waited there a fortnight. Then I requested permission of Heydrich to return to Berlin, but was told to stay in Gleiwitz. Between 25 and 31 August I went to see Heinrich Mueller, head of the Gestapo, who was then nearby at Oppeln. In my presence Mueller discussed with a man named Mehhorn plans for another border incident, in which it should be made to appear that Polish soldiers were attacking German troops.... Germans in the approximate strength of a company were to be used. Mueller stated that he had twelve or thirteen condemned criminals who were to be dressed in Polish uniforms and left dead on the ground at the scene of the incident to show that they had been killed while attacking. For this purpose they were to be given fatal injections by a doctor employed by Heydrich. Then they were also to be given gunshot wounds. After the assault members of the Press and other persons were to be taken to the spot of the incident. A police report was subsequently to be prepared.

Mueller told me that he had an order from Heydrich to make one of those criminals available to me for the action at Gleiwitz. The code name by which he referred to these criminals was Konserven [canned goods].

The incident at Gleiwitz in which I participated was carried out on the evening preceding the German attack on Poland. As I recall, war broke out on 1 September 1939. At noon on 31 August I received by telephone from Heydrich the code word for the attack which was to take place at eight o'clock that evening. Heydrich said: "In order to carry out this attack, report to Mueller for 'canned goods.'" I did this and gave Mueller instructions to deliver the man near the radio station. I received this man and had him laid down at the entrance to the station. He was alive, but he was completely unconscious. I tried to open his eyes. I could not recognize by his eyes that he was alive, only by his breathing. I did not see the shot wounds, but a lot of blood was smeared across his face. He was in civilian clothes.

We seized the radio station as ordered, broadcast a speech of three to four minutes over an emergency transmitter, fired some pistol shots, and left.

The army moved swiftly into Poland, followed by troops of the SS. Hitler knew that the military had codes of ethics that would not allow them to destroy the defeated enemy. He let the regular military take control of territory, then had the SS soldiers systematically murder the political and social elite within the occupied land. There was to be mass killing handled by an estimated three thousand to four thousand men in six special units (Einsatzgruppen) called task forces.

The Einsatzgruppen had to be coordinated so the Reich Central Security Office (RSHA) was created and placed under Heydrich's control. The RSHA involved the intelligence unit (SD), Criminal Police, and Gestapo. This allowed the coordination of any action necessary, from interrogation by torture through liquidation.

Many Jews were taken in this original sweep, but many of the deaths reflected Himmler's hatred of the Catholics. In one diocese alone, 690 priests were arrested, 214 of them executed before the remainder could be sent to concentration camps to die more slowly. The one exception was SS general Udo von Woyrsch who, like Hitler and Goebbels, was a rabid anti-Semite. He headed one unit of approximately five hundred men and made it his self-appointed duty to single out and murder only Jews.

Political leaders were also killed. Some were shot where they were found. Others were taken to the woods, shot, and dumped in mass graves.

The actual death toll is uncertain. The official death toll at the end of the first week was an average of two hundred Poles per day. By September 27, a little over three weeks from the time of the invasion, only 3 percent of the Polish social, political, and intellectual elite in the occupied territories were believed to remain alive.

Himmler delighted in the Polish war. He created a mobile Gestapo and SS field headquarters modeled after the one Hitler used. He arranged for a train with fourteen cars attached to be prepared for his use. It was called Special Train Heinrich and he rode it in splendor into the occupied territory. The train was elaborately equipped. Himmler had his own drawing room coach. Antiaircraft guns were mounted on one coach with additional armed coaches all around. There was food, a manservant and bodyguard, his military adjutant, and others, a total of fifty people.

⊰⊱

Another change took place in Himmler in Poland. Before 1939, Himmler had seen no reason for the mass extermination of any people so long as they were useful to the Aryan race. However, during interviews after the war, investigators from a number of different nations put together a very different picture of Himmler at this time.

Himmler went to areas where SS men had rounded up Jews who were either to be murdered or sent to the concentration camps. He explained that he wanted to show his followers the physical construction of the Jewish body. He wanted their bone structure observed, the shape of their skulls, and the other details that made them "criminal specimens."

Elderly male orthodox Jews were forced to stand up and be ridiculed by Himmler. He also had the SS men force Jewish prisoners to tear off the ribbons of each other's prayer shawls, a religious garment worn by all the orthodox Jewish men. He would not let the soldiers handle such things because "these people are vermin," he was reported to have said.

The action was repeated from area to area, becoming verbally and physically more abusive each time. By the time he had witnessed the actions of his Black Knights against the Jews, he changed his opinion of how to handle them. He decided that Hitler's and Goebbels' hatred was valid. Sometime at the end of September 1939 Himmler is believed to have approached Hitler concerning the "endgueltige Loesung"—the "final solution," the meticulous and total elimination of the Jews throughout Europe.

Little documentation exists concerning what took place. Major war criminals, including Himmler aides such as Schellenberg, claimed to know nothing about the change. The few official papers that remained used the code term Aktion 14 F 13, the meaning of which is unknown today. However, the attitude, at least toward the Polish Jews (the first people to face almost complete annihilation) was preserved in a speech by Dr. Hans Frank, the German governor-general of occupied Poland. He had been an SS Upper Group Leader and was a lawyer prior to the war. Frank's speech, delivered in Krakow, is believed to have quoted Himmler's ideas and plans accurately, based on the information that was obtainable after the war:

> As far as the Jews are concerned, I want to tell you quite frankly that they must be done away with in one way or another. The Führer once said that if Jewry should provoke another war... the Jew will have found his end in Europe. I know that many measures against the Jews are being criticized and there is talk about harshness and cruelty, but I beg you to agree with me that... we will have pity on the German people only and nobody else in the world. This war would only be a partial success if the whole lot of Jewry would survive while we have shed our best blood. My attitude towards the Jews is... that they must disappear. A discussion is going to take place with SS Lieutenant-General Heydrich in the Reich Security Main Office. A great migration of the Jews is to begin. But what shall be done with them? Do you think we shall allow them to settle...? Gentlemen, I must ask you to arm yourselves against all pity. We must annihilate the Jews wherever we find them and wherever it is possible in order to maintain the structure of the Reich as a whole.... The Jews represent for us extraordinarily malignant gluttons. We have now approximately two million five hundred thousand in the Government General [of Poland], perhaps with the Jewish mixtures and everything that goes with it, three million five hundred thousand Jews. We cannot shoot or poison those three million five hundred thousand Jews; but we shall, nevertheless, be able to take measures which will lead, somehow, to their annihilation. The Government General must become free of Jews, the same as the Reich.

And so the round-up of the Jews in Poland began. The ghettos were established. Thousands were murdered. And the concentration camps of Auschwitz and Maidaneck were established. In addition, for the first time the equipment needed for the systematic murder of large numbers of people was obtained, including a massive crematorium in Dachau.

In an aside of history, the Dachau giant crematorium was never completed, though many others in surrounding areas were finished. Work on the crematorium, like the rest of the construction of Dachau, was assigned to the prisoners. One of these was Dr. Leopold Figl, a man trained in both agriculture and surveying. He had been sent to Dachau in 1938 when, as an Austrian Catholic hostile to the Reich, he was considered a threat to the Nazis.

Dr. Figl earned the respect of his captors as a hard worker who did not cause trouble. He worked, at first, in the gravel quarry. Then he became part of a bricklayer's crew. But when the officials learned of his education, they made him the head of the engineering team that was creating the crematorium.

Dr. Figl drew the plans for the crematorium, carefully designing them so that the work could never be completed. He chose materials that seemed necessary, though had actually been included because their scarcity meant that they could not readily be obtained. He saw to it that "accidents" destroyed copies of the plans, forcing him to constantly redraw and rework them. He seemed to always be busy. His work always looked as though it was done correctly, yet for three years nothing was built and finally the idea of a crematorium for Dachau was abandoned. The Nazis never realized that everything had been deliberately sabotaged, the doctor was allowed to live and went on to positions of political leadership in postwar Europe.

❦

The first phase of Himmler's rise to power was now complete. His lust for control, his cold-blooded determination to move forward in ways never before encountered in recorded history, and the other factors that had changed him into the most dangerous man in Germany had all occurred. As Hitler would devote almost all of his time to fighting the war, Himmler would take charge of the civilian population, more directly affecting the daily lives of the people than Hitler, Goebbels, and the other leaders.

CHAPTER 9

The Concentration Camps

IT WAS NOT just the systematic murder of millions of people that made the Nazi death camps such a nightmare. People have always been the ultimate spoils of war. Occupiers of lands have raped, looted, and murdered throughout recorded history. If the scale of the Nazi atrocities was greater, it was only because global communication had become a reality by 1933 when Dachau became the first concentration camp. The systematic murder of the Jews and other non-Aryans of Poland, Germany, Austria, and elsewhere was little different, on the surface, than the Mongol hordes who once swept into a city and murdered every man, woman, and child they encountered.

The true horror of the Nazi regime came not from the deaths but from the grotesque inhumanity that became "normal" behind the barbed wire and walls of the concentration camps. Heinrich Himmler was comfortable letting the world know that his Waffen SS troops were hardened to murder. He took pride in the fact that the men who had the death's-head skull on their uniform could kill as often as directed without question or rebellion. What was not said, what was little known, was just how extreme the atrocities and perversions had become. It was as though all the demons from hell had been given a place on earth in which to practice activities more extreme than one's greatest nightmares could conceive. Even more frightening was the fact that these were not demented thugs, mentally and emotionally retarded. These were the elite, the intelligentsia, well-educated professors, physicians, and scientists, most of whom had advanced degrees from world-renowned universities. They would have been accepted as the ideal leaders within any society in the civilized world.

For example, there was the young woman, Ilse Koch just twenty-eight at war's end, who married the Standartenfuehrer (commanding officer) of the SS troops running Buchenwald, a camp that had been built when the woman was just sixteen. She was an attractive woman, energetic, delighting in sport and known to cut a strikingly beautiful figure as she rode to the hounds throughout the war. The woman was also an art lover who arranged to have one of the concentration-camp office walls dedicated to her collection of striking designs inked onto · parchment. Some were simple, others elaborate, and she was constantly on the lookout for new and different works that would be added to her collection whenever she requested it. The "parchment" was dried human flesh. Her collection was of tattoos—enlarged by murdering the man who bore what she desired, then stripping and drying the flesh before framing it for her holdings. Equally horrible was the creative way she illuminated the walls, using lamps made from nondecorated human skin so the textures of the furnishings would all be the same.

There was the doctor who made a point of getting to know selected prisoners on a somewhat intimate basis. Then, when he felt that they were no longer strangers, he had them killed and their heads carefully shrunk. These were proudly displayed, each visitor being entertained with the story of the person's background.

The interests of the researchers varied from camp to camp. Dr. Sigmund Rascher utilized Dachau inmates to help the air force. New planes were constantly being developed and the doctor decided to learn the full affects of rapid acceleration to altitudes of twelve miles or more as well as rapid deceleration from such heights. Not that the information was applicable to air force needs. The pilots were always provided with the equipment needed to function safely and effectively in whatever planes were used for the war effort. But Rascher's scientific curiosity exceeded the practical needs of the day and, since he was a friend of Himmler, he was given permission for special experimentation.

A mobile decompression chamber was brought to the concentration camp, placed in a street, then isolated from passers-by. It contained special instruments for reading altitude, pressure, and temperature. An electrocardiograph was attached to a "volunteer" from among the camp inmates. The box allowed the doctor to simulate the conditions of rapid ascent and descent on the body. There was never a question of whether or not the subject, who had been promised freedom in exchange for his cooperation, would die. The doctor only wanted to know how long death would take and when the heart would stop beating. One phase of his experiments involved killing a man, then cutting him open at various intervals after death to see if the heart activity had ceased.

There was no practical reason for these experiments; they could not even be justified as saving German lives. They simply satisfied the curiosity of Dr. Rascher, whose captured notes reveal such observations as "the blood does not yet boil at 70,000 feet."

Himmler later encouraged Rascher to experiment with freezing men and women. Russians were frequently used for these experiments, as were women brought from the Ravensbruck concentration camp to the doctor's Dachau base of operations.

The experiments were quite simple. They started with the immersion of men in water deliberately cooled to temperatures of 39 degrees to 48 degrees Fahrenheit, then left there until stiff. Later experiments varied the time, generally relying on a minimum of five hours, with the temperature going as low as minus 13 degrees Fahrenheit.

The idea was not to freeze the subjects. Himmler wanted to know different ways to warm them, seeing how quickly the survivors could move about normally. He was fascinated to learn that if a man and two women were allowed to warm each other after the immersion, they were not so effective as a man and one woman. The reasoning was that inhibitions were reduced between a naked couple compared with a naked threesome.

Again there was no practical application. The doctor was not trying to find a way to save the lives of German soldiers who might have to survive in the water or in cold mountain air as a result of battle. The researchers were merely curious and had been provided with an unlimited source of subjects for their experimentation.

The experiments would have been no less shocking if there had been a seemingly legitimate end in mind. However, they would have been in line with the routine horrors of warfare. The captive has always existed for the pleasure or benefit of the captor. Women allowed themselves to become the "mistresses" of the officers among the occupying forces— German, Russian, French, American, or some other nationality— because the alternative was usually gang rape by the infantry. Families often presented their best wine, their finest jewelry, and other valuables to soldiers patrolling their neighborhoods, knowing that by such a voluntary action, they were less likely to have their homes vandalized by the same men seeking to steal the same items.

Human experimentation in any form has always been against the moral standards of peacetime populations. Yet when such experimentation has been deemed necessary, such as when an essential vaccine has proved effective with animals but has unknown benefits for humanity, volunteer prisoners have seemed an acceptable necessity. As a result, if the Nazi doctors had limited themselves to using inmates for the final testing of medicines that might eradicate one or more of the ills of mankind, they would not have been faulted. Instead, the doctors violated every value routinely taught in medical school, torturing and killing for the pleasure of witnessing such abnormal deaths.

During the rare occasions that experimentation had a productive end for the Third Reich, the methods and expected results remained chilling. For example, during the time Himmler wanted all non-Aryans to be a slave force for the Reich, he felt that the vast majority of them would have to be sterilized. This would prevent race-mixing and control the slave population. Eventually the entire non-Aryan world would be conquered and certain territories set aside for slave-breeding. The Jews might be allowed to have Israel or some other territory in which to live and reproduce in controlled quantities. Or it might be Catholics, Americans, British, or some other group that was not important. For the moment there were enough people waiting to be conquered so that the existing prisoners would be sterilized, then worked to death for however many months or years proved practical.

Not that the people would be told of sterilization. Himmler and his doctors were aware that such knowledge could bring a stronger reaction than the fear of death.

The desire for life was so great that the fear of death often led a man to passive behavior. Prisoners accepted the most horrible of tasks, such as removing the gold from the teeth of corpses who previously had been friends, neighbors, even loved ones. They endured beatings, hunger, and cold with little complaint if such a situation enabled them to stay alive. But tell a man that he would be sterilized, let him think that his sex life would deliberately be changed, and he would fight. The resistance would not be overwhelming. The SS could handle any uprising. The problem was that the SS would have to kill many or most of the people they wanted for servants, rendering ineffective the reason for the sterilization program.

The answer seemed to be the use of drugs, according to experts with Madaus & Company of Dresden-Radebeul. Their researchers had worked with animals and felt that humans, perhaps taken from among the gypsies in concentration camps, should be next. A memo to Himmler explained:

> If we were to succeed, on the basis of these researches, in producing as soon as possible a drug that would within a relatively short time,

imperceptibly bring about sterilization in man, we should have a new and extremely effective weapon at our disposal. The thought alone that the three million Bolshevists presently in German hands could be sterilized, making them available as workers while excluding them from procreation, opens vast perspectives.

The research centered around a plant called caladium seguinum, which was native to South America. Special greenhouses were developed for its growth, since extracts from the plant caused sterility in animals. However, the plant did not grow well in controlled conditions and required its native environment.

By 1942 an alternative method seemed necessary and it was decided to use long, high doses of X-rays, which were known to cause sterility. X-rays were also known to cause severe damage to surrounding tissue as well, so there needed to be some refinement. This time Jewish men were chosen for the experimentation.

The method was simple. The strongest and brightest among the men were selected to be exposed to high doses of radiation. These were men who would make excellent workers in a slave society. Unfortunately, no one knew the exact level of dosage that was important, so variations were used.

Too high a level of radiation caused sores and abscesses within a short time of the dose. Tissue burns were quite obvious, and the experiment was deemed a failure. The men would be incapacitated and of no value as slaves. Thus those failures on the parts of the scientists resulted in the subjects being immediately gassed. There was no reason to keep them alive.

The "lucky" ones had no idea what their future would be. They were sent back to work, observers making certain that they did not slack off on their productivity due to health damage. Then, approximately four weeks later, those who had survived and done well were brought back and castrated so that their testicles could be dissected and studied. In that manner, the perfect dosage for sterilization was determined.

SS colonel Victor Brack, chief of service in Hitler's chancellery, worked with Dr. Horst Schuhmann, who had previously studied the effects of X-rays on human generative glands. He had worked with Hitler on a euthanasia program in 1939. This program had developed a questionnaire for doctors to use when examining people to be put to death. It listed such factors as race—"German or kindred blood (of German blood, Jewish, first or second degree, Jewish half-breed, Negro [half-breed], gypsy [half-breed], etc.)"—and health. The health aspect included specific symptoms, medicines, whether or not the person was bedridden, crippled, or otherwise incapacitated.

The form required statements concerning whether or not the person was a worker, how good a worker, and the exact nature of what he or she did. The idea was to separate the weakest among the prisoners for death, saving the stronger for tasks necessary for the state. Later they, too, would be killed, but the euthanasia program was meant to remove the weaker non-Aryan population in a scientific and "medically justifiable" manner.

Schuhmann delighted in the sterilization work and developed a scientific approach of which he was quite proud. Col. Brack explained his own discoveries in a memo to Himmler:

The following results can claim certainty and an appropriate scientific foundation: if persons are to be rendered permanently sterile, this can be accomplished only by X-ray dosages so high that castration with all its consequences ensues. These high X-ray dosages destroy the inner secretions of the ovaries and the testicles....

Theoretically, with top voltage, thin filter and close proximity, an exposure of two minutes for men and three minutes for women should be sufficient. But another disadvantage must be taken into account. Since it is impossible to screen other parts of the body with lead without attracting attention, the tissues are affected and radiation sickness ensues. If the radiation has been too intense, the skin reached by the rays will, in the ensuing days or weeks, show symptoms of burning, varying with the individual.

One practical method, for example, would be to have the persons to be processed step up to a window where they would be asked certain questions or have to fill out certain forms, detaining them for two or three minutes. The official behind the window could operate the equipment in such a way that the switch simultaneously turned on two X-ray tubes, since exposure must be from two sides. A two-tube installation thus could sterilize 150 to 200 persons a day, twenty installations some 3,000 to 4,000 persons a day. A larger daily load is out of the question anyway, in my estimation.

The initial action was to be applied to the European Jews at first. There were two to three million such individuals in captivity who were deemed healthy enough to be of use in a work program.

Testing took place at Auschwitz and Ravensbruck, the results being a disappointment for Dr. Schuhmann. The concept was a good one, but it was expensive and not 100 percent effective for men. Castration by operation was a better approach, the doctor explained, since the operation took approximately six minutes to complete. Unfortunately, the added time factor made such large-scale castration impractical.

Himmler wanted to know other approaches, so sterilization by injection for a thousand Jewish women was authorized for Ravensbrück concentration camp. This was the result of an idea put forth by the SS brigadier general of Konigshütte in Upper Silesia. It was believed that an irritant could cause sterility if injected into the cervix:

> Before you start with your work, the Reich Leader SS would appreciate learning from you the approximate time that would be required to sterilize one thousand Jewesses. The Jewesses themselves are to know nothing about it. In the opinion of the Reich Leader SS, you should be able to administer the injections in the course of a general examination. Extensive tests would have to be made to show the effectiveness of the sterilization. For the most part, these could perhaps consist of X-ray photographs, to be made after a certain period of time, tc be determined by yourself, which would establish what changes had taken place. In some case or other, however, there might have to be a practical test, conducted in such a way that a Jewess is locked up with a Jew for a certain period of time, any success attained to be observed.

The method worked, but too many women died for the procedure to be considered effective. There was also no way to inject the chemicals to a depth that was consistently predictable. However, the slave needs were too important to stop and continued through 1944, ending only when the realities of the impending loss of the war prevented further efforts.

Some of the other medical experiments were quasi-legitimate. Inmates were injected with various illnesses—paratyphoid A and B, smallpox, diphtheria, and the like—in an effort to learn more about their treatment. There were blood studies, including the quality of blood kept in long-term storage before transfusion. Yet always there was a bizarre twist of mind among the researchers. Even those whose work might have been approved under more normal conditions frequently had "hobbies" that made all actions more perverted than the most extreme contemporary horror movie.

For example, there was the scientist who suggested that a museum collection of skeletons and skulls of "Jewish-Bolshevik commissars" be established. The concept was so exciting to the SS leadership that 115 people were immediately chosen to be the first entrants in the museum. They were examined, gassed, then preserved in a special alcohol solution so that they later could be stripped of all flesh and prepared for display. The only exceptions came with certain male corpses who first had their left testicles removed for the private collection of one of the professors. There proved to be no time for the establishment of the museum, so the corpses were dismembered, then burned at the Strasbourg University Institute of Anatomy before they could be discovered by an occupying force.

Russian prisoners of war were frequently selected for the testing of war weapons. The men would be shot with poisoned bullets or would have sections of their skin painted with the poison gases being used in combat. Then their death throes would be observed, the researchers carefully noting where they had pain, whether or not they went blind before death, and similar details. There was no effort to try to find an antidote for the poisons and the gases, no effort to test protective clothing. The research was simply done out of curiosity since, in the midst of battle, it was impossible to fully observe how someone dies.

Year after year, in every camp, there were numerous stories of similar atrocities. It was impossible to imagine so many different individuals, often with advanced education, engaging in activities whose only purpose was to observe fellow humans living and dying in agony. These were not the torturers seeking information or making public examples of camp rebels in a desperate effort to keep the inmates from rebelling. These were men and women who would be considered the social elite of any nation under other circumstances who were engaged in activities that should have been beyond the extremes of human imagination. It was such activities, far more than the steady effort to annihilate literally millions of people, that made Himmler's camps unique in the recorded history of the world.

Many of the survivors of the camps went insane from a combination of deprivation and the horrors they either witnessed or knew about. Some of the men and women lived in such fear of becoming the next victim of one of the Nazi experiments that ultimately their minds could not handle present reality. They created their own special existence where life was more tolerable.

The perversions of the concentration camps were not widely known outside the camp walls. Representatives of the International Red Cross, Folke Bernadotte, and numerous others were aware only of the malnutrition, starvation, and murder that was taking place. Had they been aware of the extremes, some undoubtedly would have wanted to move faster in the rescue efforts. Others may have given up, so overwhelmed by the horrors that they would have felt themselves helpless to respond in any meaningful way.

What was known about the camps was largely ignored during the war. It was 1942, nine years after the construction of the first of the concentration camps, that news of what was taking place reached the outside world. Knowledge that there was the systematic murder of Jews, political prisoners, and non-Aryans taking place reached England, the United States, and various Allied nations. The reports were downplayed in the media and quickly forgotten.

In 1944, the most important witnesses to the death camps escaped. These were two Jews who managed to flee Auschwitz. They were able to provide the details of the gas chambers and the ovens. They described the intense suffering and, for the first time, a few people took notice. There were appeals to the Allied governments to intercede, the suggestion being made that the railroad lines leading to Auschwitz be bombed so that the trains could no longer transport people to their deaths. The survivors even suggested the bombing of the camps on the theory that more would survive the bombing than the camps, and the destruction would stop their use. The reaction of the Allied military was that such bombing would be impossible. Although they were routinely flying in the area and knew of the rail lines, they could not spare the bombs or the time away from regular missions.

Each camp was run somewhat differently. In Auschwitz, for example, there was a mockery of a ceremony on arrival. Music was frequently playing as the new arrivals were stripped of all possessions. Heads were shaved, clothing abandoned, and the women provided with a dress—though no underwear. There were showers and an attempt to clean everyone upon arrival.

The main concern of the commander of Auschwitz was dehumanizing the arrivals. It was important to reduce resistance to the guards, and public humiliation was a rapid way to achieve this end. Women who took pride in their modesty had to undress in front of thousands. All hair was shaved from their heads. Decent clothing was abandoned and rags provided. The use of the toilet was twice a day for everyone, and relieving oneself had to be done rapidly. The women were forced to sit over a large hole in the ground, publicly performing what had been a private act. They were like dogs being walked on the streets of the city, all eyes watching as they used a fireplug, the grass, or a tree.

The moment the new arrivals learned about tattoos, their first fear was that they would not be branded with a number. An Auschwitz tattoo meant that you would stay alive, at least for a fairly prolonged period of time. Those without numbers were deemed fit only for death, though this might be because of ill health, mental illness, extreme age, physical impairment, or because politically you were disliked.

The tattoos were applied by prisoners, some of whom had great compassion and tried to make the experience as painless as possible. Others were rude, uncaring, as though they felt that so long as they were a skilled part of the life-and-death process of the camp they would be kept alive. In times when life is cheap and death is all around, even the slightest hope, such as having an invaluable skill, becomes precious. The fact that the tattoo workers had been taught to use the needle in the camp meant that others could learn as easily, thus making everyone expendable. But such a reality did not generate adequate hope so it was ignored, some of the workers preferring to pretend they were superior to the new arrivals.

The amount of food varied with the camp. Most camps had work crews and many had prisoners who were placed in ammunition factories, plants making airplane parts, sewing uniforms, and doing other work. Himmler would have preferred to keep long-term prisoners who had needed skills. He felt that the concentration camps could be the model for the slave-labor facilities that would be used after Germany won the war. However, since his ideas did not dominate, most camps planned to work even the most skilled workers to death.

The severity of what took place varied with the commanders. Bergen-Belsen was plagued with dysentery. The commander, finding the uncontrollable diarrhea disgusting and unwilling to improve conditions, developed what he felt was a logical method for handling the problem. "If they don't eat, they won't shit," he declared, deliberately starving many of the prisoners.

Other camps felt that the steady stream of new prisoners meant that everyone was expendable though they should be used to their limits. Careful studies were made to determine how long it would take the average person to starve to death on rations that were slightly below what was needed to sustain life over a long period of time. Many of the leaders would know by looking at someone if the person would last three months, six months, or longer. The work details would be planned around this cycle, hunger always rampant in the camps yet the prisoners able to work for the Nazis for several weeks or months before they died of the effects of malnutrition and slow starvation.

Food became an obsession. Even the smallest crumbs were devoured eagerly. Many of the inmates created elaborate recipes and food combinations they planned to have when they were released. Whatever they were given was eaten as quickly as possible for fear that someone might take it away.

As starvation increased, fantasies became less complex, yet more horrible. One woman talked of eventually having a loaf of bread for herself. Then she embellished the fantasy, talking of not only having the loaf for herself, but being so well fed that when she cut the bread, she would leave the crumbs that fell from the knife.

Food was occasionally used as an instrument of torture. In Bergen-

Belsen, considered to have the most sadistic staff of all the camps, one of the games of the guards was to take two hundred fifty prisoners at random and lock them in a barracks designed for a third that number. Before the men and women were placed inside, though, the stove used to heat the barracks was carefully stoked so it was the hottest it could be. Neither food nor water was placed in with the prisoners, but a kettle of food was slowly cooked just outside the door, the aroma of the food wafting in to the dehydrated, starving prisoners. Then, after two days of the torture, the door would be opened and the guards would watch the prisoners trample one another as they fought to get out and get to the food. Some died from the stress. Some were trampled to death. And some got enough food to survive.

(When the camps were liberated food was occasionally a cause of death. Malnutrition and starvation change the body's chemistry. After seven days without food, the body begins to "eat" itself—tearing down muscle, not just body fat—in an effort to find nutrition adequate for sustaining life. Eventually, eating a normal quantity of familiar food that has been denied for a prolonged period cannot be handled. Someone eating what, with time and slow recovery, would become a normal meal often had an unexpectedly violent reaction that first time—retching, cramping, and, in some instances, dying.)

There was quality food in the camps despite the starvation of the inmates, and that food went beyond what the guards were given. Caring for the pet dogs of the SS men was a highly desirable position because the dogs were fed in a manner that even wealthy Germans would have respected. Their meals consisted of various combinations of claret wine, meat, milk, potatoes, eggs, and cereal. It was high-protein and far more vitamin-rich than anything the prisoners had seen in recent times. Those who cared for the dogs would supplement their rations with stolen scraps from the dogs' bowls.

There were several sources for food, and even the quality of the official rations varied among the inmates. Until the end of the war, the concentration camps generally had one set of rations for the average prisoner, a second set for prisoners on special work details where maintaining their strength was critical to the success of those details, a third set for the prisoners in the hospitals where regaining their health was considered important, a fourth for the SS enlisted men, and a fifth for the SS officers. Even among these five categories there were differences. Important prisoners cooperating with the Nazis, such as block leaders in the various barracks, could often obtain more or better food. Likewise, favored SS enlisted men could receive more than their one-dish meal if they had the right connections.

For example, if a camp inmate was to have a certain ration of meat and the work camp ration ranged from 14.1 ounces per week at the start of the war down to 7 ounces per week at its close, that meat could take many forms. At the start of the war it was generally quite decent because everyone in German territory had access to quality food. But as the war years progressed, the best of the meat had to go to the Nazis because it was in short supply. There was some beef, but also whale meat, horsemeat, and similar unusual forms of protein.

The meat was generally boiled to the point where the meat was rather stringy. The prisoners would receive their tiny ration of the meat with the liquid that contained most of the nutrients removed. The elite among the prisoners would also receive the liquid, though, giving them slightly more nutrition than the others. Likewise there were times when whole potatoes were available. If the skin was removed, those who were able to obtain the skin were better fed than those without since the bulk of a potato's nutrients are in or just below the surface of the skin.

Two types of sausage was prepared in some of the camps. Buchenwald had "liver sausage" for the average inmate, a "food" made from ground fishbones and a variety of unrecognizable by-products. There was also blood sausage, which seemed to have genuine nourishment and was restricted to the special-duty crews who were both needed and had to have greater strength.

Special units were generally those units who had been rented to area businesses. German industry paid the SS to have prisoners sent to work in factories and manufacturing plants. The workers were expected to be in good enough health to master the tasks assigned, then be able to work for the duration of the war if possible. Those on the standard meals would deteriorate over the next nine months on the average, eventually becoming too weak to function effectively. The superior rations enabled the people to work and the SS to earn money. However, in a number of instances the additional food was paid for, the money going into the pockets of the SS leaders. Formal complaints were filed by the factory owners who could not maintain expected productivity, but most of the complaints occurred in 1945, when they no longer mattered. The few preliminary reports coming from the SS "investigators" handling the matter revealed great surprise since they found that the additional rations were provided to the prisoners doing the work. They ignored the fact that they, too, were involved with the theft of the money and food.

The hospital units had access to eggs and other food needed by those recovering. While some prisoners were meant to die in the hospitals, others needed to be restored to health and the additional food was meant for this purpose.

The lack of food was obvious in that the typical weight loss for the first three months of captivity was fifty pounds. The majority of inmates, regardless of their height and bone structure, weighed under 110 pounds. Since the only safe weight loss caused by a diet with controlled nutrition and exercise is an average of one pound a week over that three-month period (twelve to fourteen pounds maximum loss), the dangers are obvious. Yet survival was possible with both luck and friends.

Sometimes food was stolen from the hospital or shared by the special-duty workers so that more inmates could gain the value. At other times an inmate in the hospital was helped by being kept an extra day longer than expected just so he or she could have that much more food.

There were also canteens for both the prisoners and the SS at many of the camps. These canteens provided desirable items for the prisoners who had money sent from home, as well as for the SS men who wanted benefits not available to the general population in surrounding cities.

The canteens were stocked with cakes, fine canned goods, tobacco, cigarettes, and numerous other items. Anyone who could afford the canteen prices could, in theory, live quite well in the camps. The problem was the corruption among the SS officials who ran the canteens. This was a problem for the SS, but it was worse for the prisoners because it was in the prisoners' canteens that the greatest exploitation occurred.

Sometimes this exploitation was simple economic maneuvering. Germany had a law that prevented shopkeepers from exploiting the citizens. All items had to be on sale, a simple concept but one unlike circumstances in past years when desirable items were linked with less desirable items. For example, suppose a citizen in Dresden needed a pair of suspenders. Under the laws of the National Socialists, he would go into a shop and buy the suspenders. Years earlier, when the laws were different and needed goods were sometimes in short supply, the shopkeepers would boost their business and profits by having what came to be known as tie-in sales. This meant that if the Dresden shopkeeper had an oversupply of boots that were not moving, you could buy the boots alone, but if you wanted the suspenders, they were tied in to the boots. You had to buy both the boots and the suspenders or you could not buy the suspenders at all.

Tie-in sales may have been eliminated in business but not in the camps. Thus, in order to get desired items, some prisoner canteens required the purchase of undesirable items, including spoiled canned goods or other products.

Most canteens simply would not sell the prisoners the critical items they carried at any cost. Canned vegetables might be on the shelf, but no amount of money would enable the average prisoner to get the item.

The SS man running the canteen would declare that the food had already been taken or find some other reason not to make the sale. The food would then be shifted to the SS guards or be used as a bribe to prisoners who were acting as spies or bullies, intimidating their fellow inmates as a favor for the guards.

Periodically the SS would make special shopping trips for a group of inmates. Everyone would pool their money, then an SS man would buy luxury items and delicacies. When he returned, he would distribute something, perhaps a chocolate bar to be shared by groups of three inmates, a little tobacco, and one or two other items. The bulk of the merchandise would be kept by the SS man and his family. No one complained because, even being cheated, more was available than before.

The SS enlisted men's canteen was both better-stocked and less prone to cheating than the prisoners' canteen. However, the best items still found their way to the elite units and the officers. Corruption and the good life became a relative matter in the camps, only the top officials ever truly being satisfied.

When the International Red Cross was able to supply packages to some of the inmates, most or all of the merchandise was stolen by the SS. This was also true of items sent by families of political prisoners and others deemed worthy of survival, albeit within the confines of the barbed wire and minefields. The volume of such thefts was overwhelming; one study of Buchenwald alone resulted in an estimated loss of as many as twenty-three thousand packages diverted from the prisoners to the SS.

Late in the war, because of the actions of Bernadotte and others, representatives of the Red Cross were allowed in some sections of some of the camps. The officials would scramble frantically to hide all evidence that they had Red Cross packages in their offices or quarters.

Safety precautions were ignored on the jobs handled by the prisoners because they were so readily replaced. In one munitions factory, poisonous chemicals were pressed into small land and sea mines. The chemicals periodically exploded in the process, killing one or more of the workers. They also coated the workers, often taking their lives through indirect poisoning. Most of the men handling such work lasted between four and six weeks.

Death camps made a pretense of giving hope to the prisoners. Jews were either selected to go to work each day or to be deloused. The latter would be taken to what appeared to be a bathhouse where attendants, often dressed in white, went so far as to distribute towels and soap. The prisoners undressed in front of one another, leaving their clothing neatly folded in an area where they were to return after their showers. Then they entered rooms where there were showerheads, fake drains, and everything necessary to create the illusion of safety.

Suddenly the guards would fire bullets into the room, not to kill anyone but to force them to move toward the center of the room, allowing more people to enter. Only at that instant was it obvious they would die, but only the final few people knew enough to struggle. The doors were sealed before anyone could escape.

Guards wearing gas masks used openings in the ceiling to drop poison pellets into the room. The more sadistic among them used peepholes to watch the death throes of their victims. The rest just waited the fifteen minutes necessary to be certain everyone was dead. Most were killed by the poison gas in the first three minutes, though some lasted longer and no one wanted to be bothered having to try and kill someone a second time.

Metal hooks were used to drag out the corpses. Then inmates were forced to remove wedding rings, gold from teeth, and women's hair. The gold was sent to the German national bank, Reichsbank. The hair was used as stuffing for the pillows and mattresses on which other, unsuspecting inmates, rested. Finally the bodies were taken to the ovens to be burned.

The crematoria were operated around the clock, the living developing a black humor about the constant smell of death. If a child was separated from a parent, frequently the child would be sent in the direction of the smoke. Others pointed to the chimney and said it was the way out of Auschwitz.

The Nazis felt that the most efficient use of the death camps was as a source for by-products that could benefit Aryan consumers. Even Himmler knew that there were limits the public would tolerate as he helped build the new Reich. He decided to keep secret the full range of uses, knowing that the public would rebel. Thus many Germans unknowingly purchased lampshades commercially made from human skin, soap made from human fat, industrial-grade coarse cloth made from human hair, secondhand clothing of a quality that could be cleaned and sold as new (all owned by death-camp inmates), and children's toys taken from Jewish children who had been killed. However, the public knew nothing of the materials used or their source.

Work camps were meant to instill a degree of hope in prisoners who were actually being allowed to die slowly rather than through deliberate execution. Most of the survivors of the concentration camps were inmates in the work facilities. But such survival took luck, cunning, and finding a way to function within the system in such a manner that adequate food for survival could be obtained and punishment avoided.

Himmler prepared signs for all the concentration camps: "There is a road to freedom. Its milestones are: obedience, hard work, honesty, sobriety, cleanliness, devotion, order, discipline and patriotism."

Most of the camps did not bother rewarding good behavior. Even where prisoners had a chance of surviving for months or years, they were still inferior beings. Non-Aryans were seen as little more than animals. Aryans were either political traitors who had not supported Hitler, Christians who refused to renounce their religion and follow the fantasies of Himmler and others, or people guilty of some similar offense. The non-Aryans could hope for a servant's role in the new Reich. The Aryans would be put to death if they did not change, the anger toward them far greater because they were supposedly superior individuals.

Certain crimes had established penalties. If a prisoner escaped and was recaptured, he or she would be beaten, often before being returned to the camp. Then the person would be forced to stand in a central location, often under a gallows, for several hours, regardless of the weather. A sign hung from the prisoner would read "I am back," making clear not only the crime but also the punishment. Ultimately twenty-five to fifty lashes would be administered or the person would be hung publicly.

Most of the crimes were petty, specifically designed to assure that anyone could be punished at any time for almost anything. So long as it was impossible to avoid breaking a rule, a prisoner could be "legitimately" singled out for punishment. Thus it was a crime to have your hands in your pockets during cold weather. Unshined shoes would result in punishment even though prisoners were frequently forced to work in the mud. However, if the shoes were perceived to be "too well shined," other punishment was given because that meant the prisoner had not been working. Coat collars had to be turned down, all buttons in order, and one's posture had to be correct. Saluting was necessary, a serious problem for those who were in concentration camps because of religious beliefs that made them look upon saluting as the equivalent of turning Hitler into a false god, something they would not do.

Other crimes included picking up a cigarette butt to smoke or, in some instances, smoking at all, straightening one's cramped body while doing stoop labor, foraging for any food, and stealing. Usually the people were honest and a charge of theft was created by the Nazis as an excuse for the guards to beat or murder a prisoner. On those occasions when stealing did occur, the thief faced a certain beating, not only by the guards but also by the other prisoners. There were so few personal possessions possible, so little food, that what was retained was too precious to be taken. A few crumbs of food meant the difference between life and death, and a thief who dared to take them was subject to great violence.

Oddly, a few of the newer prisoners had not reached a level of hunger where bread was essential for life. They wanted tobacco, which some of the starving prisoners possessed. The newer prisoners would steal bread, then trade it for the tobacco, an exchange they would regret, even if not caught, days or weeks later when when every morsel of food was treasured.

Arbitrary punishment could happen at any time and there was no preparation for it. For example, when a beating was to be administered, frequently it was done with ceremony and with the victim fully dressed. A rack, carried through the camp by inmates, would be placed atop a stone platform with high steps so that everyone could see what was taking place. The prisoner would be forced to climb the stones, then lay on the rack while his or her name and offense were read over the loudspeaker system. Then the beating would be administered either by a guard or a fellow prisoner.

Such beatings were the least deadly only because prisoners could prepare. They would wear several layers of material under their clothing, and other prisoners, who worked in the hospitals, would be ready to help them upon arrival. Everything possible would be done to speed the healing and help the beaten prisoner regain enough strength that he or she would not be put to death for being too weak to work.

When prisoners were forced to beat their fellow inmates, two types of action would occur. Some were extremely violent, either because they were sadistic or because they were so frightened of retaliation they wanted to please the guards. Others, especially the political prisoners, would either refuse or beat their fellow prisoners in such a way as to minimize the pain. When they were caught slacking off, they too, were violently punished, often more severely than those they had been ordered to beat. Yet they still adhered to their moral beliefs.

Prisoners being beaten either made a point of honor of being silent or, overwhelmed by the pain, screamed uncontrollably. In order to keep the beatings more pleasurable for the camp staff, musicians were often positioned by the rack to which the prisoner had been bound for the beating. They would play music to drown out the screams. In at least one instance in Buchenwald, an opera singer in the camp was ordered to stand beside the victim, singing an aria as a counterpoint to the screams.

The danger came from arbitrary beatings and brutality, often from new guards eager to prove that they were as strong as the veteran SS men. Typical was one of the most feared punishments administered in the camps. The prisoner's wrists were tied tightly behind his or her back. Then another rope would be tied around the wrists, the rope thrown over a tree branch, and the prisoner raised into the air, feet dangling. The action would dislocate the shoulders and cause excruciating pain. The prisoner would be suspended anywhere for from thirty minutes to four hours, and many died from the trauma. Those who lived, denied desperately needed medical care, were crippled to some degree for the rest of their lives.

The only punishment that worked against the guards, despite the fact that some inmates died, was group discipline, often at the whim of guards seeking to have fun. Large numbers of people, sometimes a barracks, sometimes the entire camp, would be ordered to perform meaningless tasks covering every inch of the grounds. They would be made to carry stones or lumber, to duck-walk, to roll or crawl, always at a rapid pace. Back and forth. Up and down. From one edge of the camp to the other they would move, often doing meaningless, grueling tasks for hours at a time.

The whole-camp punishment was considered by the guards the cruelest they could impose and they delighted in stepping on the bodies of men, women, and children who had collapsed from exhaustion, too weak to keep up. What they did not realize was that it also was an important way for the resistance movements within the camps to study the terrain. It was one of the few times that the entire area was seen by the prisoners—who normally were restricted to a limited section depending upon their sex, work detail, and other factors. All the members of the resistance movement would take the opportunity to try to memorize the terrain. Such efforts helped keep their mind off the pain and, for the survivors, gave them a tool for escape. Almost every flight from the camps, and there were many over the years, some having a handful of prisoners going uncaught, utilized knowledge gained during these brutal punishment sessions.

Fatigue labor was the other popular torture for large numbers of people. After work detail the prisoners being punished were ordered to stand, usually at attention, in the open air. This would last for as long as several hours. Then they would be weighed down with manure, rocks, sand, or other weights and forced to move at double time, usually until dusk. If the detail included a Sunday, they would be beaten randomly as well, the guards' method for punishing them for interrupting what should have been a guard's quiet day.

Individual deaths were always hidden from the records. A prisoner murdered by a guard was invariably "shot while trying to escape." The truth was usually quite different, but challenging the truth meant death.

For example, there was an incident in Buchenwald in 1941 when a film producer was trampled to death by an SS officer. The incident was witnessed by a work detail of almost thirty men, one of whom was the victim's brother. No one dared interfere.

The brother went to the officer in charge and reported the murder. The SS always tried to give the impression of fairness in such matters and dutifully interviewed each of the witnesses. Only the brother of the murdered man admitted to seeing anything. The rest of the work detail refused to admit any awareness of the death.

The brother thought he would be killed for his actions, but both he and the men on the detail were surprised when the brother was summoned for a second period of questioning, then released. It was as though the authorities were determined to not let the matter rest. They wanted the truth and were determined to punish the man who was guilty of murder. The brother was filled with hope. The other men adopted a wait-and-see attitude.

A few days passed and the brother was again asked to come and make a statement. The brother detailed all the abuses he had witnessed, then was removed from the others. He was killed shortly thereafter. Then the members of the work detail were summoned, a few men at a time, for questioning. They, too, were murdered despite the fact that they all maintained that they had neither heard nor seen the beating death. The SS wanted to be certain that they protected themselves from the truth.

And therein was one of the oddities of the camp. Hitler and Goebbels were openly anti-Semitic and determined to murder all Jews. Their efforts had severely decimated Europe and would expand with conquered territories.

Himmler and others were more pragmatic. They knew that Christians, especially Catholics, were the bigger threat to their future. They also wanted to limit the non-Aryan population to those people who could best serve the state in slavery, destroying all others or keeping them in reserve, their reproductive organs removed or destroyed, in case additional labor was desired. All the camps were death camps, if only by virtue of the substandard rations, even though there were those whose sole purpose was extermination. Yet despite all this, there seemed to be some vestige of moral conscience remaining for many of the guards. They tortured and killed at will, yet tried to cover actions taken without official authorization.

That was the odd aspect of the Buchenwald murder of the film producer, for example. The murder was unauthorized, the whim of the guard, yet the brother who complained and every possible witness were ultimately murdered. It was as though the SS feared the revelation of the truth, even though the truth would have been treated as a joke— a random, acceptable incident the producer probably "deserved" just for being Jewish. Limitless brutality existed side by side with nagging conscience. And perhaps it was because of that last vestige of moral memory that the actions should be considered even more cruel, since the men committing them either knew they were wrong or knew that even the hierarchy in the SS might consider them wrong.

Mail was carefully limited because its lack was demoralizing. Jehovah's Witnesses, among the first people to be placed in camps for religious reasons when Dachau opened in 1933, were not allowed to send or receive mail until 1939. Jews were given more opportunities, though usually only every few months. Political prisoners were often denied the right to send mail, but their families were provided with regular reports about the inmates. Often a family would be told that a political prisoner was long ago eligible for release except for the fact of his antisocial, uncooperative conduct.

In truth, the political prisoner being falsely maligned was often not only cooperative but sick from the brutality of the guards. He was doing whatever was necessary to stay alive, a thoroughly docile figure. However, the family, not knowing the full truth of the camps and being both Aryans and supporters of the new regime, would send him letters telling him to act right so he would be released. Such letters were passed directly to the prisoner, knowing that the family's misunderstanding of the truth of the situation would cause great emotional pain.

At other times a mail call would be held near an open fire. A prisoner would be informed that there was mail, shown the letter, then the letter burned before it could be read.

Recreation was considered necessary for the camps. This included activities such as soccer, volleyball, handball, and boxing. Oddly, many camps had younger men, still somewhat fit, who were quite willing to get into the ring for the entertainment of both the SS and the other prisoners. It was a diversion, a sense of life on the outside, a way to avoid facing the reality of impending death.

The ultimate oddity came early in 1945 when Himmler authorized the creation of special buildings to be utilized in each camp. Officials at the women's camp at Ravensbruck were asked to find young women volunteers, generally from eighteen to twenty-four in number, to be sent to each camp to work in the special buildings. The volunteers were placed under the care of two SS female non-commissioned officers in each camp and were to serve as prostitutes, charging two German marks for their services.

Most of the women came from backgrounds that were troubled and had led highly unstable lives. They were the type of individual who would be likely to enter such a profession in any city of the world during peacetime. Thus they could not be said to have been forced into the work, though the SS was obviously exploiting the unstable.

A few of the women, a very small number, saw working as a prostitute as a means of survival. They had no way of knowing that the war was almost over. They had no way to determine when freedom would come. They assumed that they would be well treated and well fed in order to keep them attractive to the men. Yet such women had an extremely difficult time adjusting to the pace—one man every twenty minutes unless he paid substantially more than usual or was of special importance within the SS. Both prisoners and guards utilized the recreation center, many of the SS women who ran the brothels joining in the "fun" with the women they supervised.

Only after the war would the full meaning of the camps become clear. In addition to all the other facets of the holding facilities, they were meant to make a profit from each prisoner. This was true whether someone was there specifically to be killed or if he or she was to be a part of the labor force.

Arrangements were made so that families of prisoners could send them money each month. Since mail was strictly controlled, the families never knew that their loved ones received little or nothing. The Nazis encouraged the families, convincing them that the health of their loved ones was being assured by the money that provided the few extra items needed.

Sometimes the money was stolen directly and added to the SS supplies. At other times the inmates received it directly, especially when someone came from a wealthy family and would only receive the funds if he or she stayed in direct contact with that family. The latter situation resulted in special extortions. For example, the SS knew that within any barracks there were rich and poor alike. If a single individual were asked for money, it might or might not be available. But if the barracks as a whole had to provide it, those without funds would put pressure on those with money to assure the survival of everyone. Any barracks that did not meet the demands was punished as a whole, no individual contributor escaping the violence.

For example, when there was an assassination attempt against Hitler, the inmates at Dachau were expected to contribute money toward the purchase of a new uniform for him. Each barracks was told to provide seventy-five marks. Those with money wanted to give as little as possible, not knowing when they would need more to stay alive. Those without money were determined to force the well-off to give at least the minimum demanded in order to protect themselves and others from retaliation. Some barracks gave more than the seventy-five marks minimum, thinking that it would buy them favorable treatment. Instead, it just diminished the funds available to all of them and put them at greater risk of retaliation in the future.

The money was never meant for Hitler even though it was collected in Hitler's name. It was one of many schemes the SS developed to become wealthy at the expense of the prisoners.

Another tactic, in addition to raising the price of canteen items actually sold to the prisoners by ten to twenty-five times normal retail, was to auction desired products. German tea was in great demand because the coffee tasted so terrible. The SS would frequently sell it to the highest bidder.

But no matter how the money was obtained, the SS made certain that every prisoner provided a profit in one form or another.

The least valuable prisoner could benefit his killers in at least one of several ways. Gold teeth were always desirable and, if it looked as though someone would stay alive longer than they might have value for providing money, a lethal injection could always be used in those camps without gas chambers. Human hair was used in manufacturing, as was skin. The by-products of cremation also had value, as did the clothing the prisoner owned at the time he or she arrived at the camp.

The value of a prisoner was based on a nine-month life in camp. If the person could be rented to a manufacturer or other businessman, the average pay to the SS was six marks a day. From this had to be extracted a tenth of a mark for clothing depreciation and six-tenths of a mark for food. This meant that more than five and a quarter marks could be used for other purposes—including cremation, which cost two marks per person.

During the Nazi war crime trials a more complete breakdown of the value of murder was shown by Franz Stangl, the commander of Treblinka. He explained what he would take in valuables in a given year. This was routine, not special, and similar statistics were available from the other camps. Taken from the prisoners and sent to Berlin were 250 kilograms (500 pounds) of gold from wedding rings (gold teeth were not included in the review), twenty freight cars of women's hair, $2.8 million U.S., 350,000 British pounds sterling, 11 million Russian rubles, and numerous other valuables, such as jewelry.

A large portion of the treasures were saved by the SS for the elite

Himmler planned to use to run the new Germany. An SS account was created in the Reichsbank under the name Max Heillger, a name that had been created to hide the account. Only Walther Funk, president of the bank, had access to the money and the chance to increase it through normal investments when desired. However, it was shipped out of the country when the Nazis began to lose the war.

Eventually the bulk of the valuables made their way to Argentine leader Juan Peron, a Hitler sympathizer. Argentina was officially neutral during the war but handled the funds after the Nazi decline, setting them aside so that the fleeing SS leaders could afford to start a new life in South America.

Other hiding places were used for such items as rare coins, art objects, and the like. The SS established hospitals in areas where they were not needed in order to ship the valuables through Germany. Ambulances were loaded with the valuables and moved from hospital to hospital, the large red cross on the side indicating the vehicles were to be neither stopped nor attacked. The system resulted in the shipment of what often amounted to millions of dollars per SS leader.

Only Himmler apparently did not hide wealth for after the war. He arranged for bribes in exchange for the release of prisoners, but he used his money for the SS. It cost thirteen million reichsmarks to develop Wewelsburg Castle, for example, and it was believed that the bulk of that money had been stolen.

The SS also invested in legitimate businesses. Among others, it owned the German Equipment Company, the German Experimental Establishment for Foodstuffs and Nutrition, the German Excavation and Quarrying Company, and the Society for Exploitation of Textile and Leather Work. All of these utilized either the concentration camps or the prisoners to reduce their costs and make high profits.

<hr>

The reality of the concentration camps went far beyond the systematic extermination of those deemed the enemies of the Third Reich. The world that Himmler helped create and run involved barbarity of a variety never before recorded—a system of torture, rape, murder, exploitation, and insanity.

CHAPTER 10

A Change in Advisers

DR. FELIX KERSTEN was raised in what began as an idyllic childhood in Lunia, Liflande, a small community in czarist Russia. His farmer father, Frederic, was of Dutch descent. Frederic was administrator of the large land holding of a wealthy Russian. His mother, Olga Stubing, the daughter of a postmaster, was a professional-caliber soprano who was also skilled in therapeutic massage, a technique she had learned from her mother.

There was a gentleness about the family, a sense of service for others that came from caring for others rather than subservience to the wealthy. Frederic helped grow the food that fed much of his community. Olga used simple massage techniques to reduce or eliminate the pain of stress-related ailments such as stomach ache, rheumatism, and neuralgia. Her singing was usually confined to charity events, but her voice was so pure that she was called "the nightingale of Liflande," The Kerstens never accumulated much money, but since money was unimportant to them it is unlikely that as a child Felix ever had a sense of being either rich or poor. The only discomfort in his young life was attending school, in which he had no interest. Felix, a dreamer, concentrated on his meals rather than his studies.

The parents decided that their son needed better discipline than he was receiving locally so, at age seven Felix was sent to a boarding school, at which he spent the next five years. He showed himself both bright and disinterested, his grades improving very little. Finally he

161

was sent to Riga, where the teachers were known to be unusually strict as well as skilled in reaching unmotivated students. Felix still did poorly, but at least he finished his secondary-school education.

The Kerstens had been farming for two hundred years; it was natural enough to assume that Felix would follow the family profession, so in 1914 Felix was sent to Schleswig-Holstein in Germany to study at the agricultural school in Günefeld. That education, which he ultimately rejected in favor of a medical career, would later assure a close relationship with Heinrich Himmler.

Within six months of his arrival the First World War was raging. Germany was officially cut off from Russia, and Felix was not able to return. His family, considered Germanic, was part of the large German-born mass of people in the Baltic states who were sent into isolation. They were all forced to go to Siberia and Turkestan to wait out the war in case they proved a threat to the internal security of Russia.

Felix Kersten had enough money to stay in school and finish his degree. At sixteen, a foreigner with a German-born father, he was too young to be considered either a threat or an asset to Kaiser Wilhelm II's government. He was left alone to complete his studies in agricultural engineering. However, at nineteen, his formal education seemingly complete, he had to join the army. The year was 1917 and he witnessed what he considered the worst aspects of German society.

The war had come as shock to Kersten. He could no longer live a hedonistic life because survival depended upon his developing work skills and self-reliance. The overnight maturity Kersten had to develop did not include adapting to the people around him, however. He respected the German work ethic and the country's culture and music but hated the all pervasive love of discipline that had led to Prussian militarism and, to him, the army's ridiculous strutting about in uniform.

There were options other than simply joining the German army when Kersten was forced to become a part of the war effort. Old alliances had changed. What would become Czechoslovakia (at the time the countries of Bohemia, Moravia, and Slovakia which, combined, formed the designated Crownland subdivision of Austria/Hungry) joined with Russia to fight against its former ally, Austria. And the Finns living in Germany formed their own legion specifically to fight against Russia. Since Felix knew Finland well from his frequent childhood holidays, he decided to throw in with the Finnish unit and fight against Russia. In this venture his timing was perfect. With the Russian Revolution raging the Czarist army was no longer there to shoot at the German army. Other Baltic countries were undergoing internal revolutions meant to determine their destinies in ways never previously allowed. Thus, by becoming an officer in the Finnish force Felix was able to avoid combat entirely, sitting out the war in Estonia.

Kersten did sustain injuries as a result of his military service, though. One entire winter was spent in the field. There were no shelters and no shelter could be built. The time was frequently spent in marshes that were muddy at best, frozen at worst. He was eventually unable to use his legs, with rheumatism diagnosed as the cause of his paralysis. In an effort to help him recover, his unit sent him to a military hospital in Helsinki.

The paralysis proved temporary and the convalescence gave Kersten a chance to think about his future. He could become a career military officer, an idea without appeal. Agriculture had only a limited interest for him, and then only if he could own his own land, something that seemed highly unlikely. His only strong career interest had developed while he was in the hospital: medicine. He thought he might like to become a surgeon and mentioned that fact to his own doctor.

The doctor was discouraging. Felix had no money. He had been reunited with his parents, who were allowed to return to their homeland, but the war had left them unable to provide their son financial support. He would face many long years of hard work at best. To have to earn a living while also being a student might prove overwhelming. Instead the doctor suggested he consider massage.

Massage was not considered a means of relaxation or an adjunct to physical therapy when Kersten was introduced to the field. It was a career unto itself, a healing profession at a time when medicine was still rather crude. Physicians often did more harm than good, and illnesses such as influenza that are today usually viewed as an uncomfortable nuisance were both life-threatening and often spread death in epidemic proportions. The drugs that could be prescribed were usually ineffectual or dangerous in their own right. But massage was a treatment that could do no harm and was often of great benefit. In Finland, for example, massage had been considered a highly respected science for many generations.

Massage training was primarily done in hospital, those with the knowledge passing it on directly, the student working alongside the teacher. Yet the hours were long, the expenses fairly high, and Kersten had to work odd jobs in order to pay his way. He was a waiter, dishwasher, and longshoreman. For two years he did whatever was necessary to complete his studies.

Kersten received his initial degree in 1921, then was told to go to Berlin for further training. There he was able to live with a friend of his parents, and his knowledge of Finnish enabled him to work as an interpreter for Finnish businessmen passing through the capital. Other jobs included that of movie extra in the rapidly growing German film industry.

His work came to the attention of a professor of surgery in Berlin. Germany was not then a nation where nontraditional medicine was respected. Acupuncture, massage, chiropractic, the use of diet and nutrition, and other alternatives to medicine and surgery were considered useless by most physicians. But this professor felt otherwise. He was convinced that men like Kersten could often heal where "conventional" medicine failed, and the youth had shown outstanding promise. As a result, the older man decided to take a hand in his training by broadening his education with other forms of massage therapy.

The result was the introduction of Eastern massage techniques to Kersten's training. His teacher arranged for Felix to meet Dr. Ko, a tiny, fragile-looking Chinese who had been raised in a Tibetan monastery. Dr. Ko had spent twenty years learning the healing methods of both the Chinese and the Tibetan-lama doctors. When they had taught him everything they knew, the monastery required that the doctor move to England to learn Occidental approaches as well. His trip was funded by the monastery and he earned his doctoral degree in London, after which he set up a private practice.

Eventually Dr. Ko planned to return to Tibet, living in parts of Europe before going back home, and chance brought him to Berlin for a prolonged stay during the time Kersten was there. Dr. Ko was anxious to learn the methods taught in Helsinki and was willing to exchange his knowledge with Kersten.

The training continued for the next three years. Kersten divided his week among classes at the traditional schools, odd jobs to supply himself with income, and private study with Dr. Ko. He also found that Dr. Ko encouraged him with other pleasures he was delighted to have as a part of his studies. Alcohol and tobacco were forbidden because they dulled the senses, a proscription with which Kersten agreed. But eating well was important to both men, and Dr. Ko explained that frequent sex with women assured the health of the nervous system. Felix Kersten, a true ladies' man, made certain his nervous system remained healthy.

The difference between Western and Eastern massage is important to this story because it would be a factor in Kersten's becoming the confidant of one of the most powerful men in the Nazi organization. Western massage required the patient to tell the doctor where the pain was located so that the doctor could relieve the problem. Eastern massage required the patient to say nothing. (Chinese medicine believes that there are four pulses and nerve centers, one or more being affected when someone is in bad health.) The doctor was to use palm and finger movements to identify the affected nerve group, diagnose the ailment, and then influence the nerves to restore health. The work required great sensitivity and extensive training that few were willing to undergo. To have a Westerner both capable of learning both approaches and willing to do so was unusual.

When Dr. Ko left Germany for Singapore in 1925, he turned over his extensive practice in Berlin to Kersten, making the young doctor instantly wealthy. Kersten moved from the quarters he had maintained with the family friend to a large apartment. He purchased expensive furniture, a luxury car, then hired a chauffeur so he would not have to drive. He also took the daughter of his family's friend, Elizabeth Lube, as his housekeeper. She was young enough to find the doctor exciting and his work fascinating, and old enough for their relationship to be like that of brother and considerably older sister or young aunt. Elizabeth was quite content to act as confidante, friend, cook, and maid, accepting his romantic involvements with numerous other women because he and she did not hold a sexual attraction for each other.

Kersten's work was noninvasive and involved no medication. Even if his techniques failed, the patient would feel better from a massage. And if the techniques worked, the patient ran no risk of suffering from the side effects of the treatment.

Kersten's efforts were frequently deemed successful, although there is no way of knowing whether he cured disease or simply reduced pain. In some instances, of course, he was dealing with psychological problems that caused physical symptoms. His efforts reduced stress, thus eliminating pain. Because much of his clientele was wealthy, and because many other doctors saw them as a source of long-term income if they eased the symptoms when they occurred rather than addressed the cause, he was perceived as healing where others failed. His fame spread quickly and he became known as a miracle worker.

Among those who learned about Kersten was Queen Wilhelmina of Holland who, in 1928, asked him to examine her husband, Prince Hendrik. The prince was bedridden with heart disease, a problem Kersten also diagnosed—but Kersten eased the pain and used a program of diet, rest, and exercise that restored his health when other doctors had given him just six more months to live.

Kersten fell in love with Holland and decided to make The Hague his legal residence. He maintained his apartment in Berlin so he could continue treating his wealthy German clients, but he made Holland his home, knowing that the reputation he had gained from helping the prince would assure financial success.

There would be a third residence for Kersten during this period of fame and great wealth. A wealthy industrialist was so pleased with the treatment that he paid Kersten a hundred thousand marks when the bill had only been five thousand. The money was used to buy an estate east of Berlin, a large spread with forests, meadows, and the ability to be self-sustaining.

By 1931, when Kersten was becoming well established in his practice and the master of three estates, Germany began changing. Adolf Hitler was heading a political organization that was obviously fatally dangerous to those in opposition. Yet Kersten paid little attention to what was taking place. If he witnessed any rallies, he walked by without stopping. He did not keep up with current events. If his patients were heads of government, they were there for their health. A discussion of world politics did not seem appropriate in the treatment room. And he made a point of not reading newspapers, his attitude being that if he could not make a change in society, what good did it do to know about a problem?

In 1934, however, word of Hitler's excesses became a part of office conversation. Kersten's social life was spent taking women to eat, to parties, and to bed. He did not realize what was happening until his patients began speaking of their fears of arrest. They were intellectuals, teachers, members of the upper-middle class, well educated, not seducable by propaganda, or the extremely poor. The latter he treated without charge—but they, along with the wealthy, faced arrest, torture, and the concentration camps. Many feared Nazism. Others felt that it was a national shame, a blight on a great nation's history. There was no way of knowing to what extremes the increasingly powerful party might go, but already it was something to be concerned with.

Kersten's supporters see him as apolitical during this period. If something did not affect him directly, it might as well not have been taking place.

Kersten's detractors see him differently. They feel that though he may may have had no interest in politics, he shared the fairly common anti-Semitism of the day. He would treat anyone who was sick, regardless of race, religion, or nationality. But he allegedly looked upon Jews as somewhat disreputable individuals who deserved second-class treatment in housing and business. He was probably comfortable with the ghettos, perhaps believing that the Jews were best off in isolation. He may have tolerated the concentration camps, though even his detractors never claimed he supported the deaths. Eventually it would be claimed that he was more of a friend to Himmler than he wanted to admit, an assertion that cannot be proved or disproved.

Life began changing for Kersten in 1937. First there was the matter of marriage. Nearly forty, he was a bachelor who had been with many types of women for both brief and prolonged affairs. He had learned to value women for more than just their pretty faces, their delightful figures. He had learned to value their skills as cooks.

This woman's name was Irmgard Neuschaffer. He met her at a small party given for him and Elizabeth Lube. Irmgard had come from Silesia, a family friend of the people who had invited Kersten, arriving unexpectedly when the party was about to take place. Naturally she was invited to stay for dinner.

The first course served was *rassol*, a popular Baltic-region dish that had been a childhood favorite of Kersten's. He had several helpings before continuing with the rest of the meal, the rassol so delighting him that everything else about the evening seemed perfect, including Irmgard. Kersten her asked her if she was engaged. Irmgard said she was both single and uncommitted. Kersten informed her that they would marry. She laughed and informed him that they should write one another, getting to know each other by correspondence. Two months later they were engaged; the date was confirmed four months after that first and only meeting.

The marriage startled many, in part because the well-known doctor had had no physical contact with his bride other than sharing a dinner, and in part because other women apparently expected that they would be marrying him. The couple settled in The Hague, Elizabeth Lube remaining with them. Kersten did not realize that the marriage had made him vulnerable to the rising power of Nazism in ways he could not have anticipated.

In March 1939 Felix Kersten was summoned to Berlin to treat Heinrich Himmler. He had been approached several months earlier for the same purpose, but had expressed reluctance to take such a patient. Despite his deliberate isolation from politics, the SS was so thoroughly in control of so many aspects of German life that everyone had come to respect or fear them, a fact well known to Kersten. He had explained that he did not wish to get involved with such an element of society, but friends said it would help them to have him treating Himmler. They believed that Himmler could be manipulated when he was ill and that a doctor was the perfect man to influence him.

Kersten agreed reluctantly. He traveled to 8 Prinz Albert Strasse, where the headquarters for the chancellery of the Reichsführer was located. The facility was heavily guarded, though the floor Kersten was shown seemed like any well-appointed bureaucratic office. He did not know that the basement held political prisoners who were being interrogated by the Gestapo, often through torture. The only hint of special security beyond the men present was an X-ray device hidden in a wall. Kersten was asked to pause a moment by the wall—he did not realize that this was so he could be checked for a hidden weapon.

Heinrich Himmler was not at all the man Kersten expected. He was shocked to discover that the Reichsführer was small, his hair thinning, his chin receding, and his features Mongoloid rather than Aryan. When he took off his shirt he revealed narrow, round shoulders, flabby skin, poor muscle tone, and a pot belly. He also had intense stomach pains, a recurring problem none of his previous doctors could correct. It was for the pain, excruciating enough to leave him almost crippled during the attacks, that he sought treatment.

Kersten quickly found the nerves that were causing Himmler's problem. The doctor began the massage—gripping, kneading, probing. The treatment lasted ten minutes; when it was done, Himmler was completely free of pain. He had tried all the major doctors in Germany, as well as such pain killers as morphine, all to no avail. Yet Kersten had freed him of the agony in just a few minutes. He not only insisted that Kersten treat him daily for so long as he was in Berlin, he also wanted to make Kersten a full colonel in the SS—the highest honor Himmler could give and the last honor Kersten wanted to accept.

Kersten agreed only to take Himmler as a patient for the next two weeks. The treatments always alleviated Himmler's pain. By the end of the second week, Kersten was shocked to find Himmler talking freely to him about the plans for the Third Reich. Although Poland had yet to be invaded, Himmler mentioned that the nation would soon be at war, a situation that delighted him yet surprised the doctor. He asked Himmler why, then made a diary note of the reply later in the day—a habit he would follow for the next few years, ultimately providing an important look into the mind of Heinrich Himmler.

"The Führer wants war because he believes it is important for the good of the German people. War makes men stronger and more virile," Himmler was reported to have explained. "And anyway, it will be a little war: short, easy, and victorious. The democracies are rotten at the core. They will soon be brought to their knees."

Three months later Hitler took control of all of Czechoslovakia, and by the summer of 1939 Himmler desperately requested that Kersten come to Munich, where the Reichsführer was staying. The pain he was experiencing seemed overwhelming and he needed the doctor's healing touch. The doctor agreed. It would be one of the last voluntary treatments he would make. Himmler soon made it clear that Kersten could continue the treatments as a free man, his family kept untouched by the violence that Hitler was bringing to the world, or the doctor would be eligible for the concentration camps. Kersten chose to save his own life by treating Himmler, not realizing that with that decision, he would influence the saving of thousands of lives.

Questions would arise about Kersten's true sympathies. Was he actually pro-Nazi, creating an elaborate, self-serving story about his innocence only after the war? Or did he do the best he could, walking a fine line between being a part of the Nazi inner circle and being sent to the concentration camp for his sympathy for those Himmler considered enemies?

What mattered was that he became Himmler's closest confidant other than Heydrich. And when the time came for Heydrich to be murdered, Kersten would be the most influential man in Himmler's inner circle.

<hr/>

"In dealing with members of a foreign country, especially with members of some Slav nationality," Himmler proclaimed, "we must not start from German points of view, we must not endow these people with decent German thoughts and logical conclusions of which they are not capable, but we must take them as they really are.... Obviously in such a mixture of peoples there will always be some racially good types. Therefore, I think it is our duty to take their children with us; if necessary, remove them from their environment. We either win over the good blood that we can use for ourselves and give it a place in our people... or we destroy that blood. For us the end of this war will mean an open road to the east, the creation of the Germanic Reich in this way or that... the fetching home of thirty million human beings of our blood, so that still during our lifetime we shall be a people of one hundred and twenty million Germanic souls. That means that we shall be the sole and decisive power in Europe. That means that we shall then be able to tackle the peace during which we shall be willing for the first twenty years to rebuild and spread out our villages and towns and that we shall push the borders of our German race five hundred kilometers farther to the east."

<hr/>

The invasion of Poland, which changed the power structure of the SS, not only proved Reinhard Heydrich's brutality, it also moved him into a position from which he had to be eliminated. He became known as "Heydrich the Hangman" for the mass murders he arranged as each new territory was subjugated. His associates, other than Himmler, also felt that he was using such violence to prove himself worthy to replace Himmler as Reichsführer SS. Although he never spoke of the fact, Himmler apparently understood the potential risk. Ultimately Himmler's intelligence gathering would alert him to an assassination attempt against Heydrich, and he would choose not to alert his associate to the danger. Thus it would be Heydrich's strength in occupied Poland that would also alert both the enemies of the Nazis and the SS officer's associates to the need for his elimination.

Heydrich had been concerned about the troops assigned to the Einsatzgruppen killing squads. He noticed that many of them were showing signs of uneasiness when attacking civilians instead of military targets. On September 20, 1939, a secret Fourteenth Army report noted: "The troops are especially incensed that, instead of fighting at the front, young men should be demonstrating their courage against defenseless civilians." Himmler was always ready to deal with such problems, and he began his resettlement program that October. He convinced the SS troops that the East belonged to them.

The plan, announced on Himmler's thirty-ninth birthday, October 7, 1939, called for the removal of most non-Aryans (primarily Slavs and Jews) from Poland and other captured territory. The few allowed to remain would be used as servants. Heydrich was assigned the leadership of the resettlement program and also ordered to redistribute property so that the Germans could benefit from the hard work of others. Clothing, furniture, housing, and all other valuables were given to the Nazi supporters.

Several agencies were given responsibility for handling the work, all of them placed under the Reich Commission for the Strengthening of Germanism (RKFDV). The new organization was headed by Ulrich Greifelt, a former manufacturing-plant manager. He understood the handling of such a bureaucracy and also had other skills that could be used, including helping German industry. He arranged for ethnic Germans to be brought back to the motherland to fill the half-million jobs that existed in critical manufacturing plants. However, he also came into conflict with Himmler over the resettlement program, eventually having an emotional breakdown from the stress, and the work was ultimately handled under the direction of Himmler and Heydrich.

This movement was one of the Nazis' early mistakes of the war years. There was the presumption that the ethnic Germans would be so pleased to be helping the Führer that they would accept the hardship of relocation. Certainly they had a better life than the Jews, who were being forced into concentration camps. Yet they were still being subjected to radical, unwanted change that took them from their homeland, their possessions, everything familiar. The move led to bitterness; complaining led to death.

For the ethnic Germans whose purity was uncertain, there were further hardships. They were placed in resettlement camps, with entire families often separated in the process. Then they would have to go through a series of measurements, photography sessions, analysis of their hair color, documentation of their ancestry, X-rays, and other meaningless pseudoscientific procedures. Once the analysis was done, the individual would be assigned a code number of anything from IV-3-C (essentially a death warrant because the person was declared an ethnic reject) to I-a-M/1, a person who was pure Aryan and of great importance to the Reich. Those who fell in between would often have to stay in the settlement camps for additional testing.

Life in the resettlement camps was far superior to the conditions for those who were forced to leave entirely. The evacuation involved a million and a half Poles, both Jews and non-Jews, who were forced to leave the western region during the harsh winter of 1939–1940. The temperature dropped to forty below zero, which made survival extremely difficult. Many a boxcarload of people shifted from one region to another along the railroad was so lacking in heat that everyone froze to death. The warmth of the bodies jammed together could not defeat the bitter cold.

Even the SS guards began to waver as they opened railroad cars and found stiff corpses upright—a horror beyond comprehension for the young men, far different from their early training. Recognizing this, Himmler went to visit the men assigned such duty, telling them how strong they were. Only the elite could endure such horrors, he explained. They should be proud of their inner strength. Himmler told them that "In many cases it is much easier to go into battle with a company of infantry than it is to suppress an obstructive population of low cultural level, or to carry out executions, or to haul people away, or to evict crying and hysterical women."

Himmler's pursuit of racial purity was taken to an extreme in Poland, then continued in the months that followed as Germany invaded Russia. The Reich needed men and women to work in the factories and on the farms, but they had to be trusted Germans. Some of these efforts came from forcing ethnic Germans and those who looked as though they might be to register for racial typing. If the decision was made that they were of pure blood, they were forced to go where Himmler desired:

"Where racial Germans have not applied for entry in the ethnical German list, their names must be turned over to the local State Police." His order continued: "If they do not register within eight days they are to be taken into protective custody for transfer to a concentration camp."

The reaction was swift. Fear, anger, and frustration weakened whatever support might previously have been possible. Even humor was used against the SS high command, one joke being: "And if you do not want to be my brother, I shall smash your head."

The other racial-purity action involved children. The SS sent special officers into the streets of Poland to examine children wherever they might be encountered. They checked the orphanages and playgrounds. They wanted either children of mixed heritage who looked properly Germanic or children of unknown parentage who looked Aryan. These were then kidnapped for the Lebensborn, where they were given new identities (including non-Jewish names) and then turned over to SS couples willing to raise them as future Nazi workers and leaders. More than two hundred thousand children's identities were changed in this manner.

The SS was using Poland to expand its independence from the central German government as well as Hitler's control. Himmler arranged for SS takeover of several different businesses. These were successful enterprises working for the benefit of the SS, not the Reich. Himmler was establishing a source of income so that SS operations could function no matter what anyone else did. It was an effort that assured a lack of opposition since he would not only control police, intelligence, and other forms of security, he would also not be dependent upon the budget whims of the central government.

Sometimes the business takeovers were made with legitimate financing at prices that approximated market values. The money for such efforts was frequently supplied by German industrial giants such as Krupp. The existing industrialists knew that if they acted as Himmler's short-term bankers he would leave them alone. He also would supply them with slave labor from the concentration camps, enabling them to continue with their manufacturing and sales, making higher profits than with a normal payroll.

On April 9, 1940, the war came to Scandinavia. German troops invaded Norway and Denmark. The Danish government agreed to the occupation, planning to use passive resistance to support its people who, the leaders knew, were heavily outgunned by the Germans. The

Norwegians put up intense resistance, though, a fact that led to a German memorandum meant to convince the people that Germany intended to save them from the forces of the West:

> The German troops therefore do not set foot on Norwegian soil as enemies. The German High Command does not intend to make use of the points occupied by German troops as bases for operations against England as long as it is not forced to.... On the contrary, German military operations aim exclusively at protecting the north against the proposed occupation of Norwegian bases by Anglo-French forces.
>
> ... In the spirit of the good relations between Germany and Norway which have existed hitherto, the Reich Government declared to the Royal Norwegian Government that Germany has no intention of infringing by her measures the territorial integrity and political independence of the Kingdom of Norway now or in the future....
>
> The Reich Government therefore expects that the Norwegian Government and the Norwegian people will... offer no resistance to it. Any resistance would have to be, and would be, broken by all possible means... and would therefore lead only to absolutely useless bloodshed.

The German newspapers announced that Germany was the savior of Denmark and Norway. The occupation forces were not meant to cause problems for anyone. Instead, they had assured the two countries that they would not face violence from Britain, France, or any other Allied nation. The headlines frequently stressed that Denmark and Norway had been "saved."

For the first time since Hitler began the war, Folke Bernadotte was forced to face the radical changes in his country. He was part of a conference among government leaders who had to decide how to handle their alliances and position in Scandinavia.

The answer was made obvious by the political and military realities they were experiencing. Russia dominated Finland and the Baltic countries, still in alliance with Germany. Denmark and Norway were in the control of the Nazis. They could take arms against the Germans and be destroyed or they could remain neutral, placating everyone to the minimum degree necessary for survival.

The Swedes decided to avoid alliances. They did not allow the Allied troops to traverse their territory on the way to Finland, though they had provided weapons to Finland before that territory fell to the Soviets.

This time the decision was reached to do nothing to protect Norway. That country needed guns and gasoline, both of which Sweden could have sent but chose not to. Sweden allowed the Germans to send a trainload of medical supplies and doctors to their troops in Norway, but the movement of troops through Sweden was not permitted until after Germany had triumphed in Norway. Even then, only replacement troops were permitted. This meant that approximately 140,000 German soldiers left Norway the first six months following the fighting. In exchange, an equal number of German soldiers traveled by train into Norway as their replacements. The new troops were rested and had fresh arms, but neutrality was maintained.

Later King Gustav V of Sweden would be severely criticized for his actions. However, Sweden was in a position to help concentration-camp victims and other prisoners later in the war only because of this elaborate political maneuvering. The decision proved the best possible course of action for saving the most lives, though Bernadotte did not truly understand what was happening at the time. Despite being on the committee that worked out the compromise, he seemed reluctant to consider the full face of war.

On June 21, 1941, Hitler launched Operation Barbarossa, the invasion of the Soviet Union. The Third Reich would capture the Soviet people, killing millions, resettling others, and gaining vast territory for the expansion of the Reich.

For Himmler, the capture of Russia was to be a major step in creating the world of the new SS. He invented a series of towns of twenty thousand people, Germans, ethnic Germans, and Germanized Russians (the exact racial standards involved were perpetually confusing since they seemed to change with the conditions of the war, the whims of the scientists, and Himmler's own vagueness). Each town would be surrounded by thirty to forty family farms, supposedly run by SS families who were living from the soil yet were well-armed and well-trained. The farm families would be a first line of defense against attack from within and without until, presumably, generations later, everyone would be an integral part of the Nazi system.

There was tension among Hitler's top leaders concerning who would have the chance to control the fate of captured Russian territory, but Hitler had made his decision. He arranged for Himmler, the SS, and whatever regular army troops the SS desired, to handle "special tasks for the preparation of the political administration" within Russia. They were executioners, and Heydrich was to be their leader.

Unfortunately for Hitler and the rest of the Third Reich, the invasion of Russia did not go according to plan. After tremendous initial successes, the German army found that the Russian troops fought with unanticipated ferocity and ruthlessness, employing an effective scorched-earth policy in their retreat. The Russian civilian population, despite a hatred of Stalin that Hitler hoped to fan into open revolt, became determined to repel the German invaders or die trying. And many other military factors, including the Luftwaffe's inability to dominate the skies, the unexpected peril posed by the Russian winter, and Hitler's own strategically inept orders, combined to doom the Nazi efforts on the Russian front.

Himmler was unconcerned about the problems with the Russian front. He and Heydrich relished handling the problem of the people they were to remove from the Ukraine. At first the Ukrainians welcomed the German troops, bringing a respite for everyone. Stalin had been extremely repressive in the Ukraine; the young people, especially, were not able to imagine anything more repressive and deadly than the government they had to endure. The Germans appeared to be liberators, kind soldiers out for a good time who dated the young women and delighted in local activities.

Attitudes changed quickly. The Ukrainians were fun, but they were also "subhuman." Russian prisoners of war, sometimes hometown boys who had not wanted to join the army, were shot for no reason other than they were a nuisance. Young women flirted innocently with the soldiers, then were raped in return by the Waffen-SS. Anyone who complained was shot.

Some of the violence came from the regular army soldiers whose families or friends had been hurt by violence from Russian soldiers. However, most of it was limited to the SS troops who seemed to delight in creating as much terror as possible.

The Waffen-SS fighters were among the bravest of soldiers, but their bravery was without careful analysis of what they were facing. They were so determined to prove their loyalty that they would put themselves into positions where death was certain. By February 1942, forty-three thousand Waffen-SS men were dead or wounded severely enough to take them out of the war. By the following year, one-third of the Waffen-SS men committed to Operation Barbarossa were out of commission.

The intense death toll did not diminish the popularity of the Waffen-SS units. There were more than two hundred thousand such men in uniform by the start of 1943, and more than double that number a year later. However, the new recruits were often as undertrained and ridiculous in appearance and skills as Himmler had been when he had first marched for Hitler so many years before. The quality diminished to the point where the earlier fanaticism was almost nonexistent.

Himmler and the SS troops not assigned to the front were concerned with handling the populace after battles were over. Action groups (Einsatzgruppen) were established for mass extermination. An estimated thirty million people would have to be killed in the occupied lands.

The men chosen for the action groups were an odd lot. Poachers were taken from the concentration camps because, though they had committed crimes, they were also skilled trackers. It was believed that they could be used to track partisans in hiding. To supplement the SS men, criminals known for their violence, including convicted murderers, were also selected from the camps. So long as someone was capable of murdering to order, he would be useful in the mopping-up operations.

The Ukraine was the first area where murder was critical. However, even the Jews had a brief honeymoon period after the Nazis moved into the area. The action groups had to deal with the fact that the Jews had a strong economic impact on the Ukraine. Killing them outright might reduce essential goods and services. Equally important was the fact that the Jews did not represent a serious threat to the soldiers. They were not Stalinists. They had mounted no opposition as a group, and while there were individuals among them committing terrorist acts, they were very much a part of a disorganized minority.

The violence, when it happened, was extreme. Between 150,000 and 200,000 Ukrainian Jews were gathered together, a few dozen at a time, by the Ukrainian militia and volunteers from the German army. They were taken to public areas and shot. The sound of the gunfire seemed continuous, in many instances White Ruthenian natives (the people of Ruthenia, a province of Czechoslovakia that is now West Ukrainia S.S.R.) being murdered at the same time. Those White Ruthenians who were not shot were often clubbed, the blows crippling some, killing others.

City after city was affected, the Jews forced into ghetto areas, then systematically slaughtered. Occasionally those deemed of value to an essential business were granted safety, but the vast majority were set to die.

Frequently the deaths were planned to be a surprise. An entire ghetto area would be surrounded late at night. Arc lights erected earlier would be turned on and teams of four to six SS men or militia members would simultaneously enter each house. Sometimes the people were surprised in their beds. Sometimes they placed barriers against their doors and windows to try to buy more time. Always the military triumphed, forcing the people who survived into waiting freight cars for transport to wherever they were to be murdered. The corpses of those who were killed before they reached the train (often there were elderly as well as infants with crushed skulls) were piled into farm carts.

Everyone determined to be a Jew or a Communist was destined for death. The rich could bribe guards to use them as slave labor, but that simply delayed death.

Himmler was pleased with the atrocities against the Russians: "I will not make any agreement [concerning proper treatment under the Red Cross convention to which Russia had not been a signatory] involving the verminous Russians. I will not allow my men to be restricted in their dealings with these subhuman types."

The Russians were later able to determine what had happened to the soldiers and civilian prisoners. One report stated: "Many of the prisoners were unable to walk as a result of continuous beating and exhaustion. On the Bolshaya Sovetskaya Street... the Black Guards opened a disorderly fire on the column. The prisoners attempted to escape, but the SS men overtook and shot them. In that way nearly five thousand were fatally shot. The corpses were left lying about the streets for several days."

And the labor camps were even worse. Sick men were sent to do heavy labor in order to kill them. Others were starved to death or allowed to die from dysentery, typhus, freezing, and other ravages that were common. Prisoner of War Camp 126 alone saw more than sixty thousand prisoners slaughtered.

Reports also revealed how the Germans operated. One SS man dressed in the uniform of a Russian prisoner of war, then mingled with the Soviets, randomly beating them. Another innovative murderer, identified as SS private Rudolf Radtke, used aluminum wire to make a special lash for beating the prisoners.

After the war the Russians found mass graves in which corpses were layered. Each grave held between 350 and 400 bodies, and between 10,000 and 12,000 corpses were found in each mass gravesite.

The prisoner of war and detention camps were among the worst of the concentration camps which were not established for mass extermination. By the start of World War II, there were four types of camps—detention, resettlement, prisoner of war, and extermination. The detention camps were sources of labor for the SS and the Reich. The POWs were also expected to work, but the number of inmates in such camps was unpredictable. Only in the detention camps could the SS make long term plans for labor commitments to both SS and nearby industries, the latter of which often rented inmates from the camps.

The POWs were forced to live on a ration that never exceeded 700 calories while doing work that required more nourishment than that for survival. Fuel and water were lacking. Insects and rodents were everywhere. People were housed in quarters so cramped that they literally had to sleep on top of one another. Since five or six would die each night in some wards, it was not unusual for the living to be forced to try to rest on the rotting flesh of a corpse.

Some of the Russians were transferred to Auschwitz concentration camp to be murdered. There they would be taken to a killing room apparently created specifically for them. The men would undress in one room where a radio blared to hide the sound coming from the next room. Then each man was taken to a second room with an iron grid and a drain in the floor. The man was placed against the wall, the back of his head against a slot. Then a German sniper would shoot him. However, the snipers were just far enough back to miss occasionally, creating a more difficult situation.

The blood was washed down the drain, the corpse removed by two German prisoners. Then the process would be repeated. Since there were occasional mistakes, the system was changed. The new approach was to tell the prisoner he was going to be measured and back him against the wall. Then an iron plate, ostensibly a measuring device, was slowly, gently, lowered on to his head. Once in place, a ramrod shot out, smashing the back of the prisoner's head, killing him instantly.

Other methods were used as well. Special vans, appearing to be cabin trailers, were designed for transporting civilians to the burial sites. The vans were loaded with prisoners, then sealed and a poison gas released into the air. By the time the vans had driven the ten to fifteen minutes needed to reach the mass burial site, all the people in the vans were dead.

The vans were a problem for the soldiers, though. The people came to know what the vans meant and would resist getting inside. There was also a tendency for the soldiers to separate the deaths from the war effort. It was felt that there would be much better civilian cooperation and an easier time for the military if, instead of the gas vans, the soldiers could simply execute the people with a bullet through the neck. Such executions by gunfire were believed to be more comfortable for everyone. They also prevented the maintenance problem caused by the van's victims defecating at death, forcing the SS men to have to clean the vans each time they unloaded the corpses.

The Russian winter did not halt the killings, but it slowed them and brought Germany its first defeat. The generals were irate with Hitler. His orders had been foolish, his tactics naive, and the losses too great for the necessities of other battles. Only Himmler drew close to Hitler because Himmler believed in the capture of Russia, the seizing of the land, and the use of those few people whose race made them a natural, albeit unknowing, part of the new order he was creating.

There were other activities taking place during this period, activities that would directly affect Bernadotte. The first was the appointment of Heydrich as the acting Reich Protector of Bohemia and Moravia, an action that would prove his death warrant and eliminate his influence with Himmler. The second action, occurring shortly after this period, was Walter Schellenberg's visit to Sweden.

The Schellenberg mission to Sweden had two purposes. Himmler was anxious for the Swedes to understand the racial teachings of Hitler and the religious beliefs that were uniquely Himmler's. (Not that Himmler knew he stood alone among the top Reich leaders—he tended to project his views onto them, believing in this manner that they were shared.)

The second purpose, a self-appointed one, was to penetrate the Soviet intelligence network in Sweden. Schellenberg knew that Himmler's purposes were foolish. He did not intend to waste his time extolling the Nazi party beliefs. Instead, he wanted to find ways to infiltrate his agents into the intelligence apparatus the Soviets maintained. He wanted them to move as high in the Soviet ranks as possible in order to maintain an ongoing awareness of Soviet plans to counter the German invasion. So long as the war effort was floundering in Russia, the greater the intelligence gathered, the better the chances of victory.

Sweden maintained a Communist party, the members of which were theoretically loyal to Russia. It was too small to have political clout, but party members acted as couriers throughout Central and Western Europe, distributed money, and assisted Russian agents with their work.

One of the former members of the Swedish Communist party was Nils Flyg. Flyg had left to join the National Socialists, doing similar work for the Nazis, and publishing the *Volkets Dagblad*, a newspaper with a circulation of approximately a thousand subscriber/sympathizers. However, Schellenberg suspected that the switch was actually a way of infiltrating the Nazis for the Russians. He wanted to learn whether Flyg was loyal, a double agent, or a potential triple agent who would ultimately work against the Russians who may have established him in his new position.

Before the main work of the trip took place, Schellenberg took two days' vacation in Stockholm, time he used to reflect on the future. He was quite comfortable with his role in the Nazi party. His loyalty was intact, but he was also enough of a realist to know that the circumstances in which the Nazis had found themselves in Russia were quite different from the original formulation. Russia had not been swiftly defeated. This war could not ultimately lead at worst to a negotiated settlement. Instead, it was obvious that, unlike Hitler's belief when he first invaded Poland, the European war would end with total victory or total defeat.

Schellenberg was a pragmatist. He was loyal to the Nazi cause and had proven himself brutal enough to rise in power within the SS. Yet he also realized that the Nazis could lose the war, and if they did, his position could result in his death. He wanted to see if there was a way he could use the secret service he was directing to make contacts among all the warring factions. Such contacts would prove useful in obtaining a negotiated settlement following the war should Germany not be the victor.

When Schellenberg approached Flyg, he had decided that he wanted to maintain a dialogue among the warring factions. He wanted Flyg to arrange for ten loyal Nazis within his group to officially break with the National Socialists and return to the Communist party. From their new positions they would be expected to attack the Nazis, Flyg, and his newspaper in order to prove their loyalty. It was a normal type of intelligence work, but what Schellenberg did not explain was that it would also help give them access to the Russian leadership in a different manner than before.

The seemingly unimportant efforts made at the end of 1941 were the first movements toward some greater contact. But it was the change in Schellenberg's thinking, the awareness that life might not match German propaganda and he had better plan for the worst, that would ultimately lead him to work with Bernadotte, a man for whom he previously would have felt only contempt.

❦

Czechoslovakia, the land in which Heydrich was operating, was strongly anti-Nazi. The territory was controlled by Baron Konstantin von Neurath, Reich Protector of Bohemia and Moravia and former German foreign minister, and SS brigadier Karl Hermann Frank. Heydrich's role was to tighten the security in Prague, where Czech patriots had mounted a terrorist resistance campaign. It was necessary to viciously attack the people, killing as many as it would take to stop the resistance.

Himmler changed Heydrich's role during the 1941 Christmas season. Himmler ordered von Neurath to step down, Heydrich taking his place. It was an action that terrified the populace even though it was not meant to be hostile to the Czechs; it was a way for Himmler to maintain his own power.

Naive as Himmler might have been, he was keenly aware that his hold over his assistant was weak. Heydrich was brighter and more cunning than Himmler, and at least as ambitious. While Heydrich was loyal from gratitude for the trust Himmler had given him, there was always the threat that one day Heydrich's ambition would exceed that loyalty. Should that occur, there was no question that he could take over Himmler's position. The move to Czechoslovakia was an important one and the work was critical for the Reich, but it effectively removed Heydrich from the seat of Nazi power and reduced his influence among the high officials.

Heydrich moved swiftly in his new position. He dismissed the Czech leaders, murdering many of them, including Prime Minister Alois Elias, and sending the majority who survived to concentration camps in either Birkenau or Auschwitz. Then he stopped.

There had been a change in Heydrich in recent weeks, one Himmler had perhaps sensed before he sent him away from Berlin. The man was becoming more intellectual, less physical. He decided that terror should be a tool—not, as he once believed, an end in itself. He had analyzed the Czech people and felt that they were loyal followers who could be kept in line by removing their familiar leaders. They were skilled workers whose talents could be valuable to the Reich. Unlike the Poles (who he felt should be destroyed), the Czechs were best kept as slave workers.

Heydrich next analyzed who might become the new leaders of Czechoslovakia. He saw that the laborers had no pretensions of grandeur. They would follow anyone who seemed to make sense or who simply took control of the nation. The danger came from the educated elite—doctors, teachers, scientists. Anyone who had advanced training was likely to be articulate enough to speak out against the Nazis, and in so doing, become a de facto leader of the people.

Once the potential for power shifting in Czechoslovakia was understood, Heydrich started a second wave of terror. Those who were educated were either publicly hung or sent to concentration camps specifically to be worked to death. At the same time, he ordered that food rations and pay for the workers be increased.

As a result of the new policy a myth arose within the Reich that would ultimately have helped Heydrich against Himmler had Heydrich survived his position in Czechoslovakia. This myth was that the Czech workers came to love and respect Heydrich. The image was one of an oppressed people freed from the tyranny of their former leaders, then led to a better life by the Nazis.

The truth was something else. The working class became docile in order to survive. They were eating better, earning more pay, but they had also been witnesses to mass murder. They saw that innocent men, women, and children either died on the gallows or disappeared, their only crime being their education. The average person was frightened, resentful, and uncertain what to do. All that was safe was what was familiar—going about a daily job, working hard, feeding one's family, talking with neighbors, yet always avoiding the issue of politics and the fate of the nation. The apathy that came from a combination of fear, helplessness, and relief at being alive was mistaken for support.

Heydrich believed the myth, though, and that was his undoing. He moved into the former home of Count Coloredo Mansfeld, the magnificent Brezany Castle. He began riding back and forth to his office in Prague in an open car, accompanied by a driver and, occasionally, an assistant. He eliminated the elaborate security system and phalanx of armed guards he had utilized when he first took control of the nation. He was lulled into a false sense of security by the lack of strikes, the limited sabotage, the seeming "love" of the Czech people who generally simply chose to ignore him. And as a result, no one on his staff spotted the low-flying airplane or the parachutes in the sky when Josef Gabcik (or Gabchik) and Jan Kubis, both sergeants in the Czech army in exile, landed in the country.

Gabcik and Kubis were the type of leaders Heydrich did not realize existed. They had left Czechoslovakia, becoming part of the exile army in France, then part of the British Expeditionary Force. They had participated in the Battle of Britain, gaining combat experience as well as special training to be part of an elite force that would eventually move back into Czechoslovakia to reclaim it from Hitler.

Just as Heydrich understood that the Czech people would be more compliant with their leaders destroyed, so the two sergeants recognized that the Nazi influence and control would be reduced with Heydrich's death. They trained to assassinate the Nazi leader, then parachuted into the country carrying bombs, hand grenades, money, forged identity papers, and radios. They made their way to an area just outside Prague, establishing an impregnable hideout with the assistance of underground resistance leaders. No one could reach them without dying in the attempt.

Next came the work of identifying a weak point in the Nazi leader's schedule. For four months the men studied Heydrich's every move. They studied his routine at the castle. They studied his routine in Prague. They studied how he traveled. And nowhere did they find a weak point, a moment when they could be certain an assassination attempt would work.

The sergeants were convinced that they would have only one chance to murder Heydrich. He had been lulled into a false sense of security that had reduced the number of men surrounding him, but a failed assassination attempt would lead to a closing of all weak points. New guards would be assigned. Yet there seemed to be no place that was certain.

Then in May the two sergeants received a one-word radio broadcast: *Holesovice.* The word meant nothing to them at first. It was not a code, and when they followed the radio verification procedures they had been assigned, word came back from England that such a message had not been sent. The only answer seemed to Gabcik and Kubis that the Germans had learned of their plans and had failed to identify their hideout but had used their radio frequency to send a false message.

Kubis finally realized that Holesovice was the name of a Prague suburb—one through which he had passed several times, never paying much attention to it since it was just one of many small areas through which Heydrich drove when traveling to and from the city. Since the Nazi's driver generally drove as close to a hundred miles an hour as he could in order to reduce the chance of attack, none of the roads to and from Prague seemed to offer opportunity. Still, the radio message aroused their curiosity.

Kubis took the chance of traveling to Holesovice, risking capture, torture, and death if it was a trick to bring him out of hiding. He went alone so that Gabcik would still be available to carry out the assassination if he was caught.

Kubis carefully explored Holesvoice, looking for a clue as to why the message had been sent. Nothing seemed special until, by chance, he saw a Mercedes being driven rapidly through the streets by an SS officer. This was not Heydrich's car, but it was following the same route, and as Kubis watched, the car suddenly braked rapidly in order to take a hairpin turn. The car had to slow to approximately ten miles an hour, a fact that surprised Kubis. It was the location the two sergeants had missed during their months of observation. He hurriedly returned to Gabcik; they decided to kill Heydrich on May 27.

There are two different reports about the assassination. One has Kubis throwing a bomb into the back seat of the car. The other, the more probable, actually involved four men: Kubis, Gabcik, and two unidentified members of the Czech underground.

The day was perfect, the sun bright, the sky clear. The four men traveled by bicycle, blending with the rest of the people of the town. Gabcik stayed by the hairpin turn, a Sten gun at the ready in order to shoot the car. Just before the place the car could pull completely out of the turn and begin accelerating again, Kubis was standing. It would be his job to toss hand grenades into the car if for some reason Kubis was unable to make the kill.

The two underground men were positioned as spotters. The first man had a mirror which he flashed to the second when Heydrich, who followed no set time schedule for his trip, came into view. Then the second man would alert Gabcik, who would take the Sten gun from its point of concealment in an old briefcase he carried, aim, and fire.

Some reports say that Heydrich was driving that day. Others, apparently accurate, indicate his well-armed bodyguard, Oberscharführer-SS Klein, was at the wheel.

The car had been traveling close to a hundred miles an hour when it approached the turn. The braking was made quickly, a maneuver meant to reduce the risk of attack, and the car shifted into the turn.

Gabcik put the gun to his shoulder, sighted, and pulled the trigger. Nothing happened. The weapon appeared to be in working order but had not been tested. It proved defective and would not fire even after Gabcik tried a second and third time. However, Heydrich spotted the would-be assassin, pulled his revolver from his holster, and, waving it in the direction of Gabcik, looked for anyone else about to shoot.

Kubis was not seen as he grabbed a grenade, pulled the pin, counted to two, and threw it into the car. The grenade landed in the back seat and, for an instant, nothing happened. Then an explosion lifted the car from the ground, wounded Heydrich, and sent metal, wood, and cloth fibers into his wounds.

Heydrich did not die instantly, as was hoped. Klein stopped the car and both men leaped out, holding their revolvers in order to shoot at the men who attacked them. Kubis was spotted and a bullet just missed his feet as he raced to his bike and started pedaling rapidly. He would have been shot except that two streetcars came by, momentarily offering him protection as he pedaled between them. Klein gave chase, but once Kubis was in the open again, he was no longer within range. Frustrated, the bodyguard returned to Heydrich, whom he assumed was also relatively unscathed.

While Klein pursued Kubis, Heydrich chased after Gabcik, the two men shooting at each other. Suddenly Heydrich stopped, frustrated. His gun was empty and he either had no additional ammunition or did not feel there was time to reload and still catch Gabcik.

The sergeant began running just as Klein, seeing what happened, joined the pursuit. A bullet passed close to Gabcik's head and he realized he had to stop, aim, and try to kill the driver if he was going to escape. Frightened, his emotions racing, he turned and carefully aimed at the driver. His bullet struck Klein in the hip, not a fatal shot but a painful one that caused him to drop to the ground, no longer able to continue the fight.

A streetcar was nearby, the door open. Gabcik tucked his revolver under his clothes and jumped inside. Anyone who realized who he was and what had just happened was either too frightened or too supportive to react. He was able to ride to Prague's Wenceslaus Square, walk calmly to a different streetcar, then travel to the home of Liboslava Fafka, his girlfriend. There he heard on the radio about the assassination attempt, the news report stating:

> This morning on the twenty-seventh of May at ten-thirty o'clock an attempt on the life of Acting Reichsprotector Heydrich was made in Prague. A reward of ten million crowns is offered for the capture of the culprits. Whoever hides the criminals or gives them any help, or has any knowledge of their identity or description of their appearance and does not inform the authorities will be shot with his whole family. This is by order of the Oberslandrat in Prague. Other announcements will be made in due course.

Heydrich's momentary counterattack was probably made possible by a rush of adrenaline. The Nazi leader was bleeding profusely, his wounds deep and infected. He stood ready to fight for a few moments, then dropped to the ground, unconscious. He and Klein were rushed in a bakery truck to Bulova Hospital, where emergency surgery was performed. The SS supplied troops as bodyguards, and the finest surgeons were sent from Berlin to assist the local doctors.

Himmler was in East Prussia when he heard the news, bursting into tears and saying, "Never shall I have a man like Heydrich again." He was also in fear of Hitler's wrath, since the ability of the Czechs to assassinate an SS leader so easily cast doubts on the credibility of the SS as a protective force. The only answer was to announce that the assassins would pay for their crime even though they had not yet been identified.

The first response, while Heydrich lay dying in the hospital, was imposition of a nationwide curfew in Czechoslovakia. From 6:00 P.M. until dawn, the only people on the streets of Prague were German soldiers. Martial law was imposed. Arrests were made with and without cause, people tortured, murdered, or jailed indiscriminately. By the time the assassins were located, more than ten thousand Czechs were dead or in jail.

At the same time, Felix Kersten was dispatched to Bulova Hospital along with another doctor, Professor Karl Gebhardt. They were Himmler's closest personal physicians, men he considered the finest in the world, and he was determined that they would do everything to save Heydrich's life.

Heydrich wanted nothing to do with the "magnetism" in Kersten's hand. Gebhardt wanted to operate. Other doctors wanted to use special drugs. Yet the final decision for treatment was left to Heydrich—who lasted only until June 4, when blood poisoning and other injuries caused his death. And once again Himmler was seen weeping at the loss.

The assassins were on the run during this period, eventually being moved by the underground to the Czech Orthodox Church of Saints Cyril and Methodius. The chaplain of the church, Vladimir Petrek, was a sympathizer who placed the two men in a crypt under the floor.

The crypt was so unlikely a hiding place that it was hoped the sergeants would survive. The air was limited and rather stale. There was little light. The walls were cold and damp. And the chaplain was not suspected of being anti-Nazi.

The funeral was a major state occasion. Held on June 9 in Berlin, Hitler and six hundred leading members of the political and industrial elite gathered to pay their last respects. Himmler spoke glowingly of his immediate subordinate, still grief-stricken but able to show how much Heydrich would be missed.

The Czech people also seemed to show their anger over the assassination. President Emil Hacha and his staff expressed their outrage, and fifty thousand Czech workers marched to protest the crime. However, that show of support was not enough for Hitler.

On June 10, the day following Heydrich's burial, SS investigators found that a man named Horak, formerly a miner working in Kladno, was part of the Czech army fighting from Britain. It was also learned that Horak's father was the mayor of the village of Lidice, twenty miles from Prague.

The possibility of a plot seemed obvious, so the SS searched the mayor's home, where they found a radio. The mayor, who was not involved with the assassination, admitted that he used the radio to listen to Czech-language broadcasts transmitted by the BBC in London. Himmler decided that he would use Lidice as the scapegoat.

The revenge was enacted in the swiftest, most brutal way possible. Nothing was said to the people. No warning was given. And the SS knew that no one in the small mining community had been involved with the assassination. Thus the people were in shock when they awakened to find their village surrounded by an SS police regiment.

The SS men worked in stages. First the cattle were driven off and all the food taken from the homes. It seemed as though the punishment for the residents was going to be that they would be forced to go hungry until supplies could be obtained, but that was not the plan.

Next, trucks were brought in and all the women and girls loaded on them for transport to concentration camps. All infants were sent to the Lebensborn, from which they were evaluated for possible dispersion to Aryan families who would raise the children as Nazis.

(A year later, with many of the children from Lidice and other areas surviving, Himmler wanted to see how many of them could be considered racially pure enough to be made Germans. He wrote SS colonel Max Sollmann, the chief of the Lebensborn: "I order you to get in touch with SS Obergruppenführer Frank in Prague; it would be best if you visited him. The problem to be solved is the maintenance, education and accommodation of Czech children whose fathers and parents respectively have been or are to be executed as members of the resistance movement. The Germanization must be carried out in a clever manner. Bad children should be sent to certain homes, racially good ones who might become dangerous avengers of their parents if they are not educated in a correct way should, I imagine, be examined in Lebensborn homes before being handed over to German foster-parents." The end result was that seven Lidice orphans were sent to a special home, forty-six children were executed, and the whereabouts of any others were uncertain. Even before these statistics were determined, no more than between twenty and fifty of the children were ever expected to meet the standards necessary to be allowed to live.)

Finally, the 143 men and boys of the village were placed against the walls and shot. Then explosives were planted in all the buildings and fires set in the rubble. By the end of the day, Lidice no longer existed.

Kubis and Gabcik were devastated by the news of the Lidice massacre. They had been given poison pills and decided to go to the center of Prague, place signs around their necks stating that they had killed Heydrich, then take their own lives. However, Petrek convinced them that their actions would not stop the reprisals. He also showed that they would be giving the Nazis a victory.

SS general Kurt Daluege replaced Heydrich, with Karl Hermann Frank acting as his deputy. Frank offered a reward of twenty million Czech crowns and protection against reprisal to anyone revealing the identity of the assassins. After the terror of Lidice, the reward was enough to reveal the identity of Gabcik and Kubis.

The man who presented the information to the Nazis was Karel Cruda, another Czech who had trained in England, then been parachuted back into Czechoslovakia. He was living on his mother's farm near Prague and could not stand the idea that his family might be killed when he and other members of the underground were discovered. On June 14, he decided to take the train to Gestapo headquarters in Prague. There he told everything he knew, the identities of the assassins as well as the names and addresses of all underground fighters. He did not know the exact hiding place of Kubis and Gabcik, but his information was critical to their eventual discovery.

The SS began making systematic visits to the homes of each of the Czech resistance fighters. The underground members were murdered, tortured, or committed suicide. Some revealed bits and pieces of information. Others died in silence.

On June 17, Gabcik and Kubis were sharing the church with four other Czech parachutists who had sought what appeared to be the safest refuge in the city. Kubis was keeping watch with one of the new men, staying on the balcony while Gabcik and the others rested in the crypt. It was to be their last day in Prague, all of them moving to Kladno the following morning.

At 5:30 P.M. Kubis and the other spotter saw SS troops move into position around the church. The two spotters were well armed and decided to begin shooting since they could not return to the crypt without being seen. They had high ground fire and could easily hold off the much stronger force.

The battle lasted two hours ending only when the Germans managed to toss a grenade onto the balcony and critically wound Kubis. The other fighter, wounded less severely but unable to continue fighting, took a poison capsule and died. Kubis was rushed to a hospital so he could be saved long enough for questioning and torture but he died on the operating table.

Cruda was brought to the hospital to identify the corpses in the presence of Karl Frank. He recognized Kubis but explained that the other man was not Gabcik. Frank was convinced that both men would have stayed together and ordered the troops to return to the church.

Petrek revealed nothing, though a careful search of the church led to the crypt's entrance. The SS men opened the door and were shot by a burst of machine-gun fire. The door was immediately sealed and no one dared re-enter.

The crypt had a ventilation slot that opened onto the street. Frank ordered tear gas grenades thrown inside, but the resistance fighters expected such a tactic and threw the grenades back onto the street.

Next a floodlight was brought in and aimed into the hole. This was meant to temporarily blind the partisans, but Gabcik shot it out.

A smokemaking machine was brought to the church and a hose placed through the crypt's opening. Instead of being choked out, the partisans stuffed the hose with cloth so the machine stopped working.

Firemen were brought to the crypt. They inserted a hose and pumped six hundred gallons of water a minute into the hole until Gabcik cut off the nozzle and managed to push the jagged edge of the hose back outside.

Hour after hour the attacks and defensive moves took place. Then, six hours into the siege, the SS men brought in explosives experts to blast open the long-sealed main entrance to the crypt. It had been walled over years earlier and the men inside did not expect such a method of entry. The hole appeared before they could resist, the SS then retreating momentarily before the partisans could respond.

The Czechs were outnumbered and outgunned, yet there was enough cover for them to remain unhurt until their ammunition was almost gone. As the SS men began rolling grenade after grenade into the crypt, the partisans used their final bullets to commit suicide.

Retaliation against the Czechs continued for the next few weeks. Petrek and everyone else connected with the church, including the bishop and the elders, were executed. In addition, a total of sixteen hundred others were killed.

The carnage was so intense, the evidence so damning, that it was used as the primary proof that the SS was a criminal organization when the Nuremberg War Crimes Tribunal met in 1946. Because of the one series of actions in Czechoslovakia, as well as the pride with which they were carried out, all men and women who served with the SS were declared to be criminals.

But the full story was not known at the time. The actions of the Czech partisans in Britain were better known to Heinrich Himmler than anyone realized. He had known well in advance of the assassination plot against Heydrich and saw it as the way to eliminate the one man who could rival his ultimate power.

Himmler was unaware of exactly who would handle the killing and did not know the names of Kubis and Gabcik. But Himmler knew that if he alerted the Czech underground to the potential for assassination in Holesovice, and if he did it in a way that would not be connected with the SS, a careful check of the town would reveal the hairpin curve where the murder could take place.

The man Himmler used was a trusted underling, Hauptsturmführer-SS Siegfried Hamler. He knew that Hamler would remain silent, determined to retain Himmler's favor. In fact, not until after Himmler's death, the end of the war, and the start of the Nuremberg investigation did Hamler feel comfortable admitting his role in setting-up Heydrich.

And so it was that by the end of 1942, a radical change had occurred in the German high command, a change whose impact would not become clear for many more months. The murder of Heydrich meant the end of a man who probably would not have tolerated the negotiations with Himmler that resulted in the release of thousands of prisoners from the concentration camps. Either Heydrich would have made a move to consolidate his power, taking control of the SS and manipulating Hitler to allow him to replace Himmler, or Himmler would have hardened his stance in fear of such a move by Heydrich. Although conjecture, Himmler's mixed feelings that caused him to both remain silent about his advanced knowledge of Heydrich's assassination and to exact a blood penalty from the Czech people indicate that even while Heydrich was not a true threat, Himmler would not tolerate his underling's amassing more power. When Himmler ultimately went against the wishes of Hitler by negotiating with Folke Bernadotte, a man such as Heydrich could have orchestrated Himmler's downfall and probable assassination.

CHAPTER 11

The Making of an Assassin

Yitzhak Yzertinsky* (known as Yitzhak Shamir after the successful revolt against the British) was being held in the Mizra detention camp near Acre when Avraham Stern was murdered by British intelligence. He was a leader in LEHI (Lehame Herut Israel), less narrow-minded than Stern yet equally fanatical. Some say he thought of himself as a Canaanite, having little sympathy for the horrors being experienced by the Diaspora at the hands of the Nazis. Others say he recognized that there was little the Jews could do concerning the European war, much they could do to stop the British control of Palestine. Still others say he was accepting of both realities—the need to stop the Nazis and the need to have an independent Jewish homeland free from British influence. Whatever the case, Yzertinsky had been found to be brilliant at organization, dedicated to the removal of the British, and undaunted by the overwhelming odds against success.

Neither Yzertinsky nor any of the other former leaders of LEHI were perceived as a threat to the British by 1943. Stern was dead. The retaliations on both sides seemed over.

The war was also winding down, in some ways. The Americans were firmly in the war and the Russians had not collapsed after the initial

---

*Also Itzhak Yizernitsky and Yitshak Izernitsky. The differences are the result of different transliterations from Hebrew rather than different identities.

191

losses to Germany. The Nazi push into Egypt had not succeeded, nor was such a move on Cairo likely to take place again. LEHI was considered defunct and the Irgun was so concerned with stopping the Nazis that it was not considered a threat to the British. It seemed as though there would be peace in the Middle East, at least until a victory was achieved against the Axis powers.

Both the British and the Jews who opposed the Stern gang underestimated the dedication of the LEHI members, most of whom were in Mizra. Their beliefs had not been altered by their imprisonment. Instead, men like Yzertinsky felt that the prison time should be used for two purposes. The first and most important was an analysis of LEHI's failings. Their leader was gone. Support within the broader Jewish community of Palestine was almost nonexistent. The important members of the organization were either in jail or in hiding. Yzertinsky and the others needed to analyze what had happened, to correct the problems within the organization that had resulted in its near-destruction. The second concern was escape. They could not lead a revolution against the British from within the prison walls.

The analysis of LEHI's position in Palestine society was a discouraging one. Pressures from the Nazis in the Middle East had been reduced when the United States joined the Allied forces. Suddenly there were too many other fronts with which Hitler had to be concerned for him to be thinking about Arabs and Jews (who could be handled after he was victorious elsewhere). Likewise, the British were less oppressive because they had greater concerns than the Palestine occupation.

The problem, in the minds of LEHI members, was with Irgun. They felt that Irgun had become solely a resistance movement, willing to stand against the British but not willing to consider overt action against them. LEHI felt that armed revolt was the only way to rid Palestine of British occupying forces. They also felt that such action should take place regardless of how the war continued.

The lessons in the Mizra detention camp were conducted by LEHI members who had studied underground resistance in other areas. They knew of the Irish actions against the British as well as historic underground defenses mounted in Russia and China over the centuries. Yet nothing seemed to relate to the Palestine circumstances where two cultures—Arabs and Jews—were the victims of an occupying force that was decidedly biased toward one side. The only answer appeared to be ongoing violent harassment, hit-and-run terrorist attacks, sometimes meant to isolate British leaders, sometimes meant to upset the occupying forces.

The LEHI analysis also determined that their members had not maintained adequate secrecy. They realized that Irgun, Haganah, and Jewish Agency groups had probably worked with the British CID, the intelligence division tracking down Stern and the other members.

The answer to the problem was to create a total underground operation. Instead of relying on others to supply safe houses, they would obtain their own so that only LEHI members had any awareness of where they were. Should that prove impossible, then the isolation of large areas in and around Palestine would be utilized toward their end, building bunkers in locations where the British would not think to look. In addition, the members would obtain new identities, then take legitimate jobs. They would use physical disguises where necessary and generally blend with the population except when on a mission. They would cut off all ties with people other than in LEHI, abandoning families, old friends, and anyone else who was not a part of LEHI.

Some of the conversations involved political philosophy. There were meetings held to discuss the teachings of Avraham Stern, as well as more practical questions about the world. Should they be in touch with Arab nationalist movements also concerned with independence from Britain? What would be the threat or benefit from Russia in a postwar Europe? Was Israel meant to exist because of prophecy, a nation that would exist no matter what occurred in the world because God's covenant assured them of having the land?

But no matter how political, theological, and/or philosophical some of the discussions might be, the most important concern for everyone was violent action against the British occupation forces. With few exceptions, the LEHI membership in the Mizra internment camp was dedicated to violent action. That was what had brought them into the organization, since anyone who wanted to negotiate and resist more peacefully could belong to Irgun or one of the other groups.

Having determined the course of action, Yzertinsky and some of the others began looking for an escape plan. The internment camp was not a dangerous place for those imprisoned there. The Jewish population in the center compound varied in numbers of from 100 to 160 men. Arabs, political prisoners, and enemy aliens each had their own sections apart from the Jews. The security was not particularly high, though the British used th ? south side of the camp for both military training and to house an antiaircraft unit.

Every compound was identical except for location: a number of huts, a central kitchen, toilet area, showers, and an exercise area/parade ground. There were four compounds with barracks for guards, a central office section, and warehouses. The perimeter of the camp was made up of a loosely guarded wire outer fence.

The British were not unconcerned about security, but all the inmates had come from circumstances just foreign enough to the surroundings that any escape would lead to immediate capture. Italian prisoners of war speaking only their native language would be spotted immediately. The same was true with German prisoners. Even the LEHI members had become so hated by the general Jewish population (and, in many instances, so well known) that they would be like aliens in a familiar land. Or so the British assumed.

It was decided that any escape should be small, involving critical leaders, and not involving any outsiders who would have to risk discovery and capture. Yzertinsky and Eliahu Gil Adi were the men selected.

The men made their move in January 1943. Security guards let them and several others leave the Jewish compound to go to the commissary for food, a routine procedure. Yzertinsky and Gil Adi did not go inside, instead slipping around the side and hiding in a storage shed until night.

When the other men returned they were joined by two Italians who also carried food. The Italians were also prisoners, kept in a different compound but allowed to socialize with the Jews. The two men involved frequently played bridge with two of the Jewish prisoners.

The timing was flawless. The alien compound, where the two Italians were kept, had a count just before the men slipped away. Everyone who should have been present was present. Then a prisoner count was held in the Jewish compound immediately upon the return of the Jews from the commissary. Because the Italians blended with the others, that count was also correct.

When the guard changed in the Jewish compound, the new guards were told that the count of Jewish prisoners was complete; everyone was present. There was no new count, so when the Italians left, the new guards thought that they had been viewed separately. The card game was ongoing, so their presence was not suspicious. So long as the numbers were right, no one was concerned.

A volleyball game, another common event, was taking place among the Jews. Men were everywhere and the game went longer than normal. The excitement was so great that the guards assumed everyone was caught up in the match. Nothing to arouse suspicion.

The Italians went back to the aliens' compound, were counted, and everything was fine. The guards in the Jewish section let the volleyball game go to completion, then hurried everyone to the showers. Again things were slow, much joking taking place, before the men gathered to talk more about the game. The guards, understanding the enthusiasm but with a job to do, had everyone separate and go to their huts for another body count. Although the timing was much later than normal, everything still seemed all right.

The guards were not allowed to take a count until all the men were inside their designated hut. But the men were still milling about, forcing the guards to go hut by hut, sometimes counting everyone at once, sometimes having to wait for all the men to gather back inside. It was slow, yet still no one worried. The guards all knew that escape, while possible, was ridiculous.

The first hut was counted, then the second. Each hut had the right number of men. Then came the third, the fourth, the fifth. The count was still accurate, the guards not realizing that it was the eighth in line where there would be two Jews fewer than expected.

Just as the guards reached the last hut, before they could start the count that would signal a lockdown for the night, a prisoner raced out to get water for the night. This was not usual, but not unusually odd. The men were allowed to have water in their huts for the night since they had no plumbing for water and had to carry it in containers. Usually they did it earlier, but with all the excitement, the guards accepted the fact that the man had forgotten what needed to be done.

The moment the guards stepped back to wait for the prisoner's return, the inmates of the hut opened a window and threw a blanket over a wire that linked them with one of the huts where the count had taken place. It looked like laundry on a line, again not an unusual sight. In reality, it was a makeshift tunnel through which two of the already-counted men from another hut were able to sneak into hut eight.

The inmate returned with his water, the guards entered the last hut, and the count took place. Once again, all prisoners were accounted for, or so they thought. Names were not called. Identities were not known to the guards. All that was certain was that the right number of inmates for each hut had been counted in those huts. The entire compound was locked for the night, no alarm having been raised because no shortage was noticed.

Yzertinsky and Gil Adi waited until the guards were relaxed and away from where they were hiding. Then they moved to the fence, cut the bottom with wire clippers, slipped underneath, and walked to Haifa. They met with Anshuel Spilman, a trusted LEHI member who had remained free, and split up. Yzertinsky was provided with a Polish soldier's uniform, a disguise that would let him pass freely through Israel, and made his way to Tel Aviv, where he could hide in the orange groves.

The next few months were spent trying to quietly rebuild LEHI and eliminate critical enemies as well as the few men and women outside the prison could. Robbery was used sparingly, as was sabotage. There were too few people available for an elaborate mission and too little public sympathy to risk any mistakes.

It was in September that the first important assassination took place. Israel Pritzker had been a leader in the Irgun and a contact man between the Irgun and LEHI prior to the mass arrests. He was also a double agent, working as an informant for the British.

The problems with Pritzker were suspected because he was frequently the only man who could have alerted the British to Irgun plans, but only when Menachem Begin took over as the leader of Irgun in 1943 was Pritzker left with diminished support in both the Jewish and British communities. LEHI then felt relatively safe to shoot and kill the man despite a warning by Irgun leaders that the murder should not take place.

A second major escape occurred that fall in the Latrun detention camp between Tel Aviv and Jerusalem. A growing number of LEHI members had been jailed there by the time Yzertinsky made his escape. But unlike Mizra, fleeing from Latrun was extremely difficult.

Latrun was built for security and could be used for either criminal or political detention. Wire fences, wire nets, watchtowers, and huts were positioned for maximum visibility all around. The earth was parched in the summer heat, cold and thick with mud in the winter. The food was adequate, the official activities limited to language lessons, exercise programs, volleyball, card games, and similar pastimes. The unofficial activities, created by the prisoners, added lectures on Zionist history and military tactics to be used against the British. No one would die from neglect. No one was tortured. It was an endless, monotonous life from which there was no predictable escape, a fact that added to the desire for freedom.

The problem with all detention camps, no matter how well run, is that they offer the prisoners no hope. A traditional prison holds men and women who have been given specific sentences. It was easier for an inmate to adjust to the idea of a year, five years, or whatever, than to remain with no knowledge of when release was possible. Even those with expectations of short stays, such as six months, were more likely to want to escape, to become unruly, to fight the system, than those with longer but definite sentences.

The difficulties were compounded in Latrun because the men of LEHI were anxious for physical action. They had been living on the edge, their lives a constant adrenalin rush each time they went on a mission, hid in a safe house, heard a siren or a knock at the door. They had been running scared, ready for action, perpetually overcoming the natural fear for life and safety that enabled them to continually mount whatever attack was necessary for the group.

A group of LEHI men in what was known as Hut 4, the barracks located nearest the outside wire fence, decided that they had to escape. The lack of action and the indeterminate detention made them ready to try anything, even the impossible.

Latrun was not like Mizra. No battle of wits was possible here. No one could creatively leave the compound without being seen. The only hope was to build a tunnel from the inside of the hut, straight down, then over more than two hundred feet. Huge masses of dirt would have to be removed. The walls would have to be reinforced to prevent cave-ins. Lights would have to be provided. Air would have to be brought in to prevent oxygen deprivation to the workers. It was a straightforward engineering process that probably would have been deemed impossible had the men had any hope of release. Since there was no hope, and since there would be no punishment severe enough to deter them (torture and execution, though used by the British in the past, were not a part of the Latrun policies; only further detention in a different facility might occur), the tunnel was begun.

The basic hut was originally designed for both cost effectiveness and security. There was a stone floor, twenty narrow cots, wooden walls into which nails had been driven to hold clothing, and nothing more. Empty suitcases that once contained the personal items of the men interned there were piled on one side. The guards made a thorough inspection of each hut every three days, too frequently for any changes to be made without detection.

The answer for the inmates of Hut 4 was to become model prisoners. They would make the detention camp a better place in which to work and live. They would beautify their hut and the surrounding yard. They would be an example for all.

First came the gathering of wood, nails, and other tools. Because the camp was escapeproof in any traditional manner, the men had enough freedom to obtain such items. The regular inspections would reveal anything improper, and if the inmates did something that was of no harm to the others, it was a sign that they were keeping busy.

Inmates Yehuda Ben-David and Mattiyahu Shmulevitz developed the escape plan. They organized the men into a construction crew, building a large wooden wardrobe that they positioned against the wall closest to the fence. It was large enough to hold the clothing of all twenty men as well as their suitcases. No longer would shirts, pants, and underclothes be draped over nails. No longer would there be a pile of luggage blocking one side. Their hut would be neat and orderly, the best hut in the camp.

The guards and camp officials were delighted. These were men with pride, dignity, and ingenuity. They were an example to all, and all the Jewish hut leaders were brought to see their handiwork.

Next came a sudden interest in gardening. The land surrounding the hut was excellent for the growth of flowers. A garden would beautify the camp, making it a more pleasant place in which to live. And Hut 4, the model hut, had twenty willing gardeners who were given permission to improve their surroundings.

With the preliminaries accomplished, the stone floor beneath the wardrobe was chipped away. Two stone triangles were fashioned to serve as the new floor. One was propped from below so that it could not be moved and would seem solid if tapped. The other was carefully designed so that wooden handles could be inserted on each side, then the stone triangle shifted aside. Fake cement was used to fill the cracks when the triangles were in place and the men not working in the tunnel.

Once the cover was made, the digging began. The prisoners made special oversized underclothing, the leg holes kept tight against their flesh by means of a drawstring. Then the underpants would be filled with dirt, their pants put on over the ungainly affair, and the men would go out to work on the garden. They would move about the plot, quietly pulling the drawstring so that the dirt would run down their legs and spread evenly on the ground. So long as they kept working the soil, it was impossible for the casual observer to notice that anything unusual was taking place in the yard.

At first everything seemed fine. Then the men realized that if the British were suspicious of any hostile activity, their suspicions would be intensified during the anniversary of an event important to the rebels. February 12, 1943, was the one-year anniversary of the murder of Avraham Stern. Most of the inmates had been rounded up either at the same time or immediately after the killing. It was a sore point for the Jews, and the British were likely to think that there might be an attack against them.

Not taking any chances, in the beginning of October a new floor of cement was made in the wardrobe. The stone triangles were in place as always, but the cement would have to be chipped away to get to them, whether by the British or themselves. It was the best they could do to protect themselves, the greatest camouflage they could create under the circumstances.

Four in the morning is the safest time for a surprise attack. All humans have a biological low point during this period. Exhaustion sets in; people who are driving cars tend to have the most one-car accidents. Even soldiers prepared for violence are least effective then. The British knew this and chose that time on February 12 to raid every hut in Latrun. They did not want to be violently surprised during the day.

The men were roused from sleep and ordered to stand in front of their cots for the search. Everything was checked, including the base of the wardrobe in Hut 4. The police used were familiar to the prisoners but not always the regular guards. They did not want any friendships that may have developed between the prisoners and the security forces to cause something to be overlooked.

One of the officers began scratching the cement at the base of the wardrobe. Then he tapped it, listening for hollow sounds. The men would later report that they instantly heard the difference when he tapped over the triangular stone that served as their entrance to the mine. However, none of the police reacted and no one was certain what had happened. Some thought that they had gotten away with hiding the tunnel. Others were certain that the tunnel had been detected and that the police would eventually trap them, either caving in the tunnel as they worked or setting up a perimeter watch so they could shoot the prisoners as they emerged outside the fence.

The reality did not matter to the inmates. They were men of action and determined to escape. They decided to continue, regardless of the possible consequences.

Actually, the British had detected nothing, but problems constantly arose as the tunnel progressed. First was the need for wood to shore up the walls. Bed slats were used until the beds were in danger of sagging all the way to the floor and being caught by the guards. Then bits of board were scrounged wherever possible. They were taken from wall areas that could be covered. They were taken from empty huts. They were taken from trash. And always they had to go unnoticed because, if seen taking more wood, the guards would have been curious to know what the ingenious and model prisoners of Hut 4 were creating.

Wire was stolen more easily in order to create electricity to light the tunnel. Some of the men had electrical skills and found no difficulty in tapping into the camp's supply without arousing suspicion. They put a hidden control switch in the hut that held the toilets. They knew that guards never became suspicious of a man using the toilet because anyone could have stomach problems requiring them to remain for a prolonged period. Lookouts would sit on the toilet, then throw the power to flicker the tunnel lights if it looked as though there might be a surprise head count or some other unexpected problem. When the men working in the tunnel saw the light signal, they got out immediately and covered the opening with the stone.

The only problem that could not be solved was oxygen deprivation. The further the tunnel progressed, the less oxygen reached the work area and the faster the men became ill. They would develop severe headaches and extreme nausea, symptoms that took longer and longer to overcome the deeper they went. Eventually it was found that a man could only dig for fifteen minutes, then had to come out and rest for the next forty-eight hours before recovery was sufficient to return. The fact that there were twenty men to share the work load helped, but it was still too slow.

One of the inmates decided to try to build an air pump with a length of discarded hose. The pump was successful, but the hose had been discarded because of numerous holes along its length. The oxygen did not reach the work area and the men had to continue their fifteen-minute work shifts until the tunnel was far enough past the perimeter of the fence that air holes could be drilled through to the surface.

The men had difficulty telling directions the longer they worked. Finally they began risking a signal that would help those in the hut guide those in the tunnel. Every few yards a tiny white flag would be pushed to the surface and used as a sight by the inmates. If it seemed to be progressing in a fairly straight path to their destination, the work would continue. If it did not, the men in Hut 4 would alert the diggers to begin moving a bit to the left or the right.

Days became weeks and weeks became months. The work continued undiscovered, progressing more rapidly in the fall when they were far enough past the fences that air holes could be drilled. By October the tunnel was more than two hundred feet in length and ended in a ravine that was dry except during the rainy season.

The ravine was the only safe exit. It was angled in such a way that it could not be seen from the guard towers. It was also far enough out that the men could move along it to safety without being heard.

The escape took place on October 31. One of the LEHI members from Hut 4 had escaped from a hospital where he had been taken for what appeared to be a life-threatening illness. It was his job to coordinate the rescue of the others as they emerged from the ravine. Since the escape had occurred in the hospital and not from the internment camp, no one connected it with possible problems that might arise. All twenty were able to flee successfully, their actions not known until November 1, when morning rollcall revealed Hut 4 to be empty.

With the escape LEHI, the new Stern gang, was complete. Yitzhak Yzertinsky was the military leader. Tough, aggressive, skilled in terrorism, it would be his job to rally supporters and prepare them for battles, both covert and open. He had let his hair and beard grow long, then adopted the clothing and posture of an orthodox rabbi in order to move freely among the British, the Arabs, and the Jews. He called himself Rabbi Shamir, and he would use that last name for the rest of his life, including when he became prime minister of Israel.

There were two other leaders. Dr. Israel Scheib was the philosopher of LEHI, the man who shaped the vision of the future in much the manner of the intellectual Avraham Stern. He did not believe in personal violence. He was a scholar who delighted in teaching others. Yet he was also a contradictory moralist. He would not bear arms against any man, yet he helped the LEHI and other revolutionaries against the British understand why it was important for them to kill others. His ideas motivated the terrorists to actions he refused to do himself.

The third leader was Nathan Friedman-Yellin (aka Yellin-Mor and Gera), the most dedicated Zionist of them all. He had been a schoolteacher in Poland before the war, but his skill was in publicity. Ironically, his ability to rally supporters for a cause was identical to that of Joseph Goebbels, the man dedicated to the extinction of the Jews.

❧

The new LEHI was both the same as and different from the Stern gang. The dedication was as intense as ever, though the leadership was less narrow in its thinking than Stern had been. But its goal, to end British occupation of Palestine or die in the effort, began to attract others, Jews and non-Jews. There were Communists claiming to be atheists, Sephardic Jews, former members of Irgun who had decided that the defense unit was not aggressive enough, immigrants who spoke only the language of their native country, and numerous others. Some were dedicated Zionists. Others gave little thought to a time other than when Palestine would be free to find its own way. What they shared was mutual respect, a common cause, and the determination to use violence to achieve their desired end.

LEHI gained support again in January 1944 when Begin, the leader of what might be called the new Irgun, made an effort to join forces with Shamir. Unlike previous leaders, Begin was comfortable with both overt and covert violence. The two men coordinated bomb attacks on British government offices in Tel Aviv, Haifa, and Jerusalem. And Irgun began training its men to act alone. A war had been declared, though the British did not yet know what it meant.

British intelligence (CID) began a counterattack during those increasingly violent months. Terrorists were almost routinely killed "resisting arrest," even when all the shots fired had to come from the police because the man who was killed was unarmed. Interrogations could be brutal, and there was growing hatred by the occupation force against all Jews since the patrols had no way of knowing who was friendly and who might try to kill them.

The supreme act of violence so far as the British were concerned, the assassination that would most shock humanity until Folke Bernadotte's, was the murder of Lord Moyne.

The Right Honorable Walter Edward Guinness, the first Baron Moyne, was British minister of state in Cairo, a senior official in the Middle East and actively involved with the issue of the Jewish homeland. One of his proposals was to divide a large section of the Middle East into four units: Greater Syria, Christian Lebanon, the Jewish state, and a Jerusalem state. The Jerusalem state would be a British protectorate. Greater Syria would include the current Arab areas of both Palestine and Lebanon, along with the Transjordan and Syria. However, opponents of the measure showed that many of the Arabs would be deprived of a port. The best land was in the Jewish state, but the Jewish state would be an equal mix of Arabs and Jews.

The plans and the rhetoric did not matter. Not only were none of the ideas acceptable to either the Arabs or the Jews, Lord Moyne had shown his true feelings during a time when some British officials thought that it would be possible to rescue Hungarian Jews by bringing them to the Middle East before they could be placed in concentration camps. Moyne had vetoed the idea, reportedly saying "What would I do with a million Jews?" Even worse, by the time of his death he had become so strongly pro-Arab that it was impossible to consider him a man who would ever soften to the Zionist cause. He had to die.

Cairo was a cosmopolitan city toward the end of 1944. A Nazi invasion was no longer a threat. Expensive hotels and restaurants teemed with activity. Every nationality could be found doing business in the city. Men who might have been enemies if involved with the war raging throughout Europe and Asia shared meals and business ventures. Banking, agriculture, importing and exporting of merchandise, and almost every other business flourished in the city where camels and sheep traveled the same streets as taxicabs and Land Rovers. The nightclubs were filled with revelers, the prostitutes made a good living, and the bars catered to patrons around the clock. Where once there had only been rich and poor, a growing middle class of upwardly mobile men working in lower-level positions in banks and the military were gradually making their presence known.

The city itself was filthy. The streets were littered with animal waste. Some areas were among the most modern in the world and on the next street there could be abject poverty where people lived in little more than hovels. Yet it was this very contrast that made it extraordinarily popular. It also was a diversity that would allow a stranger to enter without detection.

Eliahu Hakim, twenty, was one of the strangers who moved freely about the streets of Cairo. He had been born in Beirut, a sephardic Jew whose family moved to Palestine, raising him in Haifa.

The Hakim family was a comfortable one, Eliahu wanting for nothing. He had no interest in politics, no sense that the British were a threat until he was innocently walking the streets during a demonstration. A British policeman, looking on everyone in the area as an enemy, lashed him with a whip so viciously that he could think of nothing but revenge. Seeing that LEHI was the one group that shared his anger, he took training while still in school.

The Hakims were frightened by their son's anger and feared that he might be arrested. They hoped to channel his tendency toward violence into the fight against the Nazis and persuaded him to join the British army. Instead of going to Europe, he was part of the armed force in Cairo, where he continued his LEHI activities by becoming a weapons smuggler. He also participated in some terrorist activities after deserting from the British army, the other members of LEHI recognizing in him both courage and dedication.

Hakim was assigned to kill Lord Moyne with a partner, twenty-three-year-old Eliahu Bet Zouri, a native-born Israeli who was raised in Tel Aviv and expelled from high school for his political interests and activity. He had been an independent terrorist, working with two friends on self-appointed assassination missions, before joining LEHI. He wanted to fight and was totally dedicated to the removal of the British at any cost.

Hakim was familiar with both Cairo and the LEHI underground that had been established in that city. He and Bet Zouri took a small room at 4 Sharia Gheit el-Noubi in what was known as the Mouski district. It was an appropriate action for men of modest means, as were their activities. The restaurants where they ate, the clubs where they went dancing, all were appropriate to their apparent circumstances. They were simply two young men enjoying the city, no threat to anyone or unusual enough for anyone to remember them. What was not obvious was that they were actually spending the bulk of their time observing Lord Moyne, studying his patterns, looking for a time when he would be vulnerable to the handguns they carried.

On Monday, November 6, 1944, Lord Moyne, his aide-de-camp Captain A. G. Hughes-Onslow, and his secretary, Dorothy Osmond, left for lunch at 1:00 P.M. The British leader had a Packard Saloon driven by a lance corporal named Fuller, an infrequent driver sent to replace the sergeant who normally chauffeured him but who was sick that day.

It took ten minutes for the car to reach the home of Lord Moyne, where they would eat and he would take a brief nap. Two youths were near the gate when Capt. Hughes-Onslow stepped from the car, but nothing unusual was happening. However, as he opened the gate and turned back toward the car, he was horrified to see two young men, one blond, the other dark, holding revolvers and rushing to the car. The back door was wrenched open and Lord Moyne was shot three times. Lance Cpl. Fuller rushed to help and was also shot three times.

Fuller fell to the ground and died as Dorothy Osmond reached to help him. Lord Moyne drifted in and out of consciousness while help was summoned. He was rushed to the hospital, where he died approximately seven hours later.

Hakim and Bet Zouri succeeded with their mission, but they did not escape. They had vowed that no Egyptians would be killed, firing only warning shots when Egyptian police gave chase. Their pursuers ignored the warnings, coming at them from all sides after the alarm had gone out. As a result, they were quickly captured, though they refused to say who they were or why they had committed the murders.

British and Egyptian authorities were both shocked at first. Cairo was a safe city. LEHI had an underground operation there, but the authorities were unaware of its presence. It was the one location where assassination was not expected.

Eliahu Hakim was identified first. He was first called Cohen and then was identified as Moshe Cohen Itzak. Later it was found that he had been known as Private Samuel Bernstein. However, British army records soon revealed his real name and deserter status.

Hakim refused to identify his partner, who was listed as either Saltzman or Zalzman. Whatever his name, he admitted to shooting Lance Cpl. Fuller, and Hakim said that he killed Lord Moyne.

The two youths continued their bluff with the British authorities for twenty-four hours, determined to give the members of LEHI a chance to go underground. Then they told of their mission, though refusing to explain how they had operated.

The British investigation was fairly successful. For the next several weeks, every Palestinian in Egypt was investigated; several LEHI members, including four young women, were arrested. It was also found that the weapons used for the assassinations, weapons that had been part of a LEHI arsenal provided as needed to the members, had been used for the assassination of eight British and Arab leaders beginning as early as November 14, 1937.

The British could not understand the motivation of the killers, especially since they were arrested, in part, because they refused to shoot Egyptian pursuers. They had a cause and would not deviate from it by killing someone they felt was innocent.

The trial's end was a foregone conclusion. The two youths would be sentenced to death because, under the law and with their confessions, the court could go no other way. But the dignity of the youths and their statements in the courtroom brought their story to the world, momentarily calling attention from the war being fought in Europe and Asia.

Some may say we have no right to attack the English because it is thanks to them that we live in Palestine. [Bet Zouri explained.] There is no truth to this argument. We, the Hebrews, the natural sons of the land of Israel, fought for Palestine before the Balfour Declaration. We are the natural and legal owners of the country. We do not recognize England's right to give us Palestine or take it away from us.

Let me make clear to the court: My ideas are not Zionist ideas. We don't fight to uphold the Balfour Declaration. We don't fight for the sake of the National Home. We fight for our freedom. In our country a foreign power rules. In our country England is a stranger who does what she wants.

The crimes she commits are without number. I can give you names, dates, addresses: nothing can refute my accusations. To the English everything is "the law." When an English policeman clubs a Hebrew young man in the street in Jerusalem in nineteen thirty-nine and leaves him dead, "that is the law." When another English policeman shoots a deaf old man and leaves him dead on the ground—"that is the law." When Captain Morton breaks into a house in Tel Aviv and murders Avraham Stern, shooting him in the back, "that is the law."

In Palestine the Jews are trying so desperately to do wonderful things, but they are blocked and stopped. Young Palestine is full of initiative; its citizens seek its progress. But the English Administration is not ready to hear any suggestions. They will not listen. Whatever they want in our country, "that is the law." I wish I could tell you—my English is not good enough to express how badly the Administration rules. It rules with fear and torture. The English torture chambers are always full in Palestine. The CID tortures those who fall into their hands, to get information. They do it scientifically; they know anatomy and the most sensitive parts of the body. They go far beyond what is called in the United States the third degree. I will call witnesses who will tell you the truth of what I say. And when the English arrest and torture, "that is the law."

Bet Zouri was interrupted with the question of whether or not there was a way to protest without using a gun, to which he replied:

To whom could we protest? In a country which has a parliament, a cabinet, which has freedom of press and speech, you can protest against injustice, corruption and cruelty. But these freedoms do not exist in Palestine. If we have turned to the gun, it is because we were forced to turn to the gun! When we found every other effort would not help, we understood then that the only way to fight a rule based on violence is to use violence. That is why we decided to fight the English by using their own means, to attack the representative of their government, which is responsible for all our misfortunes.

He continued: "I am not telling you why we fight, I am telling you why we fight so severely. If you think that what we want is to change a bad government to a good government, you mistake us. What we want is to tear it out by the roots and throw it away!"

Hakim was also given a chance to speak, but he was less articulate than Bet Zouri, whose speech astonished the courtroom. Witnesses were deeply moved by the fervor of the youth, even if they disagreed with both his actions and his reasoning. Yet in the end they were sentenced to death by hanging as expected.

The youths were quickly executed, both proudly walking to the gallows. Despite their ages, they were true fanatics, dedicated to the cause of a free Palestine. And in the murder and their execution, they began to call the world's attention to a problem that had been ignored for more than two decades.

Throughout Palestine a document was circulated after the deaths of Lord Moyne's assassins. It made a statement that, for the first time, began to unify Jewish resistance, setting the stage for the ultimate confrontation with Britain and the death of Folke Bernadotte:

The curtain is not down. The hanging of Eliahu Hakim and Eliahu Bet Zouri is not the end: it is but one of the pages in our history. The book is open and its pages are written in letters of blood. We do not always see clearly the meaning of the blood that is shed. But these two names will illuminate our lives, for there was a meaning to their life and a meaning to their death. They lived and died according to the laws of honor which bind all freedom fighters from one generation to another. They sacrificed themselves in our war for a better future. They died so that the will to freedom should be rekindled in the heart of the nation. The fire that burned in their souls they sent out to kindle other sleeping hearts, to wake them for the fight for freedom. This fire will not be extinguished.

The curtain is not down. At no time and at no place in the world did a tyrant succeed in putting an end to the fight for freedom by executing its fighters. The more he seeks to subdue us, the more hangmen he employs, the more the number of rebels, the greater the rebellion.

The two who died in Cairo were not alone. There are many more. We know that every youth in the homeland is like Hakim and Bet Zouri: ready to give their lives. We shall draw fresh strength from their bravery and self-sacrifice. Our generation has been educated to suffer and to sacrifice. In the end we shall stop the occupation of our homeland by strangers.

Their names will shine in the darkness.

They believed that the objective for which they gave their young lives will come true. And because they gave their lives for their country, they have the right to say to you, to order you: Fight until victory!

PART V

Freeing of the Damned

CHAPTER 12

The $Bernadotte$ $Mission$

In early 1945, with Heydrich dead and the German army bogged down in Russia, Himmler and the other leaders were being forced to re-evaluate their actions within the Third Reich. Hitler no longer seemed an invincible military leader. Himmler, always slightly estranged from the Nazi leadership even though he grew closer to Hitler, had fewer advisers he could trust. It was easier to consider men like Heydrich too great a threat to his future and to rely on Schellenberg and Kersten, whose loyalty seemed unwavering. The fact that Schellenberg was a pragmatist more concerned with his future than the future of the Nazi party and that Kersten wanted to continue enjoying the good life without being too political with either side was not important. Himmler narrowed his counsel and with that action made himself vulnerable to what would take place during the final year of the war.

Walter Schellenberg's brilliant career resulted from both his intellect and his ability to survive in a world where shifts in power, though often violently abrupt, could be weathered by reading subtle changes in relationships over a long period of time. He became a chameleon, not only as a spy but also as a bureaucrat. Ever the pragmatist, he maintained thirteen separate identities so that he could travel anywhere at any time, both for spy missions and to escape personal enemies. He also rewrote history to suit his own involvement.

Schellenberg, who would become involved with the SS and the negotiations with Folke Bernadotte, knew that a direct connection with the

211

extermination of the Jews might adversely affect his postwar life. He sought to cloak this connection, and his work with Bernadotte helped him raise the notion that he was a humanitarian. Also, his job as head of Hitler's foreign intelligence service enabled him to claim that he was so busy gathering intelligence that he was not aware of the atrocities taking place domestically. And *The Labyrinth*, the memoirs he wrote after serving just three years in prison, were meant further to separate himself from the horrors of the damned.

For example, although admitting that Hitler was a student of the Austrian Schönerer Movement, a group that believed that the origins of Nordic culture were such that the Aryan race was supreme, Schellenberg tried to imply that the intense anti-Semitism did not occur until the end of 1943. In truth, the death camps had been operating almost a decade, but that point was nicely avoided in Schellenberg's memoirs by discussing Hitler's alleged Parkinson's disease.

Medical records do indicate that by the end of 1943, Hitler seemed to be suffering from the chronic degeneration of his nervous system. This was the result of the apparent onset of Parkinson's disease, though that diagnosis is uncertain.

As Schellenberg wrote in *The Labyrinth:*

> Heydrich was informed about the smallest detail of Hitler's private life. He saw every diagnosis made by Hitler's doctors and knew of all his strange and abnormal pathological inclinations. I saw some of these reports myself when they were transferred to Himmler's office after Heydrich's death. They showed that Hitler was so ruled by the demonic forces driving him that he ceased to have thoughts of normal cohabitation with a woman. The ecstasies of power in every form were sufficient for him. During his speeches he fell, or, rather, worked himself into such orgiastic frenzies that he achieved through them complete emotional satisfaction. But the inroads thus made upon his nervous system—and perhaps his own awareness of the disquieting strangeness of such a condition— drove him to seek medical advice from his friend, Dr. Morell, and also from Dr. Brandt. Dr. Morell's diagnosis and treatment, however, did not lead to an alleviation of this condition; on the contrary [they] intensified it. For Morell believed that these symptoms were inseparably bound up with Hitler's power of mass suggestion, that it was this intensity which worked upon his audience as a magnet works upon iron filing. It was in this period of mental and physical breakdown that Hitler reached his decision to destroy the Jews.

In other words, Schellenberg was just doing his job. He was upset to learn the truth, and while he wasn't in a position to stop Hitler, by helping Bernadotte after Hitler's mental state deteriorated, he countered some of Hitler's evil. This attempt to distance himself from Hitler's actions and even the man himself were also belied by his office. In the summer of 1941, Schellenberg was given a massive room in which to work. There was a rolling cart, known as a trolley table, covered with telephones and microphones connected directly to Hitler's chancellery as well as all major places of importance. Microphones were hidden under the desk and in the walls, lamps, and elsewhere so that all conversations would be instantly recorded.

The large mahogany writing desk was also meant to be a weapon. Two automatic machine guns were built into it, designed to follow the movement of each visitor without that person seeing weapons or mechanism. If Schellenberg perceived a threat, he needed only to push a button. The constantly aimed guns would eliminate his guest in a spray of bullets.

A second button built into the desk activated a siren that signaled guards to both come to the rescue and simultaneously surround the building. In addition, a perimeter system that combined photoelectric cells, electrically charged mesh screens, and other devices prevented anyone from gaining close access to the outside of the building without alerting security personnel.

Beyond the protective measures, Schellenberg was routinely fitted with an artificial tooth and a special signet ring each time he went abroad. The tooth was filled with poison meant to kill within thirty seconds. The signet ring had a cyanide-filled gold capsule hidden under a large blue stone. Having a single device with which to kill oneself was routine for spies, and anyone capturing such a person routinely looked for the suicide apparatus. They did not look for two, which is why Schellenberg maintained the back-up.

It is uncertain where Schellenberg's ambitions would have taken him if the Reich had survived. His memoirs speak of his love for Sweden, and especially for Stockholm. Yet he established a spy network there, a network where assassination was as likely to be a tool as the gathering of information.

Any change in Schellenberg's loyalty toward Hitler and his enjoyment of his increasing power in the Reich came with the realization that Hitler had become a madman. Hitler's true friends, such as Joseph and Magda Goebbels, never saw the change. That couple and their children shared his life in the concrete apartment building that was his bunker. Magda, especially, believed every word and delightedly showed off the medal Hitler gave her several days before they all took their own lives and the lives of the Goebbels' children. But when it became obvious that the war might be lost, when Hitler had suffered an attempt on his life by the generals, he had a meeting with Schellenberg.

Suddenly [Hitler] rose, looked at me piercingly, and said in a deep voice which vibrated angrily, "I read your reports regularly." There was a long pause and the words seemed to stand, suspended accusingly in the air of that room. I noticed that Himmler began to show visible signs of uneasiness. Involuntarily I had retreated two steps. But Hitler followed me, and said in the same voice, "Remember this one thing, Schellenberg: in this war there can be no compromise, there can only be victory or destruction. And if the German people cannot wrest victory from the enemy, then they shall be destroyed." I shall never forget his concluding words: "Yes, then they deserve to perish, for the best of Germany's manhood will have fallen in battle. Germany's end will be horrible, and the German people will have deserved it."

This was in 1944, and Schellenberg knew he had to work all sides. When the Bernadotte proposal came along, the spy realized that he had found a way to survive.

ஒஜ்ஜ

More peaceful but equally important changes were taking place in Sweden. The eighty-three-year-old Prince Carl, a vibrant, much beloved, brilliant man who had headed the Swedish Red Cross, felt that it was time for him to step down. The changes in the war were coming so rapidly he feared that he could not maintain the pace that would be needed to cope with them.

Already Prince Carl had been responsible for the relief work that helped care for prisoners of war. He had established internment camps for people of various nationalities who, through defection, retreat, seeking asylum, being shot down from the sky, and numerous other reasons, were in the country. But the war between Russia and Germany appeared to be changing the future.

The Germans were increasingly frustrated by what was taking place in Russia. The troops and their leaders were angry. What had been expected to be a lightning-fast victory was becoming a frustratingly slow battle with extensive loss of life on both sides. The Germans might decide to do anything needed to win, take any territory that might seem to be of strategic importance, including violating Sweden's avowed neutrality. If Sweden was invaded or forced to take sides in the escalating conflict, the Swedish Red Cross would be needed more than ever. Prince Carl feared that he would not be able to supply the intensity of leadership needed for such a disaster. He also felt that unless he stepped down before the crisis, there would not be time to adequately train a successor.

The chairman of the Swedish Red Cross was, by tradition, a member of the royal family. While many of the men were well qualified, the only one available to assume the role of Vice President of the Swedish Red Cross in 1943 was Count Folke Bernadotte.

It is often said that individuals have no idea of what they are capable until they are challenged by circumstances they have not previously encountered. Such was the case with Folke Bernadotte, a man who had failed in every business venture he had attempted, whose major successes in life had come from hosting parties and working with the Scouting movement.

In hindsight, it is possible to point to a maturing process in Bernadotte's life. He and his wife experienced great personal tragedy with the deaths of two of their children, losses to which they reacted by becoming involved with young people through Scouting.

In addition, in 1940, Bernadotte accepted responsibility for heading an organization that was meant to oversee the internment of foreign personnel. As the Germans overran various countries, thousands of soldiers ended up in neutral Sweden. Between four thousand and five thousand Norwegians, large detachments of Polish soldiers, and even members of a British invasion force took refuge in that country. The men could not be allowed to continue fighting because such an action would negate Swedish neutrality. They could not be returned to their native countries because it was believed they would simply return to battle and that would imply that Sweden was working with the Allies. Instead, they were interned in camps, fed, clothed, and entertained.

Such a life might seem ideal, but this was still early in the war and the men were anxious to fight. They tried to escape the camps by going into the woods or seeking their legations to arrange for a way out of the country and back to the battlefields.

The men who fled were sought by the Swedish police and four hundred thousand-man military. They were forced to return to the camps, the vast majority eventually accepting the situation both they and the Swedes were in. Until proper passage home could be arranged among all combatants, the men would be interned. However, so long as they obeyed the rules, every effort was made to make their stay pleasant. They were given passes to go to Stockholm, Falun, and other nearby central Swedish cities. Sometimes they enjoyed the wild life of the big city. At other times they developed quiet, serious relationships that led to romances with Swedish girls, and, in some instances, postwar marriages.

Bernadotte began to develop an empathy for the stress individuals could experience when isolated from family, friends, and loved ones in a strange country where even language could be a barrier. The circumstances for the military men were all as positive as possible, the soldiers being safe, well fed, and knowing they would eventually return to the life they had known. Yet he realized that the nature of any forced change is such that there can be depression, anxiety, and frustration. Ultimately this growing awareness would be an aspect of his motivation to help those in other camps, even though his actions would be taken without a full awareness of the horrors that existed in the Nazi dominated lands.

In 1941 the number of internees under Bernadotte's care grew as the crews of Russian ships, as well as soldiers fleeing the Baltic republics, sought asylum. Some of the troops, especially the Russians, were terrified of the Swedes. They were certain the camps would be rough and crude, but Bernadotte established facilities designed both for comfort and to allow as much isolation as the internees sought from one another.

When the United States became more involved with the war, approximately a thousand American airmen came to Sweden, men who had run into trouble while flying special missions.

The only problems that arose came from the Swedish people, who demanded that Bernadotte and the other organizers of the internment camps treat all internees alike. At the time, there were guarded camps for the Russians, Poles, and Germans, while the British and Americans were allowed more freedom, staying in hotels and boarding-house-style facilities. What the Swedes did not realize was that Bernadotte wanted all the camps to be open, with all the interned men to be free to enjoy Sweden; the leaders treated. The Russians, for example, were fearful of the soldiers seeing the material goods that Sweden had to offer since the style of living was so far superior to what Moscow had been able to provide under Stalin's Communist "Workers' Paradise."

The German camps were the only ones where the guards were necessary to protect the prisoners from the Swedes. It was estimated that no more than 5 percent of the Swedish population had ever been pro-German. Large numbers of Swedes were overtly hostile to the Nazis, and there was fear that there might be incidents in which the Swedes might attack the soldiers as representatives of the Nazi government. Since every effort was made to keep the Germans comfortable within the controlled camps, and since there was danger all around, Bernadotte's actions were deemed valid.

Bernadotte was officially named chief of the internment section of the

Swedish General Staff, a title he held until 1945, when his negotiations with Germany for the Swedish Red Cross took precedence. He was directly responsible for twelve thousand internees and indirectly responsible for entertaining six million victims of the war. He had 1,275 performers put on 990 shows for the internees, the total attendance figures for all the shows being a million and a half. He also arranged for the Swiss defense forces to have newspapers, magazines, and circulating libraries. There were vocational and correspondence courses available for everyone. In addition, the film and theatrical entertainers arranged for anything Bernadotte wanted so that the men could see movies, stage plays, and enjoy singers, dancers, and comedians. Bernadotte's work resulted in an estimated forty thousand film showings over a period of six years.

Obviously the work was much like that necessary to be a leader in the American USO program. It was work where Bernadotte thrived, but it did not show his statesmanship abilities. It also did not get him directly involved with the realities of the war as the countries invaded by Germany were experiencing them.

Bernadotte set two priorities for the Swedish Red Cross when he accepted his new position. The first was to provide humanitarian aid for the civilian population, long a standard service of the organization. The second was to work to exchange prisoners of war. In this effort the naive Bernadotte would seemingly blunder into a situation that enabled him to save far more lives than almost any other person involved with the war effort.

In Bernadotte's mind, there were still gentleman's rules for battles and their aftermath. There would be losers, of course, and many of them would be prisoners. But after the fighting was over, the winners were expected to let the losers go home. After all, they had won fair and square so there really was nothing more with which to be concerned. As he wrote in 1945:

> Opportunities for Sweden to assist prisoners of war have proved fewer than I had hoped in September, 1943. The entire question of prisoners of war has been dealt with after the war [World War I] in a very unsatisfactory manner. The now existing conventions for prisoners of war are not explicit as to the fixed time within which prisoners should be repatriated. Some people are even of the opinion that the Geneva Conventions cannot be applied today. Although the world cannot be considered at war, the belligerent parties have not yet concluded the peace. It is a crime against humanity, from the moral viewpoint, that hundreds of thousands

of prisoners of war who are still kept by some of the Allied countries have not been permitted to return home. One may contend that it is only reasonable that, for example, German prisoners of war are used for reconstruction work in the countries which have suffered under the Nazis. In the long run, however, such a concept is morally untenable. Certainly, repatriation of German and Austrian prisoners of war has gone on from the very beginning. The United States, for example, has not kept any. But there are still hundreds of thousands of Germans who would be glad to return to their homeland and to their families, but who are used in forced labor, not only in Eastern Europe and Asia, but also in some Western European countries.

Hitler's idea of warfare was unlike any that had been taught in the civilized surroundings of military academies. The enemy was to be destroyed or placed in slavery. There would be no shaking hands and returning to noncombatant status. Internment camps were tolerated only because the men were concentrated in a known area, unarmed, and unable to return to battle. Ultimately such camps would be death camps, though after the major operations were finished.

Bernadotte's naivete was also to prove his strength. He saw no reason to limit one's endeavors to those tasks for which one could be adequately prepared and for which there was a definite chance for success. He felt that, instead, a person should take on a challenge for which success could not be determined, a challenge that would stretch the limits of one's ability.

In the past the challenges he had faced were so menial that his failures made him a laughingstock. He was a thorough incompetent in business, his brief role as an arms merchant resulting in nothing but losses. He seemed to have no leadership abilities except within a large, well-established, regulated organization such as the Scouting movement. Even his work with the internment camps seemed more a case of someone who was good at planning parties. Although far more complex, he still seemed to have played out roles not much different from those of wealthy socialites putting on charity balls.

Bernadotte did have one vital quality, which had previously not seemed overly important: compassion. Even if he had fully understood the realities of Nazi Germany, the degree of Hitler's hatred, and the viciousness of his actions, Bernadotte would not have been deterred. He cared about the suffering, about men and women kept from their homes and loved ones. He wanted everyone to be happy again, whether Nazis or Russians, Americans or British, Poles, Latvians, Norwegians, Danes, French—everyone who was suffering. It was as though the outcome of the war did not matter so long as everyone could be made happy again. This attitude kept him from being deterred by the hostility of some of the people he encountered.

For example, on November 22, 1944, Bernadotte met with the chief of the foreign section of the German Red Cross, the only non-Nazi in a position of power in Germany. However, while he shared many of Bernadotte's views, his superior, Obergruppenführer Professor Grawitz, did not. Grawitz explained that the idea of concern for humanity was outdated, that the young should be educated for war. Even the word *humanity* should be changed, perhaps replaced with the idea of chivalry.

Such concepts were foreign to Bernadotte, though they were his first glimpse into the Nazi mind. Bernadotte was not discouraged, though, because earlier that month, on November 3, Bernadotte had been in Paris having lunch with several Swedish leaders, including Consul General Raoul Nordling. Nordling had been somewhat of an idol to Bernadotte ever since the consul general had acted as a go-between during the liberation of Paris. Nordling served as negotiator among the Allied forces, the French underground, and the German occupation forces. Although criticized for working with the enemy, the consul general had been able to save large numbers of Frenchwomen and men from being deported to Germany and probable death.

Bernadotte was convinced that he, too, could be of value. When Nordling told Bernadotte that it was important for the count to work to save as many people from the concentration camps as possible, Bernadotte began to see himself in a role as important and heroic as the one he felt Nordling had occupied.

Other influences were coming to bear during this period. Among these were the efforts of Hilel Storch of the World Jewish Congress, who was helping to coordinate various Jewish groups' attempts to ransom Jews held by the Nazis. Contacts with the Germans during the previous four years had resulted in several concerns. The first was the attitude, ranging from uncaring to strongly anti-Semitic, of most free-world governments, who were refusing to admit Jewish refugees despite their awareness of mass murders. The reasons varied, but the reality had long been that an increasing number of men, women, and children were dying.

The second situation had been betrayal by Himmler. From time to time he would agree that individuals could be purchased for a set fee. Money was spent to ransom their lives, then at least some of the Jews identified in the agreement were ordered murdered. Sometimes the bribes were direct. Sometimes the bribes were used to obtain visas to neutral countries such as Mexico. But frequently the Jews were not released.

The third situation had been occurring occasionally in the past, though with increasing frequency after Heydrich's murder and Schellenberg's personal determination that Germany might lose the war. This was the successful release of small numbers of concentration-camp inmates in exchange for money (other than the WJC bribes) and/or material goods.

Pressure was being placed on a growing number of world leaders and their spouses (American Jews met with Eleanor Roosevelt in October 1944, for example, to plead with her to exert influence on her husband) to involve themselves with the rescue. There were also occasional contacts with both Himmler and Felix Kersten, the former reluctant to allow changes in policy on a large scale yet increasingly willing to free small numbers of prisoners. He was aware that the war was not going well and that the more respected he was in the eyes of the world, the greater his chance to take control of Germany in the postwar period.

Tragically, the inmates often tried to avoid what truly was their one chance for freedom during some of these small exchanges. When Switzerland became the first country to actively seek internees, the concentration-camp inmates feared boarding the trains. "We are being sent to Osweicz [the Auschwitz concentration camp], not to Schweiz [Switzerland]," was the common fear. Ultimately only 1,210 Jews boarded the train on February 5, 1945, no one relaxing until they were over the border. Others hid, having no way to be certain they had reason to trust what was taking place.

In the United States, there was criticism of what was taking place because only Jews were being rescued. So many nationalities were in the concentration camps, so many religions represented, that the idea of bribes going for Jews alone brought a harsh backlash. The Americans also feared that the paying of bribes would lead to further blackmail. The demands of the enemy would never stop. A nation untouched by the direct violence of war, lacking fear of invading forces, having none of its civilians in concentration camps was able to adopt an angry attitude toward the demands.

Storch's constant efforts did find some sympathy within the German government. Felix Kersten and Walter Schellenberg both began putting pressure on Himmler to reduce the violence against the Jews. More humane treatment was to be forthcoming, they promised. The possibility of releasing large numbers to neutral Sweden would be explored.

This behind-the-scenes pressure, as well as Himmler's growing awareness that the war was not going to end as he hoped, aided Bernadotte's seemingly impossible rescue mission.

❧

The Third Reich had degenerated into madness by 1945. The Russians had managed to begin occupying Reich territory, the British and Americans poised for their Rhine offensive. In Berlin, the Nazi capital, four out of five homes in the central city had been destroyed by Allied bombing. Old men too feeble to fight and young boys, filled with the enthusiasm of Western children playing a game of cowboys and Indians formed defensive units on Hitler's orders. The old men knew they were useless. The boys would only discover their childish impotence when real bullets, bombs, and blood shattered their fantasies, their friends "taking their deads" for eternity.

The people of Berlin had grown tired of the war, tired of the nonsensical posturing of the Nazi leaders. Yet curiously they did not waver from their acceptance of Hitler, aged before his time, living in a concrete underground apartment with Joseph and Magda Goebbels, the Goebbels children, Eva Braun, and his guards. Some evacuated the shattered city. Others remained, living in the cellars of bombed-out homes or finding other forms of shelter where they could. They endured the hardships, the limited water, food, and lack of communication. They also participated in the construction of what the people often called the "one hour and two minutes" barricades. These were makeshift obstructions established on the roads to Berlin in order to stop the advances of the Allied troops. According to the people who built them, the barricades were so flimsy that they would invariably bring the armies to a halt for one hour and two minutes. Upon encountering them, the soldiers would laugh uncontrollably for one hour. Then they would take their tanks, Jeeps, and other equipment and demolish them in two minutes.

Ariane Ritschel, the half-sister of Magda Goebbels, was a teenager in 1945. Like other privileged children of the Reich, she was in a school separated from the violence, aware only of what she heard on the Nazi-controlled radio.

There was awareness of the bombings, of course. The children had learned to identify aircraft passing overhead. They knew which were the planes of their government, which the fighters and bombers of the Russians, the French, the British and the Americans. They were members of the Hitler Youth, too young to join the Nazi party (something you could not do until you were seventeen), but they were still being trained to serve the Führer.

"We used to practice fire drills," said Ariane. "We learned how to rescue people from buildings that had been bombed. We learned how to give first aid." To the children raised under Hitler, the bombings, the training, the helping of the nation, all were a part of daily life. The Reich was all they had ever known, none of them having learned to read before the nation had become a totalitarian state.

Ariane remembered listening to the radio with the other girls in her school early in 1945. "Hitler was asking if we were ready for 'total war,'" she explained. "We shouted back, 'Yes, total war!' We didn't know what that meant. The war was almost over and Germany was losing, but none of that meant anything. The leaders had been building mansions for themselves in the mountains and I knew the work was continuing. I knew that we couldn't possibly be losing the war if they were still doing the construction. Hitler asked if we wanted total war and we shouted back that we did. It was very exciting for us. We didn't know how bad things were."

Ariane, being one of the privileged, would also be one of the few outside Berlin to discover how much the world had degenerated into madness. She was eventually summoned to the bunker in Berlin. Magda wanted to see her half-sister one more time, to hold her, dine with her, then send her to safety in Mecklenburg until the occupation by the Allied troops was complete.

"I was shocked to see the devastation of Berlin," Ariane recalled. "Everything was in ruins. I was driven to the bunker in a Jeep, and everywhere we passed lines of people slowly leaving the city."

Ariane witnessed no hostility toward Hitler though her half-sister, Magda Goebbels, was the person people wished to see before they left. "She had always been the style leader of Germany. She used to wear fancy clothing and make-up when women of the Reich used neither. She was Hitler's favorite. He would use her as his hostess and to represent the ideal woman of Germany. She taught me how to use make-up. She took me to parties. I used to play with Hitler, who would give me hot cocoa and toys, like a paratrooper you would toss into the air and a little parachute would open so he could float down. Eva Braun wasn't as important to Hitler as Magda."

It was because of the relationship with Hitler that Magda had endured her husband's philandering over the years. Goebbels had a club foot and a face that was far from handsome. But his role as propaganda minister had given him great power and, for many women, power was the ultimate aphrodisiac. He thus was able to have affairs with everyone from movie actresses to common Aryans in whom he took an interest.

Magda may have been humiliated by her husband, but she reveled in her special relationship with Hitler. She was known as the first lady of the Third Reich and, in the waning days of Hitler's life, he presented her a medal he had worn for most of the years he was in power. He wanted her to have it, a final gift, symbolic of their closeness.

Several years later, biographers and historians would try to apologize for Magda, to imply that she had no idea of the true extent of the horrors of the Reich. They tried to picture her as naive, sheltered from the realities of the death camps, the anti-Semitism, the viciousness of Hitler's regime. The truth, according to her adoring yet brutally objective half-sister, was that Magda understood everything and did not care. She was the most powerful woman in Germany, perhaps the most powerful woman in the world. Her husband and Hitler had always been committed to the extermination of the Jews, a situation with which she was quite comfortable despite conflict about this issue within her family. (Oscar Ritschel, Magda and Ariane's father, ran an underground railroad to help Jews flee Germany from the mid-1930s until his death in 1941. Ariane's childhood best friend was a Jewish girl who was sent to the death camps. Ariane's mother was an ardent Nazi until her death in the 1980s.)

"Magda told me that she and Goebbels were going to commit suicide, that they were going to kill their children as well. I began crying. I told her that I wanted to die with them. I didn't want to go on without them.

"Magda wouldn't let me. She said that I would be safe in Mecklenburg. She explained that she did not have to die, that she and the children would be safe when the Allies took control. She was going to die because she didn't want to live unless she could have the power and fame of being the most important woman in the nation. She did not want to settle for less.

"And she was. I was there just before they killed themselves and the people fleeing the city were bringing her whatever luxuries they had managed to obtain. There were chocolates, strawberries out of season, all sorts of things. Not for Hitler. For Magda. That's how much they loved her, even at the end."

Hitler was ashen-faced, according to Ariane. He knew he had to die. He knew that all was lost for him, yet he seemed to remain lucid. And no one blamed him for the troubles the nation was enduring.

The deaths of Hitler, Eva Braun, and the Goebbels family were several months away when Heinrich Himmler agreed to meet with Count Folke Bernadotte in Berlin. Yet the situation early in 1945 was just as obvious as it would be when the leaders committed suicide. Himmler had risen to commander of the German armies on the Oder front, was in full control of the police, the concentration camps, and other aspects of the government, and was finally the most powerful man in Germany. He continued his allegiance to Hitler, yet he no longer saw the eventual change in leadership to be along the lines of that of the Catholic church's approach to the succession for the pope. Whatever leadership changes would ultimately occur for the Thousand Year Reich (and the Reich would endure even if there was a short-term military defeat of the nation), he would be the next Führer. Although the decision was probably not a conscious one, Himmler was ready to begin making those changes necessary for a transition of power. And negotiating with Bernadotte seemed a first step.

If Himmler was unrealistic about how the world would ultimately view the man who had created and run the death camps, it was probably the result of the enormity of his crimes. Despite the thousands of books published worldwide exploring all aspects of World War II, it took almost fifty years to understand what Hitler instinctively knew from the beginning. Kill one person and the world becomes angry. Kill a hundred people and there is outrage, fear, and a desire for vengeance at all cost. But kill millions and the enormity of the crime is beyond comprehension. There is denial or, worse, acceptance because the numbers are overwhelming.

The horrors of the death camps revealed the degree of suffering millions endured before their deaths. But neither those incidents nor the often-repeated numbers of Jewish victims who were part of an attempt at genocide—six million—revealed the full magnitude of what occurred.

The earliest victims were not Jews but intellectuals, political leaders, and even members of the Nazi party who were seen as a threat to Hitler, Himmler, and others. The deaths began in 1933, and by the time the final camps were liberated, from nine million to twelve million people had been systematically slaughtered. The Jews comprised the largest single group, numbers so massive that Hitler almost succeeded in their eradication in Europe. Yet as Himmler had explained, they were a minor problem compared with the Catholics and other Christians who would have been his next targets for mass extermination.

Still the numbers mounted. The Russians endured losses of twenty-six-million soldiers and civilians in the fighting. Another thirty million people also died during this era, their fate determined by Joseph Stalin, a man who deliberately took more lives than Hitler yet whose crimes were so well covered that they were not revealed until many years later. The fact that Stalin did not target just one type of citizen and that his plans did not include world domination and mass enslavement of all but a relatively small number of chosen people as Hitler had done also helped. Between the actions of the Russian and German leadership from 1930 through 1945, it is believed that more people died than it would take to populate many of the smaller European countries. Between sixty-five and seventy million people, equivalent at the time to almost half the population of the United States or almost half the population of Russia had been killed.

When Count Folke Bernadotte made his first humanitarian overtures on behalf of the Swedish government and the Swedish International Red Cross, in February 1945, there was a mixed awareness of what was taking place in Nazi Germany. Enough information had come from survivors of the early days of Dachau and the other camps, from those who had escaped the later extermination centers, and from the statements by the Nazi leaders themselves that the intelligence officers of the free-world governments were aware of many of the horrors.

The last stage of Bernadotte's maturing process came when he arrived in Berlin in February 1945. Officially he was on a mission which the Swedish government felt the Germans would accept. He was to arrange to have Swedish women who were not in concentration camps allowed to return to Sweden if they so chose. These were women who had willingly married Germans, then lost their homes during the violence of the war. They had no family in Germany. Many of their husbands were dead or in the German army, and they were isolated from all they had known. Allowing them to return to Sweden for the duration of the war did not seem a matter that would cause much debate among the Nazi high command.

There was a greater cause, though. Prince Carl, when still president of the Swedish Red Cross, and other Swedish government leaders wanted to see about saving the lives of Norwegians, Danes, and a few Swedes who were prisoners of war. The Swedish government wanted the Nazis to allow their transfer to internment camps within Sweden itself. This would assure the Nazis that the Scandinavians would not be returning to military units to again fight the Germans. At the same time, the Swedes knew that such action would save many lives and allow the Scandinavians to be restored to health.

Whatever mental pictures Bernadotte may have had about the war and his mission were shattered when he reached Berlin. Here he saw the endless lines of once-proud people slowly leaving the ruins of the city. No matter what their politics, no matter what their deeds, they had lost everything. Their homes were twisted masses of wood, bricks, and steel. Most of their possessions had been destroyed, their places of work closed or ruined, all of them uncertain whether the conquering armies would be merciful or vengeful. They were starting on a journey to an uncertain fate, hopeful that it would be better than that which might await them if they stayed.

By contrast, there was Joachim von Ribbentrop, the Reichsminister for Foreign Affairs, who insisted upon receiving Bernadotte in the Foreign Office. They met in one of the rooms so far untouched by the bombs. Ribbentrop was extremely concerned with learning what business the count had with Himmler (the two men were at odds). He also insisted upon providing Bernadotte with a view of political history that showed the madness of so many of the top leaders toward the end of the war.

Joachim von Ribbentrop was as obsessively anti-Communist as Adolf Hitler was anti-Semitic. In his mind, the entire system Russia had created worked against the average man. Bolshevism insisted on the liquidation of the privileged class, either through death or the seizing of all property. National Socialism, by contrast, stressed the retention of all classes of society. The only reason Germany had worked with Russia, a country Ribbentrop was convinced had planned to attack Germany in 1941, was for purposes of intelligence.

Ribbentrop explained that the German front on the east had to be maintained to protect the world from Bolshevism. Germany was the free world's last stand against such extremism. Should his nation lose the war, Soviet bombers would attack Stockholm in six months. Plans had already been made for the Bolsheviks to invade, capture the royal family, and murder them. Even Bernadotte would be a victim, so it was definitely in his self-interest to convince Sweden to support Hitler and the Nazis against Stalin.

Other countries needed to be more understanding of the Russian agenda, the German stressed. Russia was going to take control of China, India, and all of Europe. Bernadotte should be using his influence to convince the United States and England to stop bombing Germany because it was the German army that was protecting the world.

Bernadotte was then shocked to hear a sudden reversal. Ribbentrop conceded that the war might be lost, in which case it would be to Germany's advantage to have the Russians occupying Europe. Surrendering to England and America, he felt, would be too dangerous. Ultimately he seemed to believe that the fate of Europe would be a dual reign, Russia and Germany dominating with equal political and military might.

The words were rambling, as Bernadotte's notes recalled them. Ribbentrop complained that Germany had been too lenient with the populations of the occupied countries. Then he said that Hitler had done more for humanity than any man alive. He also said that Germany should have occupied Norway because the alternative was having British troops there, and the British troops would not respect the integrity of the Swedish border.

With all his ranting, Ribbentrop still desired to improve relations with Sweden. Knowing that telling the real reason for his visit to Himmler would create problems, Bernadotte said that he wanted to arrange for the Swedish Red Cross to do a certain amount of work in the concentration camps. This seemed a positive move to Ribbentrop, who could imagine Swedish delegates bringing packages of food and clothing, being shown only the healthiest inmates in the nicest parts of the camps. The items might be given to the prisoners or they might be kept by the Nazis. It did not matter because Germany would gain an ally either way. Or so he seemed to believe. There were no further obstacles to the meeting with Himmler.

On February 12, 1945, Walter Schellenberg drove Bernadotte to a hospital seventy-five miles outside the city where Himmler was staying. "When I suddenly saw him before me in the green Waffenschutzstaffel uniform, without any decorations and wearing horn-rimmed spectacles, he looked a typical unimportant official, and one would certainly have passed him in the street without noticing him," Bernadotte wrote later. "He had small, well-shaped and delicate hands, and they were carefully manicured, although this was forbidden in the SS. He was, to my great surprise, extremely affable. He gave evidence of a sense of humor, tending rather to the macabre. Frequently he introduced a joke when conversation was threatening to become awkward or heavy. Certainly there was nothing diabolical in his appearance. Nor did I observe any of that icy hardness in his expression of which I had heard so much."

Himmler was in turmoil. He was in command of the Oder front, Germany's primary defense against a Russian invasion. He had strengthened that area, closing a gap of more than two hundred miles where Stalin's forces could have made their offensive. It was an action of which he was proud, since the distinguished military career of his past—a career about which he bragged to Bernadotte—existed only in his imagination. And the internal structure of the nation was on the verge of collapse. As much as he talked about the fierce determination of the German people to continue the war, he knew that the effort was lost.

Relations with Hitler had also deteriorated. "You may think it sentimental, even absurd, but I have sworn loyalty to Adolf Hitler, and as a soldier and as a German I cannot go back on my oath," Himmler told

Bernadotte. "For that reason I cannot do anything in opposition to the Führer's plans and wishes."

The statement was only partially true. In Himmler's mind Hitler had become a fallen god. He was founder of the Thousand Year Reich, yet his role on earth seemed to have been played out. In the quasi-religion Himmler had created, it was possible to view Germany entering a new state of existence, a time when the leaders would change, when Hitler would be revered but others might take action on their own.

This Himmler had already done. Jean-Marie Musy, formerly the president of the Swiss Confederation, had helped convince Himmler to release Jews from the Theresienstadt concentration camp. Himmler and Musy had met in the Black Forest on January 12, 1945. Drawn up by Schellenberg and others at Wildbad-Schwarzwald, the agreement stated that a first-class train would evacuate approximately twelve hundred Jews to Switzerland every fourteen days. In addition, Musy's various Jewish organizations would work actively with Himmler to solve the "Jewish problem." At the same time, the Jews would work to alter the propaganda effort against Germany.

An exchange of money was involved, to be paid to the International Red Cross through Musy. The first payment of five million Swiss francs was made at the end of February 1945.

The first shipment of Jews did go to Switzerland, and from there to the United States, an action that went against everything Hitler believed in. Even worse, Hitler obtained a coded message from Spain (apparently a fraud, deliberately prepared to mislead) saying that Schellenberg, acting as Himmler's agent, had negotiated with Musy to secure Swiss asylum for 250 unnamed Nazi leaders. The outraged Hitler issued orders that any German who helped a Jew, an American, or a British prisoner to escape was to be executed instantly.

❦

The foreign press was alerted to the impending release of more Jews and some journalists were able to reach Hitler for comments. Outraged that such a development could take place without his knowledge or approval, he demanded to see Himmler at once. Hitler wanted to know what concessions had been gained by the release. A Jew could be allowed to live, but only at a price that benefited the Third Reich.

Himmler explained that there had been no concessions. He felt that the release would help improve Germany's image in the waning days of the war. He was looking ahead to a postwar Reich, a world quite different from what they all had known when the first violence had occurred in 1939. He wanted Germany to remain respected and strong, not risking the humiliation it suffered following World War I.

Himmler was unable to realize that the world's powers would not allow Nazi Germany to continue. And Hitler could not imagine that the release of the Jews held any value. He ordered the transportation stopped after only a relatively small number had been freed. He also ordered Himmler to do nothing further along these lines unless so ordered by Hitler. The result was that the Swiss and Musy found that they no longer had ready access to the SS chief. The Swedes and their few allies within the Nazi government, such as Kersten, were the primary hope.

There were other powers at work within Himmler's entourage. Walter Schellenberg understood that the nation had reached a stage in the war where every leader had to protect himself. The Allies were going to win. There would be executions and trials of the fallen leaders. He knew that his position with intelligence, as well as the brutality he had shown when earning the respect of Heydrich and the others who had once been his superiors, threatened his future. He could not undo the past. He could only try to find a way to obtain sanctuary in a neutral country, perhaps escaping any penalty for his war work.

As a result of these forces, of which Bernadotte was mostly unaware, he was able to help firm the arrangement despite the certainty of Hitler's wrath if the Führer learned what was taking place. The Musy incident had left everyone wary, yet Himmler had become convinced that it was time to act in a manner that would assure the future of the Reich after Hitler was gone.

When the talks were over, Himmler asked Schellenberg if a good chauffeur had been selected to take the count back to his quarters. There were tank traps and other impediments throughout Berlin. Himmler warned that if anything happened to the count, "the Swedish papers might come out with big headlines: WAR CRIMINAL HIMMLER MURDERS COUNT BERNADOTTE ."

The First Rescue

The inmates of Sachsenhausen, the concentration camp north of Berlin, were frightened. There had been a time when the camps themselves were feared, and death was still the primary occupation of the guards assigned to them. But with the war coming to an end, rations for even the soldiers becoming limited, weapons in short supply, and Allied bombers operating with impunity, the psychological aspects of the camps had changed. In many instances the guards were the prisoners, the inmates psychologically free.

Having been through hell, the inmates could sense their impending release. Some would walk through the camps' gates. Others would die before they could achieve physical freedom. Yet the potential for freedom made them struggle against death, while the brutality they had experienced caused them to accept death as a valid, though not preferred, release.

Whatever their fate, the prisoners still had a will to live and a sense of triumph in what was taking place. The guards sensed the hopelessness of their position for the first time in years. Now it was the guards who had no future, the guards who faced unknown abuse at the hands of foreigners. The murders continued unabated, yet within the nightmare of routine, each new day became a blessing for the inmates, not a curse.

It was the idea of being moved from a camp by the Nazis that created the last terror for the inmates. Movement meant helplessness once again. Movement meant being crammed suffocatingly close in sealed trucks, cattle cars, and other conveyances. Movement meant people standing in their own waste, sometimes fatally deprived of oxygen, being pressed face to face against what might be a corpse by journey's end with no place to move, no way to shift the dead body. Movement meant machine-gunning, mass graves, enduring a painful, humiliating death.

The fact that the trucks were white and clearly marked with the Red Cross meant little to the inmates. Count Bernadotte's abilities to speak English, some French, and Swedish meant nothing. There were linguists among the Nazis. Red Cross vehicles had been misused in the past. The idea of transportation in such a manner could be a sick joke of a type they had witnessed before.

There were officially 2,200 Scandinavians to be transported between March 15 and March 30 (more actually made the trip). The Swedish legation was housed in Schönhausen, one of Bismark's old estates, 125 miles east of Berlin. From there the transportation team was coordinated for the first evacuation efforts.

Dachau was releasing 600 men, women, and children. Another 1,600 men, all former policemen in Norway and Denmark, were being released from several different camps northwest of Dresden. The thirty-five Red Cross vehicles would have to make seven trips in all in order to free the people, each trip taking an average of 1,100 miles round trip. The effort was made even more rewarding by the fact that, ultimately, 2,700 people were released during this time, not just the 2,200 of the original agreement. However, Himmler was annoyed with the backlash from that release.

"When I let 2,700 Jews go into Switzerland, this was made the subject of a personal campaign against me in the Press, asserting that I had only released these men in order to construct an alibi for myself," Himmler, later told both Kersten and representatives of the World Jewish Congress negotiating for the release of more Jews during the final days of the war. "But I have no need of an alibi! I have always done only what I considered just, what was essential for my people. I will also answer for that. Nobody has had so much mud slung at him in the last ten years as I have. I have never bothered myself about that. Even in Germany any man can say about me what he pleases. Newspapers abroad have started a campaign against me which is no encouragement to me to continue handing over the camps."

Bernadotte was not permitted inside the heart of the concentration camps during his negotiations. He was not one of the rescue-team leaders or volunteer members of the transportation crew. He would probably have been personally barred from viewing what was taking place even as other outsiders got a glimpse of the nightmare world in which the rescued had lived. However, he was given a pass that enabled him to drive anywhere on the public roads during a period when such movement was carefully restricted by the police. The drive enabled him to begin to witness the horror of what had been taking place.

First he passed women prisoners from the concentration camps who were being used outside the secluded areas. There were hundreds of them, all either Aryan Germans accused of working against the Nazis or foreigners who were not Jewish. They had entered the camps in excellent condition, strong, healthy, well-nourished, and so they had survived the brutality, the lack of privacy, the denial of adequate food. They were the survivors, yet as they were marched to their jobs, their bodies were often stick-thin, their skin pulled taut over deteriorating bone and weakened muscle. Some managed to hold their heads high, defiant in captivity. Others kept their heads down, their shoulders hunched, one foot moving in front of the other like automatons capable of movement rather than life. Many were living dead. Growing dehydration from uncontrollable diarrhea and a lack of Vitamin C and B complex that caused their hearts and the cell walls of their blood vessels to deteriorate had combined to cause such interior damage that they would never recover. They might drop as they walked or worked. They might be unable to awaken one morning. Whatever the case, their vital organs had been so damaged that at some point they would just stop. Even their rescue at the point Bernadotte witnessed their movement might not have saved the healthiest of the inmates.

There were also lines of Germans traveling from East Prussia. The government claimed that there were centers where they would be housed and fed, and an effort was made to provide them. However, the inability to sustain a relief effort during the closing days of the war was obvious from the appearance of the road.

The refugees had created a crude wagon train. They used farm wagons to hold their goods and their families, covering everything as best they could. They attached whatever horses remained alive, forcing them to pull too heavy a load. Sometimes families began throwing away once-precious possessions to lighten the burden for everyone, giving them a better chance to flee. At other times they pushed onward, not knowing or not caring that the burden had grown too great for the emaciated horses. The animals suffered heart attacks and died, collapsing onto the roads and having to be dragged to the side so the endless stream of refugees could continue their walk to whatever fate might await them.

From time to time Allied planes would appear in the sky and many of the people would race for the ditches by the side of the road as the bombers dropped low over the highway. Others no longer looked up, even when bombs occasionally dropped all around them. They had become fatalistic about their lives. They would move or they would die. Survival was in the hands of God. They would make no extra effort to try to assure their own safety.

A few months earlier the bombers would have been met by German defensive units flying fighter planes. Anti-aircraft rounds from nearby ground units would have filled the sky, creating a deadly wall of metal destroying any plane unable to veer from its course.

Now the guns were mostly silent, the German fighter planes seldom seen. The people did not know if the Luftwaffe had been destroyed, if the pilots had been killed in combat, or if the idea of fighting to the death for the fatherland no longer appealed. They also did not care.

The Allies wanted the destruction to continue unabated until Hitler guaranteed that he would surrender unconditionally, something the Führer refused to do. The various Allied leaders had warned the Swedish government that they would not honor any symbol, including the Red Cross, in their aerial attacks. The soldiers were uninterested in killing demoralized, unarmed civilians. Nor did they want to interfere with genuine missions of mercy. But they traveled where the war took them, bombing and strafing wherever there was even the hint of a military target. And if they accidentally strayed or were forced from their original objective, they would use their ammunition to destroy anyone connected with the Nazi years.

The Germans tried to fight this attitude by using prisoners as human shields. The top floors of several important buildings were used to house Jews, Scandinavians, political prisoners, or anyone else whose lives might be valued by whatever attacking enemy the Nazis wanted to influence.

Such a ruse no longer assured protection. The prisoners were viewed as expendable so long as anyone or any operation of importance among the Nazis could be destroyed.

Bernadotte's closest brush with death during the evacuation period came on April 20, when he had a meeting with Himmler. This was not a time when he was part of a convoy. That initial effort was completed. This time he was attempting to negotiate the release of more prisoners, but the air war had become more intense. As he later explained:

> I was advised to take special precautions. I took two chauffeurs, one of whom, seated on the traveling trunk at the back of the car, was to act as observer. He was instructed to signal by banging the top of the car as soon as he saw Allied planes approaching, thus warning us to stop, jump out, and take whatever cover we could find. On our way we passed through the town of Nauen, twenty-six miles west of the capital. We noticed blue and yellow flags, a signal that an air raid was on, but as nothing seemed to be happening we continued on our way until we reached the outskirts of the town. Seeing an old woman by the side of the road, we pulled up, and I asked her if a raid was on. Before she had time to reply, we heard the dull drone of a large number of Allied bombers. A few seconds later bombs were dropped on the railway station, less than a hundred yards away. We drove on out of the town and took cover in a trench that had been dug at the side of the road for the defense of the adjoining village, the plan apparently being to sweep the road with fire from antitank guns.
>
> There was brilliant sunshine and a cloudless sky as the Allied bombers swooped on towards their target. For about an hour we lay in our trench, gazing at the fascinating spectacle of Nauen and neighboring villages under heavy attack. We could see the bombs leaving the planes, after which what looked like a white column of smoke rushed towards the ground at great speed, and then there came a terrifying explosion. This was the first time I had observed anything approaching panic among the German population. A crowded shelter had been hit, a number of people killed, and men and women came running across the fields, aimlessly seeking shelter in ditches and anything that offered cover of any kind. It was as if the people of Nauen felt that nothing could save them, since not even a few fighters from the nearby field of Spandau went up to engage the enemy.

Bernadotte came to understand the full scope of the German situation a few days later, when he was in Nazi-occupied Denmark. He had been provided with an ambulance plane which the Red Cross had fueled. As the plane was preparing for takeoff, American fighters raided the field. Destroying the aircraft and damaging the field would reduce the resistance by the Germans, so it was a prime military target. However, the count had seen heavily camouflaged, well-armed German planes and was certain that he would be in the midst of an intense aerial battle. Instead he took shelter and watched the Americans attack without resistance. When he asked the German commander why no defensive measures had been taken, the man sadly explained that while they had the planes and ammunition, they had no fuel. Defensive action could no longer be taken.

The situation was worse for many of the infantry troops. Despite orders from Hitler meant to prevent retreating, ragged clusters of soldiers wandered along the roads near Hamburg. They knew all was lost. They recognized that they were neither in control of their own destiny nor was the world for which they had been fighting ever going to be a reality. Even worse, they were effectively unarmed, a handful of weapons and small quantities of ammunition shared among them. Each time guards had to be posted, the weapons that remained were passed to them.

But the loss of morale, the loss of property and manpower, did not stop the killing machines of the concentration camps. Bernadotte had saved 2,700 people in his first negotiations with Himmler. Thousands more were dying each day, even as the Allied troops shattered defenses and were taking control of what had previously been Nazi territory. Lower-level leaders within the Reich were determined that the truth of the camps not be discovered. It was better to destroy everyone than to leave living witnesses to their brutality. Only Himmler, openly taking a stand against Hitler, Goebbels, and the other top officials, could reduce or stop the ceaseless murders. And Bernadotte, working with the subtle influence of both Kersten and Schellenberg, was the only man who might convince Himmler to countermand the orders for total extermination.

On April 2, 1945, there was another meeting with an extremely anxious and somber Himmler. He explained that he had given his oath of loyalty to Hitler and would have to continue with the war because that was what the Führer wanted.

"Don't you realize that Germany has lost the war?" Bernadotte replied. "By attacking Russia in 1941 you yourselves made it a war on two fronts, and it was that which snatched victory from your grasp.

You yourself say that you are willing to do anything for the German nation, and if that is true, and if you consider his determination to continue the war a disaster to your country, involving the death of tens of thousands more on the fighting fronts as well as on the domestic front, you ought to put the welfare of your people above your loyalty to Hitler. A person in your position, bearing such an enormous responsibility, cannot obey a superior blindly, but must have the courage to accept responsibility for decisions made in the interest of the people."

When Himmler briefly left the room, Walter Schellenberg, who was also present, asked Bernadotte about the possibility of approaching General Eisenhower in order to arrange for surrender on the Western front. It was a request Bernadotte refused, saying that such a request would have to come from Himmler. He also explained that he would not negotiate because his involvement would result in the implication that the Allied forces would be willing to work out peace terms. He was fairly certain that there would be a demand for unconditional surrender and did not want to be accused of interfering.

Later in the discussions, when Himmler was back in the room, Bernadotte proposed the transporting of all Danes, Norwegians, and people interned at Neuengamme (located on the outskirts of Hamburg) into Sweden. Himmler found the idea ridiculous, though he was ready to compromise. Perhaps a portion of the prisoners could be released. In that manner, Himmler would have helped Bernadotte without risking Hitler's rage as he would if Hitler discovered such large numbers of prisoners being released.

This time Bernadotte suggested that only the sick Scandinavian men should be released, but with them should come all Danish and Norwegian women. The Danish police in Neuengamme should be returned to Denmark, where they would be interned for a period of time rather than allowed to go back on duty. And other Scandinavians should be allowed to go to Swedish hospitals or hotel facilities until the war was over, at which time they would be allowed to return to Norway, Denmark, or Great Britain. In addition, Himmler agreed to release a number of individual French citizens.

Bernadotte did not realize that much of Himmler's nervousness, as well as his willingness to offer concessions, came from pressures he had experienced from Kersten. The doctor had been in Stockholm in February, meeting with Hilel Storch. The World Jewish Congress had learned that Himmler planned to destroy all Jews in the concentration camps each time the Allied troops came close to liberating them. The WJC wanted to avert this situation as well as to find a way to get them food, medicine, and, if possible, passage to Sweden and Switzerland.

Kersten began talking with a reluctant Himmler toward the middle of March. Himmler reportedly stated: "If National Socialist Germany is going to be destroyed, then her enemies and the criminals in concentration camps shall not have the satisfaction of emerging from our ruin as triumphant conquerors. They shall share in the downfall. Those are the Führer's direct orders and I must see to it that they are carried out to the last detail." However, Kersten was able to persuade him that he would have an easier time with the Allies following the war if he acted in a more humanitarian way.

On March 12, Himmler signed an agreement with Kersten, the latter knowing that the Nazi leader had too much pride to go against anything he put into writing. The agreement stated that even though Hitler might order the destruction of the concentration camps and everyone within before the Allies arrived, Himmler would not pass on that order. Himmler said that the camps would be ordered to display a white flag and surrender in an orderly manner. There would be no further killing of the Jews, and they were to be treated like all other prisoners. And he agreed not to evacuate the camps, since forced marches resulted in extensive deaths, but to allow the prisoners to receive food parcels.

It is not known why Himmler would willingly sign his doctor's document. Kersten had become something special to Himmler in the many months they had been together—reliever of intense pain, confidante, a man who seemed to accept all of Himmler's eccentricities and actions without rebuke. Kersten was also not a threat to the Nazi leader because he sought neither power nor special privilege. With the exception of his humanitarian requests, Kersten wished only to enjoy his family and the practice of his medical specialty.

The willingness to sign a paper may have been to please the doctor who brought him relief. It may have been to humor the doctor. And he may have considered it insignificant. With Himmler seeing himself as Germany's postwar leader, his authority would be total. Should he choose to go back on his word, he would be able to do so without suffering consequences.

Whatever the circumstances, written confirmation of intent was always more certain to be followed by Himmler than any spoken agreement. However, at the time, Kersten was never certain whether or not Himmler truly understood that Germany had lost the war. Himmler maintained his loyalty to Hitler, yet he seemed to realize that Hitler would not survive. One way or another, Himmler would emerge the most important man in the Nazi government. His problem seemed to be one of trying to please the critical nations, such as Sweden, without getting caught and reprimanded by Hitler. If he could walk that fine line, he was willing to do whatever was necessary to assure himself a favorable postwar image.

The problem was that the rest of the Nazi high command did not share Himmler's vision of glory. Some had become rebellious against Hitler, Goebbels, Himmler, and the others who maintained power at the top. This was most blatant after several of the generals attempted to kill Hitler with a bomb.

Some of the high command were dedicated Hitler loyalists, blindly following their leader no matter what Germany's changing military situation might indicate was rational. And others were just trying to survive the war, to secure a new life in peacetime Europe.

But no matter what the bias of the members of the high command, none were known to share Himmler's vision. Himmler might see himself as the reincarnation of Heinrich I, but they still saw him as a toady who had somehow managed to obtain vast power, yet who would not survive the war any more than they would. And those who remained most loyal to Hitler seemed to feel that if all was ultimately lost, they wanted to destroy as many of their enemies as possible before their own deaths. They fought the idea of compromise, stressing how disloyal Himmler would be.

What the other leaders did not realize was the power move Schellenberg and Himmler had planned years earlier when establishing the SS along the same lines as the German government. Himmler's religious ideas would allow him to turn Hitler into a Germanic god, taking control himself of the "secular" world after Hitler's death or defeat. He was more comfortable with rebellion than they realized, making Bernadotte's timing flawless.

The pressures from Kersten were also effective because the doctor had become Himmler's closest adviser and most trusted confidant. Even though there is reason to believe that Kersten was far more sympathetic to the Nazi movement than his memoirs and other writings indicate, he understood that when the war was over, he needed to appear an unwilling participant in the Reich. The more he acted as a go-between for men such as Storch, Bernadotte, and the various Jewish and government leaders he encountered during his travels, the better his postwar position. It was important for him to help convince Himmler to allow the release of whomever Bernadotte desired in order to gain the support of Sweden and the allied nations.

Bernadotte met with Schellenberg on April 9. The SS leader continued to push for Bernadotte acting as a go-between with Eisenhower, and this time Bernadotte was more amenable. He agreed to make the contact providing Himmler met four criteria.

First and most important, Himmler must state that Hitler had named him to be the leader of Germany in the event that Hitler was too ill or otherwise unable to carry on his duties. It was not necessary for Hitler to make such a declaration. The count realized by then that such an event would not occur. He only wanted the statement made so that Himmler could be used as the front man for negotiations.

Next, Himmler had to declare that the National Socialist party was abolished and all its leaders had been dismissed. This was to be followed immediately by the declaration that there would be an end to the Werwolf activities. The Werwolves (sometimes called Werewolves) were SS men who were part of a special sabotage unit.

And finally, before Bernadotte returned to Sweden, he had to have official confirmation that the Danish and Norwegian prisoners were also being sent to Sweden. Obviously these combined to make a revolution in the government, something the count knew would not happen. Yet Schellenberg, anxious to please because he would later seek asylum for himself in Sweden, took them seriously and attempted to convince Himmler to agree to the conditions.

The pressures for rescue became obvious during this same conversation. Hitler was aware that the war was nearly over and that the concentration camps would be a focus for rescue efforts. He had given orders that at least two camps, Buchenwald and Bergen-Belsen, and perhaps Theresienstadt as well, were to be evacuated. All the prisoners were then to be marched 190 miles on foot, which was certain to kill them. However, Schellenberg had objected strongly, or so he claimed, convincing Hitler to let the prisoners be turned over to the Allied troops when they arrived.

This was another circumstance where it is uncertain if history was being rewritten for the protection of the man. It was doubtful that Bernadotte or anyone else outside the Nazi inner circle would know if such instructions had been given. Certainly they fit into the attitude of most of the Nazi leaders. However, there is serious question as to whether or not Schellenberg would have had the power to meet with Hitler and talk him out of such an action.

Bernadotte would not have cared whether Schellenberg was ingratiating himself or telling the truth. He was willing to go along with any stories the Nazis wanted to give him provided he was able to save lives. He had told his friend Major Sven Frykman:

It would be futile to ask the Germans to open their concentration camps and allow us to take their inmates away immediately. We must proceed by stages. First we must get the Scandinavians assembled in one place in Germany near the Danish frontier so that we can keep an eye on them in case of a breakdown of the Nazi regime and, anyway, succor the sick and try and reduce the liquidations. The next step must be to get the Scandinavians over the border into Denmark and eventually to Sweden. Having inserted the thin end of the wedge, we must then try and get hold of specialized classes of non-Scandinavian prisoners, such as relatives of prominent Swedes, intellectuals and children. In the process we must lay our hands on anybody else we can and, anyway, by showing our faces, shame the Gestapo into mitigating some of the horrors of the camps. Finally we must make a general offensive against any concentration camps we can reach and enlist the collaboration of other neutral powers, such as the Swiss. We must try and percolate food parcels and medical supplies into all camps and, if possible, introduce medical personnel. This will not be achieved by table-thumping—only by firmness, tact, and perseverance. If necessary we must talk and behave like Herrenfolk, which the German officials will understand. We must also use bribery—cigarettes, drink, chocolate or any other means we can think of—in order to achieve our purpose. We must not talk politics or get into any quarrels with the Germans. We must even, if necessary, flatter and cajole them—however much it may stick in our throats. The object is save human life and to mitigate human suffering and any means to this end is legitimate.

By April 13 Himmler realized that he was operating alone. Hitler had become paranoid about many of his followers, including the head of the SS. Hitler felt that they were betraying him by not being more successful on the fighting fronts, by not killing the people in the concentration camps, by not showing their enemies that they would triumph. He was horrified that Himmler was allowing anyone to live, that he would consider negotiating with the enemy. As Schellenberg recorded after his meeting with the SS leader:

Himmler was in great mental distress. Even openly he had been almost completely abandoned by the Führer; for Hitler had ordered the Liebstandarte Adolf Hitler to remove their armbands as a dishonoring punishment [for failing to succeed in an unwinnable conflict Hitler ordered on the Danube]. He said except for Standarten-führer Dr. Brandt [his secretary], I was the only man he could trust. What should he do? He could not kill Hitler, could not poison or arrest him in the Chancellery, or the whole military machine would come to a standstill. I explained that all this was of no importance. There were only two possibilities. Either he could go to Hitler, tell him openly of the events of the last two years and persuade him to resign. "Quite impossible!" retorted Himmler, "He would fall into one of his rages, and shoot me out of hand!" " Then you must protect yourself against this," I said. "You have enough SS leaders who can carry out a surprise arrest; or if there is no other way, the doctors must intervene."

Schellenberg noted that Himmler did not reply.

It is important to remember that Schellenberg was not anti-Nazi. He had not suddenly seen the error in Germany's ways. He was a pragmatist who had worked for the side in which he believed, had come to see that his side was going to lose the war and that Hitler was unrealistic about the ultimate fate of the leaders. The top spy wanted to save his own life, recognized that Hitler was no longer fully rational concerning the war and the fate of Germany, and realized that Himmler was the one man who could do something about it. Folke Bernadotte's mission was the means to protecting power, their lives, or whatever might be possible when Germany went down to defeat.

Despite Schellenberg's efforts, Himmler decided to forbid the transfer of Scandinavian internees from Neuengamme, a fact that Bernadotte discovered when he reached the Danish border on April 19. Hurried negotiations resulted in a slight modification of the orders. All the Scandinavians could leave for Denmark and Sweden. Everyone else in the camp, twenty thousand in all, were taken to railroad cars and other vehicles for "evacuation." These twenty thousand were then slaughtered, not relocated, the action handled hastily, secretly, and completely.

The slaughter of the twenty thousand, which Bernadotte realized had probably taken place, though there was no evidence of that at the time, was the first of three shocks the count faced during a fateful few days. He returned to meet with Himmler on the twenty-first, the day after Hitler's birthday and conference with his leaders in the Berlin bunker. It was from Himmler that Bernadotte learned why there had been a delay.

While the war was winding down and Hitler was desperate to destroy as many people as possible, the Allied troops had reached Buchenwald and Bergen-Belsen concentration camps. There they had discovered men and women looking like living skeletons. They discovered some of the horrors of the damned, the end results of the brutality, the mass starvation, the endless killings. There were charred bodies, evidence of torture beyond any imagined, and even the collection of "art on parchment," the Ilse Koch tattoo collection. The soldiers were in shock, outraged, talking to everyone who would listen, spreading the word through radio, newspapers, newsreels, and magazines throughout the world.

Only the leaders of the world had been aware of the death camps. Most people, including the press, either had only heard rumors or knew nothing about what was taking place. The few who knew either could not believe such an event was occurring or felt it was appropriate to censor such news as part of the wartime effort. The true horror was not widely understood.

With the opening of the camps, thousands of average citizens became aware of what had been taking place. The soldiers and the press who accompanied them were often average people, farm boys, the children of factory workers, high school and college dropouts who had interrupted their education to help save America. They had seen the horrors of normal warfare, the numbing exhaustion, the endless terror when bullets are flying, bombs are exploding, and the shooting at an enemy one cannot really see.

But nothing had been so horrifying as the reality of the work and death camps. Whatever compassion had existed was suddenly destroyed. The German army and the German people suddenly loomed as the most amoral in history, and there was a need to show the photographs and tell the story to anyone who would listen.

Such a discovery was embarrassing for Himmler. Through Schellenberg's prodding he had come to understand the importance of his image when the war was over. Now he had to meet with Bernadotte to try and save face. It was only natural that he would order the deaths of everyone in Neuengamme he was not releasing to Sweden and Denmark. It was also natural for him to lie.

Himmler stressed that what the Allies were saying about Buchenwald and Bergen-Belsen was not true. He knew that Bernadotte had not seen the camps himself, had not seen the inmates, so he hoped that he could convince him that the nonsense he was spouting was truth.

What happened, Himmler explained, was that when the Allies were approaching Buchenwald, one of the tanks had a freak accident and burst into flames. Maybe it was mechanical failure. Maybe some of the ammunition overheated and exploded for some reason. Whatever it was, it happened inside a vehicle that was approaching a model prison camp.

The soldiers surrounding the tank did not realize that the flames were spontaneous combustion from an internal source. They thought that the tank had been hit by a shell coming from the camp. In what they thought was self-defense, the Allies fired into the concentration camp, setting one of the buildings on fire. Many inmates were consumed in the flames, so when the Allies entered the camp, they saw charred bodies. Rather than admit that the deaths had been their own fault, they blamed the Nazis. They spread lies in order to save face, a terrible thing to do. "It is outrageous," said Himmler, "that this camp, which in my opinion was in model shape, should have become the subject of these shameless accounts. Nothing has upset me so much as what the Allied press has published about this business."

Bernadotte, Kersten, Schellenberg, and others constantly pressed Himmler, watching him vacillate between his loyalty to Hitler and his need to make himself important to the nations that would influence postwar Germany. Bernadotte was allowed to bring in forty thousand Kosher food packages to some of the camps, the food reaching the prisoners for whom it was intended. There were also other releases of prisoners to Sweden, though often they were identified as Poles or by some other designation so that Hitler would not learn that Jews had been released.

Just as the numbers of dead and dying were mounting, so were the numbers being saved. Sometimes it was a handful of important individuals. Sometimes a few hundred or a few thousand. The pressure was both quiet and continuous, and Bernadotte sought to save as many people as possible.

During the time that Hitler was celebrating his birthday in his bunker, the concrete apartment he had constructed as his headquarters in Berlin, the sounds of the advancing Russians could be heard in the distance. Göring, Keitel, Himmler, Bormann, Goebbels, and others all tried to convince Hitler to leave the city. It was doomed; nothing could be done. They talked for hours, almost around the clock, alternately celebrating and trying to give Hitler a sense of reality. It was to no avail.

The birthday had not been a joyous occasion for the people of Berlin. They had once celebrated happily during times when they felt the Führer was leading them to greatness. Now it was obvious that an unknown fate awaited those who could not leave.

Barriers had been erected along the roads. Many people were living in the basements of burned-out buildings. Children had frequently been evacuated. There were trails of people walking from the city, carrying whatever possessions they could. Others felt that they might as well await whatever would take place.

Women seemed the most vulnerable. The Russian troops—and to a far lesser extent, Americans, British, and others—had men who would rape females, young and old. Such actions were not condoned. Many of the Russian rapists were eventually ordered shot by their officers. But this did not stop the violence, the drunken soldiers breaking into homes.

Magda Goebbels' family had experienced some of this. One relative of Magda's had been gang-raped by a series of Russian soldiers, then saved by a captain who took her as his lover/mistress/prisoner. It was a supposedly voluntary living arrangement, though she knew that the day she said no she would become vulnerable to the gang rapes of the other soldiers.

Eventually the captain had compassion, reuniting her with her husband, a German soldier (conscripted, not SS) who had been a prisoner of war. But the two had been together only a short period of time in the small hovel which served as their home in a semidestroyed town near Berlin when a drunk Russian soldier broke inside, surprising them as they slept. Her husband had been tortured and was too weak to put up much resistance. He was wounded by the assailant and lay dying, watching as his wife was raped. Eventually the woman died, allegedly from the trauma, though the family suspected she committed suicide.

On that April 21, the day after the birthday and two days before the Russians first penetrated the outskirts of Berlin, Bernadotte was in a car traveling from Berlin to Hohen-Lüchen Sanatorium, where he was to meet with Himmler that night. This trip was to prove his second shock.

The roads were crowded with refugees. Frightened, hopeless civilians mingled with soldiers as they walked or rode in whatever direction seemed safer than staying in the city. In many instances the soldiers had removed their uniforms, donning civilian attire in order to avoid being shot, a fate they thought possible in the final days of the war. But the most moving experience came near the Ravensbrück concentration camp outside Hohen-Lüchen. Ravensbrück was a death camp for women from America, Britain, Belgium, China, Holland, France, Poland, and Czechoslovakia. Some had been a part of the war effort. Others had been living or working in areas that were suddenly occupied by the Germans. All of them had been involved in forced labor, literally worked and starved to death.

Two hundred of the Ravensbrück slaves were being force-marched by armed men along the road. Apparently they had been working on a hire arrangement at one of the area businesses, the SS determined to take whatever profits they could make even as the war was ending. They were all in rags, so exhausted that they could barely move their feet. Yet one of the women, as worn and tired as the others, walked with her back straight and her head held high.

The woman walking so proudly shocked Bernadotte. He later

explained that her body seemed to be saying "You can never get me down, whatever you do to me." It was the sight of the triumph of the human spirit against overwhelming odds. So long as there was life in her body, she refused to be overwhelmed.

At that moment Bernadotte remembered the rescue work his fellow-countrymen had accomplished among the Frenchwomen. He realized that such women had been torn from their homes. They were not a military threat. They were not a political threat. They were needless victims and he was determined to meet with Himmler that night to arrange to have them set free.

(Six months later, one of the former Polish concentration-camp prisoners had Bernadotte to dinner at the Stockholm Concert House as a way of thanking him. Several former Ravensbrück prisoners were there, including the woman who had so impressed him on the road. After meeting her, he commented: "This case convinces me of something I never believed before—that people who work for Right and believe in their task will attain their ends if only they keep their chins up!"—a philosophy that would eventually take him to Israel.)

❧

Bernadotte did not realize just how bad the life of the Ravensbrück inmates had become when he met with an exhausted Himmler that night. There were approximately thirty thousand female inmates in the concentration camp, a death camp where the gas chambers were in constant use, despite the fact that the camp was in the firing line of the advancing Allied troops. Berlin was being evacuated. Bombers were strafing the people and destroying the buildings. Yet all that mattered in Ravensbrück was that the women be destroyed. Since many were still able to work, and since the SS was still earning money from their efforts, the murders were limited to those women who became too sick to work and those women whose weight dropped below eighty-five pounds, even if they could still function. The low weight meant that they would soon die anyway. Killing them while they could still enter the gas chambers under their own power made more sense than waiting until they became helpless.

Himmler was torn that night between his desire to become the new leader of the Reich, taking it into the postwar world, and his dying loyalty to Hitler. He had seen for himself that his Führer was at the end of his power, and probably the end of his life. Yet he knew that there were concessions that Hitler would not make and he did not want to agree to something that would earn Hitler's wrath.

Himmler told Bernadotte that the Scandinavian prisoners being transported to Denmark, a potential area of battle, could not be allowed to continue on to Sweden. However, he did agree that if the war spread into Denmark, the remaining Scandinavian prisoners could be transported to Sweden.

Then Bernadotte mentioned the Frenchwomen in Ravensbrück. He knew that Frenchwomen had been saved in the past, so he felt that such a request was appropriate.

Himmler, sensitive to what had happened with the Allies' discovery of Buchenwald and Bergen-Belsen, was concerned with the image of Ravensbrück as well. He planned to evacuate the concentration camp, a probable euphemism for murdering everyone there. But he also believed that the world would be more horrified by the wholesale slaughter of women than men. Males had traditionally been soldiers, and the death of men in wartime was far more acceptable than the deaths of women. He told Bernadotte that not only would he allow the Frenchwomen to be removed from Ravensbrück, he would like the count to arrange for the evacuation of women of all nationalities.

Bernadotte had no idea what was involved with the permission for the evacuation. He left for Friedrichsruhe after breakfast the following morning, the day the Russians broke through the outer Berlin defenses. He visited the headquarters for the Red Cross operations and arranged for the Ravensbrück women to be evacuated. Then he left for Padborg, Denmark, just over the German border, to meet with the Danish Red Cross and see what was happening to the prisoners being aided there.

The Ravensbrück rescue effort was far more dramatic than anything Bernadotte imagined. He knew that twenty-five white Swedish buses, each marked with a red cross, would drive to Ravensbrück to remove the women. There would be doctors along as well as three nurses, one of them Countess Maria Bernadotte, his sister. That was all he knew at the time.

In February 1948, Franz Göring would issue a statement during Schellenberg's trial concerning what he witnessed when he drove to the Ravensbrück concentration camp in 1945 as a liaison between Himmler and the Bernadotte rescue workers:

> On 22 April 1945, at about 12:00 P.M., I arrived in the Ravensbrück camp. I immediately conducted an extended interview with the commandant of the concentration camp, Sturmbannführer Suhren. Through a detailed inquiry, I established that 9,000 Polish women and 1,500 women of French, Belgian, Dutch, and other nationalities, in addition to approximately 3,000

Jewish women, were presently in the camp.... Here as well, the uncooperative attitude of the camp commandant and his staff toward the release of the prisoners was in evidence. Suhren attempted to evade precise questions with unclear answers. His excuse in every instance was that, following orders from the Führer, he had already destroyed all the documents, files, and other remaining materials.... In connection with the evacuation of the women, I told Suhren that I had halted... the columns of the Swedish Red Cross, so that it was advisable to begin marching the women by foot to Malchow in order to expedite their release. I would then signal the transport columns to receive the women in Malchow. Suhren gave me his firm promise to start the women on their march to Malchow that same day.... A column of seventeen buses of the Swedish, Danish, and International Red Cross was held ready for the evacuation of the women, who ought in the meantime to have reached Malchow, according to my agreement with Suhren. When we arrived in Malchow, we learned from the camp commandant that he knew nothing about the arrival of the prisoners from Ravensbrück. We then drove back to Ravensbrück and confirmed for ourselves that Suhren had in fact not sent the women on their march as agreed. When I asked him why he had failed to keep his end of the agreement, he answered... that in accordance with the Führer's orders, the prisoners had to remain in the camp. I then telephoned the special train Steiermark from Suhren's office, in his presence, and was connected with Standartenführer Dr. Brandt, Himmler's personal assistant. I described the situation to Dr. Brandt and requested an immediate decision from Himmler. Not long afterward, Dr. Brandt called back and ordered Suhren to release the prisoners for evacuation as agreed. Suhren then declared to me in private that he was now completely at a loss, since he had explicit Führer orders to liquidate the women upon the approach of the enemy troops. Suhren now became very uncertain and confided to me that he had a group of women in the camp whom he had likewise been explicitly ordered to eliminate: fifty-four Polish and seventeen French women, on whom experiments had been conducted. When I asked him what sort of experiments, he explained that the women in question had been inoculated with bacilli, which had developed into a disease, which in turn had been cured through surgery, partly through muscle surgery, partly through bone surgery. Thereupon I had two of the women brought before me and was convinced of what Suhren had told me. I immediately pointed out to Suhren that he could not, under any circumstances, carry out the order Kaltenbrunner had given until he had received a decision from Himmler. In Lübeck, I contacted Dr. Brandt once again and apprised him of this matter, requesting that he obtain a decision from Himmler as soon as possible, and further indicating that these women ought not to be eliminated under any circumstances, especially since the women who were about to be released knew of the experiments. The experiments were known in the camp under the code name Kaninchen [Rabbit]. About two hours later I received word from Dr. Brandt that Himmler had ordered the release of the so-called Versuchskaninchen [guinea pigs]. Dr. Arnoldson of the Swedish Red Cross, whom I briefed on the whole affair, personally supervised the evacuation of these women.

Tragically, the necessity of hiding the story of Ravensbrück to assure other prisoner releases meant that the history of what happened, and the knowledge of Bernadotte's remarkable achievement, was almost completely lost. It was mentioned once or twice in the years that passed, but almost nothing was written about the horrors or the rescue.

On April 23, Schellenberg stated that Hitler had lost the war. The Führer was in Berlin coordinating the defense against the Russian invaders, an impossible cause. The chief spy of the SS explained to Bernadotte: "Himmler has decided to bring about a meeting with General Eisenhower to inform him that he is willing to give orders to the German forces in the West to capitulate. Would you be prepared to take this message to General Eisenhower?"

"It would be better if Himmler's wishes were transmitted to the Swedish government, who could then, if they were willing, transmit them to the representatives of the Western powers. But in no circumstances will I forward such a communiqué to the Swedish Minister for Foreign Affairs, Mr. Gunther, unless Himmler promises that the German forces in Norway and Denmark shall capitulate too. In any case it is most doubtful if the Western Allies will agree to capitulation on the Western front alone. But even if they should agree to it, there is no necessity for a personal meeting between Himmler and Eisenhower. Himmler need only give the order to the German supreme commander to lay down arms. And, as I have pointed out before, there is no question of Himmler's playing any part in the Germany of the future. At most, the Allies might want to use his services to carry out the surrender," Bernadotte replied.

Schellenberg understood and promised to relay the information to Himmler. That was at 3:00 P.M. Eight hours later, Hitler announced that he would give no more orders to the military. Those would come through Göring. Instead, he was contemplating taking his own life.

Only Himmler knew of the planned suicide when he met with

Schellenberg and Bernadotte later that evening, and Himmler was devastated.

It was true that Himmler had talked of taking over from Hitler. The SS had been established as a government within a government, capable of usurping the power of every Nazi agency at any time it was desired. But the innocuous little man who had so quickly risen in power had lived a life of vulnerable illusions. He had developed his own Aryan/Nazi religion. He had created his own gods, reshaping the teaching of history, genetics, and biology to fit his own racist schemes. He had narrowed his thinking and his conscience to a level where he was comfortable murdering millions, planning the deaths of millions more, resettling Aryans who did not share his dreams without realizing their hostility to his actions, and ignoring crimes greater than any previously recorded by conquering armies. He could adjust to the ultimate death of Hitler, since the death would raise his Führer to the level of a god. He could see himself as leader of the postwar Reich, carrying on as he knew the deified Hitler would want him to do. But the changes occurring in the bunker, the changes caused by the advancing armies, the encouragement of Schellenberg to go against his previous oaths were all shattering him.

Himmler could see the wisdom in following the course of action Schellenberg suggested. But to do so while Hitler was still alive was an act of insubordination he could not make. He had already compromised himself by releasing prisoners.

It was around one in the morning of April 24 that Himmler decided how to handle the crisis he was facing. He recognized that Hitler was either dead or would be so shortly, that he could act as though the Führer no longer existed. His past oath of loyalty no longer mattered. He could take control of the nation.

Bernadotte remained silent while Himmler rationalized his act of insubordination. The count saw Hitler as cowardly, afraid to take responsibility for his own actions. He had declared a war in which he presumably believed. He had led his country on a path he claimed to be right and proper. And then, when he lost, he put himself in a circumstance where death, either by his own hand or by invading troops, was inevitable. He did not have the courage to face the world. He did not have the courage to try to aid his people in defeat. He was not a leader; he was a man worthy only of contempt.

Himmler recognized his responsibility as the head of the Reich: "In the situation that has now arisen I consider my hands free. In order to save as great a part of Germany as possible from a Russian invasion I am willing to capitulate on the Western front in order to enable the

Western Allies to advance rapidly towards the east. But I am not prepared to capitulate on the Eastern front. I have always been, and I shall
always remain, a sworn enemy of bolshevism. In the beginning of the
World War, I fought tooth and nail against the Russo-German pact. Are
you willing to forward a communiqué on these lines to the Swedish
Minister for Foreign Affairs, so that he can inform the Western powers
of my proposal?"

Bernadotte explained that he did not believe capitulation on the
Western front would be allowed so long as there was fighting on the
Eastern front. He also said that he would not forward any such message to the Swedish minister unless there was a promise that Denmark
and Norway would be included in the surrender.

Himmler was comfortable with American, British, or Swedish occupation of the two Scandinavian countries, fearing only the Russian
troops. He was willing to agree to the ending of executions in
Denmark, as well as the release of Belgium's King Leopold who was a
prisoner of the Nazis.

The strategic importance of Denmark and Norway was not so evident when the German occupation was being evaluated as the Allies
would discover in the last days of the war. It was only on VE Day that
the Allies became fully aware of what danger would have awaited
them had the fighting not been halted. There were at least four hundred
thousand German soldiers in Norway, all of them well-armed, sea-
soned veterans with enough food, ammunition, and other necessities to
last them two months without resupply. A lesser number, equally experienced and well equipped, were in Denmark. They were all in good
spirits, anxious to fight, and proud, when surrendering, that they left
the countries they occupied "undefeated."

Later the Allied commanders estimated that, had the German occupation forces not left the two countries, the casualty toll would have been
much higher than anticipated. The Allies estimated that at least twenty
thousand Allied soldiers would have died in the fighting, a figure far
greater than most of the military leaders originally thought possible.

Bernadotte reached Stockholm at 9:00 P.M. the night of the twenty-
fourth, meeting immediately with the heads of the Foreign Office. He
gave his report, then summoned the prime minister for a late night
meeting to discuss the proposal. Then it was forwarded to the Allies.
President Truman sent a telegram that said (an English translation of
the Swedish translation of the original telegram):

A German offer of surrender will be accepted only if it be complete on all fronts, as regards Great Britain and the Soviet Union as

well as the United States. This condition fulfilled, the German forces on all fronts must immediately surrender to the local Allied commanders. Should resistance continue anywhere, the Allied attacks will be vigorously pressed until victory is complete.

By April 28, word of the capitulation discussion reached the world news. Folke Bernadotte's name was mentioned as the person working with Heinrich Himmler to try to arrange the German capitulation.

The initial reaction was swift and angry. Hitler was not dead, and though Himmler was going to be named the Führer's successor, his having acted behind Hitler's back was perceived as intolerable disloyalty. The enraged Hitler named Grand Admiral Karl Dönitz his successor.

It is likely that this change actually helped the Allied war effort. Dönitz was a military leader, respected by the troops. Himmler, no matter how powerful he had become, was still remembered as the meaningless little man who, as a teenager, had been laughed at by the German police, had his gun taken from him, and been sent home from the Nazi rally during which Hitler was arrested. Any capitulation Himmler arranged would probably not have been followed. Denmark and Norway might have become the last bloody battlegrounds. The war might have continued far longer than it did.

But Himmler still controlled the lives of the concentration-camp inmates. Thousands of men, women, and children could and would die if he did not agree to their release.

Himmler at first attacked Schellenberg for encouraging him to talk with the Swedes. Then he realized that some of the actions Schellenberg suggested had value despite Hitler's harsh response. He ordered Schellenberg to begin negotiating the more limited cessation of hostilities in Norway and Denmark.

Nevertheless, Himmler seemed to believe that somehow he would remain Hitler's heir. Even those Nazi leaders who disliked Himmler saw him as the logical successor. He had been the Führer's unwavering supporter, even in the disastrous confrontation with Russia. No one was certain if he would use his potential power, but the fact that he had it made them understand what they were facing and the logic of his taking the mantle.

To support Himmler's fantasies further, even during the period when Hitler no longer trusted him, Schellenberg suggested that the National Socialist name should end with the war. Instead, Himmler should head the Nationale Sammlungspartei—the Party of the National Union. This would be the transitional government that would bring together all factions under Himmler's leadership.

Curiously, even Dönitz seemed to feel that Himmler would be the likely successor. Himmler's long term, seemingly unwavering loyalty to Hitler and the Reich, made him a logical next leader. And Dönitz was enough of a politician that, had Himmler taken charge, Dönitz would have worked under his direction, not in opposition to him.

Hitler had made his final angry moves on April 28. He formalized the Dönitz succession, wrote his last will, and married Eva Braun. On May 1, Hitler was dead and Dönitz announced on the radio: "I take over the supreme command... in order to continue the struggle." He nevertheless already had plans to move toward peace.

Bernadotte did not know that Dönitz was more of a realist than his speech upon the death of Hitler would indicate. He feared that the Dönitz statements concerning carrying on the war were true. After all the work done with Himmler, there was suddenly someone else in power, someone who might prove far less willing to negotiate the release of prisoners. Yet by May 4, the fears were put to rest. Dönitz agreed to have all German forces surrender in Denmark, Holland, and northwestern Germany.

The following day Bernadotte, Schellenberg, and Eric von Post, head of the political department of the Swedish foreign office, met in Stockholm. Schellenberg, always playing to all sides, had managed to obtain credentials signed by Dönitz that enabled him to attempt to arrange for the German surrender. He wanted the Swedes to help him arrange a meeting between General Eisenhower and Count Schwerin von Krosigk, the German minister for foreign affairs. The surrender would be unconditional.

On May 7 Bernadotte received a telephone call at 10:15 A.M. He was in Stockholm, continuing to coordinate aid to both those who had been released and those he was still seeking to help. He had been working since February 16, 1945, on a constant shuttle to save those who were condemned to death, but the call was to alert him that it was over. Germany had agreed to an unconditional surrender.

It was many years before all the details could be determined. However, in the end it was estimated that Bernadotte's actions in conjunction with the behind-the-scenes pressure of Kersten, Schellenberg, and others had led Himmler to turn against Hitler. The changes resulted in the preliminary movement that ultimately led to the capitulation of German troops in Denmark and Norway. In addition, the total number of men, women, and children who were freed from concentration camps as a direct result of Bernadotte's negotiations have now been estimated to be close to thirty thousand. When these numbers are added to the estimated twenty thousand lives believed saved by Bernadotte's preventing a last-stand battle between the Allies and the

German troops in occupied Denmark, the accomplishments are all the more remarkable. Folke Bernadotte had found a skill that led to one of the greatest and least-known humanitarian actions of World War II; it was also his death warrant.

Himmler's destruction within the Reich moved more swiftly than the negotiators were aware. Dönitz remained subservient until he received the message from Hitler on April 30. Then he realized that he had to move into a full power position immediately.

First Dönitz arranged for Himmler's quarters to be surrounded by specially trained guards taken from among the crews of the U-boats. They were total loyalists and were willing to enter the barracks, either killing Himmler or taking him prisoner. However, neither action was desired by the admiral, who arranged for a personal meeting with the SS leader. Dönitz wrote later:

"I talked to Himmler alone in my room. I thought it wiser to keep my revolver hidden under a sheet of paper on my desk. I gave him the telegram to read. He grew pale. He pondered. Then he got up and congratulated me."

Dönitz said that Himmler asked if he could be second-in-command, a request the admiral rejected. He explained that the new government, if there were to be one, would have to be without politics. Sometime after 2:00 A.M. on May 1 Himmler understood that his career in the prominent hierarchy was over.

"I could not part company with him because the police were in his hands," said Dönitz. "Mark you, at the time I knew nothing about the concentration-camp atrocities and the extermination of the Jews!"

Himmler was not finished. He ordered his Werwolves commander, Hans Pruetzmann, to act as his go-between with the new Führer's headquarters. He then learned that he had been abandoned, that Hitler had left word that Goebbels and Bormann were to be high cabinet ministers. But the admiral had no intention of following Hitler's orders, a decision aided by the Goebbels family's murder/suicide.

Himmler, knowing that Dönitz had disobeyed Hitler's last request, felt that he still had a chance to fill an important position. He went frequently to the new headquarters and tried to persuade the new government that he, Himmler, should be the emissary to Eisenhower. He felt that with his SS troops, he was in the best position to handle the power struggles that might take place in Central Europe.

Dönitz dismissed him and began working on the surrender alone. Himmler finally realized that his days in power were over, his life was not. On May 5, he gathered his brother, Gebhardt and his friends, explaining that he had one more task to undertake in the career that had been such a burden for him. It was an emotional moment, but only for Himmler. To the others present, it was just another in a series of histrionic performances typical of the way he had always lived.

The following morning, Himmler disappeared in a manner he had planned for months. He shaved off his mustache, adopted a black eye-patch, put on the uniform of a rural policeman, someone he felt would have no connection with the Nazi higher-ups, and took false credentials. Then he emerged on the occupied streets as Heinrich Hitzinger, a simple German worker.

In hindsight it is easy to see how foolish Himmler was. This little man's appearance was so harmless that he easily could have walked the streets unmolested in civilian clothes, his mustache removed, the eyepatch in place. He could have taken an identity that did not use the same first name and the same last initial as his real name. He could have joined the refugees, then blended into the countryside, perhaps returning to the land, living out his life as a farmer.

But Heinrich Himmler had to follow too many patterns. He did not try to see his wife, but he could not wait to be with his mistress and their two sons. He stayed with her, hiding out in her apartment, until he thought it might be safe to move south.

Finally Heinrich "Hitzinger" made his move. He traveled to the Bremervorde British Army checkpoint where the two sentries went through the motions of checking everyone's papers. Had he been in civilian clothes he would have passed through. But the men were under orders to detain all Germans in uniform. The sentries knew that a rural policeman was not important, but they took his identity card and ordered him to come with them. It was not a serious matter and no one expected a spontaneous confession.

"It's no use," declared "Hitzinger." He spoke no English and was certain that the brilliant British sentries had seen through his disguise. He was sure he was being arrested. He knew his life was over. "I am Heinrich Himmler." His voice was almost a whisper.

The sentries were amazed. They immediately notified their superiors, holding Himmler until higher officials could arrive. Himmler was ordered to remove his clothing for a search. Then they suggested that he put on a British uniform.

The British wanted Himmler to feel comfortable. They removed his clothing because they feared he might have hidden weapons or poison capsules secreted in the fabric. The offer of the British uniform, the only other available clothing, was made out of respect. They were letting Himmler maintain his dignity in captivity.

Himmler, terrified, his imagination racing, "knew" that he was being offered the army uniform so they could claim he had tried to fake being British and escape. He would put it on and they would shoot him on the spot. It was what he would have done in their place and he could see no reason why they would not kill him. He insisted upon staying naked, though the British gave him a blanket to wrap around his body.

Himmler was transported to Luneburg, where a sergeant-major named Austin took him to a room that was being used for the processing of the Nazi leaders in the area. Certain that torture and death were imminent, Himmler took a cyanide capsule he had concealed in his mouth when he stripped off his uniform.

His British captors grabbed Himmler when they heard the crunch of the poison capsule. The lifted him by his legs, striking his back and stomach, trying to make him vomit the poison, but cyanide works too quickly. His body had absorbed a lethal dose and death came within minutes.

Himmler died on May 23, 1945. Despite his self-image, the man was not considered important enough in death to have his body treated with respect. The Allies left him in the room, covered with a blanket, the corpse slowly rotting for the next two days. Then Gebhard Himmler was located, notified of the death, and brought to the room to make the formal identification. After that, Austin reported: "I wrapped him up in a couple of blankets. Then I put two of our Army camouflage nets around him and tied him up with telephone wires. I had to dig his grave myself. Nobody will ever know where he is buried."

PART VI

Retribution of the Damned

CHAPTER 13

War's Immediate Aftermath

FOLKE BERNADOTTE EMERGED from World War II with the world unaware of his heroism. He wrote a small memoir of his experiences negotiating with Himmler, *The Curtain Falls*, that instantly became a major best-seller throughout Sweden. Yet he was little known and even less understood outside his own country.

The changes to which the world had to adjust in the weeks and months immediately following the surrender of the Axis powers were greater and more varied than anyone could have anticipated. First there was the matter of vengeance and justice. The leaders of the Axis powers had to be brought to trial, their actions investigated, their crimes exposed. Some would pay with their lives, others were sentenced to jail terms of various lengths. But while the investigations were taking place, the world was being exposed to the previously hidden horrors of the damned. For the first time, everyone who read a newspaper or magazine, listened to the radio, or watched the newsreels learned of mass starvation, tortures, and the gas ovens. The atrocities that had taken place were detailed, the survivors photographed and interviewed. The men and women who had delighted in their power were being shown to have been sadists beyond comprehension.

Jewish groups throughout the world who had understood the Holocaust only in the most general sense were horrified by the census figures that were being revealed. Poland had 3,300,000 Jews when Hitler took control—only 300,000 of them survived the war. Germany and Austria had 253,000 Jews before Hitler; 228,000 of them perished. Slovakia lost 75,000 of the 90,000 prewar Jews; Greece 54,000 out of an original population of 70,000. There were 900,000 dead in the Ukraine (1,500,000 prewar); half of all the Jews in Romania and Norway were murdered, and one in four in France. In all, 5,993,900 Jews were slaughtered out of a European population of 8,861,800. And these numbers reflected perhaps only half the people of all backgrounds who were deliberately murdered throughout the war under the orders of Hitler.

It was simplistic to think that the trials of the Nazi leaders, the camps set aside for the captured Axis soldiers, and the other routine measures of postwar rehabilitation would enable the world to return to normal. Nothing was the same after World War II, not for anyone, but especially not for the survivors of the camps.

Survival left most of those who had been concentration-camp inmates with many problems to face. Some experienced guilt for living when others close to them had died. Others felt that God must have destined them to do something special, to achieve a unique greatness. Yet the truth seemed to be that they had been lucky, nothing more. They were ordinary men and women who had managed to triumph against people who wanted them dead.

There were also feelings of guilt from actions they had taken while in the camps. Some had to face the fact that they had stolen food from someone else in order to stay alive. Others agreed to have sex with their captors, outwardly expressing pleasure, inwardly feeling raped, in order to avoid the lines for the crematorium. Still others had compromised themselves in a hundred different ways because the human mind is programmed for survival against all odds, yet trains itself in moral and ethical ways that belie this inherent instinct.

On a larger scale, there was shock at what was encountered when they left the camps. Many of the former prisoners expected to go home to the land where they were raised, perhaps where their families had lived, and loved, and worked for generations.

Sometimes homes were destroyed, bombed, or burned so that mostly rubble remained. The loss created sadness, but it was acceptable. The home had been as much of a victim as the survivor.

But other homes were intact and occupied by Germans who had either been Nazis, Nazi sympathizers, or opportunists who had taken advantage of the misfortunes of others. They could not see the indecency in remaining where they were, in insisting that the Jewish former owner had no right to the structure.

More shocking was seeing one's fine clothing worn by someone else. Many of the survivors tell of going back to their hometowns, to familiar streets, and seeing strangers wearing clothing left behind when they were arrested months or years earlier. The impact was one of physical violation, the instant knowledge that a stranger had obtained intimate knowledge of one's life and possessions. It was yet another horror they encountered outside the time they had spent in the concentration camps.

Eastern Europe, once beloved, was no longer home for many of the survivors. They were often unwanted, the anti-Semitism of the war lingering after the Nazi surrender. But always they were strangers in a familiar land, perhaps the greatest isolation anyone can endure.

For thousands of Jews who survived the camps, the answer was to turn inward to religion, beliefs, spiritual roots. They were a people who accepted what some said was the wrath of God, what others said was the suffering man always endures when challenging God's will. They turned to the Bible and the Old Testament stories of the Promised Land. Their hearts and minds turned to Palestine, to the Jewish state, to a place where they could be safe, free, and—above all—wanted. What they did not expect was to learn that the British mandate against immigration to Palestine was still in effect. The same people who had been a part of their salvation seemed determined to doom them to a life in a world at once familiar and beyond comprehension.

CHAPTER 14

The Battle for Israel

THE PALESTINIAN JEWS were shocked by the cavalier treatment they received from the British immediately following the war. The Jews had been loyal allies, many of them serving in the armed forces, all of them supporting the fight against Germany. The Arabs, by contrast, had, as a general rule, done nothing or been openly pro-Nazi despite the British having maintained immigration restrictions on the Jews during the war. While there were many individual exceptions, the truth was that the British were generally able to rely upon only the Jews, especially for dangerous spy and sabotage missions.

At war's end there were one hundred thousand Jews languishing in Displaced Persons Camps throughout Europe, Jews the British were asked to allow to enter Palestine as early as September, 1945. Yet the British refused.

The British followed the reasoning of Foreign Secretary Ernest Bevin who believed that there were still strategic needs in the Middle East that were more important than the Zionist movement. He wanted to see a united Arab State that was either a part of or dominated by Transjordan, which was controlled by the British. The Jews would be given internal autonomy, and there were be sections of Palestine split among several Arab countries. This view went directly against Prime Minister Clement Attlee's public statement that the Jews should have a "national home" that included Transjordan. However, Attlee and/or his advisers quickly disengaged from that idea, preferring to let Transjordan dominate the Jews.

The insensitivity to the Jews in the Displaced Persons Camps could be excused based on the fact that the British were faced with many postwar crises of greater urgency. Many of the rescue and relief workers in Eastern Europe understood only the need to help the concentration camp victims stay alive. The former inmates were frequently emaciated, their bodies ravaged by prolonged starvation, their minds unclear, their emotions shattered by the horrors they had witnessed. Many of the people had to relearn how to eat. They lacked any quantity of solid food for so long that they were no longer able to digest what, before they were taken prisoner, would have been a normal meal. Ways had to be found to help them recover or they would die.

There was also a need for clothing, for shelter, for letting people try to cope with the horrors by telling the stories of what they had seen and experienced. There were thoughts of educating children who had been denied schooling, of helping men and women who had come of age in captivity find training and employment, of bringing psychological peace to the elderly. There were so many obvious, immediate problems that few of the rescue workers thought about the importance of transferring the Jews to an area where they would feel safe, wanted, unafraid of the future.

The Arabs also had their concerns. There were those among them whose hatred was based solely on race and religion, but these bigots were in the minority and for the most part the Arabs had legitimate economic concerns. They were poor people, hard-working, barely able to eke out a living. The idea that more people would enter their country, take the land, require food and shelter that would make life more difficult for those already there, upset them. Their hostility sprang from a fear for their own survival rather than a hatred toward the immigrants. If they could only be certain of their own prosperity in the midst of the instantly rising population, the majority would not have objected so strenuously, if at all.

And there were the Palestinian Jews who not only hated the British as an occupying force, but who recognized how many Jews had died for want of a place to go. Numerous countries of the world had been insensitive to the need of Jews to emigrate as Hitler moved through Eastern Europe. But most of the Jews of Palestine felt that their land was where the Diaspora belonged. It mattered that quotas in the United States and elsewhere had cost probably thousands of lives, but not so much as the fact that Palestine, the area of their ancestors, the land promised by God, the land where they were wanted, could not be a receiving center. The British, they felt, had no right to make restrictions that prevented what they saw as the fulfillment of God's holy word.

Had these viewpoints been understood, arrangements could have been made that would have reduced the tensions. But each side saw only a narrow aspect of what was taking place. Each side felt that its interests took precedent over everything else because they did not understand all the viewpoints affecting everyone's concerns. And the result was growing turmoil in the Middle East.

Britain's Clement Attlee and the Labour government had claimed that they would disavow the white paper Chamberlain had created to keep Jews from migrating to Palestine. But Attlee felt that the Arabs should not have their wishes challenged to such a degree. He needed to appease them and saw no reason why there was any concern about doing otherwise. After all, the Eastern European Jews who survived the Holocaust were safe. There was no mass extermination movement. Attlee felt that they did not need to come to Palestine.

Attlee's unrealistic, insensitive attitude united the Palestinian Jews. Where once there had been factions among them, now they were facing the common cause of bringing as many refugees as possible to Palestine. They began planning the shipment of refugees on as many oceangoing vessels as they could obtain. They also found that they could use the southern Italian coast, 2,500 miles away, as a point from which refugee runs could be made.

The first of the refugees, thirty-five Jews, slipped on board a fishing boat called the *Dalin* in August 1945. No one questioned where it was heading, and no one connected with the British saw it arrive. The voyage was successful and Palestine gained the first of the illicit refugees from the concentration camps.

Other runs followed, one of the largest fishing boats, the *Petro*, making several trips with 170 refugees each time. However, the British soon learned that there was something not quite right with the fishing vessels appearing in the water. The Mossad realized that it would only be a matter of time before such boats were routinely stopped. People might get hurt, and even if they didn't, the Jews would be turned back, their efforts a failure.

Other parts of the world were used for transporting Jews after the success of the Italian launches. A Greek boat designed for forty passengers was converted so that two hundred could travel at once. The vessel, called *Berl Katzenelson*, was equipped with rowboats for silently bringing Jews to shore in Palestine. The concept proved most successful when the British intercepted the vessel. They were able to stop only eleven rowboats filled with Jews, a small fraction of those who had made the trip.

The British took the Jews they had captured to internment camps. The Haganah was able to infiltrate the camps, then sneak out most of the Jews who had been taken from the rowboats. Even the Greek crews could not be stopped. After the British sent them and their vessel back to their native land, they simply took on more Jews and returned to Palestine.

Perhaps the most dramatic of these early confrontations between the British and vessels laden with fleeing Jews came in April 1946. The British had blockaded the Palestinian waters to stop the refugee runs. They were watching for smaller vessels, but what they would soon confront was the chartered ship *Fede* with more than a thousand Jewish refugees on board.

The *Fede's* charter was a ruse made with the cooperation of the Italian authorities. It was officially licensed to carry a load of salt from La Spezia, on the Italian Riviera, to Sardinia. However, several Italian officials knew its real purpose and ignored the seemingly endless truckloads of people being brought to the docks.

Not all the Italian officials were aware of what was happening, though. There was political unrest in Spain, and a few of the Italian guards working at the docks suddenly thought they were witnessing what could be an international incident they dared not allow. The people had to be Polish fascists, the guards, unfamiliar with the Jewish struggle to reach Palestine, reasoned. They thought fascists were taking the *Fede* to Franco's Spain.

The guards quickly stopped the people gathered on the docks, then were told not only who the refugees were, but what they had experienced. Despite the Italians having sided with Hitler, there was not the hatred between the Italians and the Jews that there had been with the Germans. The guards were deeply moved and immediately helped the people board the vessel.

The delay cost the refugees their chance for subterfuge. British gunboats raced to the port and stopped the ship from sailing. The refugees were ordered to immediately leave the boat or be forcibly removed by the armed soldiers.

Yehuda Arazi was the Jewish organizer of the *Fede* expedition. He was both an experienced soldier and had an understanding of the effective use of the media.

First he stopped the British boarding by claiming that the ship was filled with explosives—a claim that was probably a lie, since the Jews were concerned with using every available space to transport more survivors. He said that if the British came on the ship, the explosives would be used to sink the ship, killing everyone on board. The impression was that the people felt that they had nothing to lose, that they would rather die than be forced to give up their hope of Palestine.

Then Arazi went to the media. He first sent messages to the three leaders of the Allied powers—Harry Truman, Joseph Stalin, and Clement Attlee. Then he encouraged reporters to come to the docks. He explained that the people on board were the survivors of the death camps. He stressed their past suffering, their close call with death, the hope they felt when it came to building new lives in Palestine.

Quickly the Italian docks became a sightseeing attraction as well. Hundreds of locals turned out each day to watch the drama and listen to the speeches. The British troops had to be moved away from the docks for fear of pro-Jewish riots.

The propaganda efforts increased. The port was decorated with Italian and Zionist flags, and a sign reading THE GATE OF ZION. Arazi created immigration certificates that had quotes from the Balfour Declaration of 1917, the 1920 world affirmation concerning the need for and right to a Jewish homeland, and passages from the Bible.

The Jewish leadership in Palestine was approached for a reaction to the events taking place in La Spezia. They had to be extremely cautious, distancing themselves from Arazi and his actions. They stressed sympathy for what the refugees were going through, but they did not condemn the British, nor did they claim to be a part of what was taking place. They knew that to admit their support, and it was unlimited, would be to invite harsh British sanctions. Arazi had to be viewed as a well-intentioned rogue.

The Italians strongly supported Arazi, though because they had lost the war and were viewed with hostility by the British, they restricted their support to private meetings, condemning him in public. They also allowed him to make his next move, one calculated to force action on one side or the other. Arazi ordered a hunger strike.

No one is certain what happened next. In theory, the passengers stopped eating. Arazi posted an hourly chart showing how many hours the people had fasted and how many were losing consciousness as a result. On the third day, many of the people were being carried unconscious onto the deck so that they could be seen. Arazi stressed that all of them would rather die than return to a Europe where their loved ones had been murdered. Perhaps it was a ruse; perhaps the emotions were that intense. All that is known is that, on the fourth day, Arazi announced that not only would the hunger strike continue, the next morning ten volunteers would commit suicide on the deck of the ship. Ten more would kill themselves every twenty-four hours until the ship was either allowed to leave for Palestine or it became a floating coffin.

The suicide threat proved overwhelming for the British. There was no way to call Arazi's bluff, if that was what it was, without risking riots from the local sympathizers. And if the people were serious, the public opinion against the British would be devastating.

On May 8 the British capitulated. Everyone could travel to Palestine, and their admission to the country would not affect the existing quotas concerning immigration. A second ship was brought to the harbor, the people divided between the vessels to ensure more comfortable travel.

The British recognized that there was more to the *Fede* issue than the lives of a thousand Jews. It could easily start a precedent for extorting greater immigration into Palestine than they wanted to allow. They had to find a way to show that the British rules concerning migration to Palestine would be enforced at all cost in the future.

The confrontation came in July 1947 with the ship *Exodus*, the one vessel whose human cargo was capable of generating international sympathy. The incident united the Palestinian Jewish leaders so forcefully against Britain that anyone in any way connected with the British was the object of intense, deadly hatred.

The problem began with more than four thousand former concentration-camp inmates who had been living in German displaced-persons camps. They were given visas to go to various South American countries, a pretext to get out of the country. The visas were forged, a fact no one in authority knew, nor would it have mattered. Any problem with the visas would have been a matter for the South American countries, no one else.

The refugees traveled to Sete, France, where they boarded the ship *Exodus*. From there they traveled to Palestine, not South America. Too large to run the blockade, the ship was boarded and the Jews forced to transfer to three British transport ships. Then they returned to Sete, where the French said they would not accept anyone unless the people left of their own free will. They were sympathetic to the plight of the Jews and were not about to allow the British to force them to act in a manner in which they did not believe.

Only 130 of the more than four thousand Jews left the British transports voluntarily. These were elderly, sick, or pregnant, too tired or too ill to continue the fight. The women wanted to give birth where they were assured of proper care. The others simply could not keep fighting. But the vast majority stayed on board, forcing the British to take other action.

The insensitivity of the British government seemed beyond comprehension by then. It was decided to order the ships to Hamburg, where the passengers would be held in the only existing facilities large enough to control so many people: former Nazi concentration camps. Jews who had survived the death camps were going to be returned to them. They would have decent beds, clothing, and food. They would have proper medical care. Everything possible would be done to keep them healthy and happy. Everything except recognizing that the psychological shock would overwhelm even the emotionally strongest among them.

Two of the three transport ships unloaded without incident. The passengers felt hopeless and agreed to go along with whatever took place. The people on the third transport were not so docile. They had been through too much to back down. They refused to leave the ship, and the British had to use force against them.

By the time the British acted the docks were filled with German civilians curious about the refugees. They watched in amazement as the British carried and dragged the Jews from the boat. Many of the Jews were beaten with clubs and rubber hoses. Blood seemed to flow everywhere. Some of the passengers had bones broken.

Winston Churchill was both horrified by the event and delighted that he had an issue to use against the opposition party. He proclaimed that the incident was "the Labour Government's war with the Jews," words not far from the truth. The soldiers were applauded by some of the Labour party politicians.

The fate of the refugees was not so horrible as might be supposed. Within a month they were taken to the British Zone of Germany and housed in the Poppendorf and Amstau displaced persons' camps. Then an active movement to smuggle them into the American Zone began in earnest. Most had fled by November. All were successfully smuggled from the camps and taken to Palestine by September 1948.

The *Exodus* incident united all factions in Palestine against the British. The previously passive moderates now shared a cause with the militant extremists of LEHI and the Irgun. There would be freedom from British rule and independence for a Jewish state or the people would die in the effort. There was no more room for compromise, negotiations, or anything else. The British had proved their insensitivity and brutality. There was no turning back.

As fall 1947 approached, the Palestinian Jews decided that the best way to confront the British was to overwhelm them. The small-boat runs had worked well for a while. The attempt to bring large numbers of refugees, as on the *Exodus*, had met with failure. But the larger boats gained press attention and forced the British to utilize more of their resources. It was decided by Irgun and others to purchase two truly large ships (forty-five hundred tons each) and confront the British with overwhelming numbers of people seeking a new life in Palestine.

The *Pan Crescent* and the *Pan York* were capable of taking a total of 15,169 people to Palestine. The numbers, as large as the population of many small cities, would expose both the severity of the problem and the insensitivity of the British. At best, the people would break through the blockade. At worst, the size of the ships and the effort to which the British would have to go to stop such large numbers of people would assure extensive press coverage.

The British understood what was happening and tried to forestall any incident that might occur. Saboteurs were sent to damage or sink the *Pan Crescent* before it could be loaded with passengers. The effort was not successful, though, as the ship was repaired in Venice, where it had docked.

The ships eventually made their way to Constanta, a Romanian port, where they were followed by British destroyers. A Russian gunboat acted as the guide, and the British took advantage of that fact to spread the rumor that the Jews were actually Communists looking to somehow take over Palestine. They said that they did not want to compromise the Arabs by allowing such a migration.

No one at the time realized just how many conflicts the fifteen thousand refugees had created. The United Nations had been established following the war and was debating the issue of a divided Palestine that would allow for a Jewish state. It was felt that if the refugees suddenly appeared, it might force conflicts that would cause the United Nations members to vote against the Jewish state.

David Ben-Gurion recognized that the issue was so volatile it might be best to delay the sending of the Jews from Romania. Likewise, Anna Pauker, a Jew who was Romanian foreign minister, was against the Zionist movement but even more hostile to the British. She wanted to encourage the ships to sail as a way to act against the British. And the captains of the ships, aware of what their 15,169 passengers had endured at the hands of the Nazis, decided that they wanted the people to at last live without fear. They vowed that they would sail, no matter what might happen, because they felt the people deserved freedom.

In September 1947 the ships moved out of the harbor, passing through Turkish waters without interference. They passed into the Mediterranean, where the British no longer dared stop them. The ships would continue until they reached the blockade.

Negotiations were intense throughout the sailing. Everyone wanted to avoid a violent confrontation and both sides needed to save face. Ultimately there was a compromise that allowed the ships to have the refugees debark at Famagusta in Cyprus. They would then travel from there to Palestine when it was appropriate under the immigration policy. The refugees were safe, away from the area that had caused so much pain, and in line for "legal" immigration.

Britain was desperate for a way out of the bind it was in. The British public was not pleased with the use of troops for handling the Palestine immigration problem. The image of refugees not being allowed a place to feel safe affected the British image in the world. And the cost of the naval blockade could not truly be justified. Fortunately, in November 1947, the United Nations agreed to the division of Palestine. The British mandate would end in May 1948.

The Truman administration in America also was a major force in the change, seemingly a radical departure from his predecessor's administration. The role of Franklin Roosevelt in regards to European Jews has been a controversial one. He was long known to be a political pragmatist when it came to American minorities, and pragmatism on the issues of anti-Semitism and anti-Zionism may have been motivating factors in his decision to limit the help provided to European Jews. One Jewish refugee-laden ship was denied the right to have its passengers stay in America during the war, for example, and those passengers ultimately returned to Germany with its concentration camps. However, in the case of the ship, its passengers were refused asylum at several ports, not just the United States.

Additional allegations relate to the refusal to make tactical strikes in areas that would have slowed or temporarily stopped the mass murders in the death camps. Yet historians are still trying to determine how much Roosevelt was a pragmatist when facing many of the humanitarian issues of World War II, and how much there may have been personal bias.

But Harry Truman, who took office upon Roosevelt's death, had a different attitude. Sympathetic to the concentration-camp survivors, he opened the American zones throughout occupied Europe so that the refugees could move freely. He also arranged for the people to be sheltered rather than treated as prisoners forced to live under harsh conditions in the displaced-persons camps. He worked behind the scenes, with his assistant David K. Niles, to force the British to allow the Jews into Palestine, and he was a supporter of an independent Jewish state.

The Truman support was coming at a time when pressures were mounting on all sides. The members of Haganah were involved with terrorist activities within Palestine. On June 18, 1946, for example,

Haganah attacked several structures in Haifa and blew up nine bridges. The British arrested three thousand Palestinian Jews in reprisal, placed a curfew on Jerusalem, and created a split between the moderates and conservatives in the British Parliament.

The violence escalated quickly. On July 22, 1946, Irgun terrorists bombed the King David Hotel in Jerusalem, an important British headquarters facility where the leading British officers and their staffs had their quarters. The attack was meant to show the British that no place was safe, no place was welcome. Yet the bombing of such a structure took many lives—British, Arab, and Jewish. Ninety-one died in all; another forty were injured. A warning had been sent to the hotel thirty minutes before the explosion, though in the aftermath no one was certain whether it was taken as a hoax or simply not conveyed by the person receiving it. In any case, the bombing was condemned by many of the Jews who had previously shifted their support to the Irgun. It was the type of structure where there was too great a risk of killing innocents for it to be considered a proper terrorist target.

The attack on the hotel had been approved by Haganah—including David Ben-Gurion, a somewhat moderate voice among the leaders of the revolt against Britain. However, when excessive bloodshed resulted from that attack, Ben-Gurion tried to distance himself from the militants.

The reprisals had also revealed the anti-Semitism of Sir Evelyn Barker, commanding officer of British troops in Palestine. A curfew was imposed with orders to shoot any violators. None of the British would be allowed to patronize Jewish-owned businesses. "We will punish the Jews in a way the race dislikes as much as any, by striking at their pockets and showing our contempt for them," he wrote.

Surprisingly, the attack solidified other nations. President Truman chose the eve of the holy night of Yom Kippur, October 4, to declare that he could see that a peaceful settlement of the British occupation could not be achieved. There would have to be a partition of Palestine:

> The Jewish Agency proposed a solution of the Palestine problem by means of the creation of a viable Jewish state in control of its own immigration and economic policies in an adequate area of Palestine instead of in the whole of Palestine. It proposed furthermore the immediate issuance of certificates for 100,000 Jewish immigrants.... From the discussion which has ensued, it is my belief that a solution along these lines would command the support of public opinion in the United States.

The Truman statement seemed a mandate that supported the efforts to transport the refugees to Palestine. However, much of the opposition resulted from Britain's Labour party leader, Ernest Bevin, a man who believed in an international Jewish conspiracy.

The Nazis had been the most blatant anti-Semites in the twentieth century, but many people were touched by their propaganda. Rather than looking at the total extremism, the rantings of men like Himmler who were trying to establish their own religion, they focused on certain lies and decided that they might be truths.

For example, one of the myths created by the Nazis was the idea of a worldwide Jewish conspiracy, and a number of books, both fiction and warped "nonfiction," discussed the "Protocols of the Elders of Zion." The "Protocols" was a forgery that was supposed to be the text for a plot by Jews for world domination. Although internationally discredited, it has been reprinted by hate groups for more than half a century.

It was the belief of such bigots that the Jews of the world had organized an international conspiracy against both Britain and Bevin. "The whole Jewish pressure was a gigantic racket run from America," Bevin claimed.

The Labour party leader was unable to see world events the way anyone else might see them. He was convinced that any time there was an outcry against British excesses in Palestine, the outcry was meant to make him look bad. There was nothing the British might do that was wrong, no matter how extreme. He focused only on the Jews, never on the British actions. Ultimately he claimed that the Nazis had probably learned their greatest excesses by studying the actions of the Jews.

The UN committee working on the issue of the Jewish state had several concerns. There were 1.2 million Arabs and 568,000 Jews in Palestine at the time it was considering what action to take. There were other Jews waiting to enter who had been prevented under the British rules, but these were not a factor. The UN felt that Jerusalem should be placed under a United Nations trusteeship. Then a Jewish state would be established from 55 percent of the land. Its population would be 42 percent Arab and 58 percent Jewish. The Arab state would be just 1 percent Jewish and 99 percent Arab, and it would consist of 45 percent of the land. Arab and Jewish militias would keep order during the transition, while a five-nation United Nations Palestine Commission would handle the partition, taking over the administration of Palestine from the British.

International pressure was rapidly building against the British. By November 29, 1947, the United Nations agreed to the establishment of independent Jewish and Arab states in Palestine. Israel would become a reality.

Among those who rejoiced the most were the scholars who had spent time in the Egyptian Museum in Cairo. Three thousand years earlier Pharaoh Mnepthah had written on a parchment that was a part of the museum's collection "Israel is no more." The failure of those words so many centuries later was a cause for celebration.

༄

There were many reasons for the ensuing violence. The fate of the Middle East, the reinvolvement in international diplomacy of Folke Bernadotte, the actions by and against the British were all linked by many problems.

The first concern was economic. It is too simplistic to discuss racial and religious hatred as the key to the hostility between Arab and Jew. There were too many periods of peaceful coexistence, too many years when there was relative harmony, the enemy being the British occupying force.

The Middle East is a desert, a fragile land with limited water, limited resources. Survival depends upon effective utilization of that portion of the land that can support life. The type of food that can be eaten, the type of businesses that can succeed, the type of life-style someone can achieve—all must be in harmony with the surroundings.

Life in a desert is always one of hardships. There are always limitations, if only in the necessity to be near water. Yet so long as the Arabs and the Jews equally shared these hardships, there was harmony. Only when one side or the other achieved a visibly better standard of living was there hostility. When everything was the same, there tended to be a live-and-let-live attitude, any other prejudice seemingly unimportant.

The division of Palestine presented an economic concern for all involved. Could each nation be economically independent? Would it be possible to farm adequate food? Would there be adequate water and mineral resources? Would there be true independence, or would one side have the riches and the other side be dependent upon imports? The economics of the division was crucial.

There were secondary but extremely important additional concerns. One was religious. Most Western religions view Jerusalem as a holy city. Muslims, Jews, Christians, and others all see Jerusalem as essential to their faith. It was the cradle of man's spiritual development, and the idea that only one faith might dominate that land created great concerns.

Another fear was strategic. The Jews were a paranoid people because one nation or another had been trying to destroy them for thousands of years. The Old Testament is filled with stories about efforts to eliminate the Jews. The Holocaust had just revealed Hitler's effort to eliminate all the Jews in the world. The extremist Arab leaders had attempted to destroy the Jews. Threats were a part of their existence and a strong defense was a part of their survival. Thus it became important for them to achieve a nation on land where they could retain strategic high points from which they could best defend themselves.

Yet some Arabs also felt threatened. Were the Jews expansionist? Were they bringing more Jews from Europe in order to expand their land holdings? Would it be necessary to enter into a defensive war from which those same heights would be important?

So many questions. So many fears. And so much violence had occurred so recently that it was impossible to allay any of the concerns for any of the parties involved.

The greatest problem was actually the issue of Zionism. The idea of an independent Jewish state was frightening and offensive in the Middle East, but the Jews themselves had often been accepted and prosperous. In fact, even after the idea of Zionism was a serious goal, there was some support. At one point, for example, King Ibn Saud seriously considered selling Palestine to the Jews for twenty-million British pounds. The money would be used by Saudi Arabia to resettle the Arabs currently living on the land.

Even near the end of the period before the United Nations mandate, talks with the Arabs were far friendlier than other events would indicate. For example, on November 27, 1947, Transjordan's King Abdullah met with Mrs. Golda Myerson, a Russian-born woman who moved to Milwaukee, Wisconsin, with her family, became a schoolteacher and librarian, and moved to Palestine in the 1920s. She had become a leader of the Palestinians and would eventually become Israel's prime minister, using the name Golda Meir.

The king said: "During the last thirty years, you have grown and strengthened yourselves. Your achievements are many. We cannot disregard you and we must compromise with you. There is no quarrel between you and the Arabs. The quarrel is between the Arabs and the British, who brought you to Palestine; and between you and the British, who have not kept their promises to you.

"Now, I am convinced that the British are leaving, and we will be left face to face. Any confrontation between us will be to our own disadvantage. I will agree to a partition that will not shame me before the Arab world. I would like to take this opportunity of suggesting that you consider the possibility of a future independent Hebrew Republic within a Transjordan State that would include both banks of the Jordan, and in which the economy, the military, and the legislature would be divided equally."

The Hebrew Republic would be a part of the Transjordanian monarchy. However, Golda Meir explained that she was concerned with what would happen after the UN action. She did agree, though, that she would be pleased with the idea of the Arab section of Palestine being controlled by Transjordan. However, it was clear that the king wanted to annex the land, not let it be an independent Arab state.

Thus there were mixed feelings about what was taking place. Yet still there were the mobs, and mob violence would affect the area even after the UN resolution of the matter.

The result of all this was a demonstration on December 2, 1947, by Arabs in the heart of Jerusalem's New City. The demonstration began peacefully enough, as a protest against the partition of Palestine by the United Nations. The Arabs thought that a peaceful three-day protest strike would call attention to their plight. The British police were present and there seemed no reason to be overly concerned.

The emotions of a mob are always unpredictable, and extremist Arabs as far back as the 1930s had always chosen to take advantage of demonstrations they might turn into violent attacks against the Jews. This one proved no exception. An Arab youth smashed the storefront window of a Jewish business. Then more glass was broken and products on display were grabbed. Someone else tossed gasoline into a building, then set it on fire. And quickly there was a frenzy of smashing, looting, and burning, all in the presence of uniformed British police.

Richard Graves, the British mayor of Jerusalem, learned quickly how much power he had. He insisted that the police stop the violence, only to be told that it would not be done. The police were under orders not to interfere with the mobs unless there were reinforcements, and there would be no reinforcements. Even worse from Graves' perspective was the fact that the mob could easily have been dispersed when the violence began.

Lieutenant General Sir Alan Cunningham, the High Commissioner for Palestine, also tried to get the British police to act. In addition, he contacted the Arab leaders and requested their help. But no one would get involved. They all felt that this was just retribution against the Jewish terrorists who had been fighting for a Jewish state. The fact that the violence was against peaceful merchants and other innocents was ignored.

What happened next has already been frequently retold. The people of Israel had been preparing for the day when the British would leave since immediately after the war. Jewish leaders in various countries of the world, especially the United States, had been approached by officials from the Jewish population of Palestine. They had been asked for assistance, both with raising money and smuggling weapons to Palestine. It was clear not only that there would be a war, but also that the Jews might be destroyed if they were not prepared for intense violence.

The Arab states were arming for an all-out attack on the proposed Jewish state. Much of the violence would come from within Palestine, where three thousand Arab volunteers were to be recruited for training as a military force. The Arab states were trying to obtain light arms, including ten thousand rifles, for distribution to the volunteers and others.

There were plans for guerrilla attacks against the Jews, attacks not all the Arab leaders supported. Guerrilla operations seemed destined for failure. The land and the people were such that the attacks would most likely be used as an excuse for both massive retaliation and the stealing of land not provided Jews under the mandate.

There was also fighting among the Arabs. King Abdullah wanted to take control of some of the Arab land, as he had made clear to Golda Meir. Other Arab leaders had their own designs. While there was a massive organized force, the leadership was divided.

Beginning January 10, 1948, troops of the Arab Legion crossed into Palestine, preparing for violence. Eleven days later, after the British occupying forces made it clear that they would not drive out the Arabs unless things somehow got out of hand, the Arab Liberation Army sent in armed soldiers. There were forty thousand British soldiers in Palestine, but the British leaders explained that they were supposed to be withdrawing from that country. They could not act as a buffer between Arabs and Jews and still retreat. They simply had to ignore what was taking place.

The violence began in earnest on February 4. The Arab Liberation Army attacked a group of Irish guards, claiming that they had mistaken them for Jews. Then, on February 16, the kibbutz of Tirat Zvi was attacked by Arab forces. This time a platoon of British soldiers, heavily armed, was sent to the area, though after the fact.

The outcome was obvious from the kibbutz attack, though. The Jews realized that everyone had to go to extraordinary measures in order to survive. What would have been unusual heroic action in wartime, became the norm for the defenders. They fought well and hard, knowing that their lives and the lives of their loved ones depended upon beating the attacking Arabs. When the battle was over, forty Arabs were dead, their forces in retreat, and only one Jew had died in the conflict. However, the Arab leader put out word that three hundred Jews had died and the Arabs had experienced a major victory.

Day after day the violence continued in one form or another, by one side or the other. There were guerrilla attacks, bombings, snipings, and massed conflicts. The Jews had not had a history of being soldiers for hundreds of years. The Arabs saw themselves as fierce, well-trained, experienced fighters. Yet they often lost their encounters. And even when they won, they usually succeeded because of surprise, still facing greater opposition than they had thought possible.

Weapons smuggling took place steadily. All manner of boats were obtained for the operation, most of the guns being brought from the United States.

At the same time, the Haganah decided to take advantage of the departing British soldiers. The Haganah sought out as many dishonest soldiers as they could find, arranging for the soldiers to steal arms from the British warehouses, paying them well for their efforts. In addition, men who had fallen in love with Jewish girls were also enlisted in the effort to obtain weapons. A few were persuaded to join the Jews, deserting the British army.

Other British soldiers were frustrated by a lack of job opportunities in their native land. They thought of emigrating elsewhere and were quite willing to assist with obtaining gasoline, trucks, and other supplies. A few, from Ireland, felt themselves an oppressed minority within the British system. They felt a kinship to the Jewish struggle, especially since the violence was no longer aimed at them.

By April 3 the Jewish forces were attacking Arab settlements. They selected those areas of strategic importance, placing themselves in a position to win any battle that might soon arise. Houses were destroyed, trenches dug, and ongoing attacks and counterattacks became routine. The British were also in the midst of the fighting, though on May 13, 1948, they finally withdrew from Palestine.

The Jewish situation was mixed. The Arabs had military forces totaling twenty-three thousand from a population of forty million. These were divided among Egyptians, who supplied the most troops, Transjordanians, Syrians, Iraqis, Lebanese, Arab Liberation Army forces, and Lebanese. The Jews had thirty-five thousand men and women from the Haganah, some extremely well trained and disciplined, some from the various home security units, and some from the Irgun and Stern gangs. The latter were dedicated and deadly in terrorist activity, but undertrained and underdisciplined for military action.

The Jews seemed to have certain tactical advantages in that many were fighting near their homes, on familiar terrain, close to supplies. However, they were widely dispersed and the Arabs had them surrounded almost everywhere. The Arabs also controlled some of the high-ground areas of strategic importance. They also enjoyed superior firepower while the Jews were still waiting for shipments of heavy weapons from the United States and elsewhere. The Arabs had military warplanes, the Jews had unarmed Piper Cubs.

On May 14, having weighed the military situation, the leaders of the Palestine Jews declared the existence of the Jewish state in Palestine, a state to be called Israel. It was a solemn, joyous, and dangerous moment. The nation was essentially in the midst of war.

❧

Formal requests for recognition from key nations were immediately dispatched. A letter to United States President Harry Truman read:

My dear Mr. President:

I have the honor to notify you that the Jewish State has been proclaimed as an independent republic within frontiers approved by the General Assembly of the United Nations in its Resolution of November 29, 1947, and that a provisional government has been charged to assume the rights and duties of government for preserving law and order within the boundaries of the Jewish State, for defending the state against external aggression, and for discharging the obligations of the Jewish State to the other nations of the world in accordance with international law. The Act of Independence will become effective at one minute after six o'clock on the evening of May 14, 1948, Washington time.

With full knowledge of the deep bond of sympathy which has existed and has been strengthened over the past thirty years between the government of the United States and the Jewish people of Palestine, I have been authorized by the provisional government of the new state to tender this message and to express the hope that your government will recognize and will welcome the Jewish State into the community of nations.

Very respectfully yours,
Eliahu Epstein
Agent
Provisional Government of the
Jewish State

At 5:00 P.M. that day, the second special session of the United Nations General Assembly was being led by its president, José Arce of Argentina. The session was working on the creation of a trusteeship for Jerusalem, the city that was so important to so many groups. The representatives present were shocked to discover that Israel had established a provisional government and that the White House had recognized it. The US delegate to the UN was as amazed as the others. While there were mixed feelings about the Israeli action, all of them realized that there would be a war.

On May 15, 1948, the Arabs attacked the Jews.

CHAPTER 15

A Hero's Fate Is Sealed

THE ARAB STATES refused to admit that they had gone to war against Israel. Their delegates explained to the United Nations General Assembly that their troops had entered Palestine in order to restore order following the British exodus. However, the United States was determined to force the issue of a UN-mandated cease-fire. It was feared that one of two situations might occur. One would be an invasion by Russia claiming to act unilaterally on behalf of the United Nations. This would enable Russia to take strategic control of an area it could use for oil and other resources.

The second fear was that there would be a massacre by the Arabs, settling the Jewish question by destroying the Jews. No one had any idea of the relative strengths and skills of the various armed forces. All that was certain was that the Arabs were more experienced and had greater numbers. In either case, the threat of massacre or Russian invasion would require that Truman commit the U.S. Marines in force.

The British, however, were pleased with what was taking place. British ambassador Sir Alexander Cadogan tried to prevent the United Nations from getting involved. While the United States asked the Security Council to order a truce and initiate sanctions against either side that failed to comply, the British stalled for time. Cadogan wanted to have a major catastrophe take place, then be in a position to return the occupation force. The land, under such circumstances, would be redivided in a manner that would be favorable to the Arabs.

On May 22, with the violence increasing rapidly, American ambassador to Britain Lewis Douglas met with Ernest Bevin in London. They discussed arranging for a cease-fire, but Bevin wanted special concessions from Israel that both sides knew would not be given. In addition, the British were quietly supplying arms to the Arabs.

The U.S. State Department prepared a top-secret plan for Truman, to be implemented if there was no truce or if the UN Security Council was unable to resolve the crisis. There would be open, large-scale supplying of arms to Israel to counter the Arab threat. Such an action would end the chance for Arab domination and work against the British plans.

Truman let Britain know the general decision that had been reached. Cadogan then called for a variation of his original proposal, allowing for a cease-fire to take place for a month's duration. This was acceptable to Israel.

The British ambassador also suggested that a mediator be appointed by the United Nations to try to work out peace between the two nations. The job was given to Count Folke Bernadotte, who was still president of the Swedish Red Cross and had remained both active and respected for his postwar work with prisoners and displaced persons. He was known to be a humanitarian, and it was also known that he had been responsible for convincing Himmler to release almost thirty thousand Jews, Scandinavians, and Europeans. There seemed to be no better neutral individual to handle such negotiations. Once again the world misjudged Bernadotte, though this time they overestimated both his abilities and his sensibilities.

Once again Bernadotte, who had no concept of the sensitivities of the various factions in the Middle East, stumbled into an explosive situation lacking any sense of what he was encountering.

Bernadotte felt that whoever dominated a country should retain it. He felt that the 1947 partition plan was ridiculous and that there should be a single Arab state in which the Jews were given special rights. Jerusalem should be given to the Transjordan, making the city an Arab center. This latter idea so intrigued him that he asked French foreign minister Georges Bidault what France would say if he openly proposed the change. The astounded Frenchman explained that "the whole Christian world would join a new Crusade."

British officials rejoiced in Bernadotte's naivete. This was a man who might be convinced to work to alter the partition plan. The Jews would obtain western Galilee while the Transjordan would take control of the southern Negev and Haifa. Jerusalem would also become a part of Transjordan. Such a settlement would obviously favor the Arabs and bring peace to the region.

Critics immediately pointed out that the changes would anger everyone involved. The Jews would feel that their land was being taken in violation of the United Nations agreement. The militant Arabs would be reluctant to let Israel continue in any form. And since both sides would be frustrated by the changes, Bernadotte felt that he would be seen as an obvious neutral. Instead, he was instantly viewed as a fool at best, a pawn of the British at worst. He was hated by all sides, a situation that limited his chance to achieve any sort of settlement.

The naive bias Bernadotte maintained was generally not known outside the British high command. To the UN, Bernadotte seemed to be the perfect ambassador. This was the man who had regularly flown between Berlin and London, by way of Stockholm, during World War II. He had willingly faced Himmler at a time when no one thought that the German leader would negotiate, never being deterred from his humanitarian mission.

Bernadotte had proved himself a humanitarian, a man who was deeply religious without regard for any particular creed. He had worked with the Swedish Red Cross, aiding people on all sides of the war, helping in the aftermath. He was as compassionate for the Nazi wounded as for those they had tried to destroy. And his successes, far greater than those of almost anyone else connected with such humanitarian efforts, seemed proof of what he could do.

Bernadotte also seemed to be a proven negotiator. The fact that he spoke adequate French and fluent English also helped, since they were the most common non-native languages of the Middle East. Thus, not knowing his personal bias or his lack of understanding for the crisis he faced, Bernadotte seemed to be the perfect man for this new mission.

The provisional state of Israel was an unusual place when Bernadotte arrived. There was a government—Dr. Chaim Weizmann as president, David Ben-Gurion as premier, and Moshe Shertok (Sharett) as foreign minister. There was recognition from the United States, the Soviet Union, and Sweden. But both Britain and the United Nations did not recognize the new state officially at that time. In fact, the Arab Legion was filled with British officers and subsidized at the rate of two million British pounds per year.

Israel's leadership felt that Britain was strongly against the new provisional state. They were concerned that not only were there seventy-five million Arabs within striking distance of their nation, but those Arabs were also receiving arms from Britain. Such facts made British sympathies evident.

Bernadotte's arrival in the Middle East was met with hostility from all sides. Israeli freedom fighters had signs that read: "Stockholm is yours. Jerusalem is ours" and "You work in vain. WE are here!"

Swedish news reporters began interviewing Arabs who had a decidedly different opinion. One Arab commented: "We shall cut the Jewish race down to a minimum. The survivors we shall send to a new Babylonian prison. Everybody who tries to stop us is our enemy. And that includes you, even though you are Swedish." A Jew followed the Arab comments with "So long as there is a single enemy of our cause, we shall have a bullet in the magazine for him."

Officially the Stern Gang was disbanded. Unofficially, the Stern Gang would not only remain active until the Arabs had been defeated or a true peace settlement attained, they also knew that they would kill Bernadotte. He was a symbol of the British to them and he would have to die.

Bernadotte, determined to renegotiate the United Nations terms in order to achieve peace, accepted the fact that he could not take sides, no matter what his personal feelings. He was determined to find a common ground for all parties involved, a situation with which they could live both during the truce and afterward. Although he arrived earlier in the month, the most serious negotiations on behalf of the United Nations took place between May 27 and June 13. During that period he traveled between Cairo, Haifa, Tel Aviv, Amman, Beirut, Jerusalem, Damascus, and Rhodes.

Bernadotte at first found that no one was quite willing to listen to him. The Israelis were having great success in the north and had been about to launch offensives both in the Triangle and at Latrun. They had been tested in battle, found to be triumphant, and were no longer so interested in an immediate end to hostilities. They wanted a decisive series of victories to assure peace with their neighbors. For the same reasons, the Arabs, who previously thought themselves invincible and wanted to avoid the truce, suddenly thought that the United Nations cease-fire was a great idea.

Then came the plans that Bernadotte had developed in order to be fair to all sides. First he wanted to restrict the immigration of all men of military age while the truce was on. He felt that such immigration would be the same as heavily reinforcing the Israeli armed forces.

Bernadotte also wanted to limit food and other supplies being brought to the New City to those levels that existed at the start of the truce. This would essentially mean resupplying amounts used rather than building extra supplies to withstand a siege, feed new settlers, and/or supply soldiers in the field.

The Israeli foreign minister strongly disagreed. He insisted upon utilizing the "Burma Road," a supply route in existence before the truce, to continue shipping supplies at whatever rate the people desired. The "Burma Road" avoided Arab territory in Latrun by running south of the main road from Deir Muchsen to Saris. Other routes not in use at the time of the truce might be limited, but not the "Burma Road." In addition, he insisted that immigration continue for refugees of all ages. The only restriction would be that men of military age who were entering the country during the truce would not be brought into the army, nor would they receive military training, until after the truce had ended. There might be a larger pool of resources from which to draw, but they would not be ready for war.

King Abdullah expressed sympathy for Bernadotte as well as understanding about the Israelis. Then he displayed the Arab hard line, forcing Bernadotte to finally face the problems on all sides. Abdullah said:

"I should like to say first that I, in common with the governments of the other Arab States, am fully convinced of your sincerity as mediator and your desire to reach a just settlement. Like myself, you are of royal blood, and you must know what it means to govern a kingdom. I am always at your disposal as your counselor, if you wish to talk things over with me, but I would not force my help upon you. I will call you brother, and I hope that you will place the same confidence in me as in your brother. I regard your views [concerning the changes Bernadotte wanted to make in the UN settlement when the count first became mediator] as just and correct. But as to Jerusalem, I cannot allow that a single drop of water or a single pound of provisions should be taken into the city during the truce."

Bernadotte answered:

"I humbly thank Your Majesty for the kind words Your Majesty has had addressed to me personally. Your Majesty must understand, however, that as head of a humanitarian organization like the Red Cross, I cannot share Your Majesty's view that the starving Arabs and Jews in Jerusalem should not receive any humanitarian aid. I cannot accept a view that goes against my conscience, and I am convinced that Your Majesty, being a great king, would not give me advice, the execution of which would mean that I was acting against my conscience."

King Abdullah recognized that he had more to gain by supporting Bernadotte than by continuing the fighting. He agreed to accept the cease-fire as it was and to continue to supply Jerusalem.

Other factors were also helping Bernadotte. The Arabs were running low on ammunition and supplies. They needed a cease-fire because, as King Abdullah commented privately to other Arab leaders, it was June, the fruit season had passed, and they would be unlikely to find even one orange to throw at the Israelis.

At the same time, the Israelis were finding that, though they were still winning their offensives, the battles were taking too heavy a toll.

Both sides realized that it was time for a cease-fire. It was in everyone's best interests.

At 7:00 A.M. on June 11, 1948, the Middle East cease-fire took place under United Nations auspices. All Palestinians, Arabs and Jews, could return to their homes, their flocks, their fields, and their businesses.

The peace was uneasy. There were sniping incidents on both sides. There was also an intense awareness of changes taking place in the relative power positions of the adversaries, and both sides felt that these had to be addressed.

The Arabs were frequently tired and discouraged. They were taking far more casualties than they anticipated. There were no reserve units and a reluctance among some of the leaders to recruit new troops. The ongoing battles seemed to be placing them in a worse position than if they had not been at war.

The Jews were also suffering. They had managed to defend every settlement provided them by the United Nations, but their casualties were high. There was a serious shortage of food and clothing. There were reports of some soldiers having to go into battle wearing pajamas, and at least one instance where a man emerged from the fighting with only his underclothes, no additional garments becoming available for him for the next three weeks.

Many of the men were deliberately skipping meals, lowering their strength and reducing their effectiveness. They explained that their families were going hungry. They felt that if they skipped some meals, the extra food might be used to feed the people at home. They felt they needed to make the sacrifice no matter what the personal cost. Yet the military leaders knew that the sacrifice was slightly altering response times, a situation that could mean the difference between victory and defeat in battle.

The Jewish leadership was also looking beyond the immediate struggle to the future stability of Israel. They had nearly been destroyed in Europe. They could see territory that they needed to control in order to ensure their safety. Such land was outside the UN mandate, but so strategically important that they felt that there would be no future for Israel without taking full control of it. They decided that they needed to use the breathing spell to gather additional arms, train more soldiers, and then strike before anyone was aware of their plans. In that way they would not be in defiance of the United Nations. They would simply present the UN with a fait accompli.

Bernadotte was not aware of all this when he worked with Dr. Ralph Bunche, the American diplomat. Bunche had achieved the highest position of any black in U.S. government service. Other UN participants included a Greek, Constantin Stavropoulos; Sweden's General Aage Lundstrom; and the secretarial staff. They were developing a deliberately vague peace proposal as a position for negotiations between Arabs and Jews. The work was done in Rhodes, then presented to all sides on June 28. As Bernadotte later wrote:

> I handed to both parties a draft of my proposals for the settlement of Palestine's future. At the same time I invited them to Rhodes for further conferences. I had intentionally made my proposals very vague in the hope that it might be easier in that way to induce the parties to continue negotiations on the basis of the draft. It was also clear to me in advance that there was no prospect that either of them would completely accept my point of view. On July 3 and 6 I received answers from the Jews and Arabs respectively. In essence they indicated that they did not want to consider my proposals as a basis for continued discussions. However, at the same time, they pointed out that this did not mean that they considered all further discussions hopeless. They left the door open, and expressed the wish that I should not tire and give up my mediation.
>
> My proposals to prolong the armistice and to demilitarize Jerusalem were accepted by the Jews but not by the Arabs. On the other hand, the Arabs but not the Jews, conditionally accepted another proposal I made about the demilitarization of the oil installations and harbor of Haifa; my thought was that the various countries in the world need not suffer because the important oil export from this town was cut off.
>
> I noticed that neither party was inclined to start war anew. A secret meeting with King Abdullah of Transjordan confirmed this as far as the Arabs were concerned.
>
> The United Nations Security Council had, if it could make a quick decision, a great opportunity for firm conduct to induce both parties to accept a more sensible attitude. In that way the whole question could be solved.

Unknown to Bernadotte, the Irgun was flexing its muscles and preparing for what could have amounted to a civil war during this period. They had decided to fight on their own, to create both an army unit and obtain extensive weapons from France. Or so goes the official story of the *Altalena* affair.

In the spring of 1947 the Hebrew Committee for National Liberation purchased the SS *Altalena,* an American vessel that was being sold as war surplus. The purchasing committee was one of several American activist organizations and the name of the vessel was derived from a pseudonym once used by Vladimir Jabotinsky.

The boat was meant to challenge the British blockade. It was able to handle more than five thousand refugees without luggage, but when everything changed, the British withdrew, and the war for survival began, it was decided to use the vessel for war. The plan was to recruit European Jews willing to fight for Israel, then transport them on the vessel. The French government was supplying a gift of weapons to aid the Jews, the supplies officially presented to Irgun representatives in Paris.

The boat's crew was comprised of American Jews who had served in World War II. All the volunteer fighters were to be commanded by Eliahu Lankin, who had been part of the Palestinian Irgun leadership before being arrested by the British. Lankin, deported to Africa, made his way to Paris, where he again began working against the British.

In May 1948 the *Altalena* was taken to southern France and docked in preparation for receiving a cargo of Irgun fighters and French arms. Menachem Begin was handling the coordination of the shipment and was alerted that there were financial problems. The men and arms were ready, but there was no money for fuel and supplemental weapons that were to be purchased before sailing. The truce had not been declared, nor had negotiations for a cease-fire been completed when Begin alerted Israel's provisional government and David Ben-Gurion.

The Haganah leaders were informed of the *Altalena's* existence and mission. Begin explained that because of the benefits, the provisional government should supply the two hundred and fifty thousand dollars still needed to bring the men and weapons to Israel. Upon arrival, the men and arms would become a part of the official armed forces that were being planned as the successor of Haganah. If desired, men recruited in Europe by Haganah, separate from Irgun, could be added to the ship. An additional two thousand to three thousand men could easily fit on board, along with the arms and the nine hundred men recruited by Irgun. Upon arrival, the *Altalena* would be a gift to the provisional government, not part of a separate fleet of Irgun ships.

Ben-Gurion claimed to want no part of what was taking place, though members of Haganah were interested. His attitude against what was happening was conveyed on May 17. Ben-Gurion was convinced that Begin and other members of Irgun were hostile to the provisional government leadership, which was seen as being moderate. The Irgun leadership had always maintained that the members of the provisional government were trying to appease the British and the Arabs, not create so strong an Israel that no one could conquer it.

On May 19 the French agreed to release the weapons. Two days later, Ben-Gurion explained that the shipload of weapons and men should not sail.

The Irgun was outraged. An official army had not yet been formed. The Haganah was acting in its place, supplemented by the Irgun and the Stern Gang, though the latter two also fought independently. It was obvious from reports coming from Israel that the success was not what had been hoped. And by May 28 the Arab Legion had temporarily occupied the Old City of Jerusalem before Jewish troops recaptured the land. Irgun decided to make its own decisions how to act until an official army, separate from the Labor Zionists who controlled Haganah, was created.

On May 31, 1948, the provisional government created the Tz'va Haganah L'Yisrael, or Tzahal. This was the new Israel Defense Force, the independent army everyone had been planning. Irgun agreed to let Begin coordinate the gradual integration of Israel's fighting units. In the meantime, there would be continued tension.

The transition of Irgun to Tzahal was formally arranged on June 1. Proper papers were signed, which should have been the end of the problem. However, other concerns remained. The New City of Jerusalem was supposed to be an international city under the UN plan. The Tzahal could not openly send men and arms to fight there. Instead, David Shaltiel took a unit of Haganah, combined it with forces from Irgun (commanded separately by Mordecai Raanan) and the Stern gang, and continued fighting there. And it was because such separation could still exist within Israel despite the supposed integration of Stern and Haganah that the *Altalena* tragedy took place.

The twenty-eight-day truce under the guidelines of the United Nations Security Council developed through Bernadotte was announced on June 2. It was to begin June 11, during which period the importation of men and armaments meant for the war areas would be stopped.

On June 8 the French delivered their weapons to the dock where the *Altalena* waited, still before the truce would take effect. There were 5,000 rifles, 300 Bren guns, 150 Spandaus, four million rounds of ammunition, several thousand bombs, five caterpillar-track armored cars for desert maneuvers, and miscellaneous military supplies. Then, at 2:00 A.M. the next day the stevedores began to load the cargo.

By accident, one of the crates opened. Several of the dockworkers were Algerians and hated the new state of Israel. They had not known about the weapons and were not about to load them onto the ship. The discovery also meant that there was a chance of sabotage, so everything had to be changed quickly.

Irgun volunteers and French soldiers took over the task of loading the ship. Then the nine hundred volunteers arrived for the voyage; everyone and everything was on board the *Altalena* by 8:30 P.M., June 11. It was the same day that the truce went into effect, a truce that Ben-Gurion was determined to honor.

Menachem Begin had not been informed of the problems, nor was he alerted when the *Altalena* sailed. He was loyal to the Irgun plans but probably would not have permitted the sailing at that time. With the truce in effect, he wanted to have the least hostility possible. He probably would have negotiated with the provisional government to find a way to best utilize the men and arms without causing a conflict. However, that possibility can only be seen in hindsight. He learned of both the truce and the sailing from a BBC report after the fact.

"Whatever our attitude to the truce might be, we were not entitled to bear the responsibility for the possible consequences of a breach," Begin later wrote. "This was no longer an underground partisan-political fight. This was a fight in the open field and the consequences of defeat might be destruction for our people." He wired Irgun's headquarters in Paris, telling them not to send the ship. It was too late, and the *Altalena* could not be reached by radio.

On June 12 Begin met with representatives from the new government, explaining what had happened. The men were shocked for many reasons. Haganah, on its own, had never been able to assemble so many weapons at one time as Irgun had done, weapons that were desperately needed. At the same time, these were in blatant violation of the cease-fire. In addition, a force of such magnitude could be used against the provisional government, changing the command so that Irgun or Sternist leaders were placed in power over Ben-Gurion's administration.

At first the weapons seemed as though they might be a blessing. Begin wanted 20 percent of the weapons to be given to the Irgun unit in the New City of Jerusalem. The remaining 80 percent would be taken by Tzahal, but Begin insisted that they only go to Irgun members within Tzahal. He felt that former Haganah leaders had been discriminating against the Irgun men in the distribution of equipment and that the French arms would correct that matter.

Others felt that the division was unrealistic. The 20 percent could still go to Irgun units in Jerusalem, but the remainder of the arms should go to Tzahal without stipulation. And always the truce violation was ignored.

On June 20, the *Altalena* moored a hundred yards from the shore of the city of Kfar Vitkin. Begin arrived to watch the landing, expecting government leaders to be there to receive the men and the weapons. But no one else appeared and the sea was too rough to land. The water did not calm until the next morning, when the unloading could not take place unobserved. Instead, the vessel returned to sea just far enough to be out of sight of the UN observers. There it waited until dark.

On Sunday afternoon, June 21, the provisional government met to decide what to do with the *Altalena*. The government refused to help unload the vessel because Irgun's ideas for weapons-sharing went against the government's best interests.

The question was raised whether or not to prevent the weapons from landing. Some thought they should be allowed to land, then be seized by the government. Five hundred soldiers from Tzahal could be used to stop any Irgun members who might be present or trying to get off the boat.

It was not known, however, whether soldiers of Tzahal would be willing to use force against members of Irgun. The idea of Jew fighting Jew for any reason was anathema to everyone.

Ben-Gurion decided to use force against the men and women of the *Altalena*. It has been argued for years whether or not he knew of Begin's plans in the beginning, whether or not he approved of them, whether or not his growing fears were valid based on the actions of the Irgun leaders as he understood them. There have been charges and counter-charges made between the two men and their aides. All that is certain is that, by the time Ben-Gurion decided to act against the vessel, the fear was that the nine hundred volunteers would be used as a revolutionary army. He suspected that he might be facing a civil war against his weeks-old government. It was a threat big enough for him to decide it was better to lose the desperately needed weapons through sinking the ship than it was to risk losing his hold on power through a revolt.

The government officials gave Tzahal a free hand to do whatever was necessary to assert authority over the *Altalena*. It was understood that the government had been told that the arms were going to arrive and would be unloaded by both Tzahal and Irgun. However, Irgun broke the agreement by failing to inform the provisional government of both when the ship would arrive and where it would unload.

The *Altalena* returned to its former mooring position after dark on Sunday night. Begin boarded the boat, then assisted the removal of 850 of the volunteers, who were taken to shore on a motor launch. He personally stayed on the boat with a defense force consisting of the remaining fifty men.

The refugees who landed in Israel thought of nothing but their safety. Although they had agreed to do battle with the enemies of the new provisional state of Israel, their concern was freedom, not battles. Many of them kissed the ground and none of them left the ship with weapons. Then they were all taken to a holding camp in Natanya, where they could rest from the voyage.

There were several reactions to the ship. First, fifteen men arrived in a small boat. These were members of Palmach, the elite special force of Tzahal, and they claimed they had no orders to be there. They began to help with the unloading of some of the arms, then explored the vessel before leaving. It was unknown whether this exploration was out of curiosity or to prepare them for an attack against the vessel if necessary. Whatever the case, they did not stay long, and during their time on board, the Tzahal regular troops were establishing roadblocks. In addition, two Israeli navy corvettes took up positions from which they could serve as escorts, attack boats, or a blockade.

The unloading of the weapons and ammunition was extremely slow. The equipment was limited, the weight excessive and the number of men available was too small for the work to proceed quickly. Begin feared that either the Arabs or observers from the United Nations forces would spot what was taking place. It was also rumored that Tzahal forces were moving in, one of the officers from Irgun suggesting that any men and arms currently on the beach should return at once to the *Altalena*.

Begin was worried about the UN observers, not Tzahal. What he did not realize, but what Irgun members later came to believe, was that the hostility to the *Altalena* was more than concern over a possible revolution. The idea of a revolutionary group of well-armed fighters for Irgun making a power play sounded dangerous enough to be taken seriously. But the real reason for Ben-Gurion's actions over the next several hours, Irgun leaders came to believe many years later, was an attempt to assassinate Menachem Begin. Such an action, under cover of the *Altalena* incident, would eliminate a dangerous political rival in a way that would not be directly linked to Ben-Gurion.

Brigadier Dan Even of Tzahal sent a message to Begin giving him ten minutes to agree to turning over all weapons on board the *Altalena* or face a takeover by force.

Begin claimed it would take more than ten minutes. He sent an aide to contact the heads of the towns of Kfar Vitkin and Natanya to ask them to intercede with the government. He also requested a chance to sit down with Even to discuss the matter.

While the start of the showdown with Tzahal was taking place, a UN spotter plane noticed the ship and the cargo that was being unloaded. The crates did not indicate what the cargo might be, and two UN observers, one French and one American, came to Begin. As he later wrote, "They wanted to know what was aboard the ship and asked for permission to board her. We told them that this could not be so at that moment. They understood and saluted us. They left and we continued unloading."

Begin's advisers all felt that the boat should move on to Tel Aviv. It had been spotted by the UN. Tzahal troops were at the ready. Tel Aviv might be dangerous, but it was also the heart of Irgun territory. Any attack against the ship would risk extreme violence from trained forces. A civil war would seem imminent, a fact that might prevent Ben-Gurion's people from resorting to violence.

Begin agreed to leave the already unloaded weapons under guard on the dock. Then he would sail with the bulk of the weapons to Tel Aviv, where he could talk directly with the Ben-Gurion people.

The time was 5:00 P.M. Begin had made his decision too late. The first rounds of ammunition that were fired struck the beach. Then other rounds reached the ship.

The Arabs had attacked. That was the only possible situation imaginable to Begin and the others on the *Altalena*. Jew had not fought Jew for centuries. Such violence was inconceivable. Yet they soon discovered that the bullets and mortar rounds were coming from Tzahal soldiers.

The decision was made to move the *Altalena* immediately. If it was stuck in the wrong place, or if uncontrollable fires broke out, the subsequent explosion might destroy the town and take many lives. In addition, all the weapons would be lost.

Begin insisted upon remaining on the beach, where Irgun members were establishing a defensive front, but the other leaders would not hear of it. There was too great a risk that he would be killed. Instead, he was forcibly removed to the motor launch they had been using to ferry the refugees to the land. They went to the ship and prepared to leave the area.

Irgun men on the beach grabbed whatever weapons they could and began fighting the Tzahal forces as the *Altalena* headed for Tel Aviv, under attack by the corvettes. Six Irgun men were killed on the beach and eighteen more wounded before they surrendered. The arms that had been unloaded were taken by Tzahal, the remaining Irgun fighters placed under arrest.

The *Altalena*, chased by the corvettes, reached Tel Aviv after midnight. The vessel did not slow on its approach, choosing to run aground near Frishman Street. Immediately troops on shore joined with the corvettes in firing rounds at the vessel.

During this time several stories were being spread among the various principals involved with the *Altalena* issue. Ben-Gurion stated that Irgun had gone against all government wishes by secretly bringing a boatload of arms to Israel. This was a very dangerous situation and, when efforts were made to stop them or confiscate the weapons, the battle had begun.

Others heard a different, and probably more accurate story about what was taking place. These men said that an effort was made to arrange for the unloading and storage of all arms and ammunition. Then, with such essential items protected from harm and from the prying eyes of the United Nations observers, it would be possible to negotiate how to handle the issues in question. Begin and other Irgun leaders could work with the Ben-Gurion government to reach an effective compromise.

Whatever the truth, and the information that has come forth in recent years seems to indicate that Ben-Gurion was using the *Altalena* incident to rid himself of Begin, the gunfire continued. This was the showdown meant to establish Tzahal as the sole army of Israel. Even though the men on the ship raised a white flag and did not return gunfire, Tzahal soldiers continued firing at the vessel.

The action was not unnoticed. Reporters and UN observers in Tel Aviv not only became aware of what was taking place, the location of the vessel was such that many of them could watch the action from their hotel balconies. Others joined the area residents on the beach.

Begin was desperately trying to get the arms and ammunition off the ship before the vessel burned or exploded. Twenty percent of the cargo had been left in Kfar Vitkin. The motor launch removed another load and brought it to the beach in Tel Aviv. When Tzahal made no effort to stop the men unloading the vessel, a second trip was made, this time encountering gunfire that struck the pilot. However, the boatload of arms safely reached the beach while Begin, on board the *Altalena*, used a loudspeaker in an effort to make the soldiers stop attempting to destroy the cargo they all so desperately needed.

More rounds struck the ship, killing several on board. Reporters began pressing forward, sensing a bigger story than what first appeared as it became obvious that the shooting was strictly one-sided. No one on board the *Altalena* was firing back. Word was relayed to other areas, and soon individual Irgun members who had joined Tzahal left their posts and tried to reach the beach, only to be stopped some distance away by Tzahal troops.

Begin called Tzahal headquarters at the Ritz Hotel. There, Itzhal Rabin and Yigal Allon, the leaders of the Palmach troops, were able to agree to a cease-fire long enough to remove the wounded men. However, after the cease-fire was agreed upon for four o'clock, spotters noticed a machine gun being placed on the deck of the *Altalena*, its barrel aimed at the hotel. Allon immediately called Ben-Gurion and received permission to fire a warning shot against the vessel to have the gun removed. If there was no positive response, the *Altalena* was to be sunk.

The three warning shells were lobbed into the water at the same time that the cease-fire had been agreed upon. Begin waited too long discussing with his men what to do. After fifteen minutes without the machine gun being removed, the heavy artillery piece that had fired the warning rounds placed a shell directly into the ship's hold. The ammunition cases began exploding and a fire raced through the ship.

The Palmach leaders at the hotel claimed that the cease-fire had been legitimate but that the orders had not reached all units. It did not matter, though. The intent of the government forces was obvious when survivors jumped into the water, only to have machine-gun and rifle fire aimed at them.

Begin was determined to stay with the sinking ship. Finally two crewmen tossed him over the side and he successfully reached the shore. By the time the vessel was lost, sixty-nine people had been wounded and fourteen Irgun members were dead.

The *Altalena* incident seemed to have little to do with Bernadotte. However, the violence that occurred was changing the attitudes of the Irgun and the Stern gang leadership. Jew had fought Jew. What should have been a war for independence against the British and Arab forces had turned into what could have become a civil war. There was intense frustration as everyone tried to restore harmony among the factions that needed to be integrated into Tzahal. There seemed to be a need to lash out against anyone who symbolically represented the troubles in Jerusalem, and that violence would soon be directed against Folke Bernadotte.

❦

The issue of the *Altalena* was clear to those involved, though not until after Ben-Gurion's death in 1973 did all points become clear. The guns had been stripped, oiled, and packed into cases. They would have had to be carefully assembled and loaded to be used for a revolution.

Two members of Haganah, apparently acting with the full knowledge and authority of Ben-Gurion, had assisted the loading of the weapons in Europe and had been on and off the ship many times prior to its sailing. When the vessel eventually reached Israel, its port, Kfar Vitkin, was Haganah-controlled. Almost none of the Tzalah troops present in the city had any history of loyalty to or connection with Irgun. And when the 850 refugee recruits disembarked, none of them carried a weapon of any sort.

Menachem Begin traveled to the New City of Jerusalem—where Irgun maintained a presence separate from Tzahal, and would continue to do so through September's violent confrontation with Bernadotte. He was deeply depressed, having witnessed the needless violence caused by the political concerns of Ben-Gurion. Jew had fought Jew, and for years, nothing would ever be completely the same.

It was assumed at one time that Ben-Gurion was a moderate and Begin the extremist terrorist. By such reasoning, the actions attributed to Ben-Gurion seemed out of character. However, when Ben-Gurion's personal diaries were discovered later, all manner of grandiose schemes were considered on its pages:

> When we destroy the Arab Legion and bomb Amman we'll also finish off Transjordan, and then Syria will fall. If Egypt dares to go on fighting—we'll bomb Port Said, Alexandria and Cairo.
>
> Perhaps we shall also bomb Damascus. I'm not particularly sorry that we did not take the West Bank. But I'm very sorry that we did not capture Jerusalem and then go as far as the Dead Sea.

Ben-Gurion and Moshe Dayan, chief of staff at that time, apparently considered establishing their own approved government in Lebanon:

> The Moslem rule in Lebanon is artificial and easily undermined. A Christian state ought to be set up whose southern border would be the Litani River. Then we'll form an alliance with it...
>
> In [Dayan's] view, all we need to do is to find a Christian Lebanese officer, perhaps no higher than a captain, and win him over or buy him with money, so that he would declare himself the savior of the Maronite population. Then the Israeli army would enter Lebanon, occupy the territory in question and establish a Christian government which would form an alliance with Israel.

The Bernadotte peace proposals were studied following the *Altalena* incident. The truce between Israel and the Arab states ended on July 9, yet the count was confident something more could be worked out. On July 10, when flying from Rhodes to Lake Success, he commented: "My negotiations are now entering the second phase. I am not pessimistic. It seems to me that the door which both parties have left ajar has opened a little wider. It is my firm resolution to concentrate all my energies during the next few days towards convincing the Security Council of the importance of their coming decision.... In a few days I hope to return to Palestine to resume contacts with the fascinating leading figures of the Middle East. It is still an open question whether or not I shall succeed. I am, however, firmly decided to try every possibility to fulfill the hopes pinned upon me."

What Bernadotte failed to understand was that his position in the Middle East was very different from his position in Germany. Heinrich Himmler, Walter Schellenberg, and the others with whom he had to negotiate may have been vicious Nazi killers, but he met them at a time when the war effort was hopeless. They were determined to arrange whatever it took to save themselves. It was easier to free almost 30,000 people once marked for death than to risk having no place in which to seek asylum when the Axis powers finally collapsed.

Israel was a different matter. Many of the Israelis, including those whose lives Bernadotte saved, saw the world as out to destroy them. They recognized that they might be fighting for their existence and saw no reason to give quarter to anyone. This was not a gentleman's war. This was not just a dispute over land. This was a matter of survival by a people who had witnessed a dictator nearly succeed in eliminating every Jew in Eastern Europe. Those who spoke as though they did not understand that fact (and Bernadotte sounded more like the British than a sympathizer with the hell they had endured) were perceived as real or potential enemies.

The Arabs, quite apart from any bias of their own, saw the Israeli action as threatening their land and their financial future. If it was a choice between developing a compromise that might reduce their standard of living and destroying the new independent state of Israel, they had no interest in stopping the violence.

The rejection of Bernadotte's plan showed both the divisiveness of the groups and his own lack of awareness concerning what was taking place. Both Israel and the Arab states were irate that Jerusalem would be offered to Transjordan when the city was so important to all of them. If the Negev was given to Egypt, as Bernadotte planned, the largest land mass that had been provided for Israel would be eliminated. The idea that western Galilee might be given to Israel in place of the Negev could not work because Israel had already taken control of the Negev during the fighting. The count had failed to look at the reality of the situation for all parties involved when he developed his peace plan.

Under such circumstances, Bernadotte's shuttle diplomacy, his determination to find a compromise all sides could accept, was unrealistic. His embrace of the program that seemed to make the most sense when it came to reducing tensions did not take into account the recent history and emotions of the people involved.

That same July 10, Bernadotte asked the Arabs and Jews to agree to an additional ten-day cease-fire. He convinced the British to suspend at least temporarily the 500,000-pound payment they had been making every quarter to the Arab Legion. But the Jews responded by seizing Ramleh and Lydda, both Arab strongholds, and the Soviet newspaper *Pravda* accused the count of increasing the hostility between Arabs and Jews.

On July 13, Bernadotte was asked to report what was happening to the United Nations Security Council, the body that had appointed him mediator. He explained that several points affected a cease-fire:

First, both Arabs and Jews had to be made to understand that the use of force would not be tolerated. A cease-fire had to be established immediately.

Next, Jerusalem had to be demilitarized. This was the most volatile situation, and it would take from a thousand to two thousand UN troops to oversee this action. Then the UN must be willing to impose sanctions if the cease-fire was not obeyed.

The cease-fire, rather than being the end in itself, must be used for negotiations ultimately leading to a complete peace settlement. At that point, the issue of the refugees had to be considered in depth. And the Security Council would have to be involved.

The Russians attacked Bernadotte. Ambassador Andrei Gromyko, supported by the delegate from the Ukraine, claimed that Bernadotte had only been asked to enforce the UN partition plan of November 29, 1947. Bernadotte explained that if that had been the case, there never would have been need for a mediator. He said that the plan was outdated because of events that had taken place, and it was his job to effect a compromise with which all parties could be comfortable.

Bernadotte then went on the offensive. He said that in order to mediate effectively, he would need at least three hundred observers. The Security Council agreed, arranging for a new cease-fire on July 16, the day that Jewish forces captured Nazareth.

The new truce began officially on July 18. The Arabs said that they wanted to cede the end to Jewish immigration during the negotiations they were facing. They also said that they wanted the three hundred thousand Arab refugees from territory taken by the Jews to be allowed to return.

Bernadotte worked constantly among the various factions. The Arab League was comfortable with the idea of demilitarizing Jerusalem. The Jews had been gaining so much territory that they were determined to take a hard line against too much Arab immigration. They did not feel that the dispossessed Arabs should return home, though they felt that there should be no restrictions on the immigration of European Jews.

(Despite Bernadotte's efforts, certain factions were determined to accomplish certain goals. Some members of the Stern gang, for example, hoped to destroy the Mosque of Omar, also known as the Dome of the Rock, a Muslim mosque that was of great religious significance because of its site. It had been built where both the first and second Temples had been built in Jerusalem centuries earlier, locations reflecting both triumph and tragedy for the Jewish people. At the northwest corner of the Temple courtyard, Herod built the fortress Antonia which was the probable site of Jesus' trial before Pontius Pilate. This was also the spot where the Prophet Muhammad ascended into Heaven, making the location one of great importance to all three major religions in the area. Such destruction, and subsequent plans to build a third Temple on the site, would have reinforced the determination of the Arabs to continue the fight against the Jews. Yet the plans were the arrogant desires of extremists, a force Bernadotte did not comprehend. To him, each group was united, even though there were factions among all the warring parties.)

Bernadotte did not have the three hundred advisers he had requested, the UN explaining that at least two months would be needed to obtain the personnel and supplies. However, he continued working among the various factions so that, by August, the demilitarization of Jerusalem had been agreed upon in principle. He also reminded the UN that during the rigors of wartime, he had been able to assemble Red Cross personnel and equipment for the evacuation of men, women, and children from German concentration camps within twenty-one days. Since peacetime offered far fewer obstacles, he felt that he was being undersupported.

On August 5, Moshe Shertok agreed to sit down with the Arabs for peace talks. However, less than a week later, the Arab League rejected the talks to avoid giving the impression that they accepted the existence of the Jewish state. At the same time, armed factions in Jerusalem began attacking one another. Much of the fighting came from Irgun, but it was obviously limited warfare, not isolated sniping incidents.

On August 12 the Latrun pumping station, which supplied water to

Jerusalem, was blown up and Bernadotte was not able to assemble a UN military force adequate to provide further protection.

Bernadotte returned to Stockholm on August 13 in order to lead the Seventeenth International Red Cross Conference. He also used that time to speak freely to the press, discussing what was taking place in Israel.

As always, Bernadotte remained optimistic about the potential to end the fighting. He noted that only in Jerusalem were the factions dangerously close to all-out war. He also noted that he had personally inspected the Latrun pumping station just two hours before the attack. He explained that just forty armed men from the UN forces could have prevented the destruction. Unfortunately, the UN was not providing such support.

Bernadotte's chief concern was not the peace but the safety and welfare of the refugees from the war. There were approximately four hundred thousand people, most of them Arabs, who had been made homeless by the battles and the shifting control of the land. He felt that they had to be fed, clothed, housed, and protected at any cost.

Perhaps it was his concern for the refugees. Or perhaps he had reached a point where he only saw the logic of his own ideas, not the concerns of others. Whatever the case, Bernadotte continued to focus on a peace plan that remained totally inappropriate to all parties. Jerusalem and the Negev would be given to the Arabs, though there would be international supervision, probably through the United Nations, of all holy places in Jerusalem. Western Galilee, already held by the Jews as a result of the war, would be formally ceded to Israel.

But the Arabs were not ready to give up territory that had been taken from them by force. They asserted their right to Galilee by virtue of the original mandate creating Israel. At the same time, while the Arabs rejoiced in gaining the Negev, the Jews would not yield the territory. The Negev was underdeveloped and mineral-rich. It was an area where new housing could be built, the land could be worked, and the people could expand. It was critical for immigration and for self-sufficiency.

The first serious peace talks between Israel and the Arab states occurred on August 22, 1948. Bernadotte arranged for a discussion that he hoped would result in the demilitarization of Jerusalem. Working with the Red Cross, he had established a Red Cross–administered no-man's land, but both Egypt and Israel had made armed forays into the region. The most serious such attack had been an Egyptian assault on the Jewish agricultural school legitimately located within the neutral zone. The Israelis had counterattacked, but both sides agreed to withdraw if peace could be maintained.

Despite the seeming willingness to talk, Bernadotte was under close protection. During July, a Jewish newspaperman working in Paris received a report that the Israelis planned to assassinate the count. The information had come from such reliable sources that the journalist passed on the information to the United Nations. Two guards were assigned to him, even attending the International Red Cross Conference.

Bernadotte refused to be worried about the death threat. He felt that he was doing important work, and that, with determination, he would be able to accomplish an end to the violence.

On September 10, 1948, Bernadotte's fate was sealed. The Stern Gang was theoretically disbanded, no longer necessary as the result of Tzalah. But the extremists within Stern, including Yitzhak Yizernitzky (Shamir) and Nathan Friedman-Yellin, refused to be a part of the Ben-Gurion government. They saw the Swedish count as having the potential to influence the provisional state of Israel in such a manner that concessions might be made. They felt that the British ideas might dominate a settlement, a situation they could not tolerate. They wanted Folke Bernadotte to die.

A meeting was held among Friedman-Yellin, Shamir, and Israel Sheib inside a Tel Aviv apartment on Ben Yehuda Street. Sheib felt that the United Nations intervention was as much a threat to the new state as the British domination had been. He was insistent that Israel be able to stand alone, to not only survive but to conquer all enemies on its own. Intermediaries, occupation forces, observers, and other such groups could not be tolerated.

The death of a stranger was always an uncomfortable act, even for the most skilled assassin. Murder was taboo to the Jews, an action that went against much of the teaching of the Old Testament. Yet the hardliners among the Stern gang felt it was justifiable given the right circumstances. Shamir, for example, was quoted as saying "A man who goes forth to kill another whom he does not know must believe one thing only—that by his act he will change the course of history."

The plotters were experienced in justifying their acts. They were the ones who had helped plan such deaths as the murder of Lord Moyne. If anything, Bernadotte was seen as more important, since he represented not just Britain but the entire United Nations. The slaying of Bernadotte would send a message that no country or group of countries had the right to interfere in the actions of the new state of Israel. It would also eliminate the threat that Bernadotte's beliefs might be accepted by the moderate Jews in power.

There would be discrepancies among the stories of the three men involved. What is certain, however, is that the murder was to take place and that the identities of the killers would be hidden. Jewish patriots would destroy a symbol of foreign intervention. Specifically to name the Stern gang would change the image to one of an action by extremists outside the mainstream political structure.

The three plotters decided to create a group called Fatherland Front that would take credit for the assassination of Bernadotte. Yehoshua Zetler was to lead a group of top Sternists in the assassination. He would primarily rely upon his assistant, Joshua Cohen, and the intelligence-gathering work of Stanley Goldfoot. Goldfoot immediately began surveillance of Bernadotte to determine when and where the murder could take place.

There was knowledge that some form of violence was going to occur, though no one was certain just where. The American consuls general of Jerusalem and Tel Aviv had both heard rumors concerning a forthcoming assassination, most likely of Bernadotte. They began seeking advice concerning the problem, but the police felt that there was too much loose talk for a serious threat. The more a terrorist spoke, the less likely he was to act. It was what was not said that could prove deadly.

The greatest concern was felt by James G. McDonald, the U.S. special representative to Israel. He had been pro-Zionist for many years. He was a history and political science professor who had worked for the old League of Nations as high commissioner for refugees in 1933. He had witnessed the consolidation of Hitler's power in Germany, saw what happened to the Jews, and become extremely supportive of the new provisional state of Israel when it declared its independence from Britain.

McDonald was certain that an important assassination might cause the U.S. Congress to stop backing the nation. Many members of Congress feared that Israel was becoming Communist-controlled. This was a period during the start of the cold war, and many people felt that Jews who had fled Russia and other Communist nations were going to unite secretly against the Israeli government. Anti-Communist factions within the State Department and the Pentagon would have liked to see the end of the state of Israel based on the potential of the refugees to turn it into a Communist state. The fact that such fears were groundless was unimportant. Fears of Communism at this time exceeded a rational analysis of intelligence data. McDonald knew that assassination of Bernadotte could change the entire issue of Middle East support.

Rumors of assassination began circulating most intensely by September. On September 16, when Folke Bernadotte's plane landed at Beirut Airport, he jokingly said to his chief of staff, General Aage Lundstrom, "Nice to see you alive." The general was one of those who had been reported murdered, though there had not been an attempt on his life.

Bernadotte did not admit that the assassination plot was real, though he was to be the target. His plan for peace in the Middle East was going to be analyzed by the United Nations General Assembly, which was meeting in Paris. It was the same general plan he had developed earlier, one that completely disregarded both the religious issues as they related to Jerusalem and the security and economic issues of the land. It was a plan the Stern gang feared might be forcibly accepted by Ben-Gurion and other moderate leaders. It was a plan that assured the count's death as a symbolic gesture, much like Lord Moyne's death had been.

Bernadotte was scheduled to travel from Arab to Jewish territory through the Mandelbaum Gate, a part of the no-man's-land region from which snipers had been operating. At least two officials had been shot from an area where houses, ruined in battle, provided extensive cover. No one lived in the homes, and the combination of freestanding walls and rubble provided excellent cover for attack.

Bernadotte decided to make the trip unarmed. He felt that so long as he was traveling for the United Nations, any display of weapons would be a provocative act.

On September 17, Bernadotte's itinerary was quite heavy. He flew in the white plane "Whirlwind," known to all to be used by the mediator, traveling between Damascus and Jerusalem, where it was to land at the Kalandia Airport. In an effort to scare Bernadotte, one of the underground units (the precise one has not been determined) sent a radio message on the frequency the United Nations used: "Urgent. Inform all aircraft against landing Kalandia Airport. They will be fired upon." But the message was meant to scare Bernadotte, not to serve as a warning. Whoever sent it was trying to disrupt the forthcoming meetings, not alert Bernadotte to an assassination plot.

Bernadotte's first meeting was with British brigadier Norman Lash, commander of the Arab Legion units, in Ramallah. Upon its completion, he was given the use of an armored car for his travels to Jerusalem. The vehicle came under gunfire as it crossed into the Old City, but the shooting was meant to show there was hostility. Both the snipers and the men inside the vehicle knew that they were safe.

The men then traveled to the Mandelbaum Gate, still without incident, though within the car. There they went to the YMCA building, which served as headquarters for the observers.

After lunch, Bernadotte and his entourage decided to visit Government House in the Red Cross neutral zone, a mansion he felt might be suited for his headquarters. He had been scheduled to stay in the Hotel des Roses in Rhodes, but thought that the hotel was inappropriate. This time there was to be no armored car.

Two cars traveled through the neutral zone. Bernadotte reached the

mansion safely, exploring the rooms, then watching some of the violence from a tower. A group of heavily armed Arabs were blowing up a
road, an event he watched without much comment. The action was in
the neutral zone and reinforced the fact that there was no safety anywhere.

Unknown to Bernadotte, Stern gang member Stanley Goldfoot had
the UN mediator and his entourage under close surveillance. The
changes in Bernadotte's activity were upsetting. Everything had been
planned around the count's original itinerary, which Goldfoot and his
men had managed to obtain a week earlier. They had placed barrels
and small piles of rocks at various points along the roadside; these
could be used to create partial roadblocks at a moment's notice. Such
blocks would slow the Bernadotte party and allow areas for assassination.

Late Friday afternoon, Goldfoot drove to the government press office
in Jerusalem to try to learn of Bernadotte's changed plans. It was a time
when the office was generally deserted. The sabbath would start at sun-
down, most of the men and women leaving early, using the sabbath as
their excuse to get off work. However, he was able to overhear the radio
being used by the press information officer, a man cleared to learn all
the plans, then to provide only so much information as could be given
out without compromising security.

The radio reported that Bernadotte would enter the New City at 5:00
P.M. and indicated the route Bernadotte would take.

There was roughly an hour to plan the assassination by the time
Goldfoot returned to camp. Four men were dispatched to create an
obstruction that would allow only one vehicle to pass at a time. A Jeep
was parked by the makeshift wall, four men and a driver sitting
inside—all dressed as soldiers and in the stance of men goofing off
under the hot sun.

The road rose to a high point approximately a hundred yards away, a
natural slowing point for anyone traveling the area. Two other men,
Goldfoot and Yehoshua Zetler, positioned themselves nearby so that
they could view what happened to Bernadotte.

Bernadotte and his party traveled to the Jewish agricultural school
located near the area where he had been able to watch the Arabs bomb
the road. The school was occupied by Israeli soldiers who claimed that
they were caretakers of the facility. The count knew that the men were
in fact using the school for strategic purposes. He decided to check the
formal truce regulations to see how to word the violation, then to com-
plain to Jewish officials so the school could be temporarily evacuated.

The information Bernadotte needed was in the YMCA. Three cars, traveling as a convoy, began the trip. The first two vehicles were United Nations cars. The third, holding Bernadotte, was driven by Colonel Frank Begley, the head of the count's security force and a former Connecticut state patrolman. Beside him was a Commander Cox, also an American. Bernadotte sat in the far right passenger seat in back, Colonel André Serot, an observer for the French, in the middle, and General Aage Lundstrom on the left. Their car was bearing the United Nations flag. The lead cars were identified by flags of the Red Cross. There was no way anyone observing the convoy could mistake it for anything other than what it was.

Since the vehicles were unprotected from sniper fire, they moved quickly through the neutral zone, slowing only at the Israeli checkpoint, where the guard seemed to not know what to do. He lowered, raised, lowered, and raised the barrier, then lowered it completely as the convoy came to a complete halt. The guard tried to explain his uncertainty about how to treat observers. However, when the driver of the lead car shouted at the guard, he raised the barrier long enough for all three vehicles to pass through. No one in the vehicles realized that the movement of the barrier had been a signal to the assassination team.

The foot of the Hill of Evil was located not far from the barrier. It was the place where Satan was said to have tempted Jesus, a fitting location for the four assassins to make their move. The Jeep in which they were riding was backed onto the road, blocking the way. It appeared that the men were trying to turn their vehicle around at a bad location. No suspicion was aroused, but the convoy had to come to a complete halt.

It seemed as though the men in the Jeep suddenly noticed the convoy. Three of them jumped out, two moving to the right, one to the left, as though they were going to make an inspection to see if the vehicle was authorized.

Again the driver of the lead car explained that they should be left alone. In Hebrew he shouted "It's all right. This is a United Nations convoy. Let us pass."

The two men on the right slowed their pace, diverting attention toward themselves as the third man started running to the last car. Inside the vehicle, Bernadotte, Serot, and the others reached for their passes. They, too, assumed that this was simply a routine check of an unfamiliar group of cars.

Suddenly the third man thrust a Sten gun through the window and began shooting. Serot was killed instantly. Bernadotte, who was wearing his Red Cross uniform, complete with decorations, at first appeared not to be hit. Then Lundstrom, who was ignored in the attack, noticed that the decorations were oozing blood. Bullets from the Sten gun had stitched holes across the medals and ribbons. He was alive, though barely.

The moment the Sten gun appeared, Col. Begley leaped out of the car and tried to wrestle with the gunman. He was not shot, but the gunfire was so close to his face that he was severely burned from the flash of the exploding powder in the bullet shells.

The two men who had been on the right fired their guns into the tires of the lead cars. The third car was not struck and Begley managed to get back inside and drive to the hospital as the assassins made their escape. Bernadotte, a hemophiliac, had no chance to survive once wounded. He was dead on arrival.

While the assassination took place, Shamir and Sheib stayed in Tel Aviv apartments that served as safe houses for the Stern gang leadership. Friedman-Yellin was deliberately kept unaware of the exact timing of the assassination, so he was handling routine matters that included preparations for a trip to Eastern Europe. And no one had considered what to do with the killers. (Two of the men were able to flee to Tel Aviv that night despite a police search. The other two hid inside an empty truck until the next morning.)

Prime Minister David Ben-Gurion was in his office when a wire received at 5:45 P.M. told him of the assassination of Folke Bernadotte. Ironically, he had been busy reading a copy of the Bernadotte peace plan to be presented to the General Assembly. The copy was secret, obtained through a spy, an American Jew connected with Bernadotte's staff.

There has been some confusion as to how much Ben-Gurion knew in advance, especially since there would be government delays in tracking the killers. However, it appears that leaders of the Palmach Harel special forces had been aware of the plans to kill Bernadotte. They had met with the Stern gang weeks earlier and knew that the assassination would take place. They had a good idea who the leaders would be, and though they in no way participated, they were sympathetic.

Ben-Gurion knew none of this. He ordered Major Shmuel Glinka to take several units of the Palmach Harel Brigade and surround the LEHI camp in Jerusalem in which the Stern gang operated. This was still a time when more than one Jewish army was acting independently in Jerusalem so the orders came as no surprise. Nor, for that matter, did Ben-Gurion's attitude. The prime minister seemed to be expressing the hope that there would be resistance, allowing the special forces to wipe out the rebels once and for all.

The LEHI camp was surrounded, but the atmosphere was nonviolent. A feeling of joy existed among the men as they talked and laughed about what had taken place. Then, without resistance, they walked to jail, everyone uncaring about what would happen.

Friedman-Yellin did not hear about the assassination until almost three hours after the event. At that time he and his wife were sitting with a friend in a café in Haifa. They were talking about his plans to travel to Czechoslovakia to obtain weapons. The Stern Gang was going to be converted to a political party and he was eager to have the support of the Eastern European nations.

By 11:00 P.M. James McDonald was desperately trying to learn what had happened and what the aftermath would be. He met with Foreign Minister Sharett, who assured him that all Sternists were being arrested and that orders had been given to kill anyone who resisted. The killers would be found and executed.

McDonald realized more than anyone that there would be a crisis in Washington. President Truman was sympathetic to Israel, but much of Congress was wavering. The only way to assure ongoing support would be for the provisional government to take firm control. Washington wanted to see a tough attitude toward the terrorists. However, McDonald did convince Truman to impose no sanctions against Israel because of the assassination.

Col. Begley, unaware of the Stern Gang's intelligence system, felt that Bernadotte's openness was the cause of his death: "Count Bernadotte declined to keep his movements in Palestine a secret," he said. "The information that he would be in Jerusalem on September 17 was printed in a Palestinian newspaper two days earlier under the headline 'Count's last tour.' At the same time Mivrak, the organ of the Sternists, carried the statement 'We know how to take care of Bernadotte and blessed be the hand that does it.' Everyone knew the itinerary that the Mediator's three-car cavalcade followed on the day of the assassination."

The attitude of at least some of the top members of the provisional government toward the murder became evident over the next few days. The Fatherland Front immediately took credit for the murder and warned all foreign officials that death would occur to anyone interfering with the effort to establish a Jewish state. However, that was a ruse by the Stern Gang. What meant more was the fact that after 226 members of the Stern Gang were arrested, the holding area where they were placed was a prison in Jaffa where they took control of the facility.

The sympathy of the guards was such that they allowed the prisoners to remove the steel bars and to open doors. The cells were expanded so that the men and women could be together as they pleased.

The only act of violence occurred when some of the prisoners beat up a policeman. The warden felt that some punishment was necessary, so he canceled family visits for a Saturday. The prisoners, outraged, threw mattresses on top of the barbed wire and walked over. The guards felt that they should do something about the matter so they fired their guns, aiming high enough that no one was at risk. The Stern Gang members felt that even that action was too much. They took the weapons from the guards, kept them while partying with their families, then returned to their cells, giving back the weapons with the understanding that the guards would be nicer in the future.

Occasionally reporters were brought to the cells. During one such visit Stanley Goldfoot arranged for a barrel of beer to be brought in to celebrate. At other times the prisoners simply walked away from the jail, either permanently or long enough to go to a café.

Only Ben-Gurion showed outrage. He fired the police guards at the jail, then transferred the prisoners to the more secure Acre Prison. The prisoners were segregated by sex and the security was much tighter. However, even there the time spent would be limited.

The two Stern leaders who were arrested, Nathan Friedman-Yellin and Matityahu Shmulevitz, were put on trial in Acre in December 1948. There was no evidence to link them with Bernadotte's murder. Instead, they were convicted of terrorist activities, Friedman-Yellin being sentenced to eight years and Shmulevitz to five years. Twelve days later, they were freed under a general amnesty. Friedman-Yellin eventually became a member of the 1949 Knesset, Israel's first parliament.

Maths Heuman, the Swedish chief public prosecutor, conducted his own investigation, less into the death of Bernadotte than into the actions of the Israeli government. His report was presented to the Swedish foreign office on March 9, 1950. In addition, a sixty-two-page press release provided a summation of what had taken place, along with enough documentation to show that the full report conclusively proved negligence after the murder. (It would be almost forty more years before the full involvement of by-then prime minister Yitzhak Shamir would be noted and acknowledged, an apology being given to the Swedish people.) Heuman's report stated in part:

> The statement in the official Israeli report, to the ef.ct that the murder was committed at an isolated spot, is directly misleading. On the contrary the murder occurred on a rather busy main road outside a shop at a place where the assassins were seen by witnesses who happened to be either out of doors or at the windows of neighboring buildings.

In the jeep were four uniformed Jews, armed with automatic weapons. The four men had been waiting with their jeep for Count Bernadotte and his party to return from their trip. They had made no attempt to conceal themselves and had been observed by a number of people and several boys about twelve years of age had even talked to them.

The actual murderer dropped or threw away, perhaps deliberately, the barrel and magazine of his weapon and fled on foot. The other three men disappeared in the jeep.

Two days after the murder a description of the murderer, based on information given by Commander Cox, one of the members of Count Bernadotte's party, was issued.

The scene of the crime was not cordoned off and the investigation of the place did not begin until more than twenty-four hours had elapsed since the murder. In consequence bullets and a large number of cartridge cases, and possibly other items of importance for the inquiry, disappeared.

It is extremely unusual to say the least that after such a grave crime children, souvenir hunters or (for all that is known) accomplices of the criminals, should be allowed to take away the highly important pieces of evidence left at the scene of the crime.

The car used by the victims was not examined until after it had been repaired; and the other car which was fired at appears never to have been examined at all.

Matters arising in the course of the examination of witnesses which might have been made the subject of further inquiry were not made use of and other clues were also neglected.

In fact the examination of witnesses gives the impression of having been merely of a preliminary nature and having been neither critically scrutinized by those responsible for the investigation nor utilized for further attempts to find the culprits. Thus, for example, no attempt was made to examine a soldier who warned a twelve-year-old girl eyewitness not to say anything about the matter to the police.

Much valuable eyewitness evidence and other clues were available concerning the jeep used by the murderer. It is astonishing that it did not prove possible to trace the jeep or to find out who had charge of it previously. Consequently one of the most valuable clues to the identity of the assassins was neglected.

On the very evening of the murder pamphlets were scattered in Jerusalem from the air declaring that an organization calling itself Hamoldeth [Fatherland Front] claimed responsibility for the assassination. No such organization is known in any other connection, previously or subsequently. It is surprising that it was not possible to find out who issued the leaflets by tracing the distributors.

It is especially remarkable that no arrangement was made to confront the witnesses with the arrested members of the Stern gang. This would have constituted one of the best chances of attaining a positive result to the inquiry. Commander Cox stated that on two occasions he requested the authorities to be allowed to confront the arrested persons. He was met with the objection that it was desired first of all to arrest all suspected persons. This objection can only be construed as an expression of unwillingness by the Israeli authorities to use the possibilities of inquiry which were available.

In explanation of the negative results of the police investigation the Israeli authorities have referred to organizational deficiencies in the newly-formed police force of Israel. But those measures which were not undertaken were of such a kind that their importance should have been realized even by an untrained investigator. The taking of the necessary steps did not require any special technical means.

The Israeli Government stated in their report to the United Nations and Sweden that the incident was characterized by a remarkable lack of both direct and indirect evidence. On the contrary the crime was in fact distinguished by the presence of evidence and clues to an extent seldom met with in cases of murder where the assailant is unknown. It is most remarkable that in a case like this, where a relatively large number of people were involved, that clues or traces leading to the tracking down of the assailants should not have appeared.

The deficiencies of the inquiry are so grave that doubt must exist whether the Israeli authorities really endeavored to bring the inquiry to a positive result.

Circumstances indicate that the four assailants could not have acted on their own but behind the murder there must have been a fairly large group of people belonging to Sternist circles.

Heuman's report guessed accurately at the motive for the slaying. He felt that one factor was that the preliminary proposal for the partition of Palestine that Bernadotte advocated would have placed the new state of Israel in a bad situation. Not only would it have been completely surrounded by the Arabs, it also would have had to abandon the Negev region, so critical to both its survival and the growth that would be necessitated by the influx of refugees.

Heuman also felt that the Jews were trying to show the world that they would not have their future dictated by outside nations. In addition, he believed that Bernadotte may have been a threat to Israeli plans to take control of land that would give them a strategic advantage before any peace plan limited such expansion.

Despite the outrage and anger, both with the assassination and the lack of action by Israel, Sweden gave full diplomatic recognition to Israel on July 13, 1950.

❧

And so the life of Count Folke Bernadotte ended as quixotically as it began. The man who had failed at almost everything became the subject of the greatest outpouring of love and hate anyone could achieve, all within a five-year period.

It is easy to dismiss the greatness of Bernadotte's work at the end of World War II by saying that his timing was flawless. Certainly he arrived when it was obvious that the German leaders would want to save themselves. Himmler and his immediate coterie were willing to sacrifice their beliefs to gain the affection of a neutral nation. Yet the reality of Bernadotte was that he was so intensely driven toward humanitarian ends that he would have continued meeting with the leaders regardless of the eventual outcome. He was a man of fierce compassion matched by dogged determination.

If there was a tragic flaw to Bernadotte, it was not callousness, or being pro-British or anti-Semitic—charges leveled at him at one time or another after he agreed to work for the United Nations. Instead, the flaw was that he was not a scholar—he failed to keep apace of the history and culture of the region where he worked. Just as he had early been motivated by a fellow countryman's success at saving Frenchwomen, he came to Israel more like a schoolteacher seeking to bring peace to a playground where unruly elementary schoolchildren have gotten out of hand. He looked at his plan for peace based on a fair division of the land and the power. Had he understood what took place before his arrival, the attitudes of the refugees, the economic problems, the agricultural and strategic concerns, he undoubtedly would have handled his diplomacy in quite a different manner.

But Folke Bernadotte was what he was—a simple man despite his high birth, a gentle man, filled with compassion, with love, with courage, and dedication to a cause. He was as comfortable walking with the damned as he was in his mansion, living the good life of a gentleman who was always good for a party or a laugh.

Perhaps it is, ultimately, only the simple who triumph in a world gone mad. The numbers vary with the telling, but it is reasonably certain that Folke Bernadotte saved approximately thirty thousand lives through direct intervention, and perhaps twenty thousand more by facilitating an end to the violence in Norway and Denmark. In this regard, he may be the greatest unsung hero among the civilian negotiators of World War II.

There is an irony in Bernadotte's death at the hands of people he rescued. Many of those he saved had turned against him for his stand on the creation of Israel. Some may have been involved in the protection of his murderers.

The ultimate price Bernadotte paid was the cost of his naive blundering. Yet it was this same attitude, unconnected, at first, with understanding for what he was encountering, that had brought him his greatest triumph.

In the end, Bernadotte's murder became just another part of the violence in the Middle East and the growing cold war among the world's major powers. The Stern gang maintained that the shelling of Jerusalem and the many civilian deaths were the responsibility of Bernadotte. They claimed that he failed to act against the gas chambers and cremation camps despite knowing about them as early as 1943. And they said he was biased against Jews.

The Sternists also said that Bernadotte was prohibiting immigration and hurting Jewish victories. They claimed that he wanted an Arab-controlled Jerusalem, despite the fact that he had recognized the error in such thinking and had abandoned the idea. And there was the claim by some anti-Stern Zionists that the murder somehow proved a link between Russia and the Stern gang.

In return, the Soviets claimed that it was the British who actually had murdered Bernadotte. Oddly, they also claimed that he was a British agent as well as an agent for American big business interests ranging from Wall Street to the oil companies.

The provisional government of Israel brazened out the incident. Several weeks after the murder, the nation applied for membership in the United Nations. The application was supported by both the United States and Russia. And when an uneasy truce between Arab and Jew assured the continued life of the Jewish State, many experts believed that achievement was ultimately the result of the negotiating skill of Count Folke Bernadotte. For a time, there was a brief flurry of headlines concerning the murder, and the funeral was a state occasion. But the shooting, like the full results of his work, soon faded from memory. He walked with the damned, knowing triumph and tragedy in ways that elevated to almost mythic proportions both the love and hate with which he was remembered. In the end, though nearly forgotten, he remains an individual of unexpectedly extraordinary importance concerning two of the twentieth century's most important events—the Holocaust and the creation of the Jewish state.

Selected Bibliography

Bar-Zohar, Michael. *Ben-Gurion, The Armed Prophet*. Englewood Cliffs, N.J.: Prentice-Hall, 1968.

————.*Ben-Gurion: A Biography*. New York: Delacorte Press, 1979.

————.*Facing a Cruel Mirror: Israel's Moment Of Truth*. New York: Charles Scribner's Sons, 1990.

Bauer, Yehuda. *American Jewry and the Holocaust: The American Jewish Joint Distribution Committee, 1939–1945*. Detroit: Wayne State University Press, 1981.

Begin, Menachem. *The Revolt*. New York: Nash Publishing, 1977.

Bentwich, Norman De Mattos. *Mandate Memories: 1918–1948*. New York: Schocken Books, 1965.

Ben-Ami, Yitshaq. *Years Of Wrath/Days Of Glory: Memoirs From The Irgun*. New York: Robert Speller & Sons, 1982.

Bernadotte, Count Folke. *Instead of Arms*. London: Hodder and Stoughton, 1949.

————.*The Curtain Falls: Last Days of the Third Reich*. New York: A.A. Knopf, 1945.

————.*To Jerusalem*. London: Hodder and Stoughton, 1951.

Bramwell, Anna. *Blood and Soil: Walther Darré And Hitler's 'Green Party'*. Buckinghamshire, England: The Kensal Press, 1985.

313

Breitman, Richard. *The Architect of Genocide: Himmler And The Final Solution*. New York: Alfred Knopf, 1991.

Brissaud, André. *The Nazi Secret Service*. New York: W.W. Norton & Company, 1974.

Browder, George C. *Foundations of the Nazi Police State: The Formation of Sipo and SD*. Lexington: The University Press of Kentucky, 1990.

Calic, Edouard. *Reinhard Heydrich*. New York: William Morrow & Co., 1982.

Clarke, Thurston. *By Blood And Fire*. New York: G.P. Putnam's Sons, 1981.

Cohen, Michael J. *Palestine: Retreat from the Mandate*. New York: Holmes & Meier Publishers, 1978.

Cohen, Naomi. *The Year After the Riots: American Responses to the Palestine Crisis of 1929–1930*. Detroit: Wayne State University Press, 1988.

Dawidowicz, Lucy S. *A Holocaust Reader*. New York: Behrman House, Inc., Publishers, 1976.

———.*The War Against the Jews: 1933–1945*. New York: Holt, Rinehart and Winston, 1975.

Delarue, Jacques. *The Gestapo: A History of Horror*. New York: Paragon House, 1987.

Denham Henry. *Inside the Nazi Ring: A Naval Attaché in Sweden 1940–1945*. New York: Holmes & Meier Publishers, 1984.

Derogy, Jacques, and Carmel, Hesi. *The Untold History of Israel*. New York: Grove Press, 1979.

Deschner, Gunther. *Reinhard Heydrich*. New York: Stein & Day, 1977.

Eisenberg, Azriel. *Witness to the Holocaust*. New York: The Pilgrim Press, 1981.

Flapan, Simha. *The Birth of Israel: Myths and Realities*. New York: Pantheon Books, 1987.

Frank, Gerold. *The Deed*. New York: Simon and Schuster, 1963.

Frischauer, Willi. *Himmler, the Evil Genius*. London: Odhams Press, 1953.

Gilbert, Martin. *Final Journey: The Fate of the Jews in Nazi Europe*. New York: Mayflower Books, 1979.

———.*Auschwitz and the Allies*. New York: Holt, Rinehart and Winston, 1981.

———.*The Holocaust: A History of the Jews of Europe During the Second World War*. New York: Holt, Rinehart and Winston, 1985.

Goebbels, Joseph. *The Goebbels Diaries, 1939–1941*. New York: Penguin

Books, 1984.

———.*Final Entries, 1945: The Diaries of Joseph Goebbels*. New York: Putnam, 1978.

Graber, G. S. *The Life and Times of Reinhard Heydrich*. New York: David McKay Company, 1980.

Grant, Neil. *The Partition of Palestine, 1947: Jewish Triumph, British Failure, Arab Disaster*. New York: Franklin Watts, 1973.

Grunberger, Richard. *Hitler's SS*. New York: Delacorte Press, 1971.

Haestrup, Jorgen. *Secret Alliance: A Study of the Danish Resistance Movement 1940–1945*. 3 vols. Copenhagen: Odense University Press, 1976.

Hewins, Ralph. *Count Folke Bernadotte, His Life and Work*. Minneapolis: T.S. Denison 1950.

Hilberg, Raul. *The Destruction of the European Jews*. New York: Holmes & Meier Publishers, 1985.

Hirschler, Gertrude. *Menahem Begin, from Freedom Fighter to Statesman*. New York: Shengold, 1979.

Hitler, Adolf. *Mein Kampf*. New York: Reynaud and Hitchcock, 1939.

Hoess, Rudolf. *Commandant of Auschwitz: The Autobiography of Rudolf Hoess*. Cleveland and New York: The World Publishing Company, 1959.

Howarth, Stephen. *August '39: The Last Four Weeks of Peace*. San Francisco: Mercury House, 1989.

Hyamson, Albert Montefiore. *Palestine Under the Mandate: 1920–1948*. Westport, Conn.: Greenwood Press, 1976.

Kahn, David. *Hitler's Spies: German Military Intelligence in World War II*. New York: Macmillan Publishing Co., 1978.

Kee, Robert. *1939: In The Shadow of War*. Boston: Little Brown & Company, 1984.

Kersten, Felix. *The Kersten Memoirs, 1940–1945*. New York: Macmillan, 1957.

Kessel, Joseph. *The Man with the Miraculous Hands*. New York: Farrar, Straus and Cudhay, 1961.

Koehl, Robert Lewis. *The Black Corps: The Structure and Power Struggles of the Nazi SS*. Madison: The University of Wisconsin Press, 1983.

Kogon, Eugen. *The Theory and Practice of Hell*. New York: Berkley, 1950.

Kurzman, Dan. *Ben-Gurion, Prophet of Fire*. New York: Simon and Schuster, 1983.

Letulle, Claude J. *Nightmare Memoir: Four Years as a Prisoner of the Nazis*.

Baton Rouge: Louisiana State University Press, 1987.

Lorch, Netanel. *One Long War.* New York: Herzl Press, 1976.

Louis, William Roger, and Stookey, Robert W., eds. *The End of the Palestine Mandate.* Austin: University of Texas Press, 1986.

MacDonald, Callum. *The Killing of SS Obergruppenfuhrer Reinhard Heydrich.* New York: The Free Press, 1989.

Manvell, Roger, and Fraenkel, Heinrich. *Heinrich Himmler.* New York: Putnam, 1965.

Mattar, Philip. *The Mufti of Jerusalem: Al-hajj Amin Alhusayni and the Palestinian National Movement.* New York: Columbia University Press, 1988.

Meissner, Hans Otto. *Magda Goebbels: The First Lady of the Third Reich.* New York: Dial Press, 1980.

Mirchuk, Petro. *In the German Mills of Death: 1941–1945.* New York: Vantage Press, 1976.

Morse, Arthur D. *While Six Million Died.* New York: Random House, 1968.

Mosley, Leonard. *On Borrowed Time: How World War II Began.* New York: Random House, 1969.

O'Donnell, James P. *The Bunker.* New York: Houghton Mifflin Company, 1978.

Padfield, Peter. *Himmler, Reichsfuhrer–SS.* New York: Henry Holt, 1991.

Paine, Lauran. *German Military Intelligence in World War II.* New York: Stein & Day, 1984.

Peis, Gunter and Wighton, Charles. *Hitler's Spies and Saboteurs.* New York: Henry Holt, 1958.

Penkower, Monty Noam. *The Jews Were Expendable: Free World Diplomacy and the Holocaust.* Urbana and Chicago: University of Illinois Press, 1983.

Perl, William R. *Operation Action: Rescue from the Holocaust.* New York: Frederick Ungar Publishing Company, 1978.

Perlmutter, Amos. *The Life and Times of Menachem Begin.* New York: Doubleday, 1987.

Peukert, Detlev J.K. *Inside Nazi Germany: Conformity, Opposition, and Racism in Everyday Life.* New Haven: Yale University Press, 1987.

Postal, Bernard. *And the Hills Shouted for Joy: The Day Israel Was Born.* New York: David McKay Company, 1973.

Quarrie, Bruce. *Hitler's Teutonic Knights: SS Panzers in Action.*

Wellingborough: Patrick Stephens, 1986.

————.*Hitler's Samurai: The Waffen–SS in Action.* Wellingborough: Patrick Stephens, 1986.

Rempel, Gerhard. *Hitler's Children: The Hitler Youth and the SS.* Chapel Hill: University of North Carolina Press, 1989.

Rings, Werner. *Life with the Enemy: Collaboration and Resistance in Hitler's Europe 1939–1945.* Garden City, N.Y.: Doubleday & Company, 1982.

Rolf, David. *Prisoners of the Reich: Germany's Captives; 1939–1945.* London: Leo Cooper, 1988.

Rothchild, Sylvia, ed. *Voices from the Holocaust.* New York: New American Library, 1981.

Rutledge, Brett. *The Death of Lord Haw Haw.* New York: The Book League of America, 1940.

Sachar, Abram L. *The Redemption of the Unwanted.* New York: St. Martin's/Marek, 1983.

Sachar, Howard Morley. *A History of Israel: From the Rise of Zionism to Our Time.* New York: Alfred Knopf, 1976.

————.*A History of Israel.* New York: Alfred A. Knopf, 1970.

Sanders, Ronald. *The High Walls of Jerusalem.* New York: Holt, Rinehart and Winston, 1983.

————. *Shores of Refuge: A Hundred Years of Jewish Emigration.* New York: Henry Holt and Company, 1988.

Schellenberg, Walter. *The Labyrinth: Memoirs.* New York: Harper, 1956.

Schiff, Ze'ev. *A History of the Israeli Army.* New York: MacMillan Publishing Company, 1985.

Segev, Tom. *1949: The First Israelis.* New York: The Free Press, Macmillan, 1986.

Shirer, William L. *The Rise and Fall of the Third Reich: A History of Nazi Germany.* New York: Simon and Schuster, 1960.

Slater, Leonard. *The Pledge.* New York: Pocket Books, 1972.

Smith, Bradley F. *Heinrich Himmler: A Nazi in the Making, 1900–1926.* Hoover Institution Press, 1971.

Snyder, Louis L., ed. *Hitler's Third Reich: A Documentary History.* Chicago: Nelson-Hall, 1981.

Speer, Albert. *Infiltration: How Heinrich Himmler Schemed to Build an SS Industrial Empire.* New York: Macmillan, 1981.

————.*Inside the Third Reich.* New York: Macmillan, 1970.

Stein, George H. *The Waffen–SS: Hitler's Élite Guard at War 1939–1945.*

New York: Cornell University Press, 1966.

Steiner, Jean-Francois. *Treblinka*. New York: Simon and Schuster, 1967.

Steinhoff, Johannes, Pechel, Peter, and Showalter, Dennis. *Voices from the Third Reich: An Oral History*. Washington, D.C.: Regnery Gateway, 1989.

Suster, Gerald. *Hitler: The Occult Messiah*. New York: St. Martin's Press, 1981.

Teveth, Shabtai. *Ben-Gurion: The Burning Ground, 1886–1948*. New York: Houghton Mifflin, 1987.

Thomas, Gordon, and Witts, Max Morgan. *Voyage of the Damned*. New York: Stein and Day, 1974.

Toland, John. *Adolf Hitler*. New York: Ballantine Books, 1981.

Trevor-Roper, Hugh. *The Last Days of Hitler*. New York: Macmillan Company, 1947.

Turner, Henry Ashby, Jr. *Hitler—Memoirs of a Confidant*. New Haven and London: Yale University Press, 1978.

Wasserstein, Bernard. *Britain and the Jews of Europe: 1939–1945*. London: Oxford University Press, Institute of Jewish Affairs, 1979.

Wegner, Bernd. *The Waffen-SS: Organization, Ideology, and Function*. Oxford: United Kingdom. New York: Basil Blackwell, 1990.

Weiner, J.G. *The Assassination of Heydrich*. New York: Grossmuller, 1969.

Wulff, Wilhelm Theodor H. *Zodiac and Swastika: How Astrology Guided Hitler's Germany*. New York: Coward, McCann & Geoghegan, 1973.

Wykes, Alan. *Himmler*. New York: Ballantine Books, 1972.

❧

Special assistance was provided by Ariane Ritschel Sheppard, the half sister of Magda Ritschel Quandt Goebbels.

Index